THE BATTLE OF LEYTE GULF

Also by Thomas Cutler

Brown Water, Black Berets: Coastal and Riverine Warfare in Vietnam

THE BATTLE OF LEYTE GULF

23–26 October 1944

THOMAS J. CUTLER

BLUEJACKET BOOKS

Naval Institute Press
Annapolis, Maryland

Naval Institute Press
291 Wood Road
Annapolis, MD 21402

First Bluejacket Books printing, 2001
ISBN 1-55750-243-9

Library of Congress Cataloging-in-Publication Data

Cutler, Thomas J., 1947–
    The Battle of Leyte Gulf, 23–26 October, 1944 / Thomas J. Cutler.
        p.   cm. — (Bluejacket books)
    Originally published: New York : HarperCollins, 1994.
    Includes bibliographical references and index.
    ISBN 1-55750-243-9 (alk. paper)
    1. Philippine Sea, Battles of the, 1944. I. Title. II. Series.

D774.P5 C87 2001
940.54'25—dc21
                                            2001044460

Printed in the United States of America on acid-free paper ♾
08 07 06 05 04 03 02 01   9 8 7 6 5 4 3 2 1

To Ann and Hans Schuler
Two of the most generous people
I have ever known and loved,
without whom many lives would be
different—especially mine

and

To Chris and Gary
Whose love, achievements, and friendship
have brought me more happiness
than any father could hope for

Everything in war is very simple, but the simplest thing is difficult. The difficulties accumulate and end by producing a kind of friction that is inconceivable unless one has experienced war.

Carl von Clausewitz, *On War*

[Clausewitz] introduces the element that others have called "the fog of war," the perennial inadequacies and inaccuracies of intelligence.

Bernard Brodie, "A Guide to the Reading of *On War*"

Contents

Part V ★ Night of 24–25 October 1944 ★

Part VI ★ 25 October 1944 ★

Part VII ★ Aftermath ★

Illustrations follow page 188.

Maps

Preface

The *Simon & Schuster Encyclopedia of World War II* calls the Battle of Leyte Gulf "the greatest naval engagement ever fought." Famed historian Ronald Spector in his history of the American war with Japan, *Eagle Against the Sun*, describes the engagement as "the largest naval battle in history." Former military editor of the *New York Times*, Hanson W. Baldwin, in one of his many successful books, *Battles Lost and Won*, entitles his chapter on this battle, "The Greatest Sea Fight."

Why is the Battle of Leyte Gulf always referred to in such superlative terms? Because it was, in point of fact, the biggest and most multifaceted naval battle in all of history. It involved more ships than any other engagement, including the gargantuan Battle of Jutland in the First World War (250 British and German ships fought at Jutland; 282 American, Japanese, and Australian ships engaged at Leyte). Nearly two hundred thousand men participated in the fight, and the geographical area in which the battle was fought spanned more than a hundred thousand square miles. Dozens of ships were sunk, including some of the largest and most powerful ever built, and thousands of men went to the bottom of the sea with them. Every aspect of naval warfare—air, surface, submarine, and amphibious—was involved in this great struggle, and the weapons used included bombs of every type, guns of every caliber, torpedoes, mines, rockets, and even a forerunner of the guided missile.

But more than size gave this battle its significance. The cast of characters included such names as Halsey, Nimitz, MacArthur, even Roosevelt. It introduced the largest guns ever used in a naval battle and a new Japanese tactic that would eventually kill more American sailors and sink more American ships than any other used in the war. It was the site of the last clash of the dreadnoughts and the first and only time that an American aircraft carrier was sunk by gunfire. It was replete with awe-inspiring heroism, failed intelligence, sapient tactical planning and execution, flawed strategy, brilliant deception, incredible ironies, great controversies, and a plethora of lessons about strategy, tactics, and operations.

If all of the above is true about the Battle of Leyte Gulf, why is it not a household word like Pearl Harbor? Why have fewer Americans heard of it than the Battle of Midway or the D-Day invasion of Europe? The answer lies in its timing. Leyte Gulf occurred late in the war, after several years of conflict in which great battles had become commonplace. Names like Midway, Stalingrad, Guadalcanal, and Normandy were by then frequent fare. More significantly, however, was that the Battle of Leyte Gulf happened when most of America had accepted ultimate victory as merely a matter of time rather than as a debatable question. Midway was widely accepted as the turning point of the war in the Pacific, a dramatic reversal of what had been a losing trend. The D-Day invasion at Normandy was seen as the true beginning of the end of the war in Europe. But Leyte Gulf was seen as just another step along the way, the continuation of a trend which by that time was seen as normal and inevitable. Lacking such drama as the earlier battles had enjoyed, Leyte Gulf was then eclipsed by events like the near-reversal at the Battle of the Bulge, the ferocious fighting at Iwo Jima and Okinawa, and the cataclysmic dropping of atomic bombs on Hiroshima and Nagasaki.

But the Battle of Leyte Gulf was indeed pivotal in that it represented the last hope of the Japanese Empire and the last significant sortie of the Imperial Japanese Navy. It was vastly important to millions of Filipinos and thousands of Allied prisoners of war, whose liberation from Japanese oppression depended upon it. And, while an American victory in the battle may have been viewed as somewhat mundane by that stage of the war, an American defeat would have been a disaster of great magnitude.

Writing about a battle of such vast proportions is no simple task. Many important events were occurring simultaneously and yet must be presented in a linear format. This requires frequent shifts of scene which can become confusing if presented carelessly. I have tried to make each scene as clear as possible in terms of time and place so that the reader may keep up with the whirlwind of widespread yet interlocking events.

I have written this book making a few assumptions about the reader's knowledge. I have assumed that the reader knows that a battleship is bigger and more powerful than a cruiser and that these are, in turn, larger than a destroyer. But beyond that I have tried to explain the nature of each type of ship introduced. Readers already familiar with such things may find this somewhat tedious, but this is preferable to excluding other readers from a clear understanding. I have dispensed with the laborious practice of including the hull numbers of vessels that so many authors seem compelled to do, using instead only the ships' names. In that same streamlining vein, I have omitted from the names of individuals the frequently appended "USN" and "USNR," using only their ranks as appropriate.

Certain biases will become apparent as the reader progresses through this work. I am an American patriot and a retired naval officer, so my account will reflect a certain pride in the achievements of the U.S. Navy and a great deal of respect and appreciation for the heroism and sacrifice of the American sailors who fought at Leyte. I have interviewed and gotten to know some of these men and my admiration for them has been strengthened by that experience. But I also have an abiding and sincere respect for their Japanese adversaries. I respect anyone who has faced the terrors and rigors of combat, even those who once were *my* enemies in a different war at a different time.

This is not to say that I have pulled my punches when discussing the errors made during the battle. I sincerely believe that a true patriot must be willing to criticize constructively his beloved country, just as a loving parent will chastise the misbehaving child. Nothing is perfect, and nothing will get nearer to perfection without honest appraisal.

I have used the military 24-hour system of time—so that 3:00 A.M. becomes 0300, noon becomes 1200, 1:15 P.M. becomes 1315, etc.— because to a naval officer, using civilian time when discussing a military operation is something akin to using the word "tune" when describing Beethoven's music.

The reader will probably detect that I have a love of the sea and some readers may find my personification of ships somewhat overdone. But those are the readers who have not served in ships, who have not experienced firsthand how a vessel takes on the collective personality of the men who crew her.

A half-century has passed since the sound of gunfire echoed across the waters of Leyte Gulf, but the importance of what happened there has not diminished with time. It is fitting that we should take another look, fifty years later, at what happened at Leyte Gulf, recognizing the courage and sacrifice of those who fought there, learning from the mistakes that were made, and hoping that nothing in our future will ever rival this event for its well-deserved title of "greatest naval battle in history."

The criticisms of others found within this work are offered humbly. My purpose in questioning the acts and decisions taken a half-century ago is not to defame the men who originated them but rather to let their actions and the criticisms contained herein serve as lessons for future naval officers. Never would I claim to have been able to do better than the men I write about. I have known the awesome responsibility of handling a single ship in moments of challenge; my mind boggles at the thought of handling whole *fleets*. I have experienced the confusion that can reign on the bridge of a ship in the dark of night when all is not going according to plan; I can only begin to imagine how that would be magnified if my ship were sinking beneath me. And I have known the mind-numbing terror of combat— though never to the degree experienced by most of the men I now write about; I sincerely believe that only those who have never been shot at would disparage the actions of men under fire. I make my judgments from the comfort of a desk chair. I am surrounded by books and documents with a hundred times the information available to those on-site commanders, and I may peruse them at my leisure, pressured only by a publisher's deadline. I write on a machine that dutifully erases my errors, and I sip coffee as I write. Most of all, no one must live or die by what I do here.

So it is with the ultimate humility that I hope that my criticisms and judgments will serve as food for thought, as stimulus for further debate, but never as a substitute for what brave men did under the pressures of command and combat.

Prologue

As the sun emerges from the waters of the Philippine Sea on the morning of 24 October 1944, the stage is set for the greatest naval battle in history. In many ways, the "play" about to commence is to be a Greek tragedy. The long march of American forces across the Pacific has served as prologue, and in the acts to follow, with their many scenes of intense human drama, many noble and gallant men of two different nations will fall in battle. The chorus warns that others will find tragedy in a different form as they make their entrances full of pride and hope, only to exit as victims of the callous whims of the Fates and of their own follies. The climax will be swift and decisive, but the denouement is still being written.

As the drama is about to unfold, the major characters are on the stage or in the wings. A cast of thousands has rehearsed for this moment, but it is improvisation rather than script that will shape their performances. As in all Greek tragedies, the gods play parts as well. Poseidon as god of the sea, Thanatos, god of death, and Ares, god of war, all have obvious roles. But it is Aeolus who controls the winds, and Hermes, messenger of the gods, whose interference will have surprising effects upon the outcome. And it is Athena, sharing her wisdom with some and withholding it from others, who will determine which of the antagonists will earn Nike's laurel wreath of victory.

THE BATTLE OF LEYTE GULF

PART I

★ PRELUDES ★

1

★ CINCSOWESPAC ★

11 March 1942. The relentless shelling of the waterfront area had ceased as evening approached, and in the sudden stillness only the throaty growl of idling diesels and the crackle of flames could be heard. The general paused at the water's edge and surveyed his wilting domain. Where lush vegetation and vibrantly colored tropical flowers had recently flourished, all that remained was the bleak aftermath of battle, the shattered remnants of an army on the verge of capitulation. Trees whose fronds had once brushed majestically against the beautiful Philippine sky had been reduced to mere jagged stumps. Buildings that had housed a proud garrison now lay in ruins, their ragged remnants protruding from a pall of acrid smoke that further subdued the already fading twilight. General Douglas MacArthur, twenty-five pounds lighter than he had been three months earlier, removed his gold-encrusted khaki cap and raised it in a final salute to Corregidor, the island-fortress he had been ordered to abandon.

In the gathering darkness of those early days of the war, when defeat had followed defeat, the brave but futile stand that MacArthur's forces had made on the fortified peninsula of Bataan had been a welcome ray of light. Douglas MacArthur had been elevated in the eyes of the American people to heroic proportions not equaled since Admiral Dewey had defeated the Spanish Fleet in these same Philippine waters at the close of the last century. To allow him to fall into the hands of an enemy whose propagandists predicted that they would see him publicly hanged in the Imperial Plaza in Tokyo was, simply, unthinkable. So President Franklin D. Roosevelt had ordered the general to leave the Philippines.

This was no simple order. First, there was the general's natural reluc-

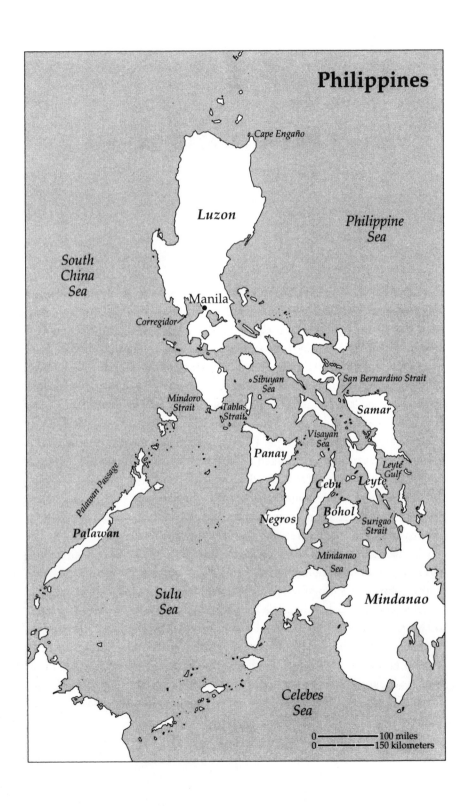

tance to abandon his command. Then, there was the realization that escape from the Philippines was more easily ordered than carried out. Japanese forces virtually controlled the air and sea approaches, so only a bold and clandestine move had any hope of success. And finally, there was MacArthur's special ties to the Philippines. His father, General Arthur MacArthur, had been both war hero and military governor there, and young Douglas's first assignment after graduating from West Point had been a tour of duty in the Philippines as a second lieutenant in the elite Corps of Engineers. He returned to the islands several more times during his career, and by the time the Japanese landed troops at Lingayen Gulf in December 1941, MacArthur had become a field marshal of the Philippine Army and commander of U.S. Army Forces in the Far East.

Now, as he stood upon Corregidor Island's weathered wooden dock, preparing to follow his commander-in-chief's orders to depart his beloved Philippines—leaving behind, to certain defeat, a combined American-Filipino army of nearly eighty thousand—MacArthur felt the color drain from his face and a sudden, convulsive twitch beneath his eyes that threatened to steal the composure he so valued. He turned his back on Corregidor and, stepping aboard the 77-foot patrol-torpedo (PT) boat that was to be his means of escape, said to the young Navy lieutenant in command, "You may cast off, Buck, when you are ready."

As evening darkness descended upon Manila Bay and rain-laden clouds erased the moon, Lieutenant John D. Bulkeley's PT-41 threaded its way through the defensive mine field and headed for the blackened waters of Mindoro Strait where enemy ships were known to prowl. On board, General Douglas MacArthur vowed to recover from this ignominious moment, to avenge the inevitable defeat, to come back as soon as possible with the forces necessary to drive out the invading Japanese, and to restore America's—and his own—honor. In a few days he would voice this determination to the world, capturing the imagination of those Americans and Filipinos who had placed their faith in him, with three small but powerful words: "I shall return."

Six days after MacArthur departed Corregidor, on the other side of the world, one of the guests at a White House dinner asked the President to reveal how General MacArthur had escaped from the Philippines. Franklin Roosevelt, with a mischievous glint in his eye that was not detected by all at the table, replied in a conspiratorial tone, "General

MacArthur took a rowboat and, disguised as a Filipino fisherman, rowed to Australia—right past the Japs. Perfectly simple. It was only a matter of twenty-five hundred miles." Not everyone laughed at the President's outlandish explanation. In fact, it appears that at least some of the guests were quite willing to believe it. In retrospect this seems rather naive, but when viewed in the context of the times, such a feat did not seem beyond the capabilities of Douglas MacArthur. Parents were christening their newborn children with his name, colleges and universities were heaping honorary degrees upon him, mothers were reportedly invoking his name to entice their children to eat spinach, organizations of every description were giving him honorary memberships—even the Blackfoot Indian tribe adopted MacArthur, conferring upon him the title of "Chief Wise Eagle." Lapel buttons bearing his image and a film about him entitled *America's First Soldier* sold well. A widely publicized news story reported that when an Atlanta junior high school teacher asked his class to name an American possession in the Far East, a pupil proudly answered "General MacArthur."

Despite all this adulation, there were many who felt quite differently about Douglas MacArthur. His many achievements—including heroic leadership in the Great War and a meteoric rise through the ranks of the Army, often becoming the youngest ever to hold key positions such as Superintendent at West Point and Chief of Staff of the Army—were offset by a towering ego that frequently manifested itself in Olympian declarations and pompous passages of purple prose. He rarely willingly shared the limelight, and his use of the first-person was legendary. His leadership during the Japanese invasion of the Philippines had been flawed, and his strong will and single-mindedness often took him to the very brink of insubordination. Yet, for all those who saw these shortcomings in MacArthur, there were probably many more who lionized and idealized him. The one constant was that he was rarely treated with moderation.

Because of these antipodal reactions toward MacArthur, President Roosevelt and his Joint Chiefs of Staff* had to be very careful how they

---

* Along with Secretary of War Henry L. Stimson and Secretary of the Navy W. Franklin "Frank" Knox, the Joint Chiefs of Staff (JCS) during World War II were President Roosevelt's closest advisers on military matters. The JCS consisted of General George C. Marshall, Chief of Staff, U.S. Army; General Henry H. Arnold, Commanding General, U.S. Army Air Forces; Admiral Ernest J. King, Commander in Chief U.S. Fleet and Chief of Naval Operations; and Admiral William D. Leahy, recalled from retirement to serve as Chief of Staff to the President and preside as Chairman of the Joint Chiefs.

utilized him. There were those among MacArthur's supporters who advocated giving him command of the entire Pacific war. Indeed, no small
bloc wanted him appointed as supreme commander of *all* American
forces, worldwide. MacArthur's enemies, of course, were violently
opposed. Additionally, American naval leaders convincingly argued that
the aqueous expanses of the Pacific, with so many islands as key strategic points, dictated that the war there would be primarily a naval one
and should, therefore, be led by an admiral rather than a general. But,
leaving MacArthur out of the war entirely was out of the question.
Besides the obvious political problem of his powerful following, there is
convincing evidence to indicate that Roosevelt respected MacArthur as a
general. The President's personal physician, Dr. Ross T. McIntire,
revealed after the war that Roosevelt "may have smiled now and then at
some of the General's purple communiqués, but always there was appreciation of him as a military genius who had worked miracles in the face
of heart-breaking odds." One of Roosevelt's most trusted advisers, Admiral William D. Leahy, wrote of MacArthur: "I had always entertained an
extremely high opinion of his ability." And Roosevelt himself told
MacArthur, while the latter was serving as Chief of Staff of the Army,
"Douglas, I think you are our best general, but I believe you would be
our worst politician." This last statement may contain an underlying reason for FDR's apparent advocacy of the popular general—that by
advancing MacArthur's interests to a degree, Roosevelt was *controlling*
those interests to an even greater degree. There is compelling evidence
that Roosevelt saw MacArthur as a potential political rival and that
keeping the sometimes difficult general in the President's camp was
preferable to making him a powerful competitor outside the President's
sphere of influence.

The sticky problem of what to do with MacArthur was ultimately
handled, as are most political dilemmas, by compromise. General
MacArthur was not given command of the entire Pacific theater, nor was
he shelved. The Pacific was carved into theaters and MacArthur was
named Supreme Commander of the Southwest Pacific Area (SWPA),
which encompassed Australia, the Solomon Islands, the Bismarck
Archipelago, New Guinea, the Netherlands East Indies (except Sumatra),
and the Philippines. The remainder of the Pacific was assigned to Admiral Chester Nimitz, who added the title Commander in Chief Pacific
Ocean Areas (CINCPOA) to his existing title, Commander in Chief

Pacific Fleet (CINCPACFLT or, more commonly, CINCPAC.* MacArthur was opposed to the idea of a divided command in the Pacific but pragmatic enough to accept the compromise. He did, however, insist upon changing his title from "Supreme Commander" to "Commander in Chief," as Nimitz had been named.

So, in the summer of 1942, the newly appointed Commander in Chief of the Southwest Pacific Area (CINCSOWESPAC) began planning to make good on his promise to the Philippines. But Douglas MacArthur's prophecy of return was not destined for fulfillment in any short order. The course of the war dictated that it would be more than two years before that return would be considered feasible. And even then, one man's promise was not necessarily his government's policy.

It soon became apparent that operations within MacArthur's SWPA theater would have to be conducted within some rather severe limitations. The first of these was imposed by the British and American Combined Chiefs of Staff,† who were determined to adhere to a policy established in a secret conference held before the United States entered the war.†† It had been decided that Hitler's Germany was a greater potential threat than the Japanese, so first priority would be given to the war in Europe. This, of course, meant that the bulk of American resources would be channeled to the European theater until Germany could be defeated.

Furthermore, the carving up of the Pacific into theaters had given MacArthur a sizable piece of geography but few assets with which to prosecute his campaign. The most significant factor was that Nimitz retained

---

* Modern readers familiar with the military command structure may be confused by this usage of CINCPAC and CINCPACFLT as synonymous terms. Today they represent two separate commands, but in World War II "CINCPAC" was merely an abbreviated form of the title "CINCPACFLT." So Nimitz was often referred to by either title. And to make matters that much more complex, he was also sometimes called "CINCPOA" and frequently referred to as "CINCPAC/CINCPOA."

† On 14 January 1942, during the Arcadia Conference in Washington, D.C., the British and Americans agreed to form the Combined Chiefs of Staff (CCS) to plan strategy. The CCS was made up of the American Joint Chiefs of Staff and the British Chiefs of Staff (consisting of the Chief of the Imperial General Staff, the First Sea Lord, and the Chief of the Air Staff).

†† The Combined Staff Conference held in Washington, D.C., during February and March 1941.

control of the Pacific Fleet, leaving MacArthur with only the remnants of the U.S. Asiatic Fleet, a force that had been severely outdated and poorly maintained in the years prior to Pearl Harbor and, along with most of the British, Dutch, and Australian naval forces in the region, had been virtually annihilated by the Japanese in the first months of the war.

Despite these limitations, MacArthur set out on a campaign that was, over the next two years, to take him up what he called the "New Guinea-Mindanao Axis" toward his return to the Philippines. Simultaneously, Nimitz conducted his own thrust across the Central Pacific, penetrating first the Gilbert Islands, then the Marshalls, the Carolines, and the Marianas.

It is interesting to note that MacArthur is deservedly remembered for his flamboyance and dramatic posturing, and Nimitz, on the other hand, is generally characterized as quiet, reserved, and avoiding public attention whenever possible. Yet, Nimitz's Central Pacific campaign is better remembered than MacArthur's Southwest Pacific campaign. Tarawa, Guam, Saipan, and Peleliu are names that most Americans associate with the war in the Pacific, whereas Buna, Lae, Aitape, Biak, and Noemfoor are all milestones in MacArthur's march up the northern New Guinea coast, and few Americans have ever heard of them.

To discredit him, MacArthur's critics complained that the length of time it took for the New Guinea campaign to be completed was excessive, but this argument loses most of its potence when one considers that New Guinea is the second largest island in the world and, when superimposed on a map of the United States, stretches from the Atlantic Coast to the foothills of the Rockies. Initially, the campaign *was* slow to get rolling, and the earliest engagements were marred by some costly errors, but once the early inertia was overcome and mistakes became lessons learned, MacArthur's leadership, and the tenacity and courage of the forces who served him, made the Southwest Pacific campaign a model of strategic and tactical brilliance. With a paucity of matériel support and an impressively low casualty rate overall, SWPA forces steadily pushed their way up the New Guinea coast—a distance of nearly two thousand miles in some of the worst jungle terrain in the world.

As the war progressed, Nimitz's Central Pacific thrust and MacArthur's Southwest Pacific advance became very different campaigns. The former was an extremely mobile, island-hopping advance across the vast stretches of the Pacific, covered by an umbrella of self-contained air power in the form of a steadily growing fleet of aircraft carriers.* The latter was more of a land campaign, employing MacArthur's few ships primarily as transport for his troops as he moved steadily up the New Guinea coast, never extending himself beyond the reach of his land-based air power. Despite their differences, however, the two campaigns complemented one another and kept the Japanese off balance by causing them to shift forces from one theater to another in anticipation of the Americans' next move. And the two campaigns shared one other important similarity: both Nimitz and MacArthur were moving ever closer to the home islands of the Japanese Empire.

---

* Because of the nature of the war in Europe (primarily continental) and in the Atlantic (primarily submarine vs. convoy), aircraft carriers were not in great demand in that theater. As these potent ships began to emerge from American shipyards, they were sent to the Pacific, where they became part of Nimitz's fleet. From the moment he took command, MacArthur tried to convince the JCS that he needed aircraft carriers, but his requests fell on deaf ears. The restricted waters of the Southwest Pacific would have encumbered the carriers' mobility and made them vulnerable to the considerable Japanese land-based air assets located on the many airfields there.

2

★ COMINCH ★

Several Navy LCIs* circled slowly just off the north shore, their cumbersome gray hulls rising and falling on the gentle Pacific swell. On board, their crews peered up at the cliffs of Marpi Point, more than a hundred feet above the ocean's surface. There were caves in those towering rocks, and the crack of sporadic gunfire echoed from within as Japanese snipers forestalled the inevitable approach of American Marines slowly closing in on them from several directions.

A young sailor aboard one of the LCIs, peering up into the glare of the afternoon sun, said, "Oh, God, here come some more," and turned his head away. On the cliff above, a woman emerged into full view, despite the gunfire, and stumbled across the rocks to the cliff's edge. In her arms she held a motionless child as she stood swaying back and forth, staring down at the jagged rocks protruding menacingly from the undulating surf below. From one of the LCIs the amplified voice of a captured Japanese soldier blared out over the water and echoed off the sheer wall of the cliff. Though most of the Americans present could not understand the words, the desperation in that voice was unmistakable.

Suddenly, the woman, still clutching the child to her, leaped from the cliff and plummeted down the hundred feet to the water below. There was an audible *thump* that made the American sailors cringe. The sound was caused not by her hitting the rocks, but by her striking other human beings. The water was littered with hundreds of floating corpses. There

---

* LCI—Landing Craft, Infantry; a 160-foot-long seagoing craft, capable of carrying nearly 200 troops at a top speed of about fifteen knots.

were so many that the LCIs and other American craft in the vicinity were sometimes forced to run over them, their propellers mutilating the already bloated bodies. It was a sight that would haunt many of the sailors and marines who witnessed it for the rest of their lives. Battle-hardened veterans of the Pacific campaign became physically ill as mothers and fathers threw their screaming children from the cliffs and then leaped after them. Those that hesitated were frequently shot by the Japanese snipers holed up in the caves. A Navy lieutenant aboard a minesweeper in the area later reported having seen the body of a nude woman float by, the head of her partially born child protruding from her.

This was the aftermath of an American invasion, the so-called "mopping up" phase of a battle that had been the most costly of the Pacific war to date. Killed or wounded were more than fourteen thousand Americans, and nearly every man of the Japanese defending garrison—some thirty thousand strong—had perished, many of them in fanatical suicide charges that never had any hope of changing the tide of battle. A Japanese general and an admiral had committed suicide. And now, as the final curtain came down on the battle, the island's Japanese civilian population committed this last ghastly act of leaping from the Marpi Point cliffs because the Japanese governor of the island had received a message from Tokyo promising that anyone doing so would enjoy the same glory as soldiers dying for their emperor. In that tragic orgy of self-destruction, thousands more souls were added to the already monstrous death toll.

This was the island of Saipan and it was the summer of 1944.

Saipan is one of the fifteen islands comprising the Marianas archipelago. During the war in the Pacific, it was considered to be of vital strategic significance by both sides. U.S. planners wanted the island as the site for an air base that would put the newly developed B-29* long-range bomber within reach of the Japanese home islands for the first time. The Japanese saw the Marianas as a vital barrier in the defense of their empire.

The terrible and costly resistance put up by the Japanese on Saipan was relevant not only to that strategic point in the Pacific but was signifi-

---

* The Boeing B-29 Superfortress was the largest and most advanced bomber used in World War II. First appearing in mid-1944, this four-engined, heavy bomber had a maximum speed of 360 mph, a ten-ton bomb load, and a maximum range of nearly six thousand miles.

cant, in a number of ways, to the war as a whole. First, it was symbolic in that it represented the inevitability of defeat for the Japanese; they had given their all to the defense of the Marianas, and it had not been enough. Second, it was a portent of things to come: the demonstrated fanaticism, not only of the soldiers in the field but of the civilians residing on the island, gave American strategists an ominous preview of what awaited the invading force they believed would someday have to storm ashore in the home islands of Japan. While this horrid vision was never fulfilled, that same resolve would soon be evident in a new and unforeseen weapon the Japanese would call their "divine wind." A Japanese defeat might be inevitable, but that did not mean an American victory would be easily achieved. A fatally wounded animal can sometimes inflict terrible harm before it succumbs.

The third way in which this battle would have a far-reaching effect was in its influence upon the thinking (and actions) of the American admiralty. So important were the Marianas to the Japanese that they committed the bulk of their navy to what would go down in history as the Battle of the Philippine Sea. It was here that one American admiral's actions would have a decided effect upon the actions of another several months later, actions that would lead to one of the greatest controversies in U.S. naval history.

The commander of U.S. naval forces charged with conducting the assault on the Marianas was Admiral Raymond A. Spruance, a quiet, publicity-shunning man who was the ideal combination of warrior and intellectual. His impressive cerebral capabilities were manifested not in philosophical terms but by the ability to evaluate each tactical situation without emotion, to calculate probable outcomes using the available data, and to select a course of action based upon military considerations tempered by a healthy respect for his opponent. His moral courage was evident in his incorruptibility and his consistency in making choices based upon what he saw as right rather than what might benefit him or his career. His physical courage was legendary. Spruance's biographer, Thomas B. Buell, himself a naval officer, writes that the admiral "seemed oblivious to personal danger. He would gaze serenely at bombers diving upon him from above and was indifferent to projectiles from shore batteries bracketing his ship."

Spruance was not a colorful figure, but this is not to say that he was dull or uninteresting. While he was serving as Nimitz's Chief of Staff, visitors to his office at CINCPAC Headquarters were quite surprised to find

Spruance working at a stand-up desk, and because there were no chairs whatsoever in his office, few of those visitors overstayed their welcome. This touch of color notwithstanding, Spruance's lack of flamboyance and avoidance of publicity prevented him from ever becoming as well known as Admiral "Bull" Halsey or Generals MacArthur and Patton. Indeed, Buell's biography of Spruance is aptly entitled, *The Quiet Warrior.*

Yet Raymond Spruance had commanded the carrier forces at the pivotal battle of Midway in June 1942, where a spectacular American victory had changed the course of the war. And he had led American naval forces in the Central Pacific drive through the Gilberts and Marshalls, capturing Tarawa, Kwajalein, and Eniwetok. At the time of the Marianas invasion, Admiral Spruance was Commander of the Fifth Fleet, the largest gathering of naval forces to date. His orders from CINCPAC tasked him with providing air and naval gunfire support for the amphibious landing and with defending the landing force from outside attack should the Japanese Navy challenge the invasion. Because the Japanese Fleet had not appeared at any of the landings in the Gilberts or Marshalls, neither Spruance nor Nimitz believed that it would challenge the American assault on the Marianas.

They were wrong.

By 1944, the tide had turned in the Pacific. After the devastating loss of four aircraft carriers at Midway and the terrible attrition at Guadalcanal, the Japanese had been forced to take the defensive. Their great outward expansion, which had marked the early days of the war, had turned into a costly retreat as Tarawa, Kwajalein, and Eniwetok fell to Nimitz's Central Pacific drive while, simultaneously, MacArthur was moving inexorably up the northern coast of New Guinea. Before the war had even begun, Japanese Admiral Isoroku Yamamoto,* Commander in Chief of the Combined Fleet and probably Japan's greatest naval strategist, had likened the United States to a "sleeping giant" that was vulnerable while slumbering but, once awakened, a terrible force to be reckoned with.

By 1944, the giant was fully awake. American production of war

---

* In Japanese culture, surnames precede given names. However, since complying with this practice might become a distraction to Western readers, all Japanese names in this book will be transposed. Thus, Yamamoto Isoroku (correct in Japan) becomes Isoroku Yamamoto (convenient to Western readers).

matériel had reached staggering heights and the nation's manpower had been effectively mobilized. Evidence of this was abundant in June of that year. In Europe, an American army marched triumphant into Rome on the fourth, while on the sixth, Allied forces crossed the English Channel in mind-boggling numbers and stormed ashore at Normandy—in what has come to be known as the D-Day invasion. In the Southwest Pacific, MacArthur's forces landed at Biak on 15 June. And, on that same day, Operation Forager began in the Central Pacific.

"Forager" was the code name assigned to the invasion of the Marianas. Spruance's Fifth Fleet brought 112 combatant ships to the assault, fifteen of which were attack aircraft carriers. The Japanese Fleet, which sortied from Philippine waters on 15 June, numbered 55 combatants, including nine aircraft carriers. The numerical advantage enjoyed by the American Fleet was somewhat offset by several factors that favored the Japanese.

The Americans were stretching themselves over a thousand miles of ocean in order to invade Saipan and therefore were relying entirely upon their aircraft carriers for air support. The Japanese had land-based aircraft spread over several islands within range of Saipan that they referred to as their "unsinkable aircraft carriers." Additionally, because Japanese aircraft were not weighted down with armor, as American planes were, they enjoyed a significant range advantage. And because aircraft carriers must, as a rule, head into the wind in order to launch or recover aircraft, the Japanese enjoyed a further advantage owing to the predominant direction of the easterly trade wind in that part of the Pacific. Their position relative to the American forces put them downwind, which meant that they could launch and recover aircraft while heading toward the Americans, whereas the Americans had to turn away from their adversary every time they wanted to conduct flight operations.

This by no means meant that the Japanese held all the cards, however. One significant disadvantage for the Japanese was their warrior mentality, which was steeped in the tradition of the *Bushido,** a code of conduct that stressed absolute obedience, military skill, and indifference to danger. This code had served the Japanese warrior well in ancient times when combat was essentially man-to-man and technology was limited, but in modern war, where killing had become a science rather than an art and

---

* From the Japanese *bushi* meaning warrior and *do* meaning doctrine.

attrition a determining factor, *Bushido* had become a detriment to the Japanese military. This blind obedience and indifference to death and danger caused Japanese captains to go down with their ships and army commanders to commit ritual suicide in atonement for failure, noble gestures on the part of the individuals involved, but costly to the greater cause. Captains and generals are not easily replaced.

The aforementioned lack of armor in their aircraft, which gave the Japanese significant range advantage, conversely meant that their aviators were more vulnerable than their American counterparts. American aircraft were also equipped with self-sealing fuel tanks, which added more weight and therefore further reduced their range. These refinements may not have been in keeping with the Japanese indifference to danger, but they ensured that fewer American aircraft exploded in the midst of an aerial dogfight. Thus, by 1944, many Japanese aviators had perished in combat. Pilots are also not easily replaced.

To compound this problem, there was a significant difference in the training philosophies of the two adversaries. American naval aviators were rotated between combat and training duties, while Japanese aviators were kept in combat until they were lost. This meant that Japanese pilots were generally more experienced than their American counterparts, but it also meant that veteran American flyers were bringing their experience home to the training commands where it could have a favorable impact upon fledgling aviators learning their new trade. There was additional benefit in allowing American flyers a respite from the rigors of combat and life at sea.

One other factor had a deleterious effect upon Japanese aviator potential. Perhaps as many as half of those land-based flyers, scattered about on those deceptively beautiful tropical isles in the Pacific, were suffering from the debilitating effects of malaria.

So, as the Japanese Fleet headed east across the Philippine Sea toward the Marianas and the American Fifth Fleet, oddsmakers, had they been present, would probably have picked the Americans to win the ensuing battle. But the oddsmakers would have likewise chosen the Japanese to win the Battle of Midway two years before, when the numerical factors and inertia clearly favored them.

At 0959 on 19 June 1944, American air-search radar detected a large number of contacts approaching from the west, range 150 miles. The U.S. aircraft carriers turned east into the wind and launched their fighters to intercept the incoming Japanese raid. In the great melee that followed, only 24 of the 69 Japanese planes survived. The second Japanese raid that morning, consisting of 130 aircraft, fared no batter—98 planes never returned. In the meantime, Spruance's attack aircraft were bombing the nearby islands and virtually nullifying the effect of the so-called "unsinkable aircraft carriers" by destroying Japanese aircraft on the ground. To further add to Japanese woes, American submarines operating in the Philippine Sea were able to sink two of the Japanese aircraft carriers.

And so it went. By the time merciful darkness brought an end to the carnage, the greatest carrier battle in history had ended so decisively that it would forever be remembered as the "Great Marianas Turkey Shoot." Contrasted with American losses of 30 planes and one bomb-hit on a battleship, the Japanese had suffered the incredible loss of 346 aircraft and two aircraft carriers. It was a one-sidedness rarely experienced in war, and it was to have an irrevocable impact upon the Japanese.

But as night swept across the Pacific, and the skies were no longer filled with the rattle of machine-gun fire and the banshee wail of plummeting aircraft, and thousands of young men rested for a few short hours in their shipboard bunks or forever in aqueous graves, there was no rest for Admiral Spruance. He had some vital decisions to make before the dawn would again bring the clash of arms to the Philippine Sea.

Spruance had already opened himself to ex post facto criticism by not aggressively moving his fleet westward to engage the enemy when the Japanese had first been discovered. Now he had to decide whether to pursue his vanquished enemy to ensure a complete victory. The problem with this course of action, as Spruance saw it, was that he knew the Japanese had a propensity for complicated battle plans that often included dividing their forces. If Spruance left Saipan to pursue an enemy that could no longer do him any immediate harm, and a heretofore undiscovered Japanese force descended upon the unprotected American beachhead, the results could be disastrous. On the other hand, this might be a unique opportunity to annihilate the Japanese carrier force.

Spruance was not an aviator, and there were those within the U.S. Navy who decried the practice of allowing non-aviators to command carrier striking forces. Many aviators believed that "ship-drivers" were not sufficiently aggressive to make effective use of the fast carriers. This criticism might have influenced a lesser man, but Raymond Spruance was not deterred by such things. During the long night that followed the Marianas "Turkey Shoot," Spruance ordered the U.S. carriers to steam *eastward,* staying within supporting distance of Saipan. Only the next day, when it became evident that there were no other Japanese forces approaching from another direction, did he give the carriers permission to pursue. Late on the afternoon of 20 June, planes from the American carriers damaged the retreating Japanese strike force, but they did not destroy it. In the aftermath, some naval officers believed that Spruance had allowed the enemy to escape.

On 17 July a large U.S. Navy aircraft approached the island of Saipan from the southeast, nearing the end of a 600-mile flight from Eniwetok. Serving as escort, several fighter aircraft flashed about the skies, a precaution deemed necessary because the Japanese still controlled several of the nearby islands. Saipan itself had been declared secure, but there were still pockets of resistance that prompted a GI to remark cynically, "If you get shot now, you were hit in your own rear areas."

Inside the large aircraft were Admiral Chester Nimitz, CINCPAC, and his boss, Admiral Ernest J. King, known cryptically as COMINCH. This title was an incomplete acronym for Commander in Chief United States Fleet. It had come into use when Admiral King was first elevated to command all of the Navy's operational forces immediately after Pearl Harbor. King insisted upon the acronym COMINCH because CINCUS, when pronounced, sounded like "Sink us," which would never do as far as Ernie King was concerned. He was a "Sink THEM" kind of admiral.

A few weeks earlier, President Roosevelt had told his Chief of Staff, Admiral Leahy, that he would like the Navy to drop the title "Commander in Chief" from its fleet titles, thus changing Nimitz's title from "Commander in Chief Pacific Fleet" to simply "Commander Pacific Fleet" and likewise transforming King from "Commander in Chief United States Fleet" to "Commander United States Fleet." Roosevelt believed that there should be only one "commander in chief," and that should be the President, who was, according to the U.S. Constitution, "Commander in Chief of the Army and Navy." Leahy dutifully passed the President's wishes on to King, who replied that he would comply if Roosevelt specifically requested him to do it or ordered it. Again, with Leahy acting as middleman, the President sent word to King that he preferred not to order it but would merely like to have it done. King remained COMINCH.

Early in his career, Ernest J. King had vowed that he would be promoted to admiral based solely upon his abilities, and that he would not play the political games of ingratiation and clique-seeking that others deemed necessary for a successful climb to the top. He was true to his word. By the time World War II was looming just over the horizon, he had achieved admiral but was an outcast in his profession. His dreams of heading the U.S. Navy had been shelved, and he was merely marking time until his mandatory retirement in 1942.

But the coming of war changed all that. President Roosevelt recognized in King the talents necessary to revitalize an emotionally demoralized and physically emasculated Navy after the Pearl Harbor disaster. King's talents included a brilliant mind with an acute sense of strategy, a fighting spirit second to none, and a wealth of experience as a surface officer, submariner, and aviator. It is to Roosevelt's credit that he was able to see King's positive qualities through a rather dense smoke screen of negative characteristics. King was cold, arrogant, blunt to the extreme, hot-headed, devoid of humility, and seemingly ignorant of tact and discretion. Professor Robert W. Love of the U.S. Naval Academy History Department has described King's weaknesses as "other men's wives, alcohol, and intolerance." One of King's daughters described him as "the most even-tempered man in the Navy. He is always in a rage."

The large aircraft carrying King and Nimitz touched down at the airfield on the south side of Saipan and was met by Admiral Spruance and other officers who had played key roles in the capture of the island. King strode purposefully up to Spruance and told the Fifth Fleet commander that he had done "exactly the right thing" in the Battle of the Philippine Sea. "No matter what other people tell you," King said, "your decision was correct." Coming from COMINCH, this was no small vindication, but it flew in the face of a great wave of criticism that had been echoing about the wardrooms and ready rooms of the fleet. Spruance's decision to remain within protective range of the landing forces of Saipan rather than move aggressively westward to pursue the fleeing Japanese Fleet had become a highly controversial topic among real and would-be strategists in the U.S. Navy. A new saying, "the Spruance nuance," was cast disparagingly about by some, while others staunchly defended the Fifth Fleet commander. Even Admiral Nimitz, who was one of Spruance's strongest defenders, could not resist dreaming of things that might have been when he submitted his CINCPAC Summary of Action for June 1944:

> There may be some disappointment to some in the fact that in addition to the successful accomplishment of our purpose—the occupation of the Southern Marianas—there was not also a decisive "fleet action," in which we would naturally hope to have been victorious, and to have thereby shortened the war materially.
>
> It may be argued that the Japanese never had any intention of evading [the Fifth Fleet] with part or all of their forces, and making their major attack against our shipping at Saipan. From this premise it can be proved that our main body of carriers and gunnery ships could have pushed to the westward without concern for the expeditionary forces, and that had it done so, a decisive fleet air action could have been fought, the Japanese fleet destroyed, and the end of the war hastened.

Little wonder that other senior commanders in the Navy might be influenced to act differently from Spruance in the coming months of the war. All of this Monday morning quarterbacking would have no discernible effect upon Spruance himself—his performance in the remainder of the war was impeccable—but it *was* to have a profound effect on another American commander in the next battle to be fought in the waters of the Philippine Sea.

Besides the obvious tone of disappointment in Nimitz's report, there is something else revealed in those words. It is apparent that he and, it is safe to assume, other key planners in the U.S. Navy did not fully appreciate the impact that the Battle of the Philippine Sea made on the Japanese. While those taking part in the battle had enough realization of the devastating losses suffered by Japanese naval air forces to dub the incident a "turkey shoot," there was not a full understanding of just how much damage had been suffered by their foe. In truth, the naval air forces of Japan had been dealt a blow from which they would never fully recover. The escaped carriers steamed back to the Inland Sea of Japan with only 35 aircraft left onboard, and there they remained for the next four months, desperately trying to train new pilots to replace the hundreds left behind in the Philippine Sea.

As COMINCH, and Chief of Naval Operations (his other hat), Admiral King was the U.S. Navy's representative on both the American Joint Chiefs

of Staff and the Allied Combined Chiefs of Staff.* Historians generally
agree that he was the most capable strategist of the American Joint Chiefs
and was equalled among the Combined Chiefs only by Air Chief Marshal
Sir Charles Portal of the Royal Air Force. King, though recognizing the
soundness of the Europe-first strategy, had also seen the need for a limited
offensive in the Pacific. He reasoned that to ignore the Japanese while
fighting Hitler's Germany would allow them to consolidate their gains and
make their Pacific empire virtually impregnable. He also believed—and
was later vindicated in that belief—that the United States economy, once
mobilized, was capable of supporting a two-ocean war. King could see
things that other men sometimes could not, and the President could see
that in King. Roosevelt relied upon him for strategic advice more than on
any of his chiefs of staff.

King had come to the Pacific for one of his periodic visits with Nimitz
to discuss strategy, inspect facilities, and make his presence felt. He had
arrived at Pearl Harbor on 13 July and, after touring a number of facilities
there, he and Nimitz visited Kwajalein and Eniwetok before flying on to
Saipan, arriving on 17 July.

After a lunch in the heavily damaged village of Charan-Kanoa on the
west coast of the island, where Marine General Holland Smith had set up
his headquarters, King, Nimitz, Spruance, and Smith climbed into a Jeep
for a tour of the island, despite the danger imposed by remnants of the
Japanese garrison still at large and still inflicting casualties upon the
American forces there. A Jeep full of armed marines accompanied
the group, warily watching the mouths of caves, the edges of ravines, and
the many canefields that served as concealment for enemy snipers. As the
King-Nimitz group reached the north end of the island, they paused at
Marpi Point and General Smith described the lemming-like mass-suicide
that had recently occurred there. The bodies were gone now, but the horror
lingered.

Later that afternoon, the group boarded a landing craft and was trans-
ported out to the heavy cruiser *Indianapolis*, where they were greeted by

---

* Admiral Leahy, as Chairman of the Joint Chiefs of Staff, was senior to King,
but had set himself apart from the Navy by adopting what is sometimes referred to as a
"purple suit" mentality, a term that signifies the blending of the uniform colors and is
meant to convey the idea of a military ecumenism in which priorities are assigned
without being influenced by the parochial concerns of one's own service.

Spruance's chief of staff, Captain Carl Moore. Because the weather was oppressively hot, no one looked forward to eating dinner in a "buttoned-up" ship. Yet wartime conditions—particularly so deep inside what had been exclusively enemy territory just weeks before—dictated that the ship's ports must all be closed after dark so that no light could be seen by enemy submarines that might be lurking in the area. It was decided to eat dinner early, before dark, so that the ship's ports might remain open for better air circulation. This turned out to be a significant tactical error. As the meal began, swarms of large, black flies descended upon the diners. Captain Moore described the invaders: "It was the kind of fly you couldn't scare off. You had to push it. It would light on your nose, and you had to practically pick it off. . . . It was a horror, because it would be in your food [and] you kept thinking that the flies had all been eating dead Japs and were coming out to the ship for a little fresh air."

As these star-encrusted officers sat eating and swatting flies in the Mariana Islands, some three thousand miles from Pearl Harbor and only half that distance from Tokyo, it was evident that they were at a major milestone in the progress of the war. What was not so evident was just where their next move should be.

King favored a strike on the island of Formosa, just off the China coast. He reasoned that if an invasion of Japan was going to be necessary—and everything pointed to that in mid-1944—then an intensive air bombardment of the home islands would be a prerequisite. This could best be accomplished from airfields in China, which would in turn require Allied control of at least one port on the Chinese coast in order to ensure adequate supply. No port could be secure without Allied control of the South China Sea, and that, King reasoned, could best be accomplished by capturing Formosa. Joint Chiefs planners had been developing this Marianas-Formosa-China strategy under the code name "Granite II."

Nimitz favored an interim step of capturing the southern or central Philippines, believing that it would be impossible to ensure Allied lines of communications with Formosa without first establishing air bases in the southern Philippines from which Japanese air power on the northern Philippine island of Luzon could be neutralized.

And then there was MacArthur. Though he was not present at the meal in the Marianas, everyone knew where he stood. He, of course, could see no alternative to a complete liberation of *all* of the Philippines. Less than a month before King's trip to Saipan, he had sent a message to the Joint Chiefs effectively stating his case:

> It is my opinion that purely military considerations demand the reoccupation of the Philippines in order to cut the enemy's communications to the south and to secure a base for our further advance. Even if this were not the case . . . it would in my opinion be necessary to reoccupy the Philippines.
>
> The Philippines is American territory where our unsupported forces were destroyed by the enemy. Practically all of the 17,000,000 Filipinos remain loyal to the United States and are undergoing the greatest privation and suffering because we have not been able to support or succor them. We have a great national obligation to discharge.
>
> Moreover, if the United States should deliberately bypass the Philippines, leaving our prisoners, nationals, and loyal Filipinos in enemy hands without an effort to retrieve them at [the] earliest moment, we would incur the gravest psychological reaction. We would admit the truth of Japanese propaganda to the effect that we had abandoned the Filipinos and would not shed American blood to redeem them; we would undoubtedly incur the open hostility of that people; we would probably suffer such loss of prestige among all the peoples of the Far East that it would adversely affect the United States for many years. . . .

MacArthur's forces had, by this time, moved most of the way up the New Guinea coast and were within nine hundred miles of the southern tip of the Philippines. The General's plan for returning, code-named "Reno V," called for a 25 October preliminary seizure of Sarangani Bay on the southern coast of Mindanao, the southernmost of the Philippine islands, in order to provide a site for land-based air. Then his main thrust into the Philippines would take place on 15 November at Leyte, a large island on the eastern side of the archipelago. This site was chosen because its central location in the Philippines would allow the Americans to divide Japanese forces in the islands, and because Leyte Gulf was particularly suitable as an anchorage for a large invading fleet. After the capture of Leyte, Reno V called for an attack on the main Philippine island of Luzon in April of 1945.

But at this point in the war, with the momentum so clearly with Allied forces, the Joint Chiefs had not decided whether to adopt the plans of CINCSOWESPAC or yield to the desires of COMINCH. They were anxious to find ways to shorten the campaign in the Pacific. MacArthur's plan

seemed unbearably slow, and even King's idea of bypassing the Philippines and leaping to Formosa would take time, more time than most planners were at that point willing to concede.

But, acceleration was the only point of agreement. The differences of
opinion regarding where to go next had created many differing factions
within the various headquarters charged with planning the war in the
Pacific. Convincing arguments came from all quarters but consensus
remained elusive. Resolution of the matter was to come in a somewhat
unorthodox manner, the first step of which was under way as Admiral King
concluded his Pacific tour and headed back to Washington. As his plane
flew eastward across the Pacific, USS *Baltimore* plied the waters below,
headed in the opposite direction. On board that heavy cruiser was the key
to deciding where the Pacific campaign would go next.

3

★ CINCPAC ★

In September 1942, when the fortunes of war in the Pacific were hanging in the balance in a godforsaken corner of the world called Guadalcanal, a mysterious message arrived at CINCPAC headquarters in Hawaii at about 0300. The duty officer immediately called Lieutenant Hal Lamar, flag lieutenant to Admiral Nimitz, to see whether he thought the admiral should be wakened and told of the contents of the message. The duty officer informed Lamar that Marine General A. Archer Vandegrift, commander of the landing forces at Guadalcanal, was requesting one hundred gross of medical item number 75–177.

"What is the item?" Lamar asked.

"It's a rubber contraceptive," came the tentative reply.

Now this was a strange request. The only women on Guadalcanal were the natives, and they were most unlikely to be anywhere near the marines then fighting a bloody, very tenuous battle with an extremely determined enemy. Reports from Guadalcanal painted a picture of men living in appalling conditions under constant enemy threat; where tropical heat, soaking rains, insect infestations, and almost constant enemy shelling made the basic needs of eating and sleeping continuously in doubt. This hardly seemed the time or the place for the services of 14,400 condoms.

Despite his puzzlement, Lamar called the fleet surgeon, Captain Gendreau, and asked him if he could supply the "medical items." Gendreau replied that there were not that many contraceptives on the entire island of Oahu and then asked why the hell the marines wanted them. Lamar could not answer.

Putting on his uniform, Lamar went up to Nimitz's quarters and woke the admiral. Nimitz read the message over once, smiled, and said, "General Vandegrift is probably going to use them to keep the rain out of his marines' rifles."

Nimitz had been right about the condoms. Like his boss, Admiral King, Chester Nimitz could often see things that other men could not. This was one of the reasons why he had been promoted over the heads of twenty-eight admirals senior to him to command the Pacific Fleet. Together with General Douglas MacArthur, he had been charged with winning the war in the Pacific.

Despite the awesome and complex responsibility that had been given these two men, Nimitz and MacArthur almost never conferred, and to find their common superior, one had to go to the other side of the world, to the President himself. As CINCPAC/CINCPOA, Nimitz's immediate superior was Admiral King, and MacArthur answered to the Army Chief of Staff, General George C. Marshall. Although King and Marshall, as members of the Joint Chiefs, deferred to a degree to Admiral Leahy, their chairman, it was Franklin Roosevelt who was the true arbiter and the final word on matters concerning the Joint Chiefs and their conduct of the war.

Because of this awkward command structure, founded more on political expediency than upon military efficiency, Nimitz and MacArthur occasionally found themselves "butting heads," as in the Solomons and the Admiralties, where their spheres of influence abutted and overlapped. But for the most part they were able to conduct their respective campaigns independently and with amazingly little friction.

What the two men thought of each other is not entirely clear. Both were rather enigmatic, Nimitz more for his taciturnity and MacArthur because of his contradictions. It appears that MacArthur resented the more junior Nimitz receiving authority equal to his own and acted accordingly on several occasions. Nimitz, on the other hand, went to great lengths to prevent animosity between them. He would not permit members of his staff to criticize MacArthur and, on one occasion, when a naval officer on his way to join MacArthur's staff told Nimitz of the negative things he had heard about the general from naval officers in Washington, Nimitz jumped from his chair and said sharply, "Young man, that never came out of *this* office, and I want that strictly understood."

Nimitz appears to have genuinely believed that he had succeeded in preventing a rift between MacArthur and himself, because in a letter to his wife late in the war, Nimitz wrote: "Drew Pearson, in his column of last night in the *Star Bulletin*, tries to stir up trouble between MacArthur and me where *none* exists. . . . What a troublemaker he is! Apparently, many people like to read such rubbish."

But there might have been a small clue to Nimitz's innermost feelings sitting on his desk at CINCPAC headquarters. There he kept a framed photograph of General MacArthur clipped from a newspaper. When asked by a friend why it was there, Nimitz confided that the photograph served as a reminder "not to make Jovian pronouncements complete with thunderbolts."

"Jovian pronouncements and thunderbolts" were definitely not Chester Nimitz's style. He was known for his quiet manner, so much so that he was often misjudged as "soft" or too easygoing. Indeed, it took a long while for Admiral King to fully trust in him. But Nimitz was much tougher than his pale blue eyes and grandfatherly smile indicated. He knew how to stand his ground, even against the likes of a fire-breather like King. Although he never rashly fired anyone, he would get rid of any officer who persisted in not measuring up to his expectations.

Despite Nimitz's jumping over the heads of many admirals senior to him when he was chosen to replace Admiral Husband Kimmel as CINCPAC in the aftermath of the attack on Pearl Harbor, he was no reckless climber. A year earlier, he had turned down an offer to make him Commander in Chief of the entire U.S. Fleet because he thought himself too junior. Upon his assumption of command in the Pacific, he immediately announced that he would retain deposed Admiral Kimmel's staff, an act that preserved for the Navy a significant number of very capable officers and helped calm some of the head-rolling hysteria that had prevailed as the smoke slowly cleared from Pearl Harbor.

Nimitz was known for keeping staff conferences brief, for leading by example, and for listening to the ideas of others. He had little discernible ego and was both a tenacious fighter and a magnanimous victor. In sharp contrast to MacArthur, arguments concerning Nimitz's character and capabilities, among both his contemporaries and latter-day historians, focus not upon whether he was good or bad but whether he was good or *great*.

By mid-1944, these two very different commanders had successfully amputated their enemy's extremities. By the tactics of direct frontal assault on some Japanese bases and the logistical strangulation of others by bypassing them and leaving them to "wither on the vine," Nimitz and

MacArthur had successfully severed New Guinea, the Gilberts, the Solomons, the Admiralties, the Marshalls, the Carolines, and the Marianas from the Japanese Empire. The time had come to go for the vital organs, to sever those arteries carrying the lifeblood flow of oil from the Dutch East Indies to the home islands of Japan, to gain a foothold from which could be delivered the final thrust at the very heart of the empire. The time had also come for Nimitz and MacArthur to meet.

Driven by the natural engine of the northeast trade winds, slowly undulating swells swept across the unbroken surface of the Pacific as far as the eye could see. From the gently heeling deck of the heavy cruiser USS *Baltimore*, a sixty-two-year-old man peered through his pince-nez at the blue waters sparkling in the sunlight. He had long had a love affair with ships and the sea, and now he appeared to be inhaling the warm salt air as though it were an elixir that could restore the color to his sallow cheeks and erase the deeply etched shadows beneath his intelligent but weary eyes. Although he could not have known at that moment, he would be dead within a year.

But before death could claim him, Franklin Roosevelt had much work to do. Important work. And that was why this wartime president was on his way to Pearl Harbor.

Whether that work was strategic or political only Franklin Roosevelt knew for certain. The official purpose of the journey was for the Commander in Chief of the Army and Navy to meet with the two men running the war in the Pacific. But there were critics who claimed that this trip was politically motivated; that Roosevelt had no need to confer directly with Nimitz and MacArthur; that he was jumping the chain of command, bypassing his principal advisers, the Joint Chiefs of Staff, by conferring with these two subordinate theater commanders; that his real motivation was to be seen (and photographed) with General MacArthur. The year 1944 was, after all, an election year, and only the day before his embarkation in *Baltimore* on 21 July, Roosevelt had been nominated at the Democratic convention in Chicago for an unprecedented fourth term as president.

James MacGregor Burns, in his biography of Roosevelt, made the point well when he noted that just prior to the ship's departure from San Diego, the President had been informed that General Tojo had been forced to resign as premier of Japan as a result of the fall of Saipan, and that

Adolf Hitler had narrowly escaped death at the hands of would-be assassins among his senior military officers. Burns observed that although "Roosevelt could not be dismissed by an emperor or deposed by ministers or generals, . . . he was the only military commander who could be sacked by the voters."

Roosevelt may indeed have wanted to be photographed with his theater commanders so that the voters might see him in his role as Commander in Chief, as potential rival Douglas MacArthur's boss. Or he may have come to Pearl Harbor to resolve the differences among his principal advisers, to decide where American forces should go next in the Pacific. He was, after all, getting conflicting advice from those who had his ear in Washington. Perhaps it was time to hear what the on-scene commanders had to say without the filters and dilutions of the chain of command.

Whatever his motivations, Franklin Roosevelt was at sea on a warship headed for Pearl Harbor, accompanied by his chief of staff, Admiral Leahy, and his little dog, Fala. The trip had been uneventful, allowing the President a much needed opportunity to catch up on sleep and to read without interruption. Fala, on the other hand, was not to be afforded such luxuries. The famous Scottie was frequently subjected to the indignity of souvenir-seeking sailors snipping locks of his hair to send home.

Like nearly everyone with that surname, Weldon E. Rhoades went by the sobriquet "Dusty." He had been a reserve Army Air Corps captain and civilian pilot flying government contracted missions with United Air Lines when, in October 1943, Douglas MacArthur had asked Rhoades to come fly for him as his personal pilot. After conferring with his wife on the matter, Dusty Rhoades decided to accept and was soon converted "from an indifferent admirer of [MacArthur's] to a most loyal disciple." He had flown MacArthur all over the Southwest Pacific area, mostly in a converted B-17 bomber that the general had named *Bataan*, and he had sometimes been MacArthur's personal confidant, though by Rhoades's own admission, this meant that the general would talk for great lengths of time during which Rhoades was not expected to respond.

On the tenth of July, 1944, General Richard Sutherland, MacArthur's chief of staff, summoned Rhoades to his office and informed him, in great secrecy, that MacArthur would be leaving Australia to attend a "world-important" conference before the end of the month. Five days later, MacArthur himself told Rhoades of the impending trip. By now Rhoades knew the destination was Honolulu and that the general had been summoned for a meeting with Nimitz and Roosevelt on the twenty-sixth.

For this special journey, Rhoades requisitioned a passenger-equipped version of the heavy cargo C-54 aircraft then being flown into Australia under military contract by Pan American Airways. He had done this because *Bataan*'s passenger compartment was small and did not have enough headroom to permit MacArthur to do his customary pacing. Rhoades knew that the general walked back and forth almost constantly while in his office, and he reasoned that MacArthur might want to do the same during the twenty-six-hour trip to Hawaii. Rhoades also replaced three rows of the aircraft's seats with a comfortable innerspring cot so that the sixty-four-year-old MacArthur might rest during the grueling trip.

Dusty Rhoades had been right about the pacing, wrong about the cot. MacArthur did not sleep during the entire trip but paced like a caged tiger during most of it. Partway through the flight, Rhoades left the cockpit to get some food and coffee. He noted that the general ate little and seemed very tense and irritable. After the meal, MacArthur said that if Rhoades was not needed in the cockpit, he should stay and have some more coffee. This was MacArthur's signal that he wanted to talk.

Rhoades sat next to MacArthur and silently sipped coffee as the general began his monologue by admitting that he was not sure why the President had summoned him. MacArthur confided that he was worried. Why had Roosevelt called him away from his command at a time when the Japanese were on the defensive in New Guinea? Could it be that his forces were about to be reduced, thus relegating him to a mere holding action in the Southwest Pacific while Nimitz's forces would continue the assault across the Central Pacific? Or was he about to be removed from his command altogether? Perhaps it was not bad news at all, and he was going to get the green light for his long-awaited return to the Philippines. After a pause, MacArthur's brow wrinkled and he said that maybe Roosevelt had summoned him for the simple purpose of providing publicity pictures useful to his campaign. He added that he hoped this was not the case. He had better things to do with his time than leave his wartime command and travel thousands of miles for a picture-taking junket.

Many hours later, as they neared Honolulu, the sky began to fill with aircraft. The planes were assembling to fly a ceremonial review for the President, who was at that moment within sight of Diamond Head in the heavy cruiser *Baltimore*.

★ ★ ★

For security reasons, the President's visit to Hawaii had been treated as highly classified information. But some things are impossible to keep secret. As *Baltimore* stood up the channel into Pearl Harbor, there were thousands of eyes upon her, hoping to catch a glimpse of the Commander in Chief. Sailors clad in their gleaming white dress uniforms were at the rails of all the ships present, bands played martial airs, the normally continuous sound of hammers chipping off old paint and rust from the hulls of tired ships was temporarily silenced, and formations of aircraft flew overhead. As *Baltimore* made her way across the world's most famous harbor, Admiral Leahy noted that there was "no striking evidence remaining of the frightful damage inflicted in the sneak attack by the Japanese on our fleet as it rode easily at anchor on Sunday, December 7, 1941."

Admiral Nimitz and several others of the more senior officers at Pearl had come out on the pilot tug and were already aboard *Baltimore* as she made her triumphal entry. The presidential flag was hoisted to the main and former Assistant Secretary of the Navy Roosevelt was in his element.

Waiting on the pier was a line of senior officers, their silver and gold shoulder boards glinting in the afternoon sun. When the ship was moored, the senior admiral in the group ordered a "Right Face!" in preparation for their boarding. These men, upon whose shoulders rested not only ornamental gold but the responsibility for deciding the course of a world war, had seen many a setting sun since they last practiced close-order drill. Two of the admirals mistakenly turned *left*, and a great cheer went up from the sailors on board *Baltimore*.

Besides the obvious humor of that moment, one can find something ironic in it as well. Such a display by the enlisted men of *Baltimore* would never have occurred in the navies of America's enemies. In Germany, an undisciplined outburst of that nature would more than likely have resulted in severe punishment for the offenders. In Japan, there would have been no laughter and the two admirals who had faced the wrong way would have probably punished *themselves* for their inexcusable loss of face. Yet these obvious differences in disciplinary standards do not necessarily reveal an American weakness. The United States was, by this time, winning the war, and not merely by the production of vast quantities of war matériel. Those sailors who had laughed at their superiors were typical of the kind who had futilely yet defiantly thrown wrenches at strafing Japanese fighters in this same harbor more than two years before. They were the same kind of men who had sacrificed themselves at Midway and changed the course of the war. And they were no different from those who would, in just a few short months, astound the world with their courage at a then little-known place called Samar.

MacArthur's suspicions were at least partially confirmed when he was invited to pose for pictures with Nimitz, Leahy, and the President on *Baltimore*'s main deck. That evening, MacArthur fumed over being brought to Hawaii for such a purpose, and his mood did not improve when he later received a message from the President regarding a planned inspection tour of Oahu's military installations the next morning. The President wanted the general to accompany him on the tour, along with Admirals Leahy and Nimitz.

General Robert C. Richardson, the senior Army officer in Hawaii (until MacArthur's arrival), made the arrangements for the presidential inspection tour, and one of his more difficult problems proved to be the procurement of a suitable vehicle in which to transport the august party. The only automobiles he could come up with were a bright red, five-passenger car belonging to Honolulu's fire chief and a larger, more moderately colored sedan that belonged to the madam of one of Honolulu's houses of ill repute. Fearing that the latter vehicle would be recognized by too many viewing the parade, General Richardson opted for the smaller, but better reputed, fire chief's car.

That evening, the four men sat down to dinner in the cream stucco mansion on Waikiki beach that millionaire Christopher Holmes had made available to the President. The conversation at dinner was either highly classified or utterly mundane, because no record of it exists. But what was said after dinner was recorded, is no longer classified, and was far from mundane.

Roosevelt, Nimitz, Leahy, and MacArthur left the table and moved into the mansion's large living room where huge wall maps of the Pacific had been hung. Nimitz and MacArthur alternately stood before the President, occasionally pointing at the maps with a long bamboo pointer, and presented their ideas for the future strategy in the Pacific. Nimitz had come around to King's way of thinking and now advocated bypassing the Philippines in favor of an invasion of Formosa, while MacArthur steadfastly defended the imperatives of a Philippine invasion. Leahy, who was more observer of the proceedings than participant, later wrote: "After so much loose talk in Washington, where the mention of the name MacArthur seemed to generate more heat than light, it was both pleasant and very informative to have these two men who had been pictured as antagonists calmly present their differing views to the Commander-in-Chief. For Roosevelt it was an excellent lesson in geography, one of his favorite subjects." Leahy added that the President "was at his best as he tactfully steered the discussion from one point to another and narrowed down the area of disagreement between MacArthur and Nimitz." MacArthur agreed with Leahy, later recording that Roosevelt "was entirely neutral in handling the discussion." Noting that both Nimitz and MacArthur had told the President that they could carry out their respective plans with the forces then available in the Pacific, Leahy added that it was "highly pleasing and unusual to find two commanders who were not demanding reinforcements."

Nimitz's arguments made good strategic sense. Formosa was well situated geographically to block the flow of oil to Japan, and it was close to China where American planners had long hoped to establish air bases for the strategic bombing of the home islands. Formosa would also serve well as a marshalling point for an invasion of Japan when and if the time came for that. But Nimitz's arguments were almost purely *military* in their scope, whereas MacArthur's were also very *political*.

MacArthur pointed out that the Asian population on Formosa could not be counted upon to lend willing support to American forces and might, in fact, be openly hostile, whereas the Filipinos were, almost to a man, loyal to America. He cited the constant flow of information he had received from guerrillas in the Philippines since the Japanese occupation, communications that were maintained at no small risk to the Filipinos involved.

He insisted that the United States had a moral obligation to the people of the Philippines to free them from Japanese oppression as soon as possible. He resorted to opening the old wounds of Bataan and Corregidor, pointing out that America had abandoned not only the loyal Filipinos there but thousands of Americans as well. He added that there were, at that very moment, American men, women, and children languishing in Japanese concentration camps in the Philippines, suffering terrible privations as the numbered days of their wretched lives passed inexorably on. He warned that the Filipinos could forgive us for failing to protect them from the Japanese in the first place, that they would even forgive our failing in an attempt to rescue them, but what they would *not* forgive was our *not even trying* to free them. And if the Philippines alone were not incentive enough, MacArthur admonished that the eyes of all Asia would be watching what we did in the Philippines, that our postwar image in that part of the world was at stake.

MacArthur was at his best that evening. He had no notes, no prepared maps of his own, and absolutely no doubt that he was right. He used his considerable powers of persuasion with consummate skill, and by midnight it seemed that he was winning the day. Not only did Roosevelt appear to be accepting MacArthur's reasoning, but Nimitz's counterarguments were coming forth less frequently, and Leahy seemed to have sided with MacArthur as well. Just after midnight, however, the meeting adjourned, with the only definite decision being that the four would continue their meeting in the morning.

The next day MacArthur took advantage of a private moment with Roosevelt to say that if the Philippines were bypassed, "I daresay that the American people would be so aroused that they would register most complete resentment against you at the polls this fall." Never one to miss the opportunity to bring all weapons to bear, General MacArthur had fired a silver bullet with this remark. At the very least he was prodding the political animal inside of Roosevelt, haunting him with the politician's nightmare, the specter of lost votes. Some historians have gone a step further, reading into MacArthur's admonition an implied threat that he would bring his influence among politicians back home to bear against Roosevelt in the coming election if the President did not give him what he wanted. Whether MacArthur did indeed intend that threat, and whether he had the political strength back in the United States to make good on it, are debatable issues. But what does seem certain is that, for whatever reason, Roosevelt had decided that United States forces must not bypass the Philippines. MacArthur received a letter from Roosevelt little more than a week after their Honolulu conference that read, in part:

Douglas—

I am on the last leg of my return journey to Washington. It has been a most successful, though all too short, visit and the highlight of it was the three days that you and I saw each other in Honolulu. I got a splendid picture of the whole vast area—far better than I had when I left Washington. You have been doing a really magnificent job against what were great

*difficulties, given us by climate and by certain human animals. As soon as
I get back I will push on that plan for I am convinced that it is logical and
can be done.*

    *And to see you again gave me a particular happiness. Personally, I
wished much in Honolulu that you and I could swap places and personally, I have a hunch that you would make more of a go of it as President
than I would as General in the retaking of the Philippines. . . .*

So the Commander in Chief of the Army and Navy was convinced, and
this was no small ally. More hurdles lay ahead, but MacArthur had won an
important victory in Hawaii, one which brought him one giant step closer
to his promised return to the Philippines.

    Several hundred men surrounded Admiral Chester Nimitz's living
quarters, a large clapboard house on Makalapa Hill overlooking Pearl
Harbor. They were armed with picks and shovels, hammers, nails, saws,
and a large gray bulldozer, which sat momentarily motionless at the edge
of the lawn, its growling diesel engine pumping blue smoke into the otherwise pristine atmosphere. On command, the force descended upon Nimitz's
defenseless quarters and began rehanging doors, transplanting palm trees,
installing emergency landing mats, painting, drying paint with blow-
torches, constructing a driveway to the back of the house, and even raising
the admiral's toilet five inches. All of this had come about as a result of a
visit from Mike Reilly, one of the most powerful men in the world, a man
who could order entire buildings evacuated, a city's traffic rerouted,
important schedules redrawn, and even an admiral's toilet raised five
inches. He was chief of the White House Secret Service detail, and he was
preparing Nimitz's quarters for a luncheon scheduled for the afternoon of
28 July. These specialized preparations reflected, among other things, the
President's special handicap. Doors had to be rehung to allow convenient
wheelchair access, the driveway had to be rerouted to the rear of the house
because Roosevelt did not like to be seen during those awkward moments
of being helped in and out of automobiles, and the toilet had to be raised
so as to allow the President to slide across to it from his wheelchair.
    During the meal, which those in the know referred to as MacArthur's
"victory luncheon," the general assured Roosevelt that he and Nimitz had
resolved any disagreements they may have had before the conference and
said, "We see eye to eye, Mr. President."

By this unprecedented visit to Hawaii, Franklin Roosevelt had successfully arbitrated the differences between his two Pacific commanders. He had indeed proven himself an able Commander in Chief of the Army and Navy. But as he dined on mahimahi with all the flag and general officers then on Oahu, there remained many rocks and shoals in the uncharted waters ahead. Still to be convinced were his advisers in Washington and, after them, were the Allied commanders. A problem that was to remain unresolved—one that Roosevelt the Commander in Chief could have eliminated, but that Roosevelt the politician would not—was that there still was no overall commander in the Pacific, a small problem when CINCPAC and CINCSOWESPAC were operating in separate theaters with only occasional minor overlaps, but a potentially greater one when these two would soon meet in full force.

But, for the moment, these future problems were overshadowed by a grand moment for Roosevelt as he presided over lunch at Nimitz's quarters. Hal Lamar, when recalling that luncheon, said that he could not remember the exact number of officers that attended, "but it seems to me that I counted one hundred and thirty-six stars on the collars of the officers present."

Among those stars comprising that constellation of military power, four belonged to a man with a leathery face and a mischievous smile who was destined to play a key role in the unfolding drama of the Philippines. Just back from emergency leave in the United States, and about to assume command of the most powerful fleet in the world, was Admiral William F. "Bull" Halsey.

4

★ COMTHIRDFLT ★

On 27 November 1941—nine days before the Japanese attacked Pearl Harbor, ten days before the United States declared war on the Empire of Japan, and thirteen days before Germany and Italy declared war on the United States—the pilots in the squadron ready rooms of the aircraft carrier *Enterprise* were handed a mimeographed sheet entitled "Battle Order Number One." The directive began with the rather startling words, "The *Enterprise* is now operating under war conditions. At any time, day or night, we must be ready for instant action." The final words on the sheet read, "It is part of the tradition of our Navy that, when put to the test, all hands keep cool, keep their heads, and FIGHT. Steady nerves and stout hearts are needed now."

Commander William H. Buracker, the task force commander's operations officer, stared incredulously at the mimeographed sheet in his hand for a moment and then ran up the several ladders to *Enterprise*'s flag bridge where he knew he would find his boss.

"Admiral, did you authorize this thing?" Buracker asked, breathing hard from the hastened climb.

"Yes," came the reply.

"Do you realize that this means war?" Buracker asked.

"Yes," the admiral repeated laconically.

At that same moment, aircraft in *Enterprise*'s hangar bay were being fitted out with bombs, torpedoes, and a full allowance of machine-gun ammunition. And the other twelve ships in Task Force 8, then steaming southwest from Pearl Harbor on a mission of delivering aircraft to Wake Island, were fitting out their torpedoes with warheads and breaking out live rounds of gun ammunition.

"Goddammit, Admiral," Buracker said with obvious exasperation. "You can't start a private war of your own! Who's going to take responsibility?"

From beneath thick eyebrows, the admiral's eyes burned brightly as he said, "I'll take it. If anything gets in the way we'll shoot first and argue afterwards."

Nine days later, bombs cascaded from the skies over Pearl Harbor, ending America's last period of innocence and plunging the nation headlong into the greatest war mankind had ever seen. The United States Navy as a whole was not prepared for what happened that day. But Task Force 8, under the command of Vice Admiral William F. Halsey, *was*.

"Bull"* Halsey was probably the U.S. Navy's most colorful admiral. His weatherworn face was the very image of an old salt and during the war appeared countless times in newspapers and magazines. He was quoted time and again by the print media because his utterances were almost always humorous, inspiring, outrageous, or a combination thereof. One example occurred as *Enterprise* steamed slowly into Pearl Harbor just hours after the attack. Halsey had surveyed the incredible damage in silence for a while, then was heard to growl, "Before we're through with'em, the Japanese language will be spoken only in hell!"

Some of his outspokenness seems a bit childish or even racist to a modern reader, but it was apropos for the early 1940s. He began early in the war referring to the Japanese as "rats." "Kill Japs, they're rats," he often said. As the war progressed they became "bastards" for a while, and then he switched to "monkeys." Finally, by war's end, the Japanese had become to Halsey "lousy yellow rat monkey bastards."

What had made Halsey such a popular figure did not rest merely upon his colorful statements or his hardened-warrior appearance. His aggressive spirit was contagious and much needed in those early days of the war, when the American Navy had much to lament. With the pall of Pearl Harbor still shadowing the American fleet, Halsey led a carrier force deep into

---

* The sobriquet "Bull" was an invention of the press. Friends called Halsey "Bill," and subordinates often referred to him as "Admiral Bill" (but never to his face). In his autobiography, Halsey wrote: "I don't want to be remembered as 'Bull' Halsey." But the name has become a part of the Halsey legend and, despite his wishes to the contrary, Admiral Halsey will forever be "Bull."

the Japanese held Central Pacific in January 1942, striking Japanese installations in the Marshall Islands and causing minimal damage but becoming an overnight hero as a direct result. Just two months later, he commanded the task force that struck Tokyo, a virtually meaningless attack in tactical terms but of inestimable value psychologically. He was then sent in to relieve a failed naval commander at Guadalcanal and there turned the tide of battle, more by the sheer weight of his personality than by any strategic or tactical measures he had taken.

Halsey was a risk-taker and a leader of the first order. It is difficult to imagine not wanting to follow a man who, upon hearing a Japanese radio broadcast tauntingly ask, "Where is the American Navy?" turned to an aide and said, "Send them our latitude and longitude!"

Admiral Arleigh Burke, himself a World War II naval hero of no small stature, wrote of Halsey, "I would follow Admiral William Halsey anywhere in this world, or beyond. And so would thousands of other sailors, from the lowliest apprentice right up the line."

In direct contrast to Spruance, Halsey was not an intellectual. One of his several biographers, James M. Merrill, writes that "his speeches, private correspondence, and reports reveal that he often thought in clichés and that his vocabulary was narrow." Halsey's autobiography, written with the aid of a professional writer, began with the words "This will not be an autobiography, but a report. Reports are the only things I know how to write. . . ." He later added that he would "avoid fields like philosophy and politics, where I am easily lost. . . ." Like the equally iconoclastic Socrates of an earlier time, Halsey's admission of ignorance seems to say there is wisdom in knowing that one is not wise.

Nimitz held Halsey in high esteem, often defending him when he got into hot water, as risk-takers inevitably do. Later in the war, when Halsey was being criticized for allowing his fleet to be caught in a vicious typhoon and there were many who called for his censure, Nimitz responded by recalling the war's early days when Halsey's aggressive spirit had served as counterpoint to the defeatism that had permeated the Navy. Nimitz said, "Bill Halsey came to my support and offered to lead the attack. I'll not be party to any enterprise that can hurt the reputation of a man like that."

Nimitz thought so highly of both Halsey and Spruance and considered each so capable of commanding at a tactical level that he could not decide who should lead the Pacific Fleet into battle. The problem was eventually solved by alternating the two. When Spruance was in command of what had become known generally as "the Big Blue Fleet," it was officially called the Fifth Fleet. And when Halsey and his staff took the reins, it became the Third Fleet. Same ships, same crews, different commander. Halsey described this as, "Instead of the stagecoach system of keeping the drivers and changing the horses, we changed drivers and kept the horses." This arrangement had the advantage of allowing one admiral and his staff to plan for a future operation while the other admiral conducted the current one. It also served to confuse the enemy, causing the Japanese to conclude that there were two fleets to contend with, when in fact there was only one.

But what a fleet that one was! By the time Halsey was having lunch with Roosevelt at Nimitz's quarters in July 1944, just prior to relieving Spruance as fleet commander, the Big Blue Fleet was the largest gathering of naval power ever to have sailed the oceans of the world. Its main striking power was concentrated in Task Force 38 (under Spruance it was Task Force 58),* which boasted no less than fourteen aircraft carriers and more than a thousand aircraft. Accompanying those aircraft carriers were seven battleships, eight heavy cruisers, thirteen light cruisers, and fifty-seven destroyers, all of which could serve as escorts to protect the carriers from air or submarine attack or could be broken off into surface striking forces capable of providing shore bombardment during amphibious landings or directly engaging Japanese surface forces similar in composition to themselves.

This combat fleet was supported by the "At Sea Logistics Group," which consisted of many oilers, ammunition ships, escort aircraft carriers

---

* In the U.S. Navy, tactical groupings of ships follow a unique pattern: fleets are the largest tactical division and are designated by a single number, such as Third Fleet, Seventh Fleet, etc. Fleets are further broken down into Task Forces, which are identified by two-digit numbers such as Task Force 38 (being part of the Third Fleet) and Task Force 77 (being a component of the Seventh Fleet), and so on. Task Forces can be further subdivided into Task Groups and identified by an additional number following a decimal point; for instance, TG 38.1, TG 38.2, TG 77.1, etc. A further subdivision would be a Task Unit and, defying the laws of mathematics, would be numbered with a second decimal point: TU 38.1.1 or TU 77.1.3, etc. If an even more specific breakdown is called for, this would be a Task Element and would be identified by yet another decimal point, thereby becoming TE 38.1.1.1 or TE 77.1.3.1, etc. Each subdivision would consist of fewer and fewer ships and the tasking assigned would become more specific.

loaded with replacement aircraft, fleet tugs for towing disabled vessels, and a large screening force of destroyers and destroyer escorts. This support group traveled independently, rendezvousing with the main body of the fleet at designated points in order to replenish fuel, ammunition, repair parts, new aircraft, food, medicine, mail, and replacement personnel.

All of this phenomenal mobile power was turned over to Halsey on 26 August 1944 when he relieved Spruance, causing Fifth Fleet to become instantaneously Third Fleet and making Halsey Commander Third Fleet (COMTHIRDFLT).

Less than a month after Halsey had taken command of the Third Fleet, Task Force 38 appeared just off the west coast of the Philippines, within sight of the deep green mountains of Samar. It was just days before the scheduled invasion of the Palau Islands, and Halsey believed he could best support those landings by striking at Japanese land-based air assets in the central Philippines to prevent retaliatory strikes that might emanate from that region.

On 12 and 13 September 1944, Third Fleet carriers launched a series of strikes that brought only a desultory response from the Japanese but yielded amazing results. Twelve hundred sorties were flown the first day and an equal number the next. Halsey later recorded that "when the last plane had returned . . . our Air Combat Intelligence officers showed me a box score that made me whistle. We had shot down 173 planes, destroyed 305 more on the ground, sunk fifty-nine ships, and probably sunk another fifty-eight, besides tremendous damage to installations. Our losses? Eight planes in combat, one operationally, and ten men!"

In addition to these impressive statistics, Halsey was further impressed by the intelligence brought back by an American fighter pilot from USS *Hornet* who had been shot down while flying a sortie over the central Philippine island of Leyte. He had linked up with Filipino natives on the island who had helped him evade capture. Upon returning to the American fleet, the *Hornet* pilot reported that there were no Japanese on the island. This contrasted with earlier intelligence that Leyte was well garrisoned with Japanese troops. Reconnaissance flights confirmed that the only visible military installations were some airstrips that appeared to be abandoned.

Halsey sat in a corner of his flag bridge contemplating what had just occurred. It seemed obvious to him that the Japanese were far weaker in the Philippines than had previously been thought—particularly after his air strikes had decimated much of the Japanese air power there. He thought about how "the South Pacific campaign had impressed us all with the necessity of being alert for symptoms of enemy weakness and of being ready to exploit them—if a stuck door yields unexpectedly, you may fall on your face." He likened the Central Philippines to "the vulnerable belly of the Imperial dragon," termed it "a hollow shell with weak defenses and skimpy facilities," and wondered if he dared do what he was contemplating. He knew that the grand strategy of the Pacific was not his domain, that such things belonged to Nimitz as CINCPAC and to the Joint Chiefs of Staff. He knew that "it was none of my business" and "would upset a great many applecarts, possibly all the way up to Mr. Roosevelt and Mr. Churchill."

But Halsey's dilemma did not last long. Soon the contemplative scowl was replaced by a look of bulldog determination. Halsey was, after all, a risk-taker.

At the same time that Halsey's Third Fleet was pounding away at the Philippines, on the other side of the world, President Roosevelt and Prime Minister Churchill were meeting at a conference code-named "Octagon" in Quebec, Canada. With them were their attendant military staffs, and the agenda for the meeting included another look at Pacific strategy. Since Roosevelt's return from the Pacific he had applied pressure, via Admiral Leahy, on the Joint Chiefs of Staff to adopt MacArthur's plan for invading the Philippines. Without much enthusiasm, the Joint Chiefs had eventually compromised over the Philippines-versus-Formosa controversy by agreeing that MacArthur should invade Leyte in the central Philippines in late December as an interim measure. They would then subsequently decide whether to continue with the liberation of the remainder of the Philippines as MacArthur wanted or go instead to Formosa, as Admiral King had long advocated.

While the Octagon conference was in progress, a message arrived from Admiral Nimitz on 13 September, forwarding a proposal he had just received from Halsey to cancel the next three operations scheduled and proceed directly to an early invasion of the Philippines at Leyte instead. Halsey's message detailed the destruction his forces had wrought in the central Philippines and added that the "enemy's non-aggressive attitude was unbelievable and fantastic." As later events would prove, he overextrapolated the evidence at hand when he described Leyte as "wide open." But the basic idea was sound and met no significant resistance from the Octagon conferees. All were weary of the indecisiveness that had persisted for so long, and since events in China* were making the Formosa alternative seem less feasible, even Admiral King put up no resistance to the proposal.

One key piece to the puzzle was, of course, MacArthur, and the Joint Chiefs were not going to make any commitments until they had heard from him. A message was quickly sent off to CINCSOWESPAC headquarters in Hollandia, New Guinea, asking for MacArthur's concurrence. As it happened, the general was at sea at the time, about to invade Morotai, and was observing radio silence. His chief of staff, General Sutherland, could not always be certain of the unpredictable MacArthur, but this time he was fairly sure he knew what his boss would want. The proposal for MacArthur's accelerated return to the Philippines, as spelled out by the JCS to CINCSOWESPAC, included the proviso that Nimitz's forces would support the landing; Sutherland felt that this would compensate for any difficulties inherent to the accelerated schedule. Sutherland's reply, in MacArthur's name, accepting the proposed acceleration but warning that Halsey was underestimating Japanese strength at Leyte, arrived at Quebec on the evening of the fifteenth, while the Joint Chiefs were being entertained at a formal dinner by their Canadian hosts. The dinner guests excused themselves from the table and adjourned to another room for a conference, a socially unacceptable move that could be excused only in wartime. Ninety minutes later, Nimitz and MacArthur had received instructions from the Joint Chiefs to begin immediate planning for the invasion of the Philippines to take place at Leyte on 20 October, two months earlier than originally planned.

General Marshall, of the Joint Chiefs, later wrote, "Having the utmost confidence in General MacArthur, Admiral Nimitz, and Admiral Halsey, it was not a difficult decision to make."

So Bull Halsey had played a key role in the sequence of events that was to lead the Americans back to the Philippines. But this grizzled old

---

* In May 1944 the Japanese had begun a new offensive in China that ultimately forced U.S. Army Air Forces there to abandon their forward airfields. This, in turn, ruled out Allied prospects for landing on Chinese shores, a key reason for the proposed seizure of Formosa.

admiral's part in the unfolding drama was far from over. Little more than a month after he had dared to suggest a major change in the Pacific strategy, he would be embroiled in the greatest naval battle in history. And before the sailors in that battle had even had the chance to clean their guns in its aftermath, Bull Halsey would also be embroiled in one of the greatest controversies in American naval history.

5

"We Will Fight You All!"

Vice Admiral Matome Ugaki, commander of the 1st Battleship Division of the Imperial Japanese Navy, peered at the placid ocean from the bridge of his flagship. Sunlight sparkled on the sapphire waters of the Philippine Sea, and only a few scattered clouds dappled the blue of the sky above. It was one of those days at sea that help sailors believe they are the keepers of a realm that other humankind have not earned. But, despite the beauty of the day, the admiral bent to his diary, which he had faithfully kept since even before the war had begun, and wrote:

> Utterly awakened from the dream of victory,
> Found the sky rainy and gloomy.
> Rainy clouds will not clear up,
> My heart is the same
> When the time for battle is up.

It was 21 June 1944, and the cacophony of battle had just hours before faded from the sea. The Japanese Fleet was retiring from the scene of what history would call the Battle of the Philippine Sea, leaving in its wake the sunken remains of three of its aircraft carriers and the wreckage of hundreds of its aircraft. That fleet had failed to prevent the loss of Saipan, and there could be no doubt that the rest of the Marianas would soon fall as well. The admiral continued in his diary, "It's the rainy season at home but here it's fine. Yet what isn't fine is my heart."

Admiral Ugaki knew that this had been a critical moment in the war in the Pacific. When he added to the diary, "The result of the decisive battle on which we staked so much was extremely miserable," he revealed an understanding of Japanese naval strategy that had been born of an intelligent mind and two years' service as chief of staff to Admiral Yamamoto, Commander in Chief of the Combined Fleet in the first years of the war. Ugaki knew that Japanese naval planners had believed, since long before the outbreak of war, that the way to defeat the American Navy was to lure the bulk of the U.S. fleet into a major fleet engagement that would prove decisive. When originally conceived, the plan had merit, since the war had begun with the Japanese holding a decided numerical advantage over their American adversaries. But as the war progressed, that advantage had faded into the waters of the Pacific as Japanese ships and aircraft were lost in battle and American shipyards and factories began a virtual orgy of frenzied production that more than compensated their own battle losses and went far beyond Japanese industry's capability to keep pace. By the time the fight for Saipan had brought the adversarial fleets together, the hope of Japanese success in a decisive battle was greatly diminished. The numbers had changed so drastically that it was clearly the U.S. Navy who held the advantage.

But the numbers were not all that had changed. Almost without anyone fully realizing it, the face of naval warfare had changed. The role of aircraft carriers and their long-ranged broods of airplanes had rendered the battleships and cruisers virtually impotent in the big battles. The outcome was not being decided by the fire-belching guns of these great behemoths in which the maritime nations of the world had invested so much of their capital in the years leading up to the war. It was the diminutive but potent airplanes that were sending thousands of tons of shipping to the ocean floor. The great majestic dreadnoughts were left to steam about in frustration, swatting at their aerial adversaries with small-caliber weapons like an animal harried by the bites and stings of tiny flying insects, their once powerful main batteries vestigial reminders of a faded age. These magnificent monsters, which so recently had promised to rule the waves, which Japan had led the way in building, now served as mere escorts to the awkward-looking flat-topped vessels who had stolen their promised moment of glory.

The Japanese had not been alone in their myopic emphasis on the big-gun ship. All the significant navies of the world had run headlong down this mismarked path during the 1920s and 1930s, concentrating on the construction of battleships and cruisers while "dabbling" in those experimental and rather improbable newcomers with the tiny airfields on top. The United

States could afford such folly. Its huge industrial base had the flexibility to recover from such a grand miscalculation. But when the Japanese chose to build the world's largest battleships, they were making a decision that the limitations of time and resources would render irrevocable.

So the great "decisive battle on which we staked so much" had come and gone, and the outcome had left Admiral Ugaki lamenting that "the prospect of victory is fading out," and "it's only natural that my heart becomes as gloomy as the sky of the rainy season." But what this commander of battleships could not have then foreseen was that the big-gun ships were not yet ready to leave the stage. In just a few short months they would appear for a final curtain call in which their great guns would at last be sighted on American warships.

The "Marianas Turkey Shoot" had dealt Japanese air power a severe blow, prompting Admiral Ugaki to write: "It will be extremely difficult to recover from this disaster and rise again." But the Japanese were far from defeated. With a measure of luck, they might still be able to deal the Americans a costly blow. Because Spruance had not pursued the Japanese Fleet as it retired from the Philippine Sea, the Japanese Navy still had enough aircraft carriers to inflict a significant amount of damage, provided they could train enough replacement pilots and produce enough aircraft in time for the next confrontation. And their big-gun ships were still a potent force—if they could somehow get them in close to the American Navy to bring that potency to bear.

The overall commander of the Japanese forces in the Battle of the Philippine Sea had been Vice Admiral Jisaburo Ozawa. He was one of the most experienced officers in the Imperial Japanese Navy, having held key commands and staff positions since 1935. He had been a professor at the Japanese Naval Academy in the mid-1930s and had an incisive mind that earned his opinions respect in most quarters of the navy. As soon as his fleet had returned to safer waters following the battle, Ozawa commenced preparations for the next encounter with the United States Navy. Because of the damage that had been inflicted upon the carrier striking force and the terrible attrition of pilots, Ozawa took the carriers to the Inland Sea of Japan where they could be repaired, and where he could train replacement pilots. He sent the bulk of his remaining forces, the cruisers and battleships under Vice Admiral Takeo Kurita, to a place in the south of the empire called Lingga Roads, near Japanese-held Singapore. This was necessary because U.S. submarines, by waging an effective campaign against the Japanese merchant fleet,* had severely restricted the flow of oil from the southern oil fields to the home islands of Japan. Ozawa reasoned that the most effective way to guarantee that these ships would have the requisite fuel was to station them nearer to the source of supply.

The repairs to the carriers were carried out with alacrity, but training replacement pilots proved a more difficult matter. By this stage of the war, Japanese manpower had been significantly depleted and the once stringent qualifications for entry into the pilot training program had to be relaxed. The great rush to train pilots as quickly as possible was an obvious detriment as well. American naval aviators by this time were not entering combat until they had received two years of training, whereas their Japanese counterparts were being created in a matter of a few short months.

And there was a further complication. When asked, after the war, whether it was the shortage of planes or pilots that caused the most significant problem for the Japanese, Captain Mitsuo Fuchida (Air Staff Officer to the Commander in Chief of the Combined Fleet) replied, "Fuel was the worst. We had plenty of pilots but couldn't train them because of the lack of fuel." So at a time when U.S. replacement flyers were arriving in the Pacific theater with over three hundred hours of actual flying time to their credit, their Japanese counterparts were fortunate to have more than a few hours of actual flying experience.

Pilots were not the only aviation personnel who were feeling the bite of attrition in the Japanese Navy. As the islands across the Pacific fell, pilots and their aircraft were able to withdraw, to fall back within the shrinking perimeter. But maintenance personnel had no such luxury. They were left behind to wither on the severed logistical vine or to become prisoners of war. This eventually contributed to a gradual decline in the matériel readiness of Japanese aircraft. Coupled with a manpower shortage in the work force manning the aircraft production factories, the quality of Japanese

---

* The American submarine campaign against the Japanese merchant fleet was effective in part because of the Japanese warrior mentality (*Bushido*). Japanese naval officers felt it was beneath them, as warriors, to escort merchant vessels; that their role must be to seek out and destroy the enemy's combatant fleet. Hence, the Japanese were slow to establish a defensive convoy system such as had been used effectively by the Americans in the Atlantic in the war against German submarines.

aircraft, once considered the finest in the world, declined significantly.

At Lingga Roads in the south, Admiral Kurita was feverishly training the crew of his battleships, cruisers, and destroyers, hoping to overcome some of the disparities between him and his enemy. He emphasized night tactics, because the Japanese had always fared better than their enemies in night engagements. Pragmatically recognizing the problems with Japanese air power, he also emphasized antiaircraft gunnery practice and had additional smaller-caliber weapons installed on his ships to increase their available antiaircraft firepower.

But as he trained so far from home, Kurita faced a related but different problem from that faced by Ozawa in the north. Whereas fuel was abundant at Lingga, ammunition was not. Japan's ammunition factories were located in the home islands. Because of the U.S. submarine menace, Kurita was far to the south with abundant fuel but a shortage of ammunition while Ozawa was in the north with access to ammunition but a paucity of fuel.

Ozawa's plan was to reunite the fleet at the earliest opportunity. His projected training schedule called for that reunification to take place at the Lingga anchorage in mid-November, once he had trained a sufficient number of replacement pilots.

Japanese naval planners had, by this time, become familiar with their adversary's pattern of operation. Judging from the past and from current conditions, they predicted that U.S. forces would strike at the Philippines in late November. This was, of course, right on the money until Admiral Halsey "upset the applecart" by proposing that the schedule be jumped ahead to allow the landing in October instead. In retrospect, it becomes clear that Halsey's proposed acceleration was to have great significance because it meant that the Japanese would not be nearly as prepared to oppose the landing as they would have been had the original schedule stood. By landing in October instead of November, the Americans would preempt the planned unification of the Japanese Fleet.

In the aftermath of the Battle of the Philippine Sea, it was evident that the Japanese and American fleets were destined to meet one more time. The inevitable thrust of American power into the inner sanctum of the Japanese Empire left no alternative. And despite the problems confronting the Japanese and the growing power of the United States Navy, the Imperial Japanese Navy was not yet ready to concede defeat.

At the same time that President Roosevelt was meeting with General MacArthur and Admiral Nimitz in Hawaii, Admiral Ugaki picked up his soft-brush pen and recorded his reaction to the news of the mass suicides at Marpi Point and elsewhere in the Marianas:

It's only to be expected that servicemen should be killed in action, but women, children, and old men in such large number prefer death to being taken prisoner by an enemy on a helpless, lonely island. . . . What a tragedy! No people but the Yamato [Japanese] nation could do a thing like this. I think that if one hundred million Japanese people could have the same [resolve] as these facing this crisis, it wouldn't be difficult to find a way to victory.

Those words refute the arguments that have served as the white man's excuse for many of his actions in the Far East, claiming that "Orientals do not put the same value on human life as Westerners do." The black-inked ideographs on the pages of this once-private diary seem diluted by the tears of a sensitive man who was not writing for the benefit of others but only recording his innermost thoughts and feelings. Yet these words might also have been written in blood for all the fierce determination they record. The remorse here recorded is nearly eclipsed by the intensity of sincere pride and devotion that would allow this man to stand in the face of growing adversity and go forward, despite the threatening gale that blew in his face warning of the coming maelstrom. Ugaki was not naive. His diary records a pragmatic realization of what was happening to him and his "Yamato nation." He did not shrink from what lay ahead.

A few pages later, Ugaki wrote of the gathering forces that threatened him and his way of life: "Roosevelt visited Attu and Hawaii and met with the commanders. Such enemy news such as there will be a big offensive against Japan shortly, etc., have been heard. The United Kingdom seems to be reinforcing her Far East Fleet, too."

And then he wrote: "Come on! We will fight you all!"

PART II
★ THE RETURN ★

6

★ King Two ★

The impending amphibious landing operation at Leyte Gulf was assigned the code name "King Two" and planning began as soon as the Joint Chiefs authorized the acceleration in schedule recommended by Halsey. That decision was made in mid-September, which left a mere five weeks before the 20 October landing. Because the ships that were to participate were so numerous and so widespread, two of those five weeks had to be allocated just for the distribution of the plan. This left only three weeks in which to put together an operation order for an amphibious landing that was the largest and most complex yet attempted in the Pacific. Only the D-Day landing in Normandy, several months before, rivaled it in all of history.

One of the people whose destiny it was to play a key role in King Two was a Navy captain named Charles Adair. He, like MacArthur, would be returning to the Philippines. And he, too, had left under rather unusual circumstances.

When war broke in the Pacific, Adair was serving as aide and flag lieutenant to the Commander in Chief of the U.S. Asiatic Fleet, that outmoded and doomed collection of antique ships that had been "guarding" America's Pacific frontier for decades. Adair had escaped from Corregidor, not in a PT boat, as General MacArthur had done, and not in a submarine, as the president of the Philippines had done. Adair had sailed (literally) with three other U.S. naval officers, one Dutch officer, and a crew of six American and twelve Filipino sailors in a two-masted, schooner-rigged yacht. This unlikely representative of the U.S. Navy, christened *Lanikai*, displaced 150 tons, was 87¼ feet long, and was armed with two .30-caliber machine guns and a three-pounder cannon of Spanish-American

War vintage. In a thousand-mile odyssey, during which Adair and his companions sailed by night and hid the vessel close to shore by day, *Lanikai* eventually reached Australia.

Adair was subsequently assigned to the staff of the Commander Seventh Amphibious Force as Planning and Operations Officer, where he directed naval planning for MacArthur's amphibious assaults. On 18 September 1944, Adair and his boss, Vice Admiral Daniel E. Barbey, were summoned to a conference in Sydney, Australia. The meeting had been called by General MacArthur, and many of his subordinate commanders and staff members were present. Admiral Nimitz had come from his Pearl Harbor headquarters and he, too, brought many members of his staff and several Central Pacific commanders. Adair arrived to a full meeting hall and wondered "how in the world they could ever find so many people that weren't working." He later said, "I felt that with all those people there, we had almost enough to make an assault, and that [we] could have roughed out an assault plan by the time it took to get those people out of that hall."

The conference had been called to kick off planning for the invasion of Leyte and to sort out the large-scale considerations of the operation. When the meeting was over, planners like Charles Adair went to work ironing out the myriad details of the assault.

There were some major logistical problems to be considered. Because of the large number of ships that would be required, there was no single harbor large enough to accommodate them all. This meant that the ships would have to be staged at various locations in the Pacific and then brought together with precise timing at Leyte Gulf. Some of the ships would gather at Hollandia on the northern coast of New Guinea, a distance of 1,240 miles from Leyte. Others were to be staged at Manus, in the Admiralty Islands, 1,565 miles from the objective. And still others would depart from Finschhafen, on the southeast coast of New Guinea, 2,075 miles from Leyte Gulf. These great distances meant that the participating vessels would have to depart their respective harbors at various times well ahead of A-Day.* The top speed of the LSTs ("*Large Slow Targets*" as their crews had dubbed them) was a mere eight or nine knots, which meant that

---

* The day of actual assault for an amphibious operation was normally referred to as D-Day, but because the American public had grown to associate this term with the assault on Europe at Normandy in France, General MacArthur insisted that the day of assault on the Philippines should be referred to as A-Day to avoid any confusion.

they could travel only about two hundred miles a day, which meant they would need six full days, for example, to make the passage from Hollandia, the nearest of the assembly points. Finschhafen would require *ten* days' passage. Time quickly became a commodity not to be squandered. The planners worked around the clock trying to meet the rapidly approaching deadlines. Fortunately, by this stage of the war, planners like Adair had become quite adept at putting together workable assault plans in a relatively short period of time. Experience is the best tutor, and the march to Tokyo had thus far provided much of that.

When Adair and the others were finished their work, the resulting plan was more than an inch thick. It took four pages just to list who was to get copies. Six more pages told the many commanders of vessels and men where they fit into the organization, seven pages described their various tasks and functions, and twenty-five pages described the movement schedule for all units. There was a plan for planting buoys and setting up navigation lights to aid the invaders in their incursion into Leyte Gulf, and there was a twenty-five-page communications plan that listed all the frequencies and call signs to be used.

This gargantuan plan for the American invasion of the Philippines would bring together in this one corner of the vast Pacific more American sailors than had been in the entire United States Navy in 1938, less than three years before the attack on Pearl Harbor.

Nearly three years earlier, and only five days after the Japanese had begun the war, a crusty-looking fifty-three-year-old naval officer with bushy black eyebrows arrived on the devastated scene at Pearl Harbor. No record of his reaction exists, but Thomas Cassin Kinkaid must have been sickened by the sight of those wrecked battleships, their twisted iron carcasses still hemorrhaging fuel oil and their once pristine wooden decks splintered and smoldering in the aftermath of sudden war. Much of Kinkaid's naval career had been spent in big-gun ships such as these.

It is probably a safe assumption that, among the many thoughts Kinkaid must have had on that day, it did not occur to him that he would someday command five of these same ships when they faced the Japanese Fleet in a great showdown at Leyte Gulf.

Kinkaid, like his father, was an Annapolis graduate, finishing in the middle of his class in 1908. He had sailed with Teddy Roosevelt's "Great White Fleet" when it made its historic around-the-world voyage and had gone on to become an expert in naval gunnery, attending the Naval Post-graduate School's ordnance course and spending all of his sea tours in ships whose main batteries were guns, from destroyers up through battle-ships.

After Pearl Harbor, Kinkaid participated in a fruitless raid on Wake Island while commanding a cruiser division and played a minor part in the Coral Sea and Midway battles. But it was in the Solomons that he stood out as a wartime commander. Ironically, the old gunnery man found himself commanding a task force centered around the aircraft carrier *Enterprise* and acquitted himself well in three major engagements. He was then trans-ferred to the far northern Pacific to command Task Force 8 in Alaskan waters, where he once again waged a successful campaign. His reputation solidified, Kinkaid was sent to the Southwest Pacific theater in June 1943 to replace the Seventh Fleet Commander, who was having trouble getting along with his immediate superior, General MacArthur. Kinkaid had no such trouble. He and MacArthur hit it off well, so Kinkaid remained, and it was to be his destiny to command the Seventh Fleet when it carried the general and his troops back to the Philippines.

Beneath his picture in the 1908 *Lucky Bag*, the college yearbook of Naval Academy graduates, Thomas Kinkaid is described as "a black-eyed, rosy-cheeked, noisy Irishman who loves a rough-house." At Leyte Gulf he was about to get one hell of a rough-house.

For the invasion of the Philippines, it had been decided to bring the bulk of American naval power in the Pacific to bear. This meant that the forces assigned to MacArthur and Nimitz would converge at Leyte. The Southwest Pacific naval forces were represented by the Seventh Fleet, now commanded by Kinkaid; Halsey's Third Fleet was at the heart of the Central Pacific's naval power.

The Seventh Fleet had been created in March 1943, more on paper than in actuality. MacArthur had been demanding ships that he could use to support his campaign in the Southwest Pacific, and Admiral King had created the Seventh Fleet as a means of placating the general. At its inception, the "fleet" consisted of a handful of submarines and their one tender. As time went on, the few ships that could be spared from other the-aters were added. But for most of the campaign the Seventh Fleet, which had come to be known as "MacArthur's Navy," was not a formidable force, consisting primarily of troop transports and escorting destroyers. For the Leyte landings, however, things would be different.

Many ships were transferred to the Seventh Fleet for the Leyte operation, including a surface combatant force of six battleships, eight cruisers, and a number of destroyers. The battleships were not the latest versions. Halsey retained the newer dreadnoughts as escorts for Task Force 38. All six of the transferred battleships had been built more than two decades before, and USS *Mississippi* was the only one of the six that had not been at Pearl Harbor on that infamous seventh of December. As Kinkaid had witnessed upon his arrival in the Pacific, *Maryland, Tennessee,* and *Pennsylvania* had all been seriously damaged in the attack, and *West Virginia* and *California* were actually sunk and later resurrected.

Also handed over to the Seventh Fleet for the Philippine invasion were eighteen aircraft carriers. But these were not the same carriers that had been roaming the Pacific under Halsey and Spruance. They were an innovative hybrid of the species that were known as "escort carriers" or "CVEs." Those ships that made up the great striking power of Task Force 38 were the "attack carriers" (CVs) and their smaller brothers, light aircraft carriers (CVLs). With her complement of 100 aircraft, the CV was the real powerhouse of naval aviation. These ships were 700–850 feet long (depending upon the class) and were manned by crews of nearly 3,000 men. The smaller CVLs were built upon hulls that were originally intended to be cruisers but were converted when it became clear that more carriers were going to be needed. They were only 600 feet long, had a crew of approximately 1,500, and could carry half as many aircraft as the larger CV. The CVE, on the other hand, was built on a merchant hull, was about 500 feet in length, and carried a complement of only 27 aircraft.

The CVEs had their origins before American entry into the war, when President Roosevelt and Admiral Halsey appear to have come up with the same idea at about the same time. Roosevelt proposed, in October 1940, that a merchant hull be adapted to make a small aircraft carrier for convoy duty that would be capable of carrying eight to twelve aircraft that could hunt submarines in the Atlantic. Admiral Halsey, then Commander of Carriers, Battle Force, simultaneously proposed a new class of auxiliary carriers designed to provide pilot training and to transport aircraft to the battle theater. Several different models ensued until eventually the CVEs were in full production, rolling off the ways in just a few months and their numbers growing until, by war's end, a phenomenal 115 had been built. These diminutive carriers—nicknamed "Jeep carriers" and sometimes referred to as "*C*ombustible, *V*ulnerable, *E*xpendable" by the sailors who crewed them—provided antisubmarine escort in the Atlantic, as Roosevelt had envisioned, and functioned as aircraft transports in the Pacific, as Halsey had foreseen. But they also participated in amphibious operations in both theaters, providing close air support for marines and soldiers ashore. It was in this role that they had been assigned to the Seventh Fleet for the invasion of Leyte.

Also transferred to the Seventh Fleet were the amphibious components of the Third Fleet. This gave Kinkaid control of all amphibious forces in the operation and left the Third Fleet a mobile striking force able to concentrate on the Japanese Fleet, should it decide to make an appearance.

With the reshuffling of ships for the Philippine invasion, the Seventh Fleet was transformed into one of the most potent attack forces in the world. More than 700 ships now made up what had once been a "poor stepchild" of the Navy, including 157 combatants; 420 amphibious ships; 84 patrol, minesweeping, and hydrographic craft; and 73 service vessels.

For the actual assault, the Seventh Fleet would be divided into three separate groups, two of which were tasked with the actual landing and the third with direct support. The Northern Attack Force, designated Task Force 78 and commanded by Rear Admiral Barbey, was made up of ships that had been operating with "MacArthur's Navy" all along. The Southern Attack Force, Task Force 79, was commanded by Vice Admiral Theodore S. Wilkinson and consisted of the amphibious forces that had been transferred from the Third Fleet. The direct support functions—most important, shore bombardment and coordinated air strikes—were assigned to Task Force 77, which consisted of the battleships, cruisers, destroyers, and escort aircraft carriers now belonging to Seventh Fleet. Command of Task Force 77 was retained by the fleet commander, Vice Admiral Thomas C. Kinkaid.

Task Force 77 was further subdivided into numerous specialized task groups, the most significant of which were Task Groups 77.2 and 77.4. Rear Admiral Jesse B. Oldendorf commanded Task Group 77.2, the Fire Support and Bombardment Group, which contained the six old battleships, five cruisers, and fifteen destroyers. Task Group 77.4 consisted of the eighteen CVEs and their escorting destroyers and was commanded by Rear Admiral Thomas L. Sprague.

Added to all of this striking power of the Seventh Fleet was the powerful punch of the Third Fleet, under Halsey. After the transfer of amphibious assets to the Philippine invasion force, the Third Fleet consisted primarily of Task Force 38, the carrier striking force commanded by Vice Admiral Marc A. Mitscher. This massive task force was subdivided into four task groups, each of which typically contained two CVs and two CVLs. Escorting these carriers were six battleships, fifteen cruisers, and forty-eight destroyers, all assigned to the four task groups in varying proportions.

All of this American military power converging upon the Philippines would virtually seem to guarantee a successful return for General MacArthur and the United States. But military histories abound with examples of "sure things" that turn out to be anything but. There was, in fact, a proverbial crack in the American armor. The outcome of the approaching battle would be jeopardized, not by a poor American strategy, nor by bad tactics, and certainly not for "want of a nail." What would ultimately offset the great advantage enjoyed by the Americans at Leyte Gulf was a weakness in the command structure, a weakness born of politics and exacerbated by the force of individual personalities.

Creating two separate theaters in the Pacific had proven to be strategically advantageous, since the two campaigns frequently kept the Japanese off balance trying to respond to moves made by first one, then the other. But now that these two theater commanders were converging on the same objective, the need for coordination became essential. One of the simplest means of coordinating military elements, no matter how large, is to place them under a common commander. But, as has already been noted, one had to go all the way to Washington to find a common commander above General MacArthur and Admiral Nimitz.

The plan for the employment of these two forces seemed workable. Kinkaid's Seventh Fleet was actually the amphibious elements of both the Third and Seventh fleets and was tasked with carrying out the actual assault on the Philippines. The remainder of the Third Fleet, which had been reduced to Task Force 38, was ordered to play a direct support role. Nimitz's actual orders to Halsey were that he was to "cover and support forces of Southwest Pacific in order to assist the seizure and occupation of objectives in the Central Philippines," and "destroy enemy naval and air forces in or threatening the Philippines Area." This was straightforward enough and, despite the absence of a common commander, should not have proved difficult to carry out. But there was something else in Nimitz's directive, something that had not appeared in his previous operation orders, a caveat that was to have a great effect on the coming battle.

Probably because of the controversy that had rattled on ever since Spruance had opted to stay at the landing area in the Marianas rather than pursue the Japanese Fleet, Nimitz's instructions to Halsey included the following sentence: "In case opportunity for destruction of major portion of the enemy fleet offers or can be created, such destruction becomes the primary task." The actual origin of that caveat is unknown. In an interview after the war, Admiral King said that he had instructed Nimitz to include it, but in a subsequent letter to U.S. Naval Academy Professor Emeritus E. B. Potter, King seemed less sure that it was he who had ordered it. Potter, in his biography of Halsey, noting that the grammatical construction of the sentence is not typical of either King or Nimitz, suggests that the caveat may have been added by a staff member. All of the other sentences in the operation order were either numbered or lettered in outline form, but this one sentence stands alone with neither number nor letter preceding, which suggests that it may indeed have been added as an afterthought. By whom remains uncertain.

No matter who wrote the caveat, it was there, and Halsey seized upon it. He saw the Seventh Fleet's role as essentially *defensive* and his own as *offensive* in nature, and he made his intentions for the upcoming battle clear when he wrote a letter to Nimitz at the end of September:

> I intend, if possible, to deny the enemy a chance to outrange me in an air duel and also to deny him an opportunity to employ an air shuttle (carrier-to-target-to-land) against me. . . .
>
> Inasmuch as the destruction of the enemy fleet is the principal task, every weapon must be brought into play and the general coordination of these weapons should be in the hands of the tactical commander responsible for the outcome of the battle. . . . My goal is the same as yours—to completely annihilate the Jap fleet if the opportunity offers.

Nimitz never countermanded these intentions. In fact, it seems apparent that Halsey's aggressive spirit had been taken into account when this operation was devised, that Nimitz had deliberately put Halsey into a position where he would be free to go after the Japanese Fleet should it appear at Leyte. In all previous operations where Spruance had been in command of the Fifth Fleet*, the entire operation had been Spruance's responsibility. The Fifth Fleet had remained intact and had conducted its own amphibious landings while the carrier striking forces had been given the dual tasks of directly supporting the assault and defending against any thwarting moves by the Japanese Fleet. But for the Philippines operation, the amphibious forces had been stripped from Third Fleet for inclusion in the Seventh Fleet, and responsibility for the actual assault had been given to Admiral Kinkaid. This may have been done solely because of the convergence of U.S. forces, but it seems likely that an additional consideration may have been to ensure that Halsey would be free to act aggressively should the Japanese Fleet show up.

Nimitz certainly did not inhibit Halsey. In a letter to Halsey, written just twelve days before the landing at Leyte, Nimitz made it clear that Halsey was free to exercise his own judgment in tactical matters:

> You are always free to make local decisions in connection with the handling of the forces placed under your command. Often it will be necessary for you to take action not previously contemplated because of local situations which may develop quickly and in light of information which has come to you and which may not yet be available to me. My only requirement in such cases is that I be informed as fully and as early as the situation permits.

One other potential problem existed as a result of the improvised command setup for the Philippine invasion. With the Third Fleet now consisting essentially of only Task Force 38, the roles of Halsey and his task force commander, Admiral Mitscher, had become somewhat redundant. There were, in essence, *two* commanders of Task Force 38. If Halsey exercised tactical command of his fleet—and Halsey's aggressive nature made that inevitable—then there was little left for Mitscher to do. What effect this would have remained to be seen.

---

* The reader is reminded that Third and Fifth fleets were essentially the same entity, differing only in their respective commanders and their staffs.

7

★ "We Sailed Quietly East in the Dark of Night" ★

Just after midnight on 18 October 1944, the sound of anchor chains rattling in hawse pipes drifted across the still waters of the Lingga Roads anchorage as seven battleships, fifteen cruisers, and twenty destroyers of the Imperial Japanese Navy made preparations for getting underway. Deep in the bellies of these great steel whales, young sailors, firing their boilers, turned huge valve-wheels to regulate the flow of the oil that was now more precious than gold to the Japanese Empire. Other sailors, assigned as lookouts on the flying bridges of the many warships, peered into the darkness, accommodating their eyes to the special challenges of night vision. Months of training in the oppressive humidity of this equatorial anchorage was over, and the moment of truth had arrived for these sailors, so far from their home waters, as they sortied for a final showdown with the American Navy.

The ships slowly emerged from the complacent cocoon of the training anchorage and stood out to sea, propellers beating a steady cadence in the warm tropical waters, weapons bristling at the stars above. Most of these vessels were combat-hardened veterans of the Pacific war, many still pocked with the scars of battle, some partially debilitated by the ravages of war and long ocean transits. The cruiser *Mogami* had endured a horrific pounding at Midway, and a picture of her as a twisted wreck in the aftermath of the battle had become famous in the United States, symbolizing the American victory. Yet there she was, still afloat, still able to inflict great harm, under way now for the Philippines and a chance for revenge.

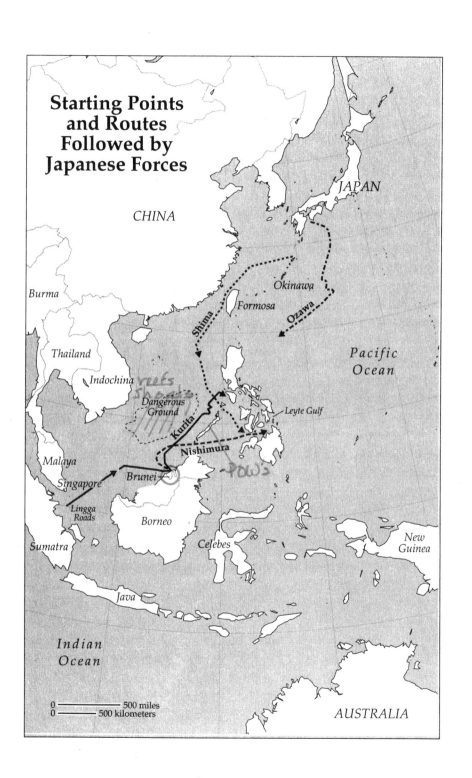

Starting Points
and Routes
Followed by
Japanese Forces

CHINA

JAPAN

Burma

Okinawa

Formosa

Shima

Ozawa

Thailand

Indochina

reefs
shoals

Dangerous
Ground

Pacific
Ocean

Kurita

Leyte Gulf

Malaya

Nishimura

POWs

Singapore

Brunei

Lingga
Roads

Borneo

Sumatra

Celebes

New
Guinea

Java

Indian
Ocean

0 ———— 500 miles
0 ———— 500 kilometers

AUSTRALIA

The battleship *Haruna*, which had struck a German mine in the First World War and had been reported sunk time and again in this one, steamed out of the Lingga anchorage, her shadowy form hauntingly vague in the subdued light of the distant stars. The destroyer *Shigure*, veteran of the Coral Sea, Solomons, and New Guinea campaigns, had been the sole Japanese survivor at the battle in Vella Gulf. Now, as her crew worked to bring her anchor into short stay, some of them surely wondered if their luck would continue through the coming engagement.

Of all the ships making up this powerful force, the most formidable were the gigantic battleships *Yamato* and *Musashi* of Admiral Matome Ugaki's Battleship Division One. They were the largest surface warships ever built. At the time that these two 862-foot, 70,000-ton behemoths entered service, they dwarfed the American 728-foot, 40,000-ton *North Carolina*–class battleships. Even their closest rivals, the German *Bismark* class, were only 823 feet in length and displaced a mere 45,000 tons.

In the earlier decades of the twentieth century the Japanese had recognized that they could not hope to rival American shipbuilding capability in terms of units produced. Their solution was to try to make each individual class of Japanese ship superior to the equivalent in the United States Navy. Hence, Japanese cruisers were equipped with torpedoes, which gave them a decided advantage over their American counterparts. In that same vein of thinking, the Japanese decided to build battleships that would almost certainly prevail in an engagement with any American battleships they might encounter. Besides the obvious consideration of ensuring a tactical victory, the oversize dimensions of the *Yamato* class reflected an important strategic consideration as well. At the time that these ships were conceived, American isolationist politics seemed to guarantee that the United States Navy would not be built up to two-ocean status, and the American Fleet would, therefore, have to rely on the Panama Canal in order to shift its assets from the Atlantic to the Pacific or vice versa, depending upon the threat at hand. The huge dimensions of the *Yamato* class, much too large to allow passage through the Panama Canal, meant that the United States could not build a similar ship without restricting it to one ocean or the other.

Building these super-battleships was no casual undertaking. Naval harbors had to be dredged out to accommodate the giants, and a significant part of the Japanese national treasury had to be expended to expand the steel-plate manufacturing facilities in order to make the armor envisioned for *Yamato* and *Musashi*.* One plate of the side armor used on vital areas of the ship was approximately 16 inches thick and weighed 68.5 tons.

A great deal of secrecy surrounded the building of *Yamato* and *Musashi*. The dock in Kure, where *Yamato* was built, was partially covered with a roof to prevent anyone from seeing what was happening from a nearby hill. Huge curtains made of sisal rope were also hung around the construction site to keep the emerging giant hidden from view. These curtains weighed 408 tons and their construction caused a serious shortage of sisal, bringing a howl of complaint from local fishermen who needed it for nets and lines.

The secrecy extended beyond the construction phase and was carried to such extremes that Admiral Kurita, commander of the fleet that included the two super-battleships, later confided that even he was not permitted to know their top speed nor the actual caliber of the huge guns that made up their main battery.

Those guns actually had a bore of 18.1 inches and were, in fact, the largest guns ever used on a naval vessel.† One turret, at the incredible weight of 2,774 tons, was more than the displacement of a heavy destroyer. So powerful was the blast from these guns that crew members exposed on the weather-decks during firing ran the risk of having the clothing torn from their bodies and of being knocked unconscious. The ships' boats could not be stowed in the open without being damaged by the blast; they had to be kept in specially built hangars. Designers also faced a very serious problem in mounting the smaller-caliber antiaircraft weapons where they could effectively defend the ship yet not be damaged by the blast pressure of the gigantic main batteries.

A single projectile from these 18.1-inch monsters weighed 3,200 pounds, which was half a ton more than those fired by the 16-inch guns of

---

* The *Yamato* and *Musashi* were the only two battleships actually built in this class. A third super-battleship was planned and construction was under way when the Japanese came to the realization that aircraft carriers, not battleships, were the decisive elements of modern naval warfare. This third ship was then converted to an aircraft carrier and completed in 1944 as the supercarrier *Shinano*.

† The British experimented with several eighteen-inch guns and actually employed them to a limited extent during the First World War, but they were improvisations at best and were short lived as well as slightly smaller in caliber.

the *Iowa*-class battleships, the largest of the United States Navy. There were three types of projectiles developed for these guns. A conventional Type HE (High Explosive) was suitable for shore bombardment and non-armored targets such as destroyers. For the armored capital ships, the Type 91 armor-piercing shell was developed. This was less conventional in its design because it had been given a hydrodynamic shape that was meant to enter the water short of a target and continue on beneath the surface, ultimately striking the victim below the waterline, somewhat like a torpedo. Least conventional of all was the Type *San Shiki* Model 3. It was something akin to a giant incendiary shotgun shell that was designed as an antiaircraft weapon. Filled with 1,500 metal fragmentation devices and rubber thermite incendiary tubes, the projectile detonated at a prescribed altitude by means of a timed fuse that sprayed a cone of fire and steel into the sky, making flying in the vicinity rather hazardous.

This large Japanese force, formidable in many ways, behind the fast-moving times in others, sailed through the narrow waters between Sumatra and the Malay Peninsula, headed for Brunei on the northwest corner of Borneo. At this moment, the men in these ships were not sure what their mission would be, though there were indications that they were going to oppose an American invasion in the Philippines.

In the rear of the long train of vessels, aboard *Yamato*, Admiral Ugaki once again opened his diary and, by the light of a red battle lamp, wrote: "We came in the early spring and left in mid-fall, but with climate and scenery making no change I had to count the time of our stay by my fingers. We sailed quietly east in the dark of night. . . ."

In Japan, at a combined meeting of army and navy staff personnel, Admiral Toyoda's staff revealed that the order had gone out to execute a plan that had been code-named *Sho Ichi Go*, meaning Operation Victory One. The army was advised that this was to be an "all-or-nothing" operation, that the navy would succeed in thwarting the American invasion of the Philippines or die trying. General Kenyro Sato, chief of the powerful Military Affairs Bureau of the War Ministry, protested that squandering the fleet on an improbable venture in the Philippines would leave the home islands open to invasion. "The Combined Fleet belongs not only to the navy but to the state," Sato said with emotion choking his voice. "Only the existence of the fleet will make the enemy cautious. So please, gentlemen, be prudent."

Rear Admiral Tasuku Nakazawa, chief of the navy's Operations Section, replied to General Sato, "I am very grateful to know that the Combined Fleet is so highly regarded by you army men." This was not offered as a sarcastic remark but with apparent sincerity. Nakazawa continued by explaining that the Philippines might be the Imperial Navy's last chance to die with honor. Tears glistened in his dark eyes as he said, "Please give the Combined Fleet the chance to bloom as flowers of death." The room was very quiet as he added, "This is the navy's earnest request."

Sato yielded, and within a few hours, the Emperor had approved the execution of *Sho Ichi Go.*

The Japanese have for centuries played a game that might be considered the equivalent of chess in Western culture. Like chess, it is a game for intellectuals as well as less cerebral types, and can be played at various levels of skill. Also like its Western counterpart, it is played on a board, and there are organizations that exist solely for the continuation and advancement of the game. Unlike chess, the pieces are identical and equal in value and far more numerous. The strategies that go into this Asian game are, in some ways simpler and in others more complicated than those of chess. The name of this Japanese game is go, which roughly translates to "battle-plan" or "operation."

Just as chess, with its monarchical Christian figures and its unique rules of movement, reflects certain aspects of Western culture and thinking, so go mirrors elements of the Japanese mind. The pieces in a chess game are all visible at the outset, making the element of surprise difficult to achieve, but in go, the pieces are not at first on the board but are introduced one at a time as the game progresses, thereby permitting the strategist to mask his intentions for a time. The chessplayer's actions reflect mobility and response to an ever-fluid situation, while the master of go patiently builds a complex and static structure that eventually overwhelms his opponent by the positioning of his pieces and by careful timing. All but the lowliest chess pieces may retreat and may even be resurrected from capture, whereas the pieces in *Go,* once committed to the board, must do or die: there is no provision for retreat, and once removed from the board they are gone forever.

So it is not surprising that the plan developed by the Japanese for the defense of the Philippines would turn out to be complex and rely heavily upon both timing and surprise for its success. It would be a strategy born of a combination of those unique Japanese cultural influences and a desperation dictated by circumstances. Earlier in the war, when the Japanese Empire had spanned a large part of the Pacific, Japanese strategists had the luxury of trading space for time. Ominous trends and other factors aside, the American offensive slowly pushing back the outer perimeter of Japanese defenses had merely meant the tolerable reduction of an immense empire. With the fall of the Marianas in the summer of 1944, however, Japanese planners were forced to change their strategic thinking. No longer could space be traded for time. The Americans had gained a base that brought the Japanese home islands within range of land-based air attack, and further losses would cut into the vitals of the empire, inflicting wounds that would, in all likelihood, prove fatal. Despite the damage inflicted by the American submarine campaign, there still existed a small but essential flow of oil and other products carried behind the screen of islands extending from Japan itself through the Ryukyus* and Formosa to the Philippines. The loss of any part of that screen would, in all likelihood, sever that last tenuous flow, isolating the Japanese home islands and dooming the empire.

The Japanese view of the importance of these last bastions of empire is evident in the comments of Lieutenant General Shuichi Miyazaki, chief of the Operations Section at Imperial General Headquarters, as he discussed the strategic significance of the Philippines:

> The Philippines were the east wing of the so-called "Southern Sphere" in the Japanese operations in the southern regions. They took the shape of the main line of defense against American counterattacks. The western wing was Burma and Malaya, and together the two wings protected Japanese access to the southern regions. Viewed from the standpoint of political and operational strategy, holding the Philippines was the one essential for the execution of the war against America and Britain.... The loss of the Philippines would greatly appropriate strategic bases for the enemy advance on Japan. If they were captured the advantage would be two to one in favor of the enemy and the prosecution of the war would suddenly take a great leap forward for the enemy.

---

* The Ryukyus are a six-hundred-mile-long arc of islands extending from the southern end of the Japanese home islands to Formosa. Included in this chain of islands is Okinawa.

Since the Japanese were not certain whether the Philippines were indeed the next target of the Americans, they devised four separate but related plans—all under the code name *Sho* (meaning "victory" or "to conquer")—to cover the areas deemed most likely to be attacked. Operation Victory One (or *Sho Ichi Go* in Japanese) focused upon the defense of the Philippines. Operation Victory Two (*Sho Ni Go*) was designed to defend Formosa, the Ryukyus, and Kyushu, southernmost of the home islands. Operation Victory Three (*Sho San Go*) focused upon the central home islands of Honshu and Shikoku, and Operation Victory Four (*Sho Shi Go*) covered Hokkaido, the northernmost of the home islands.

Since the ships of the Imperial Japanese Navy had been forced by fuel shortages and training requirements to divide up between the home islands and the Lingga anchorage in the south, and because the remaining land-based aircraft—of which there were still many—were likewise scattered all over the remaining empire, the essence of the *Sho Go* plans was to bring together all of these dispersed assets at the right time and place so that they might make one all-out, last-stand defense of the inner empire. Although the Japanese Navy, by this point in the war, had been greatly weakened, this last stand had the potential to deal the oncoming Americans a serious setback. The prerequisites for success were a good plan, carefully executed under the pressure of the moment, and a measure of good luck.

The plans that emerged were realistic and feasible, provided that the required coordination and precise timing could be effected. But two weeks before the battle for the Philippines was to begin, the Americans were to throw the proverbial wrench into the Japanese plans. And, once again, it was Halsey who was the cause.

In preparation for the upcoming invasion of the Philippines, Admiral Halsey had moved his powerful Third Fleet inside the inner screen of Japanese defenses and launched his considerable air assets against a series of targets, starting with the island of Okinawa on 10 October and then moving southward to strike at Luzon in the Philippines and then at Formosa on 12, 13, and 14 October. The attacks on Formosa had three purposes. First, since it was situated only a little more than two hundred miles north of the Philippines, Formosa was a potential staging area for Japanese reinforcements. Second, there were considerable Japanese land-based air forces already gathered there, which, if not neutralized, posed a serious threat to the U.S. forces scheduled to invade the Philippines. Third, Halsey reasoned that an attack on Formosa would provide diversion and introduce some confusion as to what really was the next target of U.S. invasion forces.

As luck would have it, Admiral Toyoda, Commander in Chief of the Combined Fleet, was in Formosa at the time of Halsey's attacks. Though he was at the actual scene of battle, he was away from his headquarters where he would have had access to all available intelligence and communications. Consequently he was forced to rely upon his chief of staff, Rear Admiral Ryunosuke Kusaka, to decide how to respond to these latest attacks. Kusaka's response was to partially activate *Sho Ni Go* by sending all available air assets to Formosa to meet Halsey's onslaught. Included in that mobilization were many of the remaining aircraft on Vice Admiral Ozawa's carriers.

As the two air armadas clashed in the skies above Formosa, Vice Admiral Shigeru Fukudome, watching flaming aircraft dropping from the sky in droves, clapped his hands in exultation and shouted "Well done! Tremendous success!" His joy was short lived when it became evident that the vast majority of those flaming aircraft were his own. He later wrote: "Our fighters were nothing but so many eggs thrown at the stone wall of the indomitable enemy formation." The earlier attrition of Japanese pilots and the deficiencies in replacement training were painfully evident. In the months prior to this engagement, the Japanese had become so desperate as a result of fuel shortages that, as a substitute for actual flight time, they had contracted the Toho Motion Picture Company to construct an artificial lake and fill it with six-foot models of U.S. warships, which were then photographed by a movie camera attached to a boom simulating different angles and speeds of approach. Such methods were innovative to be sure but hardly an adequate substitute for actual flying experience.

The unavoidable truth was that the Japanese air forces were beyond recovery and could not hope to mount a serious challenge to the American aviators now arriving in the Pacific fully trained and in ever-growing numbers. Rear Admiral Robert B. "Mick" Carney, Admiral Halsey's chief of staff, watching the Japanese counterattack on the Third Fleet from the bridge of the flagship, noted the apparent weaknesses in the enemy's air arm:

> The Nips decided to throw everything they had in the way of air attack against our forces. The attacks took the form of formations of from sixty

to eighty planes, but those of us who had seen the air operations earlier in the war in the South Pacific were immediately impressed by the fact that these aerial formations were nondescript in character, included all types of planes, and that the technical performance was not nearly of the same order as had been previously encountered.

At the end of the three days of the Formosa engagement, the Japanese had lost five or six hundred of the approximately one thousand aircraft they had committed to the huge air battle. And, of particular significance to the forthcoming struggle over the Philippines, the reduction of Vice Admiral Ozawa's already diminished carrier striking force, this time by half, left him with a mere 110 aircraft to share among the remaining aircraft carriers. This emasculation of Ozawa's forces ended all hope of effectively employing the Japanese carriers. Halsey's earlier strikes on the Philippines, back in early September, had led to the advancement of the invasion date which, as already noted, had prevented Ozawa from completing his scheduled training of pilots and from linking up his carrier forces with his surface forces in the south. By causing his enemy to commit so many aircraft to the Formosa air battle, Halsey had again disrupted Japanese planning.

Another effect of Halsey's strike on Formosa was that it effectively eliminated Ozawa as overall commander of the Japanese operational forces. The impotence of Ozawa's forces meant that all hope for success in any coming engagement would depend upon those surface forces in the south. Recognizing this, Ozawa was compelled to relinquish tactical command to Vice Admiral Takeo Kurita, who had been training those forces at the Lingga anchorage. The effect of this change in commanders can, of course, be no more than a matter of speculation, since there is no way to know with certainty that Ozawa would have acted any differently than did Kurita. But, in light of what actually did occur, and Admiral Kurita's pivotal role in these events, speculation on this matter is all but unavoidable. Monday morning quarterbacks will probably always be tempted to ask, what if Ozawa had been in command instead of Kurita? How different might have been the Battle of Leyte Gulf?

Both admirals had acquitted themselves well to this point in the war. Ozawa, a dignified and physically impressive man who was taller than most Japanese, had served in a variety of assignments that gained him extensive sea-duty experience balanced by a number of important staff assignments, including Chief of Staff to the Commander of the Combined Fleet. In the years just prior to the war, he had commanded both a battleship division and a carrier division, experience that would have served him well in the coming battle had circumstances permitted him to retain command of all operational Japanese forces. Ozawa deserves high marks for his performance as commander of Japanese forces at the Battle of the Philippine Sea the previous June, despite the outcome, when consideration is given to the comparative assets of the two sides and the extraordinary capabilities of his opponent, Raymond Spruance.

Takeo Kurita, whose fate it would be to lead the attack on the Americans in the most critical phase of the coming struggle for the Philippines, was much smaller in stature than Ozawa, yet the very model of a fighting man. Quiet, weathered, and stern-looking, he had spent most of his career at sea, almost totally avoiding administrative assignments and taking his shore tours at the Naval Torpedo School where he could work on the advancement of tactics. He had been at sea for all but two weeks of the entire war, first in command of a cruiser division, then a battleship division, and finally the Second Fleet. He was recognized throughout the Japanese Navy as a leading expert in torpedo warfare and had been blooded during the arduous fighting in the Solomons.

Kurita had chosen to make his career in destroyers, cruisers, and battleships in an era when it was aircraft carriers and submarines that were deciding the outcome of naval engagements. Yet this naval officer, who had apparently chosen the wrong path to glory, was destined to have the fate of the empire in his hands, leading a formidable force of battleships and cruisers into a final thrust at the enemy—a thrust that, by luck and by clever planning, had a real chance for success.

The outcome of that engagement and the reasons for it, including Kurita's role, would be a heated topic of discussion among naval officers and historians for decades to come.

A young hawk swept low over Kurita's fleet as it made its way across the southern reaches of the South China Sea. With wings outstretched to ride the tropical air currents, the bird circled the battleship *Yamato* and then perched on one of the towering masts of the giant ship. Vice Admiral Matome Ugaki watched from his flag bridge while several sailors cautiously approached the hawk, captured it, and then placed it in a cage to serve as a mascot. Ugaki smiled and then peered out over a placid sea covered by what he would later describe in his diary as "a faintly illuminated layer of auspicious air." The arrival of the hawk and the beautiful sea are good omens, he thought. Victory will surely be ours.

Admiral Ugaki, with good omens and an indomitable spirit to fortify him, looked forward to the days ahead. Operational Telegram Order Number 360 had arrived from Admiral Toyoda, who was now in his "first battle command post" at Hiyoshi, near Tokyo. The message ordered the commencement of Operation Victory One, *Sho Ichi Go*. Ugaki knew that the battleships in his division, including the incomparable and as yet unblooded *Yamato* and *Musashi*, might at last see the action he had long dreamed about. As events were shaping up, it seemed possible that American and Japanese surface forces might clash in battle reminiscent of the days at Guadalcanal when the Imperial Japanese Navy knew the taste of stunning victory.

Ugaki was ready for anything that might come. Later, as he wrote by the dim light of the red lamp, his optimism once again illuminated the pages of his diary. "We are not afraid of a million enemies or a thousand carriers because our whole force shares the same spirit."

8

★ "Strike!" ★

Dusty Rhoades stood on the forecastle of USS *Nashville* near the huge pelican hooks that secured the anchor chain while the ship was at sea. The cruiser was moving almost silently through the water at a mere 12 knots, a soft breeze gently marking the ship's passage and a canopy of stars twinkling above in the night sky. Earlier, at twilight, Rhoades had watched with great interest as the ship's navigator had peered at those celestial signposts through his sextant and then, under the red glow of a lamp designed to preserve the night vision of mariners, plotted the ship's position on a chart.

Rhoades looked about in the subdued light and could barely make out the shadowy presence of the other ships in the formation, all steaming completely blacked out to foil the deadly aspirations of enemy submarines that might be lurking here in the Philippine Sea. Despite their near invisibility, he knew that there were literally hundreds of American ships out there, all pressing through the dark waters on the same course, toward the same objective.

Tiny phosphorescent creatures that inhabited the tropical waters were stirred into brilliance by the passage of the great steel hull, and Rhoades watched in fascination as their eerie green glow ignited in the ship's bow wave and danced about in the turbulence like miniature fireworks. It was like a dream world one might expect to see in Disney's *Fantasia*, but it was real and Dusty Rhoades was a part of it. As General MacArthur's personal pilot, he had not expected to be invited to accompany the general when he embarked in USS *Nashville* for the historic return to the Philippines. But MacArthur rarely did the expected, and Rhoades, happily, found himself at sea with the invasion force.

It had been nearly three months since Rhoades had watched MacArthur stride purposefully across the airstrip toward his waiting aircraft, having just returned from his talks with President Roosevelt. It was apparent that the general was in good humor, so Rhoades was emboldened to fall into stride with MacArthur to ask if the general had gotten what he wanted. MacArthur glanced around to see that no one else could overhear and then replied, "Yes, everything. We are going on."

"To the Philippines?" Rhoades had asked.

"Yes. It will not be announced for a few days yet, but we are on our way."

From his elevated perch in the highlands of Leyte Island in the Philippines, Joseph F. St. John gazed in wonderment at the gulf below. The water was slate gray in the early dawn light but was everywhere mottled by the blue-black silhouettes of ships. Hundreds of ships.

St. John let the image burn into his mind for a moment, then, at last, after two and a half years of fear, privation, and desperate hope, he let himself believe that his ordeal was indeed coming to an end. He began to shout with all his strength, "*Americanos* come!"

His Filipino companions took up the cry. "*Americanos* come!" They, too, had been waiting a very long time for this moment, and now, with their American friend's confirmation of what the scene in the gulf below truly meant, they began to celebrate. The word spread like an uncontrollable fire, down the slopes of the mountain, through the villages, across the valleys, along jungle trails, and into the rice paddies. All over Leyte, the words "*Americanos* come!" resounded with great jubilation.

Then the words faded and were replaced by a new call. This one, St. John noted, was more like a chant, heavy and sonorous, almost primitive in its cadence and tone. The wild celebration had given way to a grim determination, a venting of emotion long buried beneath layers of fear and pragmatism, yet smoldering with the embers of a burning hatred. "Kill Jap" echoed across the highland slopes. "Kill Jap, kill Jap, kill Jap . . . "

On the American ships beginning to fill the waters of Leyte Gulf, men were hard at work bringing the great armada to its momentous destination. Helmsmen steered the invading ships into the restricted waters of the gulf, while radarmen watched their glowing cathode-ray tubes for the electronic warning of enemy aircraft. Lookouts peered through the morning gloom for the telltale signs of enemy periscopes or mines that might have been missed by the earlier trawls of the minesweepers. Officers huddled around planning tables for one last review of charts and orders, and stewards kept the flow of coffee continuous. Infantrymen cleaned their already pristine weapons one last time, and coxswains checked the engines of their landing craft for the hundredth time. But for many the only sign of activity was their blinking eyes peering anxiously into the growing light of dawn, wondering what lay ahead. The black outline of their island objective loomed up out of the dark waters, its amorphous mass appearing formidable to all but the stoutest of hearts. This time, the last hours before combat, is always a difficult one, when the proximity of death is the only certainty and the idle mind is left to its corrosive effect. The proverbial calm before the storm.

On the bridge of the light cruiser *Nashville*, a khaki-clad figure stood near the vessel's captain, his gold-encrusted cap reflecting fragments of the faint but growing light. He had waited two years, seven months, and three days for this moment, and with great anticipation he scanned the distant shore of Leyte for some recognizable landmark. Forty-one years before, Douglas MacArthur had stood on that very shore, a proud young lieutenant, fresh from West Point. In these Philippine Islands he had begun what would prove to be a long and glorious career, and now, to these same islands he was about to return, this time to fulfill a promise, to avenge an ignominious moment, to regain lost honor.

With a great convulsive blast, the big guns of battleships and cruisers cast their opening salvos toward the shore. The calm had instantly evaporated, and now began the great storm.

Joseph St. John saw the fire emanating from the gun barrels of the ships in the gulf several seconds before he heard the sound. From his high vantage point he had a clear view of the proceedings at first. But as the firing continued, great clouds of gunpowder smoke settled over the area, obscuring all but the muzzle flashes from the ships and the growing line of flames along the targeted shore. The firing intensified until the pulse-like detonations slurred into a nearly continuous rumble like the elongated thunder of a summer storm.

As the assault continued, St. John watched in fascination as smaller vessels emerged from the smoky shroud and moved in closer to the shore. Suddenly, hundreds of bright red needles lifted from their decks in near-perfect unison and arched their way to the beach, looking like flaming arrows as they cascaded down upon the sand. Volley after volley spewed from the amphibians, igniting the entire shoreline as they fell. St. John had heard of rockets before but had never witnessed their awesome beauty and power until now.

He saw something else he didn't recognize. Among the familiar silhouettes of chubby transports and sleek warships, he had noticed many odd-looking vessels with their superstructures mounted very near their sterns. To him they appeared as though they might at any minute tip over backwards and disappear into the sea. These were LSTs,* and they had not even existed when St. John had last seen a U.S. Navy ship.

Joseph St. John had been an Army private first class in the Fourteenth Bombardment Squadron when it first arrived at Manila back in September 1941. When the Philippines had fallen to the Japanese several months later, St. John had managed to evade capture and had spent the next thirty months as a fugitive and a guerrilla fighter. Even with the almost constant aid of friendly Filipinos, he had barely survived the harsh jungle environment and the danger of capture that had constantly haunted him throughout the ordeal. He suffered a drastic weight reduction and a permanent loss of hair. He had eaten locusts, monkeys, and dogs in order to stay alive, and he contracted malaria, dysentery, and a number of other maladies for which he had no name. Filipino bandits were a constant threat, and, more than once, he narrowly escaped capture by the Japanese.

On one occasion, St. John hid in a ditch beneath a large log while Japanese soldiers searched the area for him. When they failed to find him, the soldiers settled down just a few feet away to wait, in case he returned. Hours passed in which St. John dared not move a muscle. All the while, large Philippine ants crawled over St. John's body, constantly biting him from his nose to his toes. As if this were not enough to endure, he soon became aware of ghastly, blood-sucking leeches who had come to join the feast. For hours he lay there, unable to move, while his flesh turned to a

---

* The Landing Ship, Tank (more frequently referred to simply as an LST) was an unusual but highly useful amphibious ship that made its debut in World War II. A little over 300 feet long and displacing about 4,000 tons fully loaded, it was capable of transporting eighteen tanks or an equivalent load of other materials to a landing site where it had the ability to run its shallow bows right up on the beach and disgorge its cargo through huge bow doors.

mass of welts and his blood flowed into some of nature's most grotesque creations. Finally, the Japanese soldiers gave up their vigil and moved off to search for him elsewhere, ending his ordeal.

Little wonder that Joseph St. John had cheered madly when he saw the U.S. fleet come to take back the Philippines.

Unlike Joseph St. John, who was watching the landing from the heights of Leyte Island, Dusty Rhoades did not have a good view of the shore bombardment. *Nashville* did not participate in the firing and was too far from the action to afford Rhoades much of an opportunity to see what was happening. This disadvantage was more than made up for later that day, however, when Rhoades was permitted to accompany the general on his triumphal return to the Philippines. Rhoades was beside himself with excitement at the prospect of being a part of that historic moment. He even hid the fact that he was ill so as not to endanger his chances of being included.

At about noon, Rhoades boarded the landing craft with MacArthur, Philippine President Osmeña, and a host of other assorted dignitaries. The trip into the beach was uneventful, but as they neared the shore, Rhoades could see American dive-bombers swooping out of the clouds, peppering the hillsides in back of the beach where Japanese gun emplacements were firing at the thousands of invaders still pouring ashore. The sound of gunfire of all calibers was everywhere and the pungent smell of cordite hung heavily in the smoke-filled air. Palm trees that fringed the far side of the beach burned like giant candles, and the concussion of exploding shells flattened clothing against the human forms beneath.

The landing craft crunched up on the shore and the bow door rattled down into the surf. They were still some distance from the dry sand of the beach, so the general and his entourage had to step off into knee-deep water and wade the rest of the way in. It was one of those moments that would become a graven image in the American heritage, photos of which would flash around the world in newspapers and then settle indelibly into thousands of history books as icons of restored national honor.

Dusty Rhoades waded in on the general's right, a few yards behind, and followed him across the sand to a waiting microphone. He watched as MacArthur took the handset and held it close to his lips.

"People of the Philippines," MacArthur said in his resonant voice, "I have returned."

The gray skies above suddenly opened and rain cascaded from the clouds like tears, so fitting to this emotional moment.

"By the grace of Almighty God," MacArthur continued, "our forces stand again on Philippine soil—soil consecrated in the blood of our two peoples."

With the sounds of mortal combat still thundering around him, soldiers of both sides dying not far away, this man, who many characterized as an egotistical demagogue and others worshiped as a military saint, sent his words out over the Philippine Archipelago to a people who had long awaited his return. "The hour of your redemption is here," he intoned, and countless numbers of Filipinos rejoiced. "Your patriots have demonstrated an unswerving and resolute devotion to the principles of freedom that challenge the best that is written on the pages of human history."

In the years that would follow, MacArthur's detractors would pan this moment. They would accuse him of grandstanding, which is undeniable. They would criticize his use of the first person, which is certainly questionable. Some would even characterize his speech as trite and overblown, which is arguable. But an objective observer could hardly deny the deep emotions that America's return had stimulated in many of the Filipino people, emotions that were manifested in the cheers of *"Americanos* come" and the ominous chant of "Kill Jap" that Joseph St. John had witnessed in the highlands of Leyte.

"Rally to me," MacArthur challenged. And many did. In the months following the landing at Leyte, many Filipinos laid down their lives, fighting as guerrillas in the Japanese rear as the Americans pushed inexorably on through the islands. These people had listened when MacArthur said, "Let the indomitable spirit of Bataan and Corregidor lead on. As the lines of battle roll forward to bring you within the zone of operations, rise and strike. Strike at every favorable opportunity. For your homes and hearths, strike! For future generations of your sons and daughters, strike! In the name of your sacred dead, strike!"

PART III
★ FIRST BLOOD ★

9

★ Of Sorties, Submarines, and Coffee ★

U.S. submarines had been playing a major role in the Pacific war since the beginning. It was an American sub that had carried Philippine President Osmeña to safety in early 1942, when the fall of the Philippines was imminent. Throughout the war, American submarines had carried men, supplies, and information in and out of the Philippines and other areas of the Pacific, where coast watchers and guerrillas clandestinely opposed the Japanese conquerors. Even in the early stage of the war, when poorly functioning American torpedoes had taken much of the sting away from these ubiquitous denizens of the deep, submarines had prowled the vast reaches of the Pacific, serving as effective reconnaissance units by keeping tabs on Japanese Fleet movements. Once the torpedo problem had been solved, American submarines began to take their toll against units of the Imperial Japanese Navy, and, more important, had mounted an increasingly effective anti-commerce campaign that eventually put an economic stranglehold on the empire.

By 1944, U.S. submarines had become a major nemesis for Japan, making the movement of Japanese supplies, troops, and naval units a very risky business, though there were still not enough subs to effectively blanket all areas used by Japanese shipping. Available submarines were assigned to patrols in operating areas that had been code-named for identification, some with colorful sobriquets such as "Convoy College" (the waters between the Philippines and Formosa) and "Maru Morgue"* (waters sur-

---

* *Maru* is Japanese for "ship."

rounding the Ryuku Islands southwest of Japan). The area designated "Hit Parade" covered the waters adjacent to the eastern coast of Kyushu and the southern coasts of Honshu and Shikoku and included the approaches to the Inland Sea and to Tokyo Bay itself. In the second week of October, several U.S. submarines were assigned to patrol the Hit Parade area to detect any sorties of the Japanese Fleet from the home waters of Japan. While other units patrolled the approaches to Tokyo Bay, the submarines *Besugo*, *Ronquil*, and *Gabilan* arrived on station on 10, 11, and 12 October, respectively, and began prowling the waters outside Bungo Strait, one of two channels connecting the Inland Sea with the Pacific.

The three submarines remained submerged during daylight hours and patrolled on the surface during the night. Their primary mission was reconnaissance, watching and reporting the movement of Japanese shipping through the area, but their orders included the option for attack when the situation called for it. On 16 October, *Besugo*, operating in the western sector of the patrol area, sighted two ships identified as unescorted heavy cruisers. Among World War II submariners, cruisers, battleships, and aircraft carriers were considered plum targets, so *Besugo* maneuvered into position and fired a spread of six torpedoes at the two ships. The submarine scored one hit and both Japanese vessels retreated into the Bungo Strait. Postwar analysis of Japanese war records confirms the attack and the hit, but the records also reveal that the two vessels were *not* cruisers but were, in fact, the destroyers *Wakatsuki* and *Suzutsuki*. This was not an unusual mistake. Anyone who has ever been to sea will sympathize with lookouts and watch officers who must try to identify other vessels at the ranges required and under the adverse conditions imposed by wind and wave. During wartime, these difficulties are exacerbated by the necessity for added caution and the exaggerating effects of massive doses of adrenalin. Such misidentification was to prove an important factor in the events soon to come.

The next several days were uneventful for the three submarines operating off Bungo Strait. Unknown to the American submariners, there was a flurry of activity going on in the Inland Sea, as Admiral Ozawa's forces made ready for sea. When they were ready, this Japanese force, which included nine ships that would be considered plum targets by the submariners then lying in wait, would sortie via the Bungo Strait. But Commander T. L. Wogan, tactical commander of the three-sub wolf pack, had been watching the flow of Japanese shipping in the area through his periscope for several days now and had deduced that the enemy was intent upon security rather than battle, since many more ships were headed *into* the Inland Sea than were exiting. Wogan decided to invoke the secondary aspect of his mission, the destruction of Japanese shipping, and moved *Besugo* and *Ronquil* farther west in hopes of finding some fat merchant pickings along the eastern coast of Kyushu.

On 19 October, Wogan's immediate superior, Commander Task Force 17, wanting to cover the other passage connecting the Inland Sea to the Pacific, ordered the *Gabilan* to move east and patrol the approaches to Kii Strait between Shikoku and Honshu. This proved a fateful decision, because it left the eastern approaches to the Bungo channel uncovered.

So it was that on the afternoon of 20 October, at about the same time that General MacArthur was making his triumphant return to the Philippines, no American submarine was on hand to witness the emergence of a column of Japanese ships from the eastern side of Bungo Strait. The cruiser *Isuzu* and four destroyers came out first and immediately set up an antisubmarine screen. In their wake came the remainder of Vice Admiral Ozawa's force: the large carrier *Zuikaku*; three light carriers, *Zuiho*, *Chitose*, and *Chiyoda*; two more cruisers, *Oyodo* and *Tama*; and the very unusual battleships *Ise* and *Hyuga*.

Called "hermaphrodites" by naval analysts, *Ise* and *Hyuga* were tangible proof of the evolutionary process then under way in the world's navies. Built originally as conventional battleships, they had entered the shipyards at Kure and Sasebo for a major conversion shortly after the Battle of Midway. Because the Japanese had lost four of their carriers in that battle, and because they finally recognized that the battleship had indeed relinquished to the aircraft carrier its role as capital ship of the world's navies, four of the twelve large-caliber guns had been removed from the after sections of each ship and were replaced by a flight deck. This strange configuration allowed aircraft to take off but not land. Consequently, the air complement of these vessels had evolved into a mix of seaplanes and normally land-based aircraft, which would serve as reconnaissance and attack aircraft, respectively.

When Halsey's forces had attacked Formosa, all the aircraft assigned to *Ise* and *Hyuga* had been detached from the ships and sent to the battle, so the "hermaphrodites" were once again merely battleships as they steamed south for the Philippines—battleships with fewer guns than they once had owned.

So Admiral Ozawa had eluded his American watchdogs and was headed south for Leyte Gulf with an unusual array of ships. More unusual than his ships, however, was the nature of his mission.

Ensign Andy Kerr had an important decision to make. In fact, it might well be the most important decision of his life. It was about 1600 in the afternoon of 20 October, and Ensign Kerr's ship, the light cruiser USS *Honolulu*, known to her crew as the "Blue Goose," had been firing her six-inch batteries for the better part of three days in support of the Leyte landing. Japanese land-based aircraft had been sporadically attacking the Seventh Fleet ships since the landing had begun, causing the ships to remain at battle stations most of the day. Kerr's battle station was in main battery plot, deep in the heart of the ship and he was tired.

Late in the afternoon, there was at last a lull in the action and the ship had recently secured from general quarters, setting Condition Two, which meant that only half the crew had to remain on station, releasing the others to go catch up on sorely needed sleep. Kerr's dilemma occurred when he caught the aroma of a freshly brewed pot of coffee.

Unknown to Kerr, or to any member of *Honolulu*'s crew, at that moment a Japanese aircraft was flying low over Leyte, headed for the gulf, the hilly terrain of the island concealing its approach. This aircraft was one of the land-based Japanese air assets that still remained in the aftermath of the Formosa air battle. Most of the surviving aircraft had been ordered in from Formosa to supplement those already stationed in the Philippines, and additional planes from China and Japan had also been added, bringing the total number of land-based aircraft in the Philippines to nearly four hundred. Seventy different airfields of various sizes scattered all through the Philippine Archipelago permitted the Japanese to scatter these land-based air assets so effectively that total neutralization by American striking forces was virtually impossible.

Like most sailors of the U.S. Navy, the men of the offgoing watch down in *Honolulu*'s main battery plot had long ago become immune to the effects of caffeine and many had opted to remain on station long enough to have a cup of the freshly brewed coffee before heading for their bunks. Ensign Kerr, no stranger to the habit, debated for a moment, then decided that sleep had more appeal than coffee and began to climb the ladder leading out of the plot room. He was the only man to leave at that time.

A warning flashed out over the TBS* as the Japanese plane emerged from the hills of Leyte, and several lookouts on *Honolulu* spotted the incoming plane simultaneously. Even through the veil of mist that hung low over the gulf, a large dark shape could be seen hanging from the underside of the aircraft. "Torpedo plane, port quarter" came the alarm.

By this time, Ensign Kerr had climbed up two or three ladders in the access trunk, leaving main battery plot and the coffee-drinkers several decks below. Suddenly, the ship's loudspeakers barked, "Set condition affirm. Underwater attack." This meant that all watertight doors and hatches on the ship should be closed immediately. Ensign Kerr, having just passed through an armored hatch, instinctively turned and closed it.

Topside, Captain Harry R. Thurber, *Honolulu*'s commanding officer, who seconds before had been in his sea cabin getting a haircut, arrived on the bridge in time to see a large splash in the water beneath the incoming aircraft. Quickly assessing the situation, he ordered full speed astern and threw his rudder over hard left in a desperate attempt to position his ship parallel to the wake of the incoming torpedo. His quick thinking was the most that could be done under the circumstances and probably saved the ship from an even more devastating blow, but it was not enough to escape the oncoming torpedo.

Andy Kerr had just finished dogging down the armored hatch when the torpedo slammed into *Honolulu*'s port side, just forward of the bridge. Kerr felt a tremendous jolt and all the lights went out, leaving him in total darkness. He groped about as the ship shuddered and groaned, feeling for a sound-powered telephone to establish communication with some other part of the ship. He sensed that the cruiser was listing heavily to one side and wondered if she was going to sink. Without further orders, he was reluctant to open either of the hatches above or below him for fear of allowing fire or flooding to spread, yet he was not enjoying the prospect of remaining in this dark access trunk if the Blue Goose descended to the deep.

The torpedo had caused a massive explosion, ripping a gaping hole in the cruiser's port side and allowing the sea to rush in and flood most of the forward third of the ship from keel to waterline. Extensive damage-control

---

* TBS—"Talk Between Ships"—was the primary radio network used by ships to communicate with one another during World War II. Today's naval personnel would recognize this net as PRITAC or "Primary Tactical."

measures were under way to shore up the damage and to right the ship's list.

Andy Kerr was not the only man in *Honolulu* who was wondering about his survival. Radioman Third Class Leon Garsian had been sleeping in the radio compartment below decks when the torpedo hit. Fortunately the space had maintained its watertight integrity, for within seconds, the compartments above had been flooded with water and oil. Garsian was cut off from his shipmates and would spend the next sixteen hours alone in the radio compartment while the spaces above him were pumped out and acetylene torches burned away at the four-inch armor plate that had him temporarily entombed.

The hatch above Ensign Kerr clanked open and a voice called down, "Is anyone down there?" Neither he nor the Blue Goose would perish that day.

But others were not so lucky. As Andy Kerr was soon to learn, all sixty-five men in main battery plot had been killed. Only his timely exit had saved him from the same fate.

The ship's ordeal continued as nearby American ships, exercising poor firing discipline in their zeal to shoot down Japanese aircraft making strafing runs in the gulf, fired into the pall of smoke surrounding *Honolulu*, killing five more men and wounding an additional eleven. The Blue Goose would eventually limp out of Leyte Gulf, barely able to make way because of the extensive damage, arriving at Manus thirteen days later.

But Ensign Kerr's ordeal was not yet over. Because he was the only survivor of those assigned to battle stations in main battery plot, it was his misfortune to have to return to that devastated compartment after the ship was safely tucked into drydock at Manus. He would help identify the remains of his fallen shipmates, who by that time had been submerged in warm tropical water for nearly two weeks. The details of that experience are better left unrecorded.

Ironically, it appears that USS *Honolulu* may have been the victim of a case of mistaken identity. Hours after the torpedo attack Radio Tokyo erroneously broadcast the news that General MacArthur's ship had been hit and sunk in the Philippines. *Honolulu* was a sister ship of USS *Nashville*, MacArthur's flagship.

At Brunei, many of the ships comprising the Japanese armada were still filling their fuel bunkers with the fossil-generated elixir that had been one of the major causes of this war in the Pacific. The verdant Borneo mountains surrounding the anchorage, rising in places to more than 12,000 feet, shielded Kurita's force from detection, both visual and electronic. It didn't matter, however, because there were no Allied submarines or aircraft in the region to sound the alarm. In fact, at that moment in the early evening of 21 October, the U.S. Navy was not sure where the bulk of the Imperial Japanese Navy was, nor what it was up to.

Had an American reconnaissance aircraft flown over the anchorage at that moment, its crew would surely have been awed by the sight of the mighty *Musashi* and *Yamato*, five other battleships, thirteen cruisers, and nineteen destroyers. The Americans might also have been curious to know why there were several small craft clustered near the cruiser *Atago*. They might have deduced that this was the fleet's flagship, and that the boats nearby had brought the commanding admiral's subordinate commanders to the cruiser for a pre-sail briefing.

On board *Atago*, Vice Admiral Ugaki and the other assembled officers listened intently while they were briefed on the upcoming plan by one of Admiral Kurita's staff. The *Sho* plan, as devised by Combined Fleet planners in Japan, instructed the fleet to thwart the invasion of the Philippines by attacking the enemy's troop transports. While all the Japanese officers were prepared to carry out these orders, there were many who privately objected to this seemingly misguided prioritization of targets. To these dissenters it seemed inappropriate and tactically unwise to attack such a relatively benign target when there might be enemy carriers and battleships within their reach. Some still sought the "decisive engagement" that had dominated their thinking since the war's beginning. Others shared Rear Admiral Nakazawa's conviction that this was the Imperial Japanese Navy's last chance to die with honor, and to do so while attacking troop transports, rather than the heart of their adversary's power, was no way for the fleet to "bloom as flowers of death."

Kurita himself was one of the dissenters, as was his chief of staff, Rear Admiral Tomiji Koyanagi. While Kurita's fleet had been training at the Lingga anchorage, Koyanagi met with representatives of the Combined Fleet staff in Manila. Rather than try to get the Tokyo planners to completely reverse their decision, he decided to attempt a more subtle approach and asked, "According to this order, the primary targets of First Striking Force are enemy transports, but if by chance carriers come within range of our force, may we, in cooperation with shore-based air, engage the carriers and then return to annihilate the transports?"

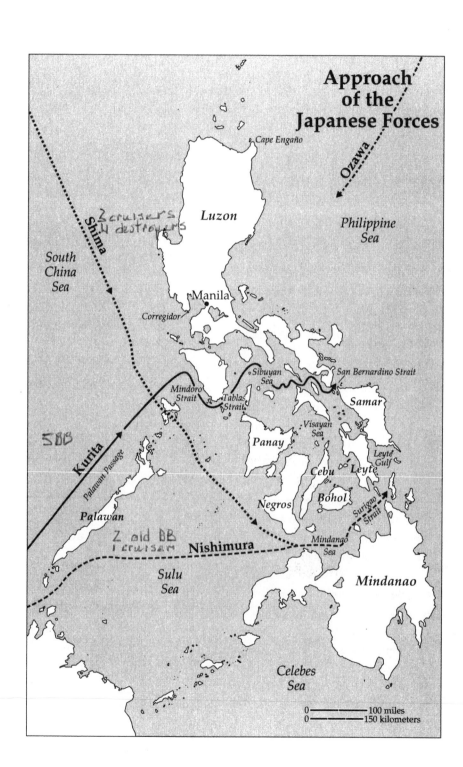

Approach
of the
Japanese Forces

Cape Engaño

Ozawa

Luzon

Philippine
Sea

Shima

2 cruisers
4 destroyers

South
China
Sea

Manila

Corregidor

Sibuyan
Sea

San Bernardino Strait

Mindoro
Strait

Tablas
Strait

Samar

588

Visayan
Sea

Kurita

Palawan Passage

Panay

Cebu

Leyte

Leyte
Gulf

Negros

Bohol

Surigao
Strait

Palawan

Z old BB
1 cruiser

Nishimura

Mindango
Sea

Mindanao

Sulu
Sea

Celebes
Sea

0 ——————— 100 miles
0 ——————— 150 kilometers

Koyanagi's circumspection paid off. Combined Fleet headquarters agreed to this proviso.

Despite this reservation about the mission itself, and a constant hope that circumstances would allow them to invoke the proviso and engage carriers instead of troop transports, Kurita's staff worked hard to prepare for the coming battle. They carefully studied nautical and topographical charts, pored over tactical doctrines, and frequently conferred. They paid particular attention to three points in the Philippines they deemed most likely to be the site of an American invasion: Lamon Bay in the north, Davao Gulf in the south, and Leyte Gulf in the center.

So when the word came that the Americans had arrived at Leyte Gulf, Kurita and his staff were ready. Their plan called for Kurita to divide his forces into two elements that would hit the American forces from two different directions in what is traditionally called a "pincer attack." The larger of the two elements, which would include Ugaki's Battleship Division One, would remain in Kurita's tactical command and proceed northward from Brunei, then cut through the Philippine Archipelago using the Sibuyan Sea as passage.

Once across this rather narrow inland sea, this force would pass through San Bernardino Strait, proceed south along the coast of the island of Samar and attack the American landing forces at Leyte Gulf from the north.

Meanwhile, the other, smaller element, consisting of the battleships *Yamashiro* and *Fuso*, the heavy cruiser *Mogami,* and four destroyers, was placed under the command of Vice Admiral Shoji Nishimura. It would sortie from Brunei after Kurita's force, taking the shorter but more hazardous route through the Philippines via the Sulu and Mindanao seas. With proper timing, Nishimura would pass through Surigao Strait and enter Leyte Gulf from the south at about the same time Kurita's force was attacking from the north.

Dividing one's forces is always a risky venture because it creates two elements, each of which must, by definition, be weaker than the whole. It also complicates the commander's problem of control by requiring coordination over greater distances. But the advantages gained can offset these problems under the right circumstances. A pincer attack, where separate elements approach an enemy's force from different directions simultaneously, can be very effective because it causes the enemy to divide his forces and his attention. It can even be effective if the two forces do not attack with perfect simultaneity, because the force being attacked may shift its assets to meet the thrust of the first force, leaving another side vulnerable to the oncoming attack, the other part of the pincer. In the case of Leyte Gulf, where the target was the landing forces then assaulting the shores of Leyte island, this type of attack was particularly well suited, since it was hoped that one Japanese force would draw away the defending U.S. warships, leaving the second Japanese force a free hand with the then highly vulnerable American amphibious forces.

An amphibious landing renders a naval force somewhat vulnerable by its relatively static nature—"one leg ashore, one leg afloat" as one naval historian and analyst described it. Such an operation forces the navy guarding the landing into a defensive role, thereby negating the advantages of mobility and offensive attack normally enjoyed by a fleet not so encumbered. For the Japanese—who had spent most of the war on the defensive, and who had more recently endured the devastating ramifications of Bull Halsey's mobility and offensive power—gaining even a slim hope of a tactical advantage was no small consideration.

The biggest problem facing the Japanese was that the Americans had such an overwhelming advantage in available forces. Japanese intelligence reports, though not perfect, were providing a reasonably accurate assessment of what was waiting at Leyte. The Japanese were aware of the large amphibious fleet (Kinkaid's Seventh) that was spearheading the invasion. If this were the only force to contend with, Kurita's two-pronged attack would have an excellent chance for success. But the Japanese knew that Halsey's forces were also lurking about, spoiling for a fight with a gargantuan agglomeration of naval striking power. Halsey and Kinkaid together had more than enough forces available to take on any number of pincer elements, coming from any number of directions. How, then, could the Japanese hope to contend with such overwhelming odds?

The answer lay in the age-old weapon that has served inferior forces for as long as there has been warfare. *Deception* was to be the offsetting element that might negate some of the preponderant American advantage. Although the Japanese knew that their carrier striking forces had been rendered impotent by their lack of trained pilots, they reasoned that the Americans might not fully appreciate this fact and might still consider the carriers a force to be reckoned with. So it had been decided that Ozawa's role in the forthcoming battle would be to approach from the north in a straightforward manner, hoping to be detected in order to lure some portion of the American forces away from Leyte Gulf. With luck, it would be the U.S. carrier striking forces that would be lured away, giving Kurita's powerful surface forces a fighting chance for carrying out their mission against the amphibious forces at Leyte. The success of the plan depended upon how much of the U.S. Navy's air power could be drawn off to give chase after Ozawa. Except for the support that could be provided by land-based air forces stationed in the Philippines, Kurita would be very vulnerable to air attack by the Americans once he moved within range of their aircraft.

Operation Victory One would be a long shot for the Japanese. The chances of success were slim, at best. Yet it was a workable plan. With good timing and a bit of luck, the Japanese Navy might yet pull off a spectacular setback for the oncoming U.S. Navy. While a Japanese victory in the war was, by this time, all but impossible, a U.S. setback in the Philippines might have consequences favorable to the Japanese in the American presidential election just days away. Turning the tide of battle might cause President Roosevelt to be ousted from office, or at least significantly weakened, which could conceivably force a change in policy. The United States might be compelled to retract its demand for an unconditional surrender and might be willing to negotiate an end to the war more palatable to the Japanese.

As the briefing aboard *Atago* drew to a close, Admiral Kurita stood before his assembled subordinates and, uncharacteristically, began to address them. His message was pragmatic and fatalistic, yet not devoid of the devotional inspiration so characteristic of Japanese warriors like Matome Ugaki, then standing a few feet away. Acknowledging that the war was going poorly, Kurita said, "Would it not be shameful to have our fleet remain intact while our nation perishes?" He told the men before him that they were being given a "glorious opportunity" and exhorted, "You must remember that there are such things as miracles. What man can say that there is no chance for our fleet to turn the tide of war in a decisive battle?"

With that, Ugaki and the others responded with loud cries of "*Banzai!*" and departed to their respective ships to prepare for the sortie from Brunei.

10

★ Dangerous Ground ★

The twenty-second of October was supposed to have been their last day on station, and the crew of the American submarine *Dace* busied themselves with preparations for the voyage back to friendlier waters. The navigator and his quartermasters worked on the charts that would guide them back to Australia from the uncertain waters west of the Philippines. Storekeepers inventoried provisions and engineers carefully checked fuel and lubricating oil levels. Off-duty sailors put the finishing touches on long letters they would at last be able to post.

This patrol, like most of those conducted by submarines in the Pacific during World War II, had consisted of endless hours of boredom, punctuated by moments of high excitement, followed by periods of postpartum depression as the excitement waned and the hours of boredom returned. Earlier in the patrol *Dace* had bagged an oiler and a transport near the coast of Borneo, and just three days ago she had unsuccessfully attacked a destroyer, which had then retaliated with an equally unsuccessful depth-charge attack. There had also been several promising moments when contact with elements of the Japanese fleet seemed imminent, but these had led only to disappointment as the sighting reports proved bogus or the potential prey outmaneuvered them. Compared to some of *Dace*'s previous exploits—delivering commandos into enemy-held territory, a near-ramming by a Japanese destroyer, and a daring reconnaissance mission into Sarangani Bay in the southern Philippines—this was not the most fulfilling patrol a submarine skipper might hope for. So it is not too surprising that when *Dace* received a midday report of a Japanese convoy headed south toward her position, her captain, Commander Bladen D. Claggett, decided to postpone their departure.

By this time, *Dace* and another submarine, USS *Darter*, skippered by Commander David H. McClintock, were operating in an area east of Palawan Island near an area identified on their nautical charts as "Dangerous Ground."

With the steady vibration of powerful engines gently massaging his feet as they rested upon *Yamato*'s steel deck, Vice Admiral Ugaki wrote in his diary: "With regard to the movement of the Fifth Fleet, there have been some arguments but finally it was decided to charge into the anchorage from the west entrance of Surigao Strait following the Second Force in the early morning of the 25th. Sometimes it's better to reserve some strength, too."

By the "Fifth Fleet" Ugaki was referring to a force of two heavy cruisers, one light cruiser, and four destroyers that had not been at Lingga with Kurita's large surface force when *Sho Ichi Go* had been activated. These ships, entrusted to Vice Admiral Kiyohide Shima, had been operating to the north around Formosa and the coast of China. As indicated by Ugaki's diary, there had been a great deal of indecision as to what to do with this additional cluster of ships, but at last it was decided that Shima would follow on the heels of Nishimura through Surigao Strait into Leyte Gulf. Now there were four separate Japanese forces converging on the Americans at Leyte Gulf: Ozawa coming from the north, Kurita on his way to San Bernardino Strait, and both Nishimura and Shima headed for Surigao Strait.

Despite Ugaki's unsatisfying explanation that it is sometimes "better to reserve some strength," a question immediately comes to mind. Why did the Japanese not merge Shima's force with Nishimura's, rather than plan for them to arrive separately? Together they would present a more formidable force. "Reserving strength" does not seem an appropriate tactic when the overall strategy is an "all-or-nothing" attack.

The answer may lie in personalities. Shima and Nishimura were very different, and there is evidence that they did not get along. Whereas Nishimura was a seagoing admiral who shunned politics and had earned his reputation and promotions on the decks of ships, Shima had spent much of his career in staff and school assignments, where his proficiency had been in administrative rather than operational arenas and where he had cultivated advantageous relationships with the Japanese admiralty. While it is nowhere officially recorded, it is quite possible that the decision to keep these two men—and therefore their forces—apart was predicated on their dislike for one another and because their merger would have put the less-experienced, but nonetheless slightly senior, Shima in command. In this matter, the usually outspoken Ugaki was taciturn. His diary only confirms that the two forces were to arrive independently.

On another matter, Ugaki is also strangely laconic. The formation that Kurita had ordered for the transit north consisted of two sections, each having two major columns made up of the battleships and heavy cruisers with three columns of light cruisers and destroyers placed on either flank and between the two major columns. What is inexplicably odd about this formation is that these were known submarine waters and, while Kurita's disposition provided good protection from a flank attack, it left him open to a head-on attack. Leading the way of this massive formation was a line-abreast consisting of two destroyers, the light cruiser *Noshiro*, the heavy cruiser *Myoko*, and Kurita's flagship *Atago*, also a heavy cruiser. To put such high-value targets as cruisers in the front rank without a screen of destroyers ahead of them is less than prudent when the threat of submarine attack is high. The narrowness of the waters the ships were then traversing magnified the need for emphasis on the leading ships since any enemy submarine present would be constrained by the narrow corridor ahead. The best that can be said for this formation under these circumstances is that the battleships were nestled into its most secure area. While Ugaki was not usually so myopic, perhaps this is why, as commander of Battleship Division One, he did not question the wisdom of the formation, since *his* ships were not endangered by it. It seems, from his diary entry, that he may even have approved of the formation because he described it as "an alert formation against submarines."

Be that as it may, this was to be the formation of Kurita's armada as it pressed northward along the western side of Palawan, the southwestern-most island of the Philippine Archipelago. Of the three possible ways to reach San Bernardino Strait from Brunei, Kurita had chosen this one as a compromise of time, distance, logistics, and safety. After leaving the anchorage on the northern coast of Borneo, he could have turned eastward, passing through Balabac Strait between the northern coast of Borneo and the southern tip of Palawan, and then crossed the Sulu Sea on a northeasterly heading to reach the Sibuyan Sea and San Bernardino Strait. This was the most direct route, but Kurita rejected it because American search planes based on Morotai, to the southeast, were within range of the Sulu Sea, and this route would only increase his chances of being detected. By

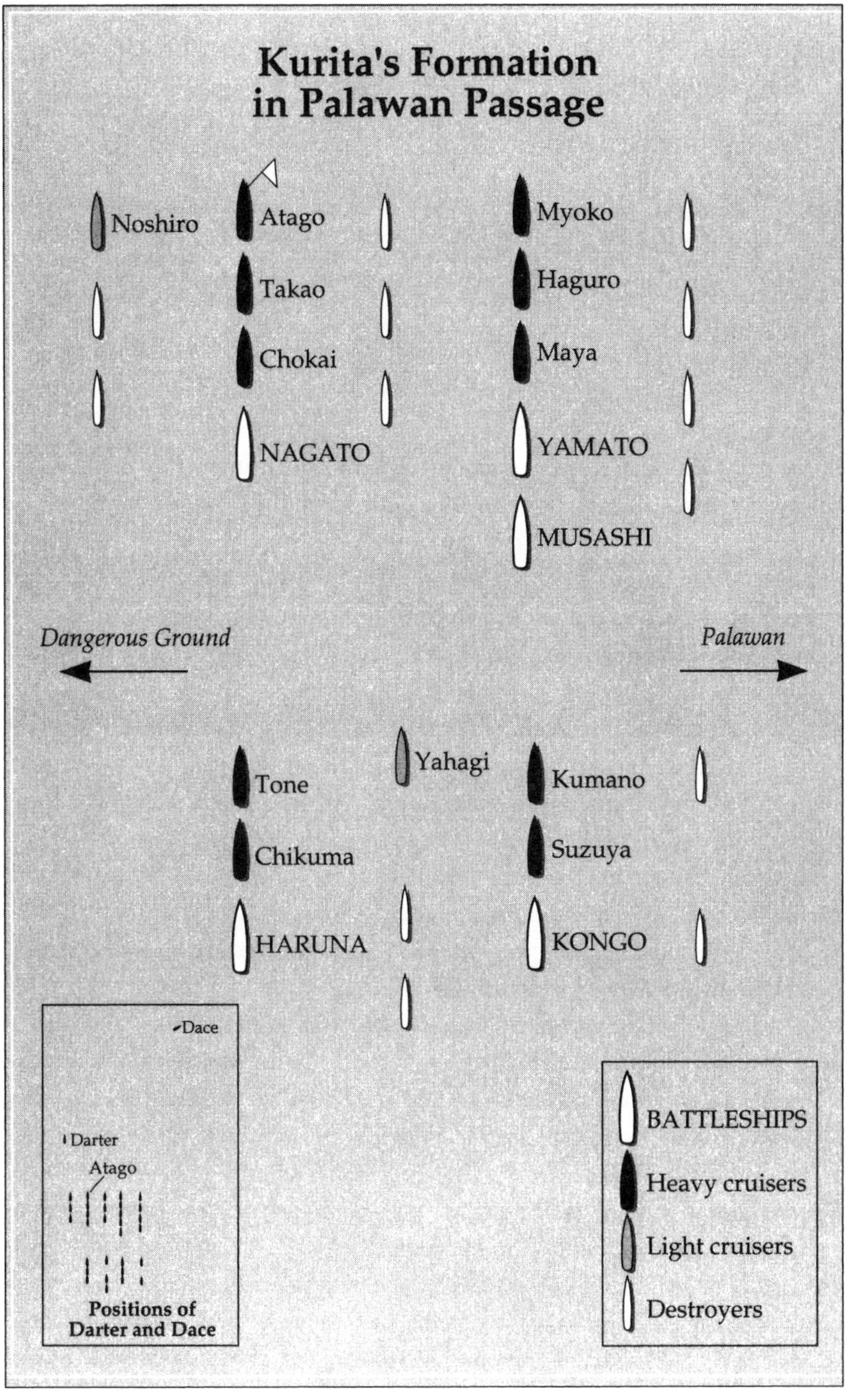

Kurita's Formation in Palawan Passage

Noshiro

Atago
Takao
Chokai
NAGATO

Myoko
Haguro
Maya
YAMATO
MUSASHI

Dangerous Ground

Palawan

Tone
Chikuma
HARUNA

Yahagi

Kumano
Suzuya
KONGO

Dace

Darter

Atago

**Positions of
Darter and Dace**

BATTLESHIPS

Heavy cruisers

Light cruisers

Destroyers

far the safest route, in terms of avoiding submarines and minimizing the chances of detection by air, would have been to proceed northwest out of Brunei, then sweep far out into the South China Sea before heading due east into Mindoro Strait to reach the Sibuyan Sea. But, being a much longer route, it would have required a refueling at sea, which would have taken too much time and was a logistic impossibility because of the shortage of Japanese tankers. So Kurita opted for the compromise route, northeast through the Palawan Passage that ran along the western side of Palawan Island and then to the Sibuyan Sea via Mindoro and Tablas straits. This route would keep him out of range of land-based aircraft from Morotai and would not necessitate another refueling, but it would also take him through a bottleneck area where the probability of submarine activity was high.

As the ships of Kurita's force steamed through the Palawan Passage, on their starboard hand lay the long and narrow Palawan Island, where American prisoners of war had been suffering terrible deprivations and cruelties since the early days of the war. On their port hand was a vast area of reefs and shoals that on the Japanese chart was identified simply as "Dangerous Ground."

At a little past midnight, the two U.S. submarines *Darter* and *Dace* rendezvoused on the surface in Palawan Passage. The pop of a line-throwing gun resounded across the dark waters, and soon the two skippers were exchanging copies of their accumulated message traffic in case either had missed anything they were supposed to receive. Both Claggett and McClintock went below to look over the messages while their bridge watches used megaphones to converse across the narrow ribbon of water flowing between the two submarines.

At sixteen minutes after midnight, *Darter*'s radar operator reported a contact southwest of the submarines. At first, the sailor watching the radar scope thought the contact was a rain squall headed up the passage, but soon *Dace*'s radar operator had the contact as well, and the fuzzy image began to take on definition, leaving no doubt that they were seeing ships. *Many* ships.

There was great jubilation on board the two subs as they broke away from each other and came up to full speed to close the distance to the targets. Because the night was very dark, the subs were able to remain on the surface as they stalked their newfound prey over the next several hours.

As senior skipper, McClintock made several radio contact reports, alerting his superiors to the presence of the massive flotilla coming up the passage. Carefully, he studied the geometry of the problem, trying to work out the positions that would give the two submarines the best angle of attack yet allow for any sudden course changes the enemy might make.

As the night wore on, with *Darter* and *Dace* working their way into a favorable firing position, the initial elation of the submariners had given way to a more serious evaluation of what lay ahead. Jokes became scarce and conversation gradually died as the two Davids moved ever closer to Goliath.

On board the super-battleship *Yamato* the routine morning order "All hands to quarters" was passed. More than two thousand Japanese sailors were soon moving about within the great armored shell as it plowed the waters off Palawan at 18 knots. Admiral Ugaki climbed to his bridge in the towering superstructure and peered out at the dark sea. Off the starboard side he could make out the faint image of one of the destroyers back-lighted in the violet glow of dawn. It was a peaceful scene.

Yamato's bow began swinging to port as the ship changed course in compliance with the latest leg of the zigzag plan then in effect. Such periodic course changes, executed by all ships in the formation, were designed to complicate the targeting solution of any submarines that might be lurking in the area. Many a torpedoing has been foiled by such measures. But such was not the case on this fine October morning.

Ugaki was watching the stern of the cruiser *Maya* ahead of him when he saw what appeared to be a flame leaping out of the sea some distance off his port bow. In the sudden illumination he saw a great column of water rise up and knew instantly that the Americans had drawn first blood.

Almost immediately, the signal "green green" caused the formation to execute a simultaneous emergency turn to starboard, and as Ugaki felt *Yamato* heel slightly to port in response to her rudders, he saw a second explosion in the same general direction as the first. In response to a lookout's report that a ship had indeed been hit, Ugaki hurried to the port side of the bridge to get a better look. Hoping to see that the hapless victim was a destroyer, he was sorely disappointed when he saw, in the growing light of dawn, that there were *two* ships that had been hit, both cruisers. One was listing heavily and a great column of white smoke rose from the other. Ugaki recognized one of the cruisers as *Takao*, which had been second in the port main column. But it was the other ship—the ship apparently more severely damaged and almost certainly sinking—that riveted his attention. It was Kurita's flagship, *Atago*.

At 0510 *Darter* had slipped beneath the waves to hide from the coming dawn, and moments later, *Dace* had done the same. *Darter* had taken up a position ahead of the nearer column of approaching Japanese ships and would initiate the attack. At McClintock's direction, *Dace* had positioned herself five miles northeast of *Darter* in case the enemy formation turned to starboard.

At 0532, with the lead ship sighted in his crosshairs and only a little more than a mile away, McClintock fired six torpedoes from his bow tubes, then put his rudder over hard left to bring his stern tubes around to bear on the Japanese formation. As he swung his periscope around to the right to counter the submarine's movement, he shifted to the second ship in the column. *Darter* completed her turn and began steadying on a reciprocal course, and the sound of five successive explosions signaled that *Darter*'s torpedoes had found their target. McClintock quickly fired all four stern tubes at the second cruiser, then shifted his scope back to the first. He later recorded what he saw in an official patrol report:

> Whipped periscope back to first target to see the sight of a lifetime. (Cruiser was so close that all of her could not be seen at once with periscope in high power.) She was a mass of billowing black smoke from the number one turret to the stern. No superstructure could be seen. Bright orange flames shot from the side along the main deck from the bow to the after turret. Cruiser was already down by the bow, which was dipping under. Number one turret was at water level. She was definitely finished. Five hits had her sinking and in flames. It is estimated that there were few, if any, survivors.

Ugaki was now in command. All communications with Kurita had ceased and *Atago* was unquestionably in her death throes. Several destroyers were moving in to lend assistance to the wounded cruisers while the others dashed out in search of vengeance. From what sense he could make of the incoming reports of periscope sightings and sonar contacts, Ugaki erroneously deduced that there must be at least four enemy submarines in the area. As the formation disintegrated into chaos, Ugaki stared out at the nearby Palawan Island mountaintops, silhouetted against the growing glow of the coming sun, and quickly evaluated the situation. Palawan Passage is only about twenty miles wide at the site of the torpedoing, so Ugaki knew that radical maneuvering was not an option. He saw the coming daylight as both an asset and a liability, and felt that the loss of two cruisers was serious but by no means decisive. The mission must go on.

Ugaki decided to increase the formation's speed so as to clear the area and leave the submarines behind. He knew the enemy could not hope to keep up while submerged and, with daylight breaking, they would not dare to surface. He came up with a makeshift formation that would restore some order and was about to put it into effect when two significant things happened. First, the destroyer *Kishinami* reported finding Admiral Kurita in the water near his stricken cruiser. Second, there was another explosion almost dead ahead of *Yamato*.

Onboard *Dace*, lying in wait to the northeast, Captain Claggett had watched through his periscope as *Darter* successfully torpedoed the two lead ships of the column nearest her. "It looks like the Fourth of July out there," he said for the crew's benefit, confirming what they had assumed when they heard the sound of multiple detonations resonating through the sub's hull. "The Japs are milling and firing all over the place," Claggett continued. "What a show!"

After several minutes of watching and describing the "show," Claggett suddenly said, "Here they come." What semblance was left of a Japanese formation had turned and was headed right toward him. McClintock's positioning of the two submarines had been perfect.

"Stand by for a setup!" Claggett said, his eye glued to the periscope. "Bearing, mark!" he barked. "Range, mark!" The fire control officer and his assistant quickly calculated as the Japanese ships drew inexorably closer. "Angle on the bow, ten port." The dials of the mechanical computer spun about in search of a deadly solution. "Down scope!" Claggett ordered, and in the conning tower was an unexpressed feeling of relief as the men watched the telltale periscope withdraw into the skin of the submarine, leaving the sea above no longer marked by its presence.

The minutes passed and soon the periscope was on its way up again. More ranges, bearings, angles on the bow. The men in *Dace* waited, all of them blind to the scene above, save one, each of them dealing with amplified emotions in his own way.

Claggett watched as the column of Japanese ships loomed large in his narrow field of vision. He wished he had a lot more torpedoes. "Let the first two go by," Claggett said, then added a phrase that would have turned the most seasoned of sub skippers deep green with envy: "They're only heavy cruisers."

Claggett's selectivity, though enviable, turned out to be superfluous. Believing the third ship in the Japanese column to be a battleship, he had let the heavy cruisers *Myoko* and *Haguro* go by only to select another heavy cruiser, *Maya*, as his victim.

With a near perfect firing solution at hand, Claggett began chanting, "Fire one! Fire two! Fire three!"

Vice Admiral Takeo Kurita had been spared. He had survived the torpedoing of his flagship but had been forced to jump into the sea to keep from accompanying *Atago* to the bottom of Palawan Passage. She had gone down in eighteen minutes, taking three hundred and sixty men with her.

Kurita had been fished from the debris-laden waters of the strait and unceremoniously hoisted aboard the destroyer *Kishinami*. As he stood on the main deck with oil and water dripping from his body, he saw a series of flashes near *Yamato* and then heard the sounds of detonations rolling across the water in ominous testimony of still more death and destruction as *Maya* took her hits.

From *Yamato*'s bridge, Vice Admiral Ugaki stared straight ahead of the ship's track, where a moment before the cruiser *Maya* had been steaming ahead of *Yamato*. Now there was only a great turmoil of smoke and boiling water, and debris was raining from the skies as *Maya*'s remnants were swallowed by the sea.

There is an old saying in the Navy, "Paybacks are hell," and Commander Claggett had no desire to see confirmation of that old adage. The sixth torpedo had barely left its tube when Claggett ordered *Dace* into deep submergence and put his rudder over trying to fall into the wake of the next oncoming ship in the Japanese column. As the submarine plunged downward, two tremendous explosions could be heard by all on board. The soundmen reported that it "sounded as if the bottom of the ocean was blowing up." Claggett later wrote that "nothing could cause this much noise except magazines exploding." But as the sound of the explosions subsided, it was replaced by a strange crackling noise, like the sound of cellophane being crumpled. It began faintly, then grew in volume until the men in *Dace* were staring wide-eyed at one another. None had ever heard a sound quite like it, and Claggett feared that his submarine was yielding to the growing pressure of the dive even though she was nowhere near her test depth. He immediately ordered all stations to report the condition of their compartments and waited anxiously for their replies. After several agonizing moments, all stations had reported that the submarine was intact. Claggett then deduced that what they were hearing must be the sound of their Japanese victim breaking up. As he listened in awe to what he later described as "the most gruesome sound I have ever heard," Claggett realized that the noise was all around him, and another frightening thought swept over him. Could the Japanese ship be coming down right on top of *Dace*? The idea of being holed by the descending ruins of his victim or, worse yet, being pinned to the bottom of the sea by the dead vessel's corpse, was not pleasant to contemplate. As though echoing Claggett's thoughts, the diving officer said, "We better get the hell out of here!"

At full speed, *Dace* dashed away, frantically trying to escape, her electric motors taking long draws on the limited capacity of her batteries, the unsettling noises of her victim's demise still resonating through her hull. It was a long moment for the crew of that American submarine as they listened to the sounds of death so close at hand and wondered how contagious such things might be. At last, the terrible noises were clearly falling astern, and Claggett and his crew began to breathe once again.

Their respite was brief. A string of depth charges detonated terrifyingly close aboard, announcing the arrival of Japanese destroyers. *Dace* rocked and shuddered violently as light bulbs exploded and locker doors burst open. The executive officer, Lieutenant Commander R. C. Benitez, later recorded, "The Japs were very mad—and we were very scared."

The pounding continued for several minutes and then all was quiet. As cautious relief slowly seeped into the submarine, Commander Claggett sent a messenger to the forward battery compartment to get him a cup of coffee from a pot that had miraculously remained intact. About the time the sailor reached forward battery, another string of depth charges went off very close aboard. Another young sailor, who was a veteran of quite a few patrols despite his age, leaped into the air and shouted, "For gosh sake, let that man in!"

Again, the submarine was slapped about in the deep as the destroyers above sought retribution by sowing the sea with canisters of high explosives. At last, the attack subsided, and after another nerve-racking period of waiting for the hammer to fall, the men in *Dace* realized that this round was over and there had been no knockout punch.

Claggett remained deep for several hours before cautiously working his submarine toward the surface. By the time he arrived at periscope depth, all had been quiet for quite some time. *Dace*'s periscope broke the surface at 1100 and Claggett swept around in a 360-degree arc. The sea was empty.

Ugaki retained command of the Japanese armada until well into the afternoon. The bulk of the force raced northward, leaving behind two destroyers to watch over the crippled cruiser, *Takao*. Her rudder and two of her propellers had been blown off, and three boiler rooms were completely flooded. But she was more fortunate than her sisters *Atago* and *Maya*, whose remnants now littered the ocean floor just east of the region called "Dangerous Ground."

At 1540, the force was well clear of Palawan Passage and the destroyer *Kishinami* maneuvered alongside *Yamato* to transfer Admiral Kurita and the other survivors of the *Atago* sinking. By 1700, Kurita was again in command of his diminished force.

The day had been costly. Kurita's force had already been diminished by the three torpedoed cruisers and the two destroyers left behind to assist *Takao*, and it was still a long way to his objective. That evening, as Ugaki recorded the day's events in his diary, adding that another Japanese cruiser had been torpedoed several hundred miles to the northeast,[*] he closed the entry with, "A bad day is a bad day to the end."

Yet, despite the day's losses, Kurita still had a formidable force, and he had, after all, set out on this mission fully realizing it was going to be costly. He knew from the outset that he was going to lose ships. The real question was whether he could reach his objective—the American landing site at Leyte Gulf—with enough ships still intact to inflict significant damage on his enemy. With his five battleships still undamaged—including the powerful *Yamato* and *Musashi*—and nine cruisers and thirteen

---

[*] This was the cruiser *Aoba*, which had been detached from the main fleet units to support a convoy of reinforcement troops that the Japanese were moving from Luzon to Leyte. The U.S. submarine *Bream* fired a spread of six torpedoes, only one of which connected, but it was enough to put *Aoba* out of commission. She did not sink but was damaged sufficiently to be knocked out of the war.

destroyers still in his force, Kurita was not ready to throw in the towel.

As darkness descended, Kurita's force turned east and headed for Mindoro Strait. Tomorrow, they would cross the Sibuyan Sea, where they would face a gauntlet of another type.

The so-called Dangerous Ground is an area in the South China Sea so full of reefs and shoals—many of them named for the unfortunate ships who were their victims—that it is given a wide berth by all prudent navigators. But the exigencies of war sometimes obviate prudence. Both *Darter* and *Dace* had been operating in the waters adjacent to Dangerous Ground for days. This had been of no great consequence when they were alone in Palawan Passage, because the two submarines had been able to come to the surface and routinely obtain good navigational fixes by taking bearings on the prominent points of Palawan Island and by "shooting" twilight stars by sextant. During this period they knew where they were in relation to the navigational hazards to the west of them and could therefore stay well clear. But once the Japanese Fleet had entered their domain, dominating their attention and preventing them from coming up for a good fix, the two submarines had been forced to navigate by dead-reckoning, a kind of "best guess" form of the navigational art and always the mariner's last choice.

After *Dace* had come to periscope depth and found an empty sea around her, she had headed northward, back in the general direction of the earlier melee. Three and a half hours passed uneventfully. Then, at 1425, the tops of masts appeared on the horizon. Claggett moved in cautiously and a half-hour later was able to make out a damaged cruiser lying motionless in the water. Two destroyers were hovering nearby and Claggett decided to stand off until dark.

Meanwhile, *Darter* was also nearby, and McClintock had already tried to move in on the crippled cruiser to finish her off. He had worked his way in to a range of 7,000 yards when both destroyers seemed to have caught his scent and began moving in his direction. When the nearer of the two had closed to 3,500 yards, McClintock decided that discretion was the better part of valor and went deep to evade. He decided to wait until nightfall when he and *Dace* could move in together for a combined attack.

At sunset that night, a few fateful words were recorded in *Darter*'s log: "Too close to cruiser to surface for star sights." And with that, the fortunes of war had turned against USS *Darter*.

When Palawan Passage was once again blanketed in darkness, *Darter* and *Dace* surfaced, planned their attack, and began moving in. *Takao*, meanwhile, had managed to get under way and was limping back toward Brunei, managing only about five knots. *Darter* began circling around the cruiser, trying to do an end run to the west.

Dace also began sweeping around, trying to position so that the cruiser would be silhouetted against the eastern horizon, which was faintly visible despite the darkness of the night. At seven minutes after midnight, *Dace* received a brief but startling message from *Darter*. "We are aground."

As *Dace* approached *Darter*, there was no doubt that the latter was aground. She was so high out of the water that she looked like a vessel in drydock. Her propellers were clear of the water so it was apparent that she was not coming off that reef. The only thing to do was rescue her crew and then destroy her so that she would not fall into enemy hands.

While many of the *Darter*'s crew worked at destroying papers and equipment, others began clambering down the side of her hull into two rubber boats for transfer to *Dace*. It was slow going since the rubber boats could only carry six men at a time, and it was after 0430 when the last boat run brought McClintock to *Dace*.

Demolition charges had been set on board *Darter*, and, as the two crews now aboard *Dace* braced themselves for a great explosion, there was instead what *Dace*'s executive officer described as "a ridiculously low and inoffensive 'pop.'" The demolitions had failed to properly detonate.

Now they were in a fine fix. Under the circumstances, reboarding the foundered submarine seemed unwise. But leaving her there for the Japanese was also unpalatable. McClintock and Claggett decided to use some of *Dace*'s remaining torpedoes to put *Darter* out of her misery. One at a time, Claggett fired four torpedoes at point-blank range. Each detonated with a frightening clamor but succeeded only in blowing away small portions of the offending reef. *Darter* was too high out of the water for the torpedoes to have any effect on her.

Next they tried *Dace*'s deck gun. Twenty-one rounds later, *Darter* was damaged, but only barely. Talk began to spread among the men that the sub was somehow invincible. One of the more seasoned veterans suggested that they might all be safer aboard *Darter* than *Dace*.

As the sky to the east began to brighten, their situation was becoming precarious. A submarine on the surface is like a warrior without his shield, and one with more than twenty men out on her weather deck is like an army in open terrain. The longer they lingered there on the surface with *Dace*'s gun crew firing away, the greater the chance for discovery and attack.

Sure enough, at 0558, the dreaded event occurred. A Japanese aircraft appeared overhead and commenced an attack run. The ammunition for the deck gun was left topside as men scurried for cover inside the sub, and some scrambled headfirst down the hatch, an unconventional but speedy method of entry. But all knew that the chances were slim that *Dace* could dive to safety before the aircraft could effect his attack.

In the air above, the Japanese pilot released his bombs and down they plummeted. His target was a sitting duck. The other submarine's decks were awash and it was apparent that she was beginning to submerge, but this one remained inert, like a target ship waiting to die.

"That dumb ass of a Japanese pilot!" said one of the sailors aboard *Dace*. "He made his drop on *Darter*!"

The Japanese pilot could hardly have been blamed for his decision to attack the more inviting target. He had no way of knowing that it was an abandoned submarine that was indeed waiting to die. But to the Americans on *Dace* this "dumb-ass" act had been their salvation, and there was much jubilation as the unscathed submarine disappeared into the deep.

As it turned out, it mattered little which target the pilot had selected. He had missed. *Darter* was still high and dry and relatively intact.

Claggett and McClintock decided to remain in the area, determined to reboard *Darter* that night and try again to destroy her, this time using *Dace*'s demolition charges. During the day, they watched through *Dace*'s periscope as a Japanese destroyer arrived and apparently sent a boarding party to investigate the stubbornly thriving *Darter*.

By nightfall the Japanese destroyer had departed, and the Americans cautiously moved in. As they got to within two thousand yards, they heard the *ping* of underwater echo-ranging and knew they were not alone. Somewhere nearby lurked another submarine, and since they were certain there were no other American subs operating in the area, McClintock and Claggett decided it was time to give up on *Darter*. Enemy units were becoming a habit in the area, and it was a long way home to Australia, especially with two crews having to subsist on the rations meant for one.

After obtaining permission from his superiors, McClintock had directed Claggett to set a course for Australia and *Dace* began the long voyage back to friendlier waters. Conditions aboard the submarine for the trip back were less than ideal. In a space considered unbelievably tight and crowded under normal conditions, there were now twice as many men. Food, head facilities, and sleeping space were all at an incredible premium. Men sat on the deck in the same spot for days, moving only to make a head call or to curl up to sleep. Meals were brought to these poor sedentary souls, and soon the menu degenerated to the unvarying fare of peanut butter sandwiches and mushroom soup.

This trying situation is probably best illustrated by the sad story of one of *Darter's* officers who, having nothing to do on the long voyage, joined a running poker game in *Dace's* tiny wardroom. The game went on all day and most of each night, stopping only long enough for meals and a few brief hours of sleep. This officer's luck had all been expended on surviving the battle in Palawan Passage, and each time the game temporarily suspended, he would get up from the table loudly bemoaning his losses. After several days of this, one of the other card players could stand it no longer and snapped, "If playing hurts you so much, how come you sit in day after day?"

The hard-luck player replied, "Buddy, the only way I can get a seat on this damn boat is to buy it, and I intend to sit on a cushion from here to Australia no matter how much it hurts my feelings or my pocketbook!"

Dace departed Palawan Passage leaving *Darter* perched on Bombay Shoal as an odd but fitting monument to what had transpired there. The opening shots of the battle for Leyte Gulf had been exchanged. In the aftermath of this first round, two Japanese heavy cruisers had been sent to the bottom, accompanied by hundreds of the men who had crewed them. Another heavy cruiser was limping back to Brunei, taking two destroyers with her as protective escort. The Japanese Fleet commander had been forced to abandon his ship and swim for his life, an experience of no small physical and psychological strain. The American Fleet commanders at Leyte Gulf had been warned of their adversary's location and his approach. And the U.S. submarine *Darter* had been lost, but her entire crew had survived.

In assessing what occurred, several matters bear discussion. The first involves Kurita's ordering a formation that left him so vulnerable to a head-on attack. Was it that admirable but deleterious code of the *Bushido* warrior that motivated Kurita to put himself in the lead of his force and would not allow him to hide behind a protective screen of destroyers? Was it the reflection of a fatalist who openly admitted that he expected to lose half or more of his ships on this long-shot venture, and who had resigned himself to a predetermined outcome? Or was it simply an error in judgment committed by a man who had long born the strains of command and combat? Could it even have been the first sign of the unraveling of a heretofore highly capable and unquestionably dedicated officer? Since Kurita never revealed his reasoning in this matter, the question must remain unanswered, but speculation will no doubt continue.

The second matter that invokes discussion is Kurita's detachment of two destroyers to escort *Takao* back to Brunei. Kurita acknowledged the "all or nothing" nature of the mission, and he knew the criticality of preserving every unit possible. Yet he expended two of his destroyers at a time when the need for their antisubmarine capabilities had just been painfully proven. His decision was a humanitarian one, to be sure, for to leave *Takao* on her own, with no escort, would have probably spelled her doom, and the death toll for this engagement would have been several hundred higher. But this was at a time when the Japanese Navy, by policy, was seeking to achieve a miraculous victory or, failing that, was hoping to "bloom as flowers of death," as Rear Admiral Nakazawa had so metaphorically put it just a few days earlier. As Kurita himself had said in his speech at Brunei the day before, "Would it not be shameful to have our fleet remain intact while our nation perishes?" Yet he squandered two of his ships to protect a useless cripple when the moment of truth for both him and his navy was about to arrive. Again, his reasoning is unknown and only speculation will serve.

But it is not Kurita alone who must be questioned in this engagement. The persistence of *Darter* and *Dace* in stalking *Takao* begs explanation. After the torpedo attack, *Takao* was incapable of inflicting any further damage on U.S. units. And in light of Kurita's decision to send the destroyers to escort her, she was actually more of a tactical liability to the Japanese in her crippled state than she would have been lying alongside her sisters *Atago* and *Maya* on the bottom of Palawan Passage. Yet the loss of *Darter* to navigational error was brought on, at least in part, by this preoccupation.

McClintock, as on-scene senior skipper, bears the responsibility, although there is no evidence that Claggett or McClintock's operational senior, Rear Admiral Ralph W. Christie, Commander Task Group 71.1

(based in Fremantle, Australia) ever questioned McClintock's decision. It is probably reasonable to assume that part of what was motivating McClintock, and Claggett for that matter, was the desire for a statistical kill. A cruiser sunk looks far better on paper, and over a beer, than does a cruiser disabled.

In fairness, there wasn't much else for *Darter* and *Dace* to do at that point. Once Kurita's force had passed on, there was a distinct paucity of targets and both submarines had torpedoes remaining on board. The only other option was to return to Australia. In retrospect, it is easy to assess that this would have been preferable to what did happen, especially for *Darter*, but that *is* retrospective. Given the circumstances and the aggressive nature necessary in a submarine skipper, McClintock's decision to remain and attempt to finish off *Takao* is at least understandable, if not completely defensible.

In the final analysis, this first engagement in the Battle of Leyte Gulf must, of course, be judged a tactical success for the Americans. Three cruisers to one submarine is not a close score. It must also be deemed a strategic success for the U.S. Navy, because the radio reports from the two submarines gave Kinkaid and Halsey a "heads-up" warning as to the location and approach of a significant portion of the Japanese Navy.

But, considering the almost suicidal nature of the Japanese mission and their desire to arrive at Leyte Gulf with enough firepower to do significant damage to the American forces there, this was no major defeat. Kurita still had a potent force and it was still en route to Leyte Gulf.

PART IV

★ 24 OCTOBER 1944 ★

11

★ TG 38.3 ★

At dawn on the morning of 24 October 1944, six different naval forces were in, around, or headed for Leyte Gulf. Four of these forces were Japanese,* and they were all converging on the gulf. Vice Admiral Takeo Kurita was about to start his trek across the Sibuyan Sea toward San Bernardino Strait with his remaining force of five battleships, nine cruisers, and thirteen destroyers. Vice Admiral Shoji Nishimura had sortied from Brunei after Kurita and was headed across the Sulu Sea with his force of two battleships, one cruiser, and four destroyers. Coming from Chinese waters, Vice Admiral Kiyohide Shima had taken his three cruisers and four destroyers north of Palawan Island and was headed southeast

---

* For simplicity, the Japanese naval forces will be referred to by the name of their respective commanders throughout this narrative. These forces had other, more formal designations, but the names are confusing. Ozawa's force was known to the Japanese by the various names of First Mobile Fleet, Third Fleet, or the Main Body, while the Americans later dubbed it simply the Northern Force. Kurita's force, to the Japanese, was Second Fleet; Forces "A" and "B" of the First Diversion Attack Force; or First and Second Sections, while U.S. commanders simply called Kurita's ships the Center Force. Nishimura's group was referred to as the Southern Force by the Americans and Force C, or Third Section of the First Diversion Attack Force by the Japanese. Shima's force was the Fifth Fleet, or Second Diversion Attack Force. There is an apparent disparity between some of the names assigned to the Japanese forces and their actual missions. Ozawa's decoy force is called the "Main Body," for example, while Kurita's powerful striking force is labeled "diversionary." These apparent misnomers arise because the forces were originally named before the activation of the *Sho* plan, and at that time the names assigned more accurately reflected the intended missions of the various forces.

across the Sulu Sea, where he would eventually intercept Nishimura's track and follow him into Surigao Strait. And finally, there was Vice Admiral Jisaburo Ozawa—with his motley collection of one heavy and three light aircraft carriers, the two "hermaphrodite" battleship-carriers, three cruisers, nine destroyers, six destroyer escorts, and two oilers—coming down from the north, hoping to be detected and attacked.

Waiting for these various Japanese forces, though unaware of most of them as dawn arrived on 24 October, were Vice Admiral Thomas C. Kinkaid's Seventh Fleet and Admiral William F. Halsey's Third Fleet.

The bulk of Kinkaid's Seventh Fleet was actually inside Leyte Gulf, the transports and amphibious vessels busily putting troops and supplies ashore while the gun-toting battleships, cruisers, and destroyers provided gunfire support. Outside the gulf, where they had more room to conduct air operations, steamed the remainder of the Seventh Fleet, the tiny escort carriers (CVEs) and a small contingent of destroyers and destroyer escorts whose task it was to guard the carriers against submarine and air attack. These diminutive flattops and their escorts were attached to Kinkaid's Seventh Fleet as Task Force 77.4 under Rear Admiral Thomas L. Sprague. The eighteen carriers in the force had been further divided into three task groups, each containing six of the CVEs and several escorts. These task groups were formally designated as TG 77.4.1; TG 77.4.2; and TG 77.4.3; but were more commonly referred to by their radio voice call signs, Taffy 1, 2, and 3, respectively. Admiral Sprague retained command of Taffy 1 as a "second hat," but he had designated separate subordinate commanders of the other two task groups. Taffy 2 was commanded by Rear Admiral Felix B. Stump, and Taffy 3 was the responsibility of Rear Admiral Clifton A. F. Sprague, who despite the same last name, was not related to his boss, Thomas L. These "Taffy" forces were tasked with providing direct air support to the troops ashore and with conducting antisubmarine patrols to keep away any marauding Japanese submarines, which might be tempted to steal into the gulf where there were many hundreds of tempting targets.

Even farther from the landing site in the gulf were the powerful task groups of Halsey's Third Fleet. Rear Admiral Ralph E. Davison's TG 38.4 was closest to the Seventh Fleet forces, operating almost due east of Leyte Gulf. TG 38.2, under Rear Admiral Gerald F. Bogan, was located north of Davison's force, east of San Bernardino Strait. And Rear Admiral Frederick C. Sherman's TG 38.3 was still farther to the northwest, having taken up a position east of the main Philippine island of Luzon.

Despite its awesome power, this largest of the world's fleets had one weakness common to all armies and navies: it was manned by mortal human beings. And those mortals were tired! The practice of "changing the drivers, but keeping the horses" (as Halsey had described the Third/Fifth fleet system) was "hard on the horses." Vice Admiral Marc Mitscher, commander of Task Force 38, was concerned about the rigorous employment of his carrier striking forces, remarking that "probably 10,000 men have never put a foot on shore during this period of ten months. No other force in the world has been subjected to such a period of constant operation without rest or rehabilitation." Reports from ships' medical officers in the task force contained many references to fatigue, and Mitscher worried that the reactions of his crews had been slowed down to such a degree that "they are not completely effective against attack." Because of this, and because the first few days of the landings at Leyte had brought no discernible response from the Japanese Navy, Halsey had detached Vice Admiral John S. McCain's TG 38.1, the most potent of the four task groups, to proceed to Ulithi to replenish supplies and give the men a break from the rigors of continuous operations at sea. Halsey had also ordered Davison to prepare to take *his* task group to Ulithi the following day.

The stage was now set for the greatest naval battle in history. In the early daylight hours of the twenty-fourth the first phase was about to begin.

Darter had reported the approach of Kurita's force during the night and, in response, Halsey quickly canceled the scheduled departure of Davison's task group for Ulithi and then ordered a comprehensive reconnaissance of all the eastward approaches to Leyte Gulf. Each carrier group was assigned a specific search arc extending out some three hundred miles and covering all navigable channels among the Philippine Islands. Teams of one Helldiver bomber and two Hellcat fighters were assigned to cover each 10 degrees of arc of the search area, while other fighters were stationed at hundred-mile intervals from the carriers to relay radio reports over the great distances.

In the carrier *Essex*, flagship to Task Group 38.3, Rear Admiral Frederick C. Sherman was concerned about the large number of aircraft Halsey was sending out on reconnaissance. Sherman worried that once the enemy fleet was located the number of American aircraft remaining aboard the carriers would not be sufficient to launch the most effective strikes and still provide adequate protection to the ships of the American task force.

His pessimism stemmed from several ominous signs. To begin with, Sherman's task group, the northernmost of the three patrolling the waters east of the Philippines, had been shadowed throughout the night by enemy aircraft that seemed to be keeping track of him. He had launched night fighters to keep them at bay, and, at 0227, one of the enemy was "splashed." But five others remained in the vicinity, keeping tabs on his task group's movements throughout the night. Then, when daylight came, radar revealed a number of aircraft taking off from the airfields near Manila, and Sherman launched twenty fighters to attack them. This enemy activity indicated to Sherman that in the coming hours there might be more to deal with than just the approaching Japanese Fleet.

Admiral Sherman was right.

In accordance with *Sho Ichi Go*, the Japanese had pooled several hundred aircraft in the Philippines and were preparing to use them. The ideal plan would have called for those aircraft to support Kurita and Nishimura as their ships crossed the Sibuyan and Sulu seas, respectively. But the inadequately trained pilots did not have the skills necessary for air-to-air combat,[*] so it was decided that the vast majority of available aircraft would strike the ships of the American Fleet. By concentrating on the American carriers, the Japanese felt they could at least give Kurita and Nishimura indirect support by attacking their potential attackers. When interrogated after the war, Commander Moriyoshi Yamaguchi, operations officer of Second Air Fleet, said, "Our object was to attack your task force and by doing that we would have given Kurita indirect protection." He added, "But it was true that there were always ten planes above the fleet." It is presumed that these ten aircraft were meant to provide fighter protec-

---

[*] With all due respect (and a great deal is due) to those pilots who flew attack (bombing and torpedo) missions in World War II, a pilot with minimal skills, such as the Japanese were turning out at this stage of the war, was more likely to be successful attacking a surface target than he would be in carrying out an air-to-air (fighter) mission. Three-dimensional air combat maneuvers are complex and require split-second reactions as well as a significant dose of finesse not likely to be found in a neophyte. But a pilot having only rudimentary skills might be able to pull off a successful attack on a vessel or land target whose movements are confined to only two dimensions and are carried out at a much slower relative speed. Therefore, most of the newly acquired Japanese pilots by this time were more suited to bombing missions than the more complicated fighter assignments.

tion for Kurita's force. But Admiral Kurita remembered it differently: "I requested that they send fighters from land base, but they did not send any . . . leaving [my] fleet without the expected cover."

There were also many Japanese army aircraft in the Philippines and, in an uncharacteristic gesture of interservice cooperation, the army and navy agreed to pool their resources in the struggle against the American invading forces. This unprecedented agreement to cooperate—brought on by the pervading feeling of desperation rather than any truly ecumenical spirit—proved more verbal than actual. Kurita later confided that he never called for army air support, that his requests for fighter cover went directly to the commander of First Air Fleet, Vice Admiral Takajiro Onishi, and that "when called upon for planes, the navy would send them if they had them; if not, the navy would request them locally from the army."

Despite these problems, as the morning light painted fleecy white clouds across the brightening sky, many Japanese aircraft took to the air, their pilots determined to kill or be killed for their Emperor.

Aboard USS *Intrepid*, flagship of Admiral Bogan's Task Group 38.2, the flight deck crew labored over preparations for the morning launch. It was a strange world for these sailors, living and working on this giant among ships, this smallest of airfields. Unlike their brothers aboard the "battle wagons" and "tin cans," these mariners worked beneath the wings of mechanical birds, where spinning propellers would cleave the bodies of the unwary, where the smell of aviation fuel soaked deep into the clothing and skin, where the heat of the sun was broken by the sudden ferocity of summer squalls or the damp rot of monotonous monsoonal rains, where explosives and flammables were continuous and temperamental companions, where the roar of engines and the clatter of maintenance equipment rendered the ear a vestigial organ, where days were distinguished only by the number of sorties flown and the routine altered only by the periodic call to memorial services for fallen shipmates.

Lieutenant j.g. Max Adams threaded his way through the maze of moving men and machines on *Intrepid*'s flight deck. The ship was on her downwind leg, running counter to the fresh easterlies the aerographer had promised at the morning briefing, so the air on the flight deck was rather still. Adams stepped over fuel hoses and ducked beneath the unfolding wing of a Hellcat fighter as he headed for his own aircraft. He was a dive-bomber pilot with Bombing Eighteen, one of the three squadrons making up Air Group Eighteen, *Intrepid*'s flying complement. This triad of dive-bombers, fighters, and torpedo planes had been operating with the ship since 10 August 1944 and had flown various combat missions in the Palaus, Philippines, Ryukus, and at Formosa. Many of the pilots in this air group had grudgingly participated in the celebratory flyover that had greeted President Roosevelt upon his July arrival at Pearl Harbor to confer with Nimitz and MacArthur, and some had bought war souvenirs from the Marines on Saipan during a brief stopover there in late September. Now, they, like most of the combat forces belonging to CINCPAC and CINC-SOWESPAC, were part of the massive armada whose task it was to take back the Philippines.

Adams reached his Helldiver and, after circling the aircraft for a pre-flight inspection, climbed into the cockpit. He did an internal phone check with his companion in the rear seat, whose job it would be to watch the radar, man the rear guns, and serve as an extra pair of eyes. At a little before 0600, Adams taxied into position, and a few minutes later his wheels rolled off the end of *Intrepid*'s wooden flight deck and dangled idly in the morning air as the Helldiver's wings took over the role of supporting the growling aircraft. As Adams turned westward, putting the sun behind him, the large island of Samar loomed ahead off his port side, its foliage-covered mountaintops brightly lit by the rising sun, its sandy feet immersed in the still shadowy sea.

Adams's Helldiver was joined by four Hellcats from Fighting Eighteen, and the five aircraft flew off to the southwest to cover "sector three" of the search area. About halfway across the Sibuyan Sea, two of the Hellcats broke off to loiter and serve as radio relay while the other three continued on.

There was plenty to see along the way as they flew over the Sibuyan Sea and Tablas Strait. In sharp contrast to the monotonous stretches of open ocean that was the usual panorama for naval aviators, this reconnaissance mission took the three aircraft over waters mottled with different shades of blue and green broken by islands, some low-lying coral affairs and others that had climbed out of the sea to towering heights on the backs of powerful volcanoes. It was a scene that belonged on a postcard rather than a battle map.

As they neared the southern tip of Mindoro, the large island flanking the western side of Tablas Strait, several suspicious blips began glowing on Adams's radar screen at a range of twenty-five miles. He radioed the information to his two fighter companions and they all turned southward to investigate. The three planes were cruising at about nine thousand feet when they spotted the telltale wakes painting tiny white hyphens on the turquoise sea below. They winged over for a closer look, and the hyphens became commas as the ships below began turning. Within minutes, Adams and the other pilots could make out the ships themselves.

In his Hellcat, loitering over the Sibuyan Sea at his radio relay station, the headphones suddenly crackled in Bill Millar's ears. The call was from one of the fighters in Adams's group using the call sign "Five Fox Lucky." The laconic message was electrifying: "13DD, 4BB, 8CA* off the southern tip of Mindoro, course 050, speed 10 to 12 knots. No train or transports." This many combatants with no supply or troop ships in company could mean only one thing. The Japanese fleet was coming out to do battle. Millar excitedly relayed the message and within minutes Admiral Halsey had the word.

Bull Halsey was spoiling for a fight. Unlike Mitscher, who had seen a great deal of action while serving as Task Force 58 commander under Spruance and was most concerned about the weariness of his men, Halsey had, by bad luck and asynchronous timing, missed the large-scale, decisive battles his aggressive spirit had long yearned for, and he was hot to do battle.

Halsey's story was one of repeated frustration. He had begun the war in a seagoing command, but with so weak a force in comparison to the Japanese that all he was able to accomplish was a series of morale-building but strategically insignificant raids. Later, while he was en route to the Southwest Pacific, anticipating a major confrontation with the Japanese Navy, the Battle of the Coral Sea occurred east of Australia, while Halsey was still a thousand miles away. It was Admiral Frank Jack Fletcher who commanded U.S. carrier forces in that first great air-sea battle of the war. Just as the muses of history had brought him to the very brink of decisive battle in June 1942, Halsey had come down with a skin rash so debilitating that he had been forced to a Pearl Harbor hospital bed, and Raymond

---

* DD, BB, and CA are naval designations for destroyers, battleships, and heavy cruisers, respectively. This report was not entirely accurate, though very nearly so. By this time there actually were thirteen destroyers, but five battleships, seven heavy cruisers, and two light cruisers remained in Kurita's force.

Spruance sailed off to glory at Midway. While the "Big Blue Fleet" was growing to its gargantuan proportions and chipping away at the bastions of Japanese empire, Nimitz had needed Halsey's fighting spirit to revitalize the sagging spirit of forces in the South Pacific. So it had again been Spruance who took the fleet to sea while Halsey had operated from a shore-based headquarters, turning the tide in the important but less swashbuckling Solomons campaign. Little wonder that this admiral, whose bellicose utterances had made him famous, was anxious for a chance to place his fleet "alongside that of the enemy."*

Upon first arriving at Leyte Gulf, Halsey had broken radio silence to ask Kinkaid if San Bernardino and Surigao straits had been swept clear of mines. It was Halsey's belief that the Japanese Fleet would not commit to battle over the Leyte landings, but would move into position west of the Philippines, where it could support the movement of supplies and reinforcements from Luzon to Leyte "through the back door." If this proved to be the case, Halsey's intention was to steam through the archipelago to seek out and engage the enemy, and that was why he had queried Kinkaid about the mines. To label this intention Custer-like might be somewhat extreme, but there can be little debate that taking his fleet into the confined waters of the inland seas of the Philippines was at least risky, if not reckless, and certainly unnecessary.

Admiral Nimitz, who was following the progress of the Leyte landings from his headquarters at Pearl Harbor, was alarmed by Halsey's message to Kinkaid. It was clear that Halsey was going to provide the aggressiveness intended by the caveat to Nimitz's orders, which said, "In case opportunity for destruction of major portion of the enemy fleet offers or can be created, such destruction becomes the primary task." But it was also quite clear that Halsey had little or no compunction about abandoning the other part of Nimitz's orders, which directed him to "cover and support forces of Southwest Pacific in order to assist the seizure and occupation of objectives in the Central Philippines."

Nimitz immediately sent a message in which he reminded Halsey of

---

* This borrowing of phraseology from Britain's greatest naval hero, Admiral Horatio Nelson, is Halsey's doing. In describing his own thinking and actions in his autobiography, Halsey quoted Nelson's written order to his officers just prior to the Battle of Trafalgar: "No Captain can do very wrong if he places his ship alongside that of an enemy." Halsey wrote that this "principle of warfare is burned into my brain."

his responsibility to cover the landing, and further directed that "movements of major units of the Third Fleet through Surigao and San Bernardino straits will not be initiated without further orders from CINCPAC." Having been reined in by Nimitz, it seemed that Halsey, once again, had been thwarted from doing head-on battle with the enemy.

Darter's reports of Kurita's force in the Palawan Passage the night before had raised Halsey's hopes, but it was not until the report from *Intrepid*'s aircraft in search sector three that Halsey knew with certainty that the Japanese Fleet was coming. At 0822, Halsey lifted the TBS handset from its cradle and, with obvious excitement in his voice, repeated the reconnaissance information to his fleet. Five minutes later, he ordered his forces to consolidate by directing Sherman's northernmost Task Group 38.3 and Davison's southernmost TG 38.4 to close on Bogan's TG 38.2 in the middle. At 0837, using the collective call sign for all task groups, Halsey spoke into the radio handset once again and uttered the words that officially began the Battle of Leyte Gulf. The message was brief, but unquestionably to the point. He said, "Strike! Repeat: Strike! Good luck!"

To the north, off the east coast of Luzon, Rear Admiral Sherman received Halsey's order to strike and prepared to do so. But while his carriers were turning into the wind, radar operators in the task group excitedly began reporting a large number of air contacts bearing down on the task group from the west. Soon another large group appeared on the scopes, coming in behind the first. And then a third appeared about sixty miles to the southwest, this one larger than the other two.

Sherman's earlier concerns about the large-scale search ordered by Halsey now seemed vindicated. So many of Sherman's fighters were off on the search mission that responding to Halsey's strike order would have depleted TG 38.3's defensive capability to the point that the task group's ships would be seriously endangered by the inbound enemy aircraft. Admiral Sherman had no choice but to ignore the strike order for the moment and respond to the incoming threat. He immediately ordered all available fighters in the task group to be "scrambled."

David McCampbell had been dismissed from the Navy. He had entered the Naval Academy in 1929, the same year that the Great Depression had descended upon America. But when it was time for him to graduate in 1933, the economic woes of the nation had permeated virtually all aspects of American life, and the military was no exception. Because of funding shortages, McCampbell was not permitted to enter the Navy as an officer upon graduating, but was instead given an honorable discharge and sent home. A year later, however, the fiscal picture had brightened enough that he was recalled to active duty and commissioned—a seemingly innocuous event, at the time, that was to have no small effect on the Battle of Leyte Gulf a decade later.

David McCampbell remained in the Navy, earning his wings at Pensacola in 1938 and then flying from the carrier *Wasp* from 1940 until she was sunk at Guadalcanal in September 1942. He was a gifted pilot who amassed an enviable flying record, and by the time American forces had converged on Leyte Gulf he had risen to command Air Group Fifteen, flying from the deck of USS *Essex*.

On the morning of 24 October, McCampbell had risen at 0530, dressed in his flight suit, and headed for one of *Essex*'s two wardrooms for a breakfast of orange juice and coffee. Over the next two hours, he visited the fighter squadron's ready room to check on the day's expected weather, watched one of the morning's launches, and settled down in his office to do battle with the fighting man's worst enemy—paperwork. At a little past 0730, he went out into the morning air to watch more of his fighters take off for a sweep of the airfields near Manila. As the last plane lifted off the deck, some quick mental arithmetic told him that he now had only seven fighters left aboard.

Returning to his paperwork, McCampbell had little time to accomplish anything before he heard the ship's general announcing system warning of incoming Japanese aircraft and then calling, "All fighter pilots, man your planes." Rushing to meet the call to battle, McCampbell was stopped by an officer who told him that the chief of staff wanted him to remain on board, so he reluctantly headed to the ready room. When, a few minutes later, the 1MC again summoned all available fighter pilots, this time appending the word "immediately" to the call, McCampbell rationalized that the chief of staff must have changed his mind. Within minutes, he was strapped into the cockpit of his fighter, a Hellcat he had named *Minsi III* after a ladyfriend back in Milwaukee.

The flight deck crew was still pumping fuel into his aircraft as it was positioned on the catapult for launch. The unexpected scramble had not permitted adequate time for a full refueling. McCampbell checked his gauges as he heard the air officer in primary flight control bellow over the flight deck announcing system, "If the air group commander's plane is not ready to go, send it below!" McCampbell's centerline external tank was full, but his two main tanks were still half-empty. Two hundred seventy-five gallons. It would have to do. He waved off the crewmen with the fuel hoses and signaled that he was ready.

A moment later, the hydraulic catapult yanked *Minsi III* down the flight deck and flung the roaring Hellcat into the air. The fighter barely dipped as its wheels left *Essex*'s flight deck, a grim reminder of how light the aircraft was without its full complement of fuel.

As he climbed into the bright blue sky, McCampbell fired off a few rounds of his machine guns. All six were working perfectly. Once the other six remaining fighters of *Essex*'s air group had joined him at 6,000 feet, McCampbell and his flock headed north where the ship's radar had picked up the scent of a large inbound formation.

The enemy aircraft were approaching at about 18,000 feet, so the Americans began a rapid climb as they conformed to the intercept vector provided by *Essex*'s fighter direction officer (a young lieutenant by the name of John Connally, who would one day become Secretary of the Navy and governor of Texas[*]) in *Essex*'s Combat Information Center. McCampbell's wingman, Ensign Roy Rushing, despite a full fuel load, was able to stay with the lighter *Minsi III* as she soared upward. The other five fighters began to fall behind.

McCampbell and Rushing soon sighted a large formation ahead and above. McCampbell radioed *Essex*, "Rebel, this is Niner-Niner. Are there any friendlies in the area?" *Essex* replied in the negative, and McCampbell then said, "Well, in that case, I have the enemy in sight."

Rushing and McCampbell quickly evaluated the oncoming formation as consisting of "60 rats, hawks, and fish."[†] The enemy fighters were flying higher than the bombers and torpedo planes, and since McCampbell and Rushing had reached a higher altitude than the other Hellcats, McCampbell decided that he and his wingman would go after the rats and leave the hawks and fish to the others.

---

[*] In a further coincidence, one of Connally's closest assistants while Secretary of the Navy would be Andy Kerr, the sole survivor of USS *Honolulu*'s main battery plot, whose story is recounted in chapter 9.

[†] "Rats" were fighters; "hawks" were dive-bombers; and "fish" were torpedo planes.

As he climbed toward the enemy, it occurred to McCampbell that two American Hellcats against forty Japanese fighters were not the healthiest odds. He radioed *Essex* to see if there was any help available, but there was none. In actuality, the odds at face value were somewhat deceiving. Painted on *Minsi III*'s fuselage, just below the canopy, were twenty-one Japanese flags representing McCampbell's confirmed kills thus far in the war.

Both McCampbell and Rushing were able to climb above the enemy formation, apparently undetected. From this position of superior altitude, the two Americans watched as the Japanese fighters started a slow turn to the right and continued on around through an arc of about 270 degrees. Now McCampbell and Rushing were above and behind the Japanese formation, in an almost perfect tactical position for an attack.

One of the enemy fighters began lagging behind the formation and, like the lion who focuses her attack on the straggler from the herd, McCampbell pounced. Diving down on the unsuspecting fighter, McCampbell waited until he could see the bright red "meatball" insignia contrasting sharply with the olive-drab fuselage of the Japanese fighter. Then, easing the stick back to reduce the angle of his dive and centering the target in his gunsight, McCampbell squeezed the trigger mechanism. *Minsi III* shuddered noticeably as she coughed out a spray of deadly .50-caliber armor-piercing and incendiary bullets. Tracer rounds painted a path to the target and, within seconds, the fuel tanks near the Japanese plane's wing roots ignited. Bright yellow flame and sinister black smoke poured from the stricken Japanese fighter as it dropped its nose and began to plummet. No parachute emerged, and soon both plane and pilot were swallowed by the sea below.

McCampbell looked about and saw that his was not the only victory. Rushing, too, had severed one of the fighters from the formation and another trail of black smoke marked the way to the sea below. Astonishingly, the Japanese fighters had not yet reacted to the attacks, and McCampbell and Rushing set up for an encore. In the meantime, the other *Essex* Hellcats had engaged the bombers and torpedo planes and were embroiled in a wild melee below.

For the second time, McCampbell was able to attack a Japanese fighter and erase it from the formation. But this time, the Japanese reacted. They formed up in what American aviators call a "Lufberry," a tight counterclockwise circular formation reminiscent of Conestogas of the Old West forming a circle to defend against Indian attack. It was a purely defensive maneuver, somewhat surprising considering their superiority in numbers, but it is likely that they did not know how many American fighters were attacking them at the time.

Breaking into a Lufberry is no simple undertaking. More to the point, it can be quite hazardous to a pilot's health. No fighter pilot wants to position himself ahead of an enemy where the adversary's guns can be brought to bear. But to approach any fighter in a circle from behind, by definition, places the attacker in front of the next aircraft. A less experienced pilot, facing odds of about twenty to one, carrying less than a full bag of fuel, and facing a Lufberry, might have seriously considered returning to *Essex*.

But *Minsi III* was not adorned with twenty-one Rising Sun flags because David McCampbell was in the habit of heading for the barn when the going got tough. He nosed over and headed down again in a screaming dive of nearly 300 knots, determined to make a head-on attack. Within seconds he pulled out of the dive and swooped in toward the Japanese formation. With all six guns pounding away, he headed straight for the nearest enemy fighter, but this time he faced an adversary rather than a victim. Glaring tracers flashed past him as the enemy fought back. At a relative speed of nearly 400 knots, the engagement did not last long, and the two opponents passed one another in an eye-blink flash. Neither dropped from the sky.

McCampbell repeated the attack, and again it failed. This time he noted ugly black holes in his wings where his adversary had scored a number of hits. He hovered above the Japanese formation for several minutes trying to decide what to do next. His head-on attacks were clearly not working, and each one tried increased the chances of his taking a fatal hit. Rushing was having no better luck.

Suddenly, their dilemma was solved. The Japanese, apparently low on fuel—or merely not fond of the current situation—broke out of the Lufberry and headed back toward Luzon. With the Lufberry broken, McCampbell and Rushing were back in business. Within minutes, McCampbell had splashed his third victim. And not far behind was number four. And then number five.

A fighter pilot who downs five enemy aircraft during his career earns the title "ace." The majority of pilots never achieve it. McCampbell was already an ace four times over before that morning's engagement over the Philippine Sea, and now he had become an ace yet again—on one mission.

After kill number six, McCampbell checked his fuel gauge. It was getting unsettlingly low, and as he and Rushing pursued the fleeing Japanese planes, they were getting farther and farther from the *Essex*. Rushing, who had by this time downed four enemy fighters himself, had plenty of fuel but was running low on ammunition.

Still they pursued. And soon another aircraft dropped from the sky, smoke pouring profusely in its wake. Before long McCampbell's count was an incredible seven. And Rushing, too, had achieved single-mission ace status as his fifth kill plummeted into the sea. Luzon loomed ahead and McCampbell knew that the chances of meeting up with other Japanese fighters increased dramatically with every mile they drew closer. Still they pressed on.

Finally, as McCampbell fired at victim number nine, he heard several of his guns give out as they ran out of ammunition. Rushing had, by this time, run out completely, and McCampbell's fuel gauge was ominously low. It was time to retire.

Rushing stayed close by McCampbell as the two of them flew back, slowly descending and maintaining maximum fuel-economy rpm. After several tense moments, *Essex* at last answered McCampbell's radio call, but the response was not reassuring. The carrier's flight deck was full of aircraft preparing for a launch. There was no room for a landing, and it would be at least fifteen minutes before they could get the strike off.

McCampbell's troubles got a lot worse when he and Rushing at last spotted the American formation. One of the American ships in the task group, mistaking the two Hellcats for Japanese aircraft, opened fire. Five-inch rounds began detonating nearby, and McCampbell and Rushing descended to just above the wave tops, jinking violently back and forth in fuel-consuming maneuvers to avoid being hit by the friendly fire. The firing stopped, but then several American fighters joined the fray, diving down on the two lone Hellcats, who by now had nowhere to go but into the sea.

At the last possible moment, the diving American fighters recognized the two helpless aircraft as some of their own and broke off the attack. A few minutes later, McCampbell, to his great relief, recognized *Essex* a short distance ahead. His relief was short-lived: *Essex*'s flight deck was still covered with aircraft.

In desperation, McCampbell looked about and saw *Lexington* not far away. With a nervous glance at his fuel gauge, which now read something akin to "hopeless," he turned toward the beckoning haven. Again, frustration washed over him as he saw that she, too, had a full flight deck. He flew on to the next carrier in the formation, USS *Langley*, and was again greeted by a deck fouled with aircraft.

McCampbell was about to ditch *Minsi III* in the water when he got word that *Langley* was launching and should have room to take him aboard in just a few minutes. The question was whether he had a few minutes. His fuel gauge said he did not, but he managed to stay airborne long enough to be invited aboard.

When McCampbell at last rolled to a stop on the flight deck of USS *Langley*, his engine coughed and stopped before he had a chance to shut it off. There were six rounds of ammunition left in one gun; the rest were empty.

McCampbell was fed sandwiches and coffee aboard *Langley*, and before long was airborne again flying combat air patrol. When he finally landed aboard *Essex* later that day, he was summoned to the flag bridge. As soon as Sherman saw him, the admiral bellowed, "Dammit, I told you I didn't want you flying in these scrambles." McCampbell tried to explain but was not very convincing, so Sherman cut him off, saying, "Dammit, don't ever let it happen again."

And "it" didn't. What no one seemed to realize at the time, in the midst of the battle then under way, was that history had been made. David McCampbell had shot down nine enemy aircraft[*] in one engagement, a feat never before or since duplicated. Rushing had downed an additional six to bring the total for these two pilots to an incredible fifteen.

Full realization did finally come and, in recognition of this historic mission and another in which McCampbell downed another seven enemy aircraft, the following was later written in a citation:

> During a major fleet engagement with the enemy on October 24, Commander McCampbell, assisted by but one plane, intercepted and daringly attacked a formation of sixty hostile land-based craft approaching our forces . . . shot down nine Japanese planes and, completely disorganizing the enemy group, forced the remainder to abandon the attack before a single aircraft could reach the fleet. . . .

---

[*] He probably downed two others as well, but these could not be confirmed.

That citation was appended to the Medal of Honor.

There was another aerial hero that day. Like McCampbell and Rushing, he laid his life on the line to carry out his duty. He killed a great many of his enemy—far more than McCampbell and Rushing—and he eliminated and debilitated a significant proportion of his enemy's combat capability. Unlike McCampbell and Rushing, he was a bomber rather than a fighter pilot. And, unlike McCampbell and Rushing, his name has been lost to the anonymity that is the unfitting reward of most of those who fight and suffer and sacrifice and die in the cataclysmic events of war. And, quite unlike McCampbell and Rushing, he was Japanese.

The importance of what McCampbell and Rushing and many other American fighter pilots did that day takes on heightened significance when viewed in light of what this lone Japanese bomber pilot was able to do. Flying a Yokosuka D4Y Suisei—known to the Japanese as a "Comet," to the Americans as a "Judy"—he did not succumb to the defensive attacks of the American fighters in the area. Nor did the heavy antiaircraft fire of the screening destroyers and cruisers in the American task group deter him from his mission. At a little past 0930, this anonymous Japanese pilot, following close behind a group of returning American fighters, slipped through the defenses of the American task group and, emerging from a low cloud, fixed his sights on one of the biggest prizes of all in naval warfare.

The U.S. aircraft carrier *Princeton* was recovering aircraft completely unaware that a Japanese plane was nearby. She had taken aboard twelve aircraft when her lookouts spotted the Judy coming straight for the ship. *Princeton*'s rudder was immediately thrown over and her 20- and 40-mm antiaircraft batteries opened up, but these measures proved ineffective. The Japanese bomber continued in, undeterred by the American gunfire, and released a single 550-pound bomb. The bomb plummeted straight and true and landed almost dead center on the flight deck, just forward of the after elevator. It was apparently an armor-piercing round, because it did not explode on contact but went on through the flight deck, leaving only a small hole to mark its point of entry.

The pilot then pulled up his aircraft and dashed for the sanctity of the clouds. He escaped for the moment but was later reported shot down by *Lexington*'s combat air patrol.

Captain William H. Buracker, who had been Halsey's operations officer in the early days of the war,* was now *Princeton*'s commanding officer. He felt no great concern as he peered down from the bridge at his damaged flight deck: "I saw the hole, which was small, and visualized slapping on a patch in a hurry and resuming operations." Such was not to be. The bomb had penetrated not only the flight deck but had passed through the hangar deck, coming to a stop in the ship's bakery, where it detonated, killing all the men at work there. The explosion ripped open the hangar deck and flames quickly enveloped six torpedo bombers that were being refueled and rearmed there. Aviation fuel fed the flames, and soon the torpedo warheads began detonating.

One of the aviators who had landed aboard *Princeton* just moments before the bomb hit was Ensign Paul Drury, a fighter pilot in squadron VF-27. When the explosions had begun, Drury and the other pilots who had just returned were ordered to stand by their aircraft, which had by this time been moved to the forward part of the flight deck. Drury stood helplessly by his Hellcat fighter, feeling the shock of the explosions down below and wondering what he and the other pilots could possibly do. "I knew there was no way we were going to get airborne under those circumstances," he later said, "and I didn't think it was too likely that anyone was about to steal my plane."

The situation deteriorated rapidly as the fire-fighting crews were unable to get the fires under control, and before long, a series of massive explosions ripped great gaping holes in the flight deck. Drury watched in horrified fascination as one of the ship's massive aircraft elevators came completely out of its pit and rested at an odd angle on the flight deck.

At about 1010, Captain Buracker ordered the setting of Salvage Control Phase I, which meant that all but 490 of the ship's 1,570-man complement were to abandon the ship. The remaining men were firefighters, who would continue to try to save the critically wounded vessel, and gunners, who would protect her from air attack during the process.

Lieutenant Drury watched as a destroyer moved in close aboard *Princeton*'s port side to help fight the spreading fires and to assist in the abandonment. The sea had been mounting and there was an ugly grinding sound as the two ships were thrown together. Drury considered leaping over to the destroyer, but reconsidered when he saw another man apparently break his leg making the jump between the violently heaving ships.

---

* See chapter 4.

When ammunition in the ready-service lockers began to explode on board *Princeton*, Captain Buracker ordered Salvage Control Phase II, calling for the gunners to leave the ship and leaving only the damage control parties on board. Captain John M. Hoskins, who was scheduled to relieve Buracker as commanding officer of *Princeton* in just a few days, opted to join the fire fighters in the after part of the ship, hoping to help save his would-be command.

Paul Drury headed farther forward on the ship and considered climbing down the anchor, but saw that another man had already tried it and gotten his foot lodged in the chain. The ship, heaving up and down in the ocean swell, periodically submerged the unfortunate man who was unable to pry himself loose. Drury then headed aft, where he found a number of lines that had been suspended in the water. He quickly used one to lower himself into the surging sea and began to swim.

On into the afternoon, the remaining crew of *Princeton* fought the raging fires, trying desperately to get them under control. Several other ships of the task group moved in close-aboard to help fight the fires and to rescue men who had either jumped or been blown overboard by the explosions. Finally, at about 1330, most of the fires had been isolated to an area around the ship's after-magazine, and she was still upright, on an even-keel, and not in any danger of sinking. There was new hope that the ship would survive. Captain Buracker might still have a ship to turn over to Captain Hoskins in a few days.

The USS *Birmingham*, a light cruiser assigned to TG 38.3, was signaled alongside to fight remaining fires and get a hawser across to take the crippled *Princeton* under tow. *Birmingham*'s decks were quite crowded as the cruiser approached the carrier's port side. Towing and fire-fighting equipment was everywhere on her topside decks and, more significantly, hundreds of her crew were there as well. It took several approaches before the necessary lines could be gotten over, and the cruiser had to break away once when there were warnings of a combined submarine and air attack. So it was late afternoon, nearly 1530, when disaster struck.

Without warning, a tremendous explosion tore off a huge portion of *Princeton*'s stern as her after-magazine blew up. There was a terrible staccato of metal on metal as shrapnel of all shapes and sizes—pieces of *Princeton*—raked across *Birmingham*'s exposed decks like the deadly grapeshot canisters fired from the cannons of yesterday's sailing ships. The effect was the same. Hundreds of men instantly fell dead or horribly wounded. Within seconds, the ship's scuppers ran red with blood* as it poured forth from thousands of grotesque wounds, and severed limbs lay about the blood-smeared deck like the casual droppings on a slaughterhouse floor. The senior medical officer was away from the ship assisting in an operation on the cruiser *Santa Fe*, and the dental officer was among the first to die, which left only one doctor to deal with the incredible carnage. Many of the crew, some of them seriously injured themselves, administered first aid to those with hope and helped ease the suffering of those without. And in the midst of the horror of this gruesome scene, the ship's executive officer saw something positive and inspiring, which he later described:

> I really have no words at my command that can adequately describe the veritable splendor of the conduct of all hands, wounded and unwounded. Men with legs off, arms off, with gaping wounds in their sides, with the tops of their heads furrowed by fragments, would insist, "I'm all right. Take care of Joe over there," or "Don't waste morphine on me, Commander; just hit me over the head. . . ." Terrible as the destruction was, it is a source of supreme gratification to know the heights of courage and forgetfulness of self to which one's shipmates can rise.

And terrible the destruction was. The final casualty count aboard *Birmingham* was 229 killed, 4 missing, 211 wounded seriously, and 25 with minor injuries. The ship itself was more fortunate. Although her starboard side was perforated by hundreds of holes and nearly all of her topside weapons were damaged or disabled, she was still seaworthy. Returning to friendly waters under her own power, she was repaired and returned to the war in time to participate in the Battle of Okinawa.

Princeton, on the other hand, fared differently. Her personnel casualties were less in number than those of *Birmingham*—108 killed and 190 more wounded—but many of them were every bit as gruesome. Just after the huge explosion, Captain Hoskins, prospective commanding officer of the now badly crippled carrier, discovered that his foot was attached to his leg by only a few tendons and bits of flesh. He immediately grabbed a piece of line and made a tourniquet to stop the profusion of blood. The

---

* The official report of the incident reads as follows: "The decks ran red with blood, not figuratively but literally. . . ."

medical officer soon came to his aid and, seeing the futility of trying to save the mangled foot, cut the remaining tendons and flesh with a sheath knife. Dusting the ghastly stump with sulfa powder and injecting morphine, the doctor turned Hoskins over to two sailors who carried him through the furiously burning ship to the forecastle, where the wounded were being lowered to whale boats hovering dangerously close to the great floating inferno. As Hoskins and the two sailors emerged from the shroud of smoke onto the forecastle, they were met by Captain Buracker. Hoskins looked up at Buracker from the stretcher that would carry him to the waiting whale boat below and saluted. Smiling, he asked, "Have I your permission to leave the ship, Sir?"

Buracker was not far behind Hoskins in leaving the ship. With her stern blown off and fires now burning their way forward (where *Princeton* had another magazine), it was time to put the old girl out of her misery. At 1600, Captain Buracker ordered the ship abandoned, and by 1638, he was the last man off.

Meanwhile, Ensign Paul Drury had spent a good while swimming in the turbulent sea, trying to make his way to USS *Irwin*, a destroyer in the vicinity. He had been a member of the University of Pennsylvania swim team and was no stranger to the water, but even the strongest of swimmers will tire in open ocean swimming when the sea is up. By the time he reached *Irwin*, he was close to exhaustion and was most grateful when a sailor climbed down the cargo nets slung over the ship's sides to help him up to the deck. Drury had swallowed a great deal of saltwater during the swim and that, coupled with the physical strain of the ordeal, caused him to vomit. He was not alone. There were many *Princeton* survivors aboard *Irwin*, and many of them were likewise vomiting. Some of the destroyer sailors broke out fire hoses and began washing down the fouled deck.

By late afternoon, when *Irwin* was ordered to finish off the still upright but horribly disfigured *Princeton*, her decks were crowded with some six hundred of the carrier's survivors. *Irwin*, like several of the other ships that had moved in close to provide assistance, had been damaged by colliding with the wallowing aircraft carrier. *Irwin*'s torpedo director had been badly damaged in just such a collision so that when the first torpedo was fired, it curved away and barely struck *Princeton*'s bow, causing no significant damage. The next "fish" curved astern and completely missed. The third torpedo jumped clear of the water as it sped along, turned completely about, and headed back toward *Irwin*. Lieutenant Drury watched in horror as the torpedo came head-on for the ship. It seemed as though he had survived the ordeal on *Princeton* only to meet his demise in this ignominious fashion. *Irwin*'s captain ordered "All engines ahead emergency" and Drury felt the destroyer lurch forward. Without breathing, he watched as the oncoming wake of the torpedo began to drift slightly to the left. A moment later, the errant torpedo passed within thirty feet of *Irwin*'s stern.

Torpedoes four and five missed and, incredibly, number six repeated the earlier harrowing performance of number three, except that this one passed even closer to the destroyer. It is probably fair to say that at this point the thought of mutiny may well have passed through the minds of many aboard the hapless *Irwin*.* Drury was thinking, "I *really* don't want to do this again," when Admiral Sherman at last ordered USS *Reno* to relieve *Irwin* of the unpleasant task of finishing off the crippled carrier. Her torpedoes worked as intended, and within minutes she had placed two "fish" into *Princeton* that proved almost instantaneously fatal. An official report rather laconically described *Princeton*'s demise as a "terrific explosion in the vicinity of the forward magazines and gasoline tanks. The ship disintegrated in a matter of 45 seconds, and all that could be seen was fire on the water." By this time, Paul Drury had been through so much he was virtually numb to the sight of his ship's cataclysmic end. Mostly, he felt relief that the ordeal was over. He and the other survivors could now get on with whatever lay ahead.

That night, Drury slept atop *Irwin*'s wardroom dining table, and the next day he was transferred to *Birmingham* for the trip back to Pearl Harbor. As he moved about on the wounded cruiser during the voyage, he saw many reminders of the terrible explosion and the tragic, yet heroic, sacrifice of the men who had fallen while trying to save his ship. Jagged holes were everywhere on the cruiser's starboard side, and, despite the cleanup efforts of her remaining crew, Drury saw many patches of dried blood and pieces of flesh still adhering to the ship's steel sides. It was a sight that would "humble any man," Drury later said. "To this day, if I start to feel a little full of myself, the memory of what I saw on the *Birmingham* brings me quickly down to earth."

Captain Hoskins had, of course, missed his chance—by a frustratingly

---

* Indeed, Samuel Eliot Morison, in his *History of United States Naval Operations in World War II*, records: "More than one survivor [of *Princeton*] was thinking of taking drastic action on [*Irwin*'s] bridge. . . ."

few days—to command USS *Princeton*. And he had lost a foot. But John Hoskins was not the kind of man to be easily deterred. He was eventually fitted with an artificial foot and was expected, under the circumstances, to accept disability retirement as his lot. There had not been a "peg leg" captain in the Navy since the days when sail yielded to steam. But Hoskins petitioned the Navy to allow him to remain on active duty, and, when it was decided that one of the newly built aircraft carriers was to be named *Princeton*, Hoskins applied for her command. He insisted that he was "one foot ahead of the other applicants" and argued that he was better qualified for the assignment because, in a middle-of-the-night emergency, he could get to his battle station more rapidly than anyone else since he would already be wearing a sock and a shoe. His arguments may not have been convincing, but his spirit certainly was. John Hoskins was given command of the new USS *Princeton*.

12

★ Sibuyan and Sulu Seas ★

The "Bull" had caught the scent of battle and charged into the ring. Halsey had been given the world's most powerful fleet because he, of all the U.S. Navy's admirals, could be counted on to use it aggressively. And on the morning of 24 October, he was living up to that expectation, fully.

While Admiral Sherman's Task Group 38.3 had been preoccupied with repelling Japanese air attacks and struggling to save *Princeton*, the other two Third Fleet task groups—38.2 under Bogan and Davison's 38.4—were busy casting hundreds of their aircraft into the skies in response to Halsey's strike order. Fighters, dive-bombers, and torpedo planes flew westward across the Sibuyan Sea to attack the oncoming Japanese Fleet, which had been discovered by Lieutenant j.g. Max Adams and the others from *Intrepid*'s air group.

Attacking the enemy was what was expected of Halsey. Aggressive tactics were what had made this admiral famous, and for him to have done otherwise at this point in the battle was virtually inconceivable. But Halsey did more than merely strike out at the enemy that morning. In his actions early on 24 October, there are some omens, for want of a better word, subtle but significant indications of the inner workings of this man. These actions would have serious consequences as well as indications of what he might be expected to do as this battle developed.

The first omen is found in realizing that Halsey, by issuing orders directly to his fleet, was effectively cutting Admiral Marc Mitscher out of the chain of command. Admittedly, the command structure was not ideal, having been made somewhat redundant by stripping the Third Fleet down until it was really Task Force 38 with a bigger name. But in Marc

Mitscher, Halsey had a valuable asset that a prudent commander would not frivolously cast away. Mitscher had been instrumental in many of the Pacific war's most important battles and campaigns, and under Spruance he had enjoyed a great deal of autonomy. Indeed, the only notable occasion when Spruance had overruled Mitscher was in the Battle of the Philippine Sea, when he had held Mitscher back from pursuing the Japanese Fleet in order to defend the landing forces in the Marianas from an end-run attack that never materialized. It was this controversial decision that had hurt Spruance's reputation among many of the Navy's senior commanders, and, although it is still certainly arguable that this was the correct action under the circumstances, it is also retrospectively clear that had Spruance listened to Mitscher, the Japanese Fleet would have been destroyed and both men would have been regarded as brilliant tacticians. But Halsey apparently failed to see this, and, either by design or by oversight, bypassed Mitscher when he picked up that radio handset and ordered his fleet to "Strike! Repeat: Strike!"

Admiral Halsey was certainly within his rights to issue orders directly to his fleet, but admirals are human beings, and frequently they are human begins with larger-than-average egos. To exclude Mitscher in this way was, at the very least, undiplomatic, and such callous disregard for the feelings of so important a subordinate commander does not rank among Halsey's more sensible actions.

In order to recognize the second omen that appeared that morning, it is necessary to look back more than a decade earlier, when then-Captain William F. Halsey was a student at the Naval War College in Newport, Rhode Island. The year was 1933, and the War College was on the verge of some significant changes. A review of the theses written by the student-officers during the first few years of the 1930s reveals an unquestionable emphasis on large surface fleets such as those that had engaged in the World War I Battle of Jutland. There is, in these papers, and in the recorded comments of some of the faculty and staff at the War College, a paucity of attention to the relatively new fleet weapon, the aircraft carrier. In fact, there is a distinctly defensive tone to some of the comments regarding the future of naval warfare. This hostility is evident in the 1931 comments of Admiral William V. Pratt, then Chief of Naval Operations and, just four years earlier, president of the Naval War College. In an interview for the *Army and Navy Register*, Admiral Pratt exhorted: "There are many who believe the day of the battleship is over. It is my opinion those who hold this view don't know what they are talking about, and that most of them belong to a pure pacifist class who would like to see the Navy done away with altogether, or else they belong to that class of people who when ill go to the quack, instead of the specialist."

With that decided emphasis on the battleship, there was an attendant clinging to doctrine regarding the use of battleship-centered fleets that had been around since the days when Alfred Thayer Mahan had catapulted himself, and the War College, into the world spotlight with his thought-provoking and well-timed book, *The Influence of Sea Power Upon History.* Among Admiral Mahan's many observations, one took on a particularly dogmatic significance. In 1899, he had advised that "like the land, the sea, as a military field, has its important centers, and it is not controlled by spreading your force." He called instead for "concentration" of forces and labeled this concept warfare's "first principle." Although, in context, Mahan was advocating this "concentration" in a strategic sense (such as keeping the U.S. fleet intact in one ocean or the other rather than splitting it up to cover both), this principle was extended into the tactical realm by those who followed. By the time Halsey got to the War College, he, and many others, had accepted as "a cardinal principle of naval warfare"[*] that a commander should concentrate his forces for battle.

Such dogmatic thinking would not last forever. In 1936, the president of the Naval War College, Rear Admiral Edward C. Kalbfus, circulated among his staff and students a draft of a manual that would eventually be published as *Sound Military Decision.* Included in that manual was the admonition that the "axiomatic advice that it is unwise to divide a total force, while containing a sound element of caution, is often misleading and inadequate, for division is often necessary or desirable." But this came after Halsey had left the War College, after he had left behind his thesis, which concluded: "Command is the nerve center that directs, controls, and coordinates the strategic and tactical. They are command's right and left hands. As command controls these hands, so command controls the war. Strategy, tactics, and command may be called the trinity of war; and the greatest of these is command."

While it is not altogether clear what Halsey was trying to say in this paper, there are strong indications in his words that he was a take-charge

---

[*] Halsey's words.

kind of person, and there are hints that he was a man who might prove reluctant to recant a decision once made. But perhaps most significant of all is his apparent subjugation of strategy and tactics to command, indicating that Halsey may have seen strategy and tactics as tools to be used by the commander rather than as products of his own analytical thinking. There is a tendency for students of warfare to seek ironclad principles and axiomatic rules devised by others, rather than to see strategy and tactics as the course of action taken by individual commanders after they have analyzed a particular situation. It appears that Halsey was just such a student, and despite his later, almost prescient, recognition of the ascendancy of the aircraft carrier in naval warfare, he appears to have been unable to divest himself of some of the dogmatic baggage that had been part of the Mahanian battleship era and was still echoing about the hallowed halls of the Naval War College. Like many others of his time, Halsey continued to subscribe to what was popularly believed to be Mahan's dictum that a naval commander should always concentrate his forces in order to do battle. Indeed, as late as 1952, Halsey would write in an article published in the U.S. Naval Institute's *Proceedings* magazine that "It is a cardinal principle of naval warfare not to divide one's force to such an extent as will permit it to be beaten in detail."

So, on the morning of 24 October 1944, after receiving the reconnaissance reports of the large Japanese Fleet approaching from the west, Halsey's actions reflect that dogmatic influence he carried with him from Newport. His first reaction was to order Sherman's northern and Davison's southern task forces to converge on Bogan's in the center, thus *concentrating* his available forces. He also radioed Vice Admiral McCain, ordering him to abort his rest-and-resupply mission to Ulithi and return at once to the Leyte area. Another concentration of force.

No criticism of Halsey's actions at this point is intended. With one major enemy force on its way to do battle, it is sensible for a commander to bring his available forces together for better control and for concentration of offensive power. Although McCain's Task Group 38.1 was more than a day's steaming away, it consisted of more carriers and planes than any one of the other three task groups, so it made good tactical sense for Halsey to recall it. These actions were not incorrect, but they *were* harbingers of things yet to come.

★   ★   ★

"The Big E" had become a legend. From the earliest days of the war, she had played a key role in most of the major sea battles of the conflict. Indeed, there was a time when she had been nearly all there was that stood between the Japanese and a complete victory in the Pacific war.

USS *Enterprise* had steamed into Pearl Harbor the day after the infamous attack, fortuitously late for that engagement, but intact and bound for retribution. With Admiral Halsey in command, she had returned to sea within hours of her arrival at Pearl and began what would prove to be a grueling and glorious campaign lasting nearly four years and taking her to all corners of the Pacific. She had led the way on the road back from Pearl Harbor, launching the earliest retaliatory strikes on Japanese-held islands and accompanying USS *Hornet* for the Doolittle raid on Tokyo. *Enterprise* had been one of the key players at the Battle of Midway and was instrumental in the South Pacific struggle over Guadalcanal. She had participated in the capture of the Gilberts, Marshalls, and Marianas, and had fought at the nearly decisive Battle of the Philippine Sea. She had conducted countless raids on heavily defended Japanese bastions, including Yap, Truk, and Formosa, and now she was part of Task Force 38.4, under Halsey once again, aiding in the recapture of the Philippines. It seems only fitting that members of her air group were the first to strike at the Japanese Fleet in the opening rounds of the battle for Leyte Gulf.

At just after 0600 on the twenty-fourth, two groups of fighters and bombers from *Enterprise* rolled off her wooden flight deck and climbed into the growing light of dawn. They set out toward the southwest, each of the bombers armed with two 500-pound bombs, and the fighters carrying a full bag of .50-caliber ammunition and four five-inch rockets each. The planes crossed over the Philippine islands of Bohol, Cebu, and Negros and then soared out over the wide expanses of the Sulu Sea. At 0820, they spotted a seven-ship formation headed northward at about 15 knots. As the American flyers closed in for a better look, they could see pagoda-like masts rising upward from the broad-beamed hulls of two battleships. A cruiser and four destroyers made up the remainder of the group, the latter arranged in a square screen around the heavier ships. *Enterprise* flyers had spotted Nishimura's force on its way to Surigao Strait.

The Hellcats went in first. Plummeting out of the glare of the morning sun, the fighters roared in on Nishimura's force, leading off with the five-inch rockets, then following with long bursts of machine-gun fire.

Close behind the fighters came the bombers, diving almost straight down at the weaving ships below. As their intended targets grew larger with every split second of descent, the exploding flak grew heavier around them. The roar of the descent filled the pilots' ears as they watched the silent twinkling of Japanese antiaircraft guns through the blurred disks of their spinning propeller blades. At about 2,000 feet, the Helldivers released their bombs and sheared off to swoop low over the sea, dodging fire from the screening destroyers.

A bomb exploded on the stern of battleship *Fuso*, destroying her catapult-mounted search planes and causing a fire that raged on for the better part of an hour. The destroyer *Shigure* took a direct hit on her forward gun mount. Five men were killed, six more wounded, but this sturdy little veteran continued on with the rest of Nishimura's force, which was still intact and still bound for Surigao Strait.

Commander Fred Bakutis, commanding officer of *Enterprise*'s fighter squadron VF-20, like the other pilots who had just attacked Nishimura's force, was pulling out of his dive after attacking one of the two battleships in Nishimura's force. Ahead loomed one of the destroyers. Bakutis decided to attack rather than avoid. A fateful decision. He opened up with all six of his .50-caliber machine guns as he swooped in on the ship. Roaring over the destroyer at about 300 feet, he felt his aircraft take a hit. Smoke began to pour from his engine cowling and his oil gauge began to drop. Turning southwest to put as much distance as possible between himself and the Japanese ships, he glanced again at the oil gauge and this time saw that it registered empty. He quickly radioed the other men in his squadron and got back a reassuring, "We're all for you, Skipper."

A minute passed before the engine froze, and then Bakutis began to lose altitude. Already low over the water, it was not long before the Hellcat was in the sea. Bakutis had made a good landing—"no more severe than in the case of a normal carrier landing," he later said.

The cockpit began to fill rapidly with water, so Bakutis climbed out onto the starboard wing. It was clear that the aircraft was going down, so he jumped into the water and began inflating the life raft that had been provided for just such occurrences as this. As he struggled with the balky CO_2 bottle, his attention was momentarily diverted by the eerie sight of his Hellcat fighter slowly spiraling downward through the crystal clear water beneath him. He could see it for quite a way down before it finally merged with the shadows of the deep.

Overhead, the other pilots of VF-20 were circling, keeping a protective eye on their downed skipper in his rubber raft. There was not much they could actually do for their leader, but at least they could linger for a while to help him ward off the loneliness that would soon be his. But from Bakutis's viewpoint, the well-meaning pilots were doing him no favors. The Japanese ships in Nishimura's force, although retiring from the scene— much to the relief of Commander Bakutis and his airborne comrades— were still firing at the lingering aircraft, causing Bakutis to be showered with falling shrapnel from the rounds detonating above.

At last, the pagoda-masts disappeared over the horizon, and the Hellcats of VF-20 reluctantly turned homeward and headed back for *Enterprise*. Fred Bakutis was alone on the Sulu Sea.

On the flagships of the Third and Seventh fleets, admirals and their staffs were pondering the developing situation. They now knew that there were at least two Japanese forces en route to Leyte Gulf. *Intrepid*'s search group had pinpointed Kurita's fleet entering the Sibuyan Sea and *Enterprise* planes had located and attacked Nishimura's force in the Sulu Sea. Halsey had ordered massive strikes against Kurita's fleet, and Kinkaid's staff was already formulating plans to meet Nishimura's group in Surigao Strait that night. But the big question was, "Where are the carriers?"

None of the incoming aerial reconnaissance reports spoke of aircraft carriers among the oncoming Japanese forces. American submarines on picket stations all over the Southwestern Pacific had not spotted any of the dreaded flattops. The U.S. commanders knew the Japanese still had a number of carriers in their fleet, and the Americans were not fully aware of the weakness of the Japanese air groups. So it stood to reason that there would be serious concern about the possibility of a Japanese carrier striking force lurking somewhere about, ready to do serious damage. Abetting this concern was the realization that the Japanese had a penchant for dividing their forces into complex and potentially devastating, pincer attacks. The sighting of two separate Japanese forces apparently bound for Leyte Gulf supported that suspicion.

It stood to reason that any undiscovered forces would come from the north, since that was the direction of the home islands and the last intelligence received on the whereabouts of the Japanese carriers had placed them there. Halsey had expected Sherman's northernmost task group to conduct searches in that direction, but TG 38.3 had been too busy fighting off land-based Japanese air attacks and trying to save the crippled *Princeton*, so Admiral Sherman had not yet been able to comply with Halsey's order.

The irony was that Admiral Ozawa was hoping to be discovered. Two days before, he had deliberately broken radio silence and sent reconnaissance flights southward, hoping that they would be detected by the Americans and followed back to his force. At 0700 on the twenty-fourth, his search planes made contact with Halsey's force—Admiral Sherman's TG 38.3 specifically—but no one among the Americans noticed these carrier aircraft among the many land-based ones then attacking.

So neither of the adversarial commanders had what he wanted. Ozawa was aware of Halsey but had not managed to get the latter's attention, and Halsey was fretting over the absence of aircraft carriers among the Japanese forces so far discovered. As the day wore on with no change in this situation, Captain Doug Moulton, Halsey's Air Operations Officer, pounded his fist on the chart table and growled, "Where in hell *are* those goddam Nip carriers?" It is probably safe to assume that similar expressions of frustration were uttered in Japanese ships several hundred miles to the north.

Fred Bakutis lay in his rubber raft, surrounded by the lonely vastness of the Sulu Sea. A peaceful yet foreboding stillness had fallen about him as the raucous sounds of men and their machines faded away with the last departing *Enterprise* Hellcat. He could feel the gentle undulations of the Sulu Sea through the thin sheet of rubber that held him suspended above the gaping maw of the deep. For him, the Battle of Leyte Gulf was over. In the next few days, while the clash of arms would resound across the various waters of the Philippine Archipelago, and thousands of men would be swallowed into the abyss, Commander Bakutis would struggle in a world of near silence against the natural elements and his own fragile mortality.

His first night went well enough. There was a half-moon to oppose the darkness of the vast sea, and no rain fell. But as the retreating sun left the sea vulnerable to the intruding cold reaching up from the depths, the bottom of the raft grew quite cool, and sleeping was difficult.

The next day was more arduous. The placid sea, which had mercifully served as runway for his stricken aircraft the day before, now turned on him and began to rise up in anger. Soon it was lashing him about in that chaotic dance that can nauseate even the strongest of constitutions. Having eaten nothing but a malted-milk tablet and two hard candies since crashing the day before, he had little to throw up. He ate half of an apple he had brought with him on the fateful flight and sipped at his finite supply of water. Nighttime brought the rain.

The moon was frequently lost in the clouds as spasmodic showers robbed him of what little warmth his lightweight flight suit husbanded. He tried to collect the rain for drinking but had little success.

The third day brought added frustration as several U.S. Army B-24 aircraft flew over but at such high altitude that Bakutis could not get their attention with his signal mirror. The sea continued to be rough and, periodically, a wave would fill his raft with water, immersing him and sapping his strength as he bailed. His hands and buttocks began to show the ill effects of constant immersion; they turned a sickly white and became very sore. Near evening, a sea bird landed on his head and Bakutis grabbed it by the legs. After a struggle, he was able to wring the bird's neck. Then he cut off the head and drained a cupful of blood, which he forced himself— with no small effort—to drink. After vomiting, he cut open the bird and found a flying fish inside, not yet digested. This he ate as well.

Bakutis remembered being taught that sea birds headed for land in the evening, so he watched them as the day waned. To his consternation, the birds flew off in all directions.

After another night of intermittent showers, Commander Bakutis awoke for his fourth day to the hiss of a heavy downpour on the sea. He was able to collect some of the rainwater to replenish his drinking supply, but his hands and buttocks were getting worse and the pain was becoming more and more distracting. As the day wore on, he made an important discovery when he found that he could scoop minnows from the sea. He swallowed the smaller fish whole, but cleaned the larger ones before eating them. Seaweed served as salad for the repast.

The ordeal continued for a fifth day. And then a sixth. All the while, the long hours consisted of the painful effects of immersion, the chilling discomfort of frequent tropical rains, the sustenance of minnows and seaweed, and the frustration of an occasional American aircraft passing too far away to see him.

By the seventh day he had discovered that he could ease the pain in his hands somewhat by rubbing them with insect oil, but his buttocks by this time were covered with ugly white blisters and were more painful than ever. That night was peaceful and brightly lit by a gibbous moon. Bakutis had been sleeping soundly when he was awakened by the growl of diesel engines. Afraid that it was a Japanese gunboat, he was about to jump overboard when he saw in the bright moonlight that it was a submarine. Someone called "Ahoy," and Fred Bakutis knew his ordeal was over.

USS *Hardhead* rescued Commander Bakutis from the Sulu Sea and, the next night, transferred him to USS *Angler*, commanded by his Naval Academy classmate, Commander Frank Hess. *Angler* ultimately took him to Australia, and by 5 December he was back with his squadron, by then embarked in USS *Lexington*.

Fred Bakutis later shot down several more Japanese aircraft and ended the war as an ace, retiring from the Navy in 1969 as a Rear Admiral.

So far, the Japanese had put out of action the American destroyer *Ross* (mined during the preliminaries to the amphibious landing and towed away by the tug *Chickasaw*); the cruiser *Honolulu* (hit by a Japanese torpedo plane and sent back to Manus under her own power); the aircraft carrier *Princeton** (sunk by a Japanese bomber); and the cruiser *Birmingham* (knocked out of action by damage from the *Princeton* explosion). The cost to the Japanese so far had been the cruisers *Atago*, *Maya*, and *Takao* (all torpedoed in Palawan Passage) and the destroyers *Naganami* and *Asashimo* (undamaged but removed from action to escort the crippled *Takao* back to Brunei).[†]

On the face of it, this was not a bad score for the Japanese. Consideration of the relative sizes of the two forces somewhat diminishes the Japanese achievement because it was obvious they could not hold their own in a struggle of attrition. But the relative strengths of the forces also makes the Japanese achievements that much more remarkable.

Aircraft were another story. With the exception of the lone hits on *Honolulu* and *Princeton*, the Japanese were having little notable success

---

* USS *Princeton* was the first U.S. aircraft carrier sunk since *Hornet* was lost at the Battle of Santa Cruz on 26 October 1942.

† The cruiser *Aoba* had also been torpedoed just outside Manila Bay by a U.S. submarine but managed to get into port where she sat out the battle. This cruiser was not part of the four main forces converging on Leyte Gulf, so was not technically a participant in the battle royal. However, she was involved peripherally because she was part of the task group that was moving reinforcement troops to Leyte from some of the other Philippine islands.

with their air attacks. McCampbell's tally of nine Japanese planes shot down in one day was the record, but many other American pilots added impressive numbers of Rising Sun emblems to their fuselages that same day. And Task Group 38.3 fighters were not the only ones to score successes. Many of the Japanese planes shot down were the victims of fighters from the Seventh Fleet CVEs, and a significant number fell to the antiaircraft fire of Seventh Fleet ships. The ratio of Japanese to American aircraft lost that day was somewhere in the range of ten to one.

But the scorecard for 24 October was not yet complete. More ships and aircraft were about to be eliminated and *many* more men would die before the day was over.

Lookouts in Kurita's force had spotted *Intrepid*'s search group. Kurita immediately ordered his force to increase speed to 24 knots and prepare for battle. Tense minutes ticked by with no activity. The American planes did not attack and soon were lost in the clouds. The minutes dragged on and still nothing. Kurita surmised that what they had seen was a reconnaissance group and there would be a delay before the attack. He slowed his force back to 20 knots and, to foil the targeting solutions of any American submarines that might be in the area, he ordered the ships to resume antisubmarine zigzagging. Two hours passed in which several aircraft sightings and a periscope were reported by anxious lookouts, but still no attack materialized. The huge force continued on, rounding the north end of Tablas Island at about 1000, radar and lookouts' eyes scanning the still empty skies.

Radar was the first to detect the coming attack. Multiple air contacts coming from the east showed on the cathode-ray tubes. Then at 1025 the lookouts reported a group of about thirty aircraft off the starboard beam. One minute later, Japanese antiaircraft (AA) guns opened up on the incoming planes and the Battle of the Sibuyan Sea had begun.

This first engagement lasted only twenty-four minutes, yet it was intense and not without consequence to both sides. The extra AA guns added to Kurita's ships at Lingga had made them very prickly prey. Battleships, cruisers, and even the destroyers now bristled with hundreds more 25-mm guns than they had ever had before, and the effect was noticeable. Several of the torpedo bombers were splashed in the early moments of the attack and a Hellcat fighter soon joined them. But a number of American aircraft penetrated the wall of heavy fire and great geysers leaped skyward from the water close aboard Kurita's flagship, *Yamato*.

Rear Admiral Tomiji Koyanagi, Kurita's Chief of Staff, watched as a bomb exploded on *Yamato*'s forecastle and several others detonated in the water close near her bow. The one that had hit exploded immediately without penetrating the great ship's thick hide, so it did little damage other than knocking out one of her anchor windlasses.

Yamato's sister ship *Musashi* was also the target of several of the American planes. A torpedo struck her on the starboard side, but the great steel-plate blisters that formed a protective cocoon for just this eventuality minimized the effect. A bomb struck her at about the same time, but this, too, seemed to have little effect. The two super-battleships steamed on, the claims of their designers that they were indestructible seemingly vindicated.

No one had ever declared the heavy cruiser *Myoko* indestructible, however, and soon she was succumbing to the aerial onslaught. She had no protective blisters like *Musashi* and, when a torpedo bit into her barnacled side, she began to limp. Her maximum speed was reduced to 15 knots and she began to fall back from the formation.

As the surviving American aircraft broke off the attack and headed back to *Intrepid* and *Cabot* from whence they had come, the staff of Commander Cruiser Division 5 transferred from *Myoko* to the heavy cruiser *Haguro*, and then *Myoko* turned westward and headed back toward Brunei. Kurita had lost another cruiser. And this was only the first act in what was to be a day-long dramatic play.

The second wave of American aircraft was spotted by Kurita's lookouts at a little past noon. The planes went for the Japanese force like angry bees out of the hive. In just minutes, three of the torpedo planes had left their stingers in *Musashi*. Still she steamed on.

There was a brief respite and then another wave of U.S. aircraft appeared. On board *Musashi*, Chief Gunnery Officer Koshino pleaded with his captain to be allowed to fire the Type *San Shiki* Model 3 shells from the ship's main battery. These were the special rounds that had been designed to act like a giant shotgun shell when fired from the 18.1-inch monster-guns of the super-battleships. Because he knew that testing had shown that these unusual AA rounds could damage the bore of the big guns, Rear Admiral Toshihira Inoguchi, *Musashi*'s commanding officer, denied Koshino's request. Inoguchi wanted to save his big guns for the expected fight in Leyte Gulf.

The latest wave of American attackers concentrated again on *Musashi*, and soon she was enveloped in smoke and huge geysers of water. Several bombs struck the giant and the deadly clatter of machine-gun rounds from the fighters resounded across her topside decks and bulkheads. Another torpedo slammed into her.

Musashi's executive officer, Captain Kenkichi Kato, a twenty-eight-year veteran of service in the Imperial Japanese Navy, had been executive officer of the heavy cruiser *Chokai* at the battles of Midway and Savo Island earlier in the war. At Midway, his ship had seen no action; at Savo Island he had endured little from the defeated American cruisers. But such was not to be the case in the Sibuyan Sea that afternoon.

As executive officer, Kato was responsible for damage control in *Musashi*. When the first torpedo hits had occurred, there had been no cause for serious concern. The outer hull, consisting of those gargantuan plates that had once seriously depleted Japan's available steel supply, had absorbed the early hits and minimized the effect of the enemy torpedoes. But even the strongest fortifications will yield from repeated blows to the same location. One of the earlier torpedoes had struck the outer hull at a spot near number four engine room. A later one found its way to the same spot. This time the inner hull gave way, and soon number four engine room was flooded. Kato tried to pump water out of the large engine room but was unable. Bomb hits were having their effects on some of the pumping equipment and upon the ship's internal communications. So much water inside the hull, though confined to the engine room, put a tremendous drag on the ship and reduced her stability. This, combined with the loss of engine power from number four, caused *Musashi* to slow and begin listing to one side.

The now obvious damage encouraged Chief Gunnery Officer Noshino to renew his pleas to the captain for permission to fire the huge AA rounds. As yet another wave of American aircraft emerged from the clouds, Inoguchi relented. Even in the midst of the chaos of battle, excitement spread throughout the ship as the world's largest naval guns came to life. This would be the first time ever that these great weapons would speak in anger against an enemy. And speak they did. A tremendous concussive roar eradicated all other sound as the nine guns erupted. The shock below decks was tremendous and some of *Musashi's* crew thought the great jolt came from another enemy hit.

Inoguchi and Koshino watched the approaching enemy planes, waiting for great numbers of them to fall from the sky as the big shells sprayed fire and shrapnel into the eastern sky. The American planes opened their formation a bit but not one of them fell.

As Inoguchi had feared, one of the turrets was damaged by the firing. The remaining six guns of the other two turrets continued firing, but to no avail. The American aircraft, some sixty-five in number from *Enterprise* and *Franklin*, bore in for the attack. Within minutes they were swarming over *Musashi*, striking hard at the crippled ship. More torpedoes chewed away at the already mangled port side and bombs continued to tear at her topsides. One bomb detonated directly on the pagoda-like tower housing the command bridges. The damage was extensive and for a brief time it appeared that no one was in command of the ship. Then Inoguchi's voice emanated from a speaking tube, saying that all personnel on the main bridge had been killed and that he was shifting to the secondary bridge. Moments later, another series of explosions rained heavy shrapnel on *Musashi*'s command tower. This time, Inoguchi was not so fortunate. His distinctly weakened voice echoed in the brass speaking tube, saying, "Captain is wounded. Executive Officer, take command."

On *Yamato*, Admiral Ugaki watched helplessly as one of his ships of Battleship Division One slowly succumbed to the relentless pounding of the American aircraft. Though losing speed, *Musashi* was still making way at a rate sufficient to cause a huge wave to pile up in front of one of the giant plates of her outer hull, which had been torn loose from her port side. Smoke poured from several of her gaping wounds, and she was listing noticeably to port. A message came over from *Musashi*—by signal flag since her electric power had been snuffed out by the attacks, rendering useless her radios and signal searchlight. "*Musashi* capable of cruising at 15 knots," the message read. "Listing to port about 15 degrees. One bomb hit first bridge; all members killed. Five direct bomb hits and twelve torpedo hits."

And still the Americans came. More aircraft from *Intrepid*, *Cabot*, and *Essex* joined those of *Franklin* and *Enterprise* still attacking Kurita's force. The punishment was relentless and the carnage horrific. Had there been ringside seats from which an audience could view the violent spectacle, the nationalist American would have taken great satisfaction in seeing the Imperial Japanese Navy—that once powerful force that had bombed and strafed and torpedoed virtually helpless American battleships at Pearl Harbor—become the victim of a similar onslaught. The objective human being, on the other hand, would have found the pathetic scene difficult to watch. Without any air cover, Kurita's ships had no hope of a victory and little for survival. Although American aircraft were falling from the sky and American airmen were dying, the seemingly endless supply of planes and pilots pouring forth from Halsey's great fleet ensured the outcome. As the day wore on, the incoming strikes grew larger in number and proportionately fewer aircraft succumbed as more and more Japanese AA batteries fell silent.

This is not to say that there were not uplifting aspects to this strife. As individuals, brave men flew their aircraft into the face of great danger, while others remained at their stations, firing their weapons despite the holocaust going on around them. Pilots took risks that only they knew about, and sailors entered flaming compartments to rescue injured shipmates. Rear-seat gunners rode backwards through a whirlwind of violent aerial maneuvers while colored bursts of smoke exploded all about them and shrapnel rattled across their canopies. Men with little or no medical training ministered to the wounded, trying to suppress arterial fountains while their ears filled with sounds they had never heard and would never forget.

Musashi was falling farther and farther behind the formation. Kato reported to Inoguchi—whose left arm now lay inert in a sling—that the ship could withstand no more punishment. A message soon went out to Kurita in *Yamato*: "Speed 6 knots, capable of operation. Damage great. What shall we do?"

Admiral Kurita had probably had better days. As he stood on *Yamato*'s flagship holding the message from *Musashi*'s commanding officer, he had a great deal to think about. In the last twenty-four hours he had lost several of his ships to submarines in the Palawan Passage, had his flagship shot out from under him, been fished unceremoniously from the sea and deposited aboard a new flagship with only half his original communications personnel, endured air attacks most of this day, received no response to his repeated pleas for air cover, and watched as one of his two most valuable assets was pounded into submission.

Kurita ordered *Musashi* to retire from the battle and detached cruiser *Tone* and two destroyers to accompany her. Once again, detaching a three-ship escort for a cripple seems a curious thing to do. This is not the action of a commander who seeks mission accomplishment at all or any cost. The convoy commander, for example, will not risk the integrity of his convoy by slowing down or detaching one of his vessels to recover a man who has fallen overboard in potentially hostile waters. That may seem cruel and is by no means an easy decision to make, but it makes sense in the cold calculus of war. So does sacrificing crippled vessels when the mission calls for an attack with all available power against an enemy who is superior in number.

An indication of Kurita's thinking is found in a postwar interview in which he stated that his reasons for cruising at 22 to 24 knots during most of the voyage to Leyte Gulf was that his ships did not have enough fuel "for long distance voyages at high speed and they had to save their fuel for the trip back to Brunei." These are not the thoughts of a man on a suicide mission. Among Admiral Kurita's many considerations during this mission, survival appears to have been one.

As American aircraft in apparently endless supply continued to fill the skies above his formation, Kurita considered what lay ahead. Despite the evasive maneuvering required each time the American planes attacked, his current rate of progress across the Sibuyan Sea would have him arriving at the narrow waters leading to San Bernardino Strait while there was still ample daylight for another attack. Entering those restricted waters would prevent his ships from maneuvering under attack, making them all the more vulnerable.

Kurita's ships had already endured a terrible pounding and to subject them to even worse conditions seemed pure folly at this point. At 1530, Kurita ordered the formation to come about and head westward, which might eventually take them out of range of the attackers and would at least keep his ships out in the center of the Sibuyan Sea where they would be free to maneuver under any forthcoming attacks. He drafted an explanation of his actions and sent it to Admiral Toyoda in Tokyo at 1600:

> Originally the main strength of [my] force had intended to force its way through San Bernardino Strait about one hour after sundown, coordinating its moves with air action. However, the enemy made more than 250 sorties against us between 0830 and 1530, the number of planes involved and their fierceness mounting with every wave. Our air forces, on the other hand, were not able to obtain even expected results, causing our losses to mount steadily. Under these circumstances it was deemed that were we to force our way through, we would merely make ourselves meat for the enemy, with very little chance of success. It was therefore

concluded that the best course open to us was temporarily to retire beyond the reach of enemy planes.

It is clear that Kurita felt betrayed by the lack of Japanese land-based air support. He very pointedly referred to the promise of that support twice in the dispatch: once, in the opening sentence, by reminding Toyoda that the original plan called for coordination between the air and surface forces, and again, when he pointed out that their air forces "were not able to obtain even expected results." It is also noteworthy that Kurita sent information copies of the message to the commanders of the First and Second air fleets, probably as a dig at them for not providing him any support.

Although Kurita's message states that by turning away from San Bernardino Strait he hoped to get beyond the range of the attacking American aircraft, he could not realistically hope to do so for quite some time after coming about. Yet, mysteriously, after his formation turned westward, no new waves of American planes appeared. There was still plenty of daylight and he was certainly within range, but the skies remained empty. This was a welcome change but at the same time somewhat unsettling. What were the Americans up to?

In the unexpected quiet, Admiral Ugaki peered out his flag bridge window as the wounded *Musashi* came back into view. It was a painful sight. The great battleship had absorbed nineteen torpedo hits and nearly as many bombs. Still listing to port, most of her bow was now underwater. She had tried to run herself aground rather than sink—at least that way her great guns could remain in service as a gigantic shore battery—but damage to her steering equipment relegated her to slow circles in the Sibuyan Sea, and it seemed only a matter of time before she would succumb.

On board *Musashi*, the carnage and damage were great. Bodies torn by the fury of exploding bombs lay about the topside decks. Weapons stations and deck equipment were mangled beyond recognition. Sailors stuffed secret-code books into canvas bags weighted with machine guns and tossed them over the side so that they would sink into the depths and not fall into the hands of the enemy. Rear Admiral Inoguchi, his shoulder badly wounded, wrote in a small notebook, his words befitting not only himself but his navy, and all the world's navies for that matter, as he lamented his folly in placing so much faith in large ships with giant guns. He penned an appeal for the Emperor's forgiveness and then turned the book over to Captain Kato, ordering him to deliver it to Admiral Toyoda. It was apparent that Inoguchi intended to uphold the Japanese tradition of the captain going down with his ship, and Kato argued that he, too, should perish with *Musashi*. But Inoguchi chastised him, saying that it was the executive officer's responsibility to lead the men to safety so that they could return to fight again and avenge the death of their ship. "My responsibility is so great it can't even be compensated by death and I must share *Musashi*'s fate," he said. He then instructed Kato to save the ship's battle ensign and the Emperor's picture. The executive officer left his captain to make the final preparations for abandoning ship.

There were no more air attacks on the Japanese force in the Sibuyan Sea that afternoon, so by 1715, Kurita decided to reverse course again and head for San Bernardino Strait. Signal flags climbed *Yamato*'s halyards, conveying Kurita's orders to his fleet. Helms spun, rudders answered, and the diminished but still powerful force came about, steadying up on an easterly heading once again.

It appeared that Kurita had made the correct decision as far as his superior was concerned. After he had ordered his force to resume the trek across the Sibuyan Sea, a message arrived from Admiral Toyoda, intended as a response to Kurita's earlier dispatch: "With confidence in heavenly guidance, all forces will attack!"

By 1900, the force was again passing the dying *Musashi*. The sun was low on the horizon by then, and the angled light added to the gloom of the awful sight. For the second time, Ugaki stared out across the darkening sea at his faltering giant. His grief was profound, and he quietly resolved to share the fate of his remaining ship, *Yamato*, no matter what might befall her.

On board *Musashi*, the battle ensign had been lowered as the Japanese national anthem was played on a trumpet. Then a strong swimmer was picked from among volunteers and the flag was ceremoniously tied around his waist. Empty shell casings began to clatter down the sloping deck as *Musashi*'s list grew worse.

Kurita's force steamed on and soon was out of sight. Cruiser *Tone* had rejoined the main force as it passed, leaving the destroyers *Hamakaze* and *Kiyoshima* to watch over the deathbed. The lonely vigil was not to last long. At about 1930 *Musashi* began to roll slowly to port, gaining momentum as she went. Sailors ran along the rotating hull in the opposite direction like lumberjacks at a log-rolling contest, trying to stay on the upward side of the ship. Many were barefoot in preparation for the anticipated swim, and the barnacles encrusted along what had been *Musashi*'s underwater hull lacerated their feet as they ran. Some dove into the sea only to be sucked back into the ship through gaping torpedo holes. Within minutes, the battleship was standing on end, her gigantic propellers high in the evening sky, her bow already deep in the dark sea. She paused for a moment; then there was a convulsive underwater explosion and *Musashi* plunged into the abyss.

The destroyers moved in to pick up the survivors. Only half of *Musashi*'s 2,200-man crew remained to be rescued. Half the number of men who had died at Pearl Harbor went to the bottom of the sea with that super-battleship.

The Battle of the Sibuyan Sea was over. It had been costly but not decisive. Kurita's force had showed incredible stamina in the face of the American aerial onslaught and had lived to fight another day. That day was not far off.

13

★ "Start Them North" ★

While Kurita's force was being relentlessly attacked in the Sibuyan Sea, American reconnaissance aircraft had discovered Shima's afterthought force heading across the Sulu Sea, following in the wake of Nishimura's force. So by midday Halsey and Kinkaid knew about all the Japanese forces approaching Leyte Gulf except the one that *wanted* to be discovered. Ozawa was still approaching from the north, trying desperately to get Halsey's attention. Ironically, the Japanese had contributed to the problem by their early morning attacks on Admiral Sherman's northernmost Task Group 38.3. It was this task group that was responsible for searching northward, but the Japanese air attacks had preoccupied Sherman, preventing him from getting off his reconnaissance efforts as ordered. The big question of "Where are the Japanese carriers?" still haunted Halsey and his staff.

By the early morning hours of the twenty-fourth, Ozawa had reached a position off northern Luzon and had launched a dawn search to the south to confirm Halsey's position, but he discovered nothing. At 0820, he received a message from Japanese land-based aircraft reporting the presence of an American task force to the south of him, so he again sent out his own reconnaissance mission to confirm the location. This turned out to be a wise decision, since the report he had received from the land-based aircraft was some eighty miles in error. By 1115, Ozawa had his confirmation and decided it was time to play his trump card. For quite some time he had been deliberately breaking the traditional radio silence of a transiting naval force in hopes of attracting the Americans' attention. Now, he decided it was time to send out his few aircraft as more bait.

At 1145, forty fighters, twenty-eight dive-bombers, six torpedo planes, and two reconnaissance aircraft took off from Ozawa's carriers with instructions to attack the American force 150 miles to the south. This seventy-six-plane force represented nearly all of Ozawa's assets. Several planes were unable to take off for maintenance reasons, and Ozawa retained about twenty fighters as a defensive combat air patrol. Because some nasty squalls had been reported in the vicinity of the U.S. force, and because the fledgling Japanese pilots had little flying experience, they were directed to land at Japanese airfields ashore if the weather prevented them from returning to the carriers. Any damage they might inflict on the American forces would be a bonus for this neophyte group. Their main task was to convince the Americans that there was a carrier threat coming down from the north. The sooner they could accomplish this task, the sooner they might take some of the pressure off Kurita, who by this time Ozawa knew was being mercilessly hammered in the Sibuyan Sea.

Lieutenant John Monsarrat had been USS *Langley*'s fighter director officer for more than a year. His was a job very new to warfare. The invention of radar and the ever-increasing speeds and capabilities of aircraft had brought this young naval lieutenant and others like him to live out the long hours of the war in a darkened compartment of his ship at first called "radar plot," then later christened the "combat information center," or, more commonly, "CIC." Here, in this cavern-like space nestled deep among the vital organs of the ship, Monsarrat stalked his enemies across the glowing face of a cathode-ray tube and fought them with the power of a radio transmitter. He was the long-range eyes of the fighter pilots who flew combat air patrol over the carrier task force. His super-secret equipment, which had been merely experimental at war's beginning, shot radio waves out into the atmosphere to serve as thousands of invisible reconnaissance aircraft capable of covering hundreds of miles in split seconds. Once his enemy had been detected, Monsarrat vectored the fighters out to intercept them. Simple enough to describe, difficult to accomplish.

In the heat of battle, a fighter director officer had to keep track of tiny points of greenish light that alternately glowed and faded like miniature novas, sometimes filling his screen like the stars in the sky on a dark night. This he would do while talking with excited men who were hurtling about the skies at hundreds of miles an hour, feeding them information that often meant the difference between life and death, not only for them but for the ships they were protecting.

At 1245 on 24 October, the northeast sector of Lieutenant Monsarrat's radar screen filled with tiny blips of light. It was Ozawa's strike, inbound for TG 38.3, range about 105 miles. The flagship *Essex* was coordinating fighter direction for the task group and ordered Monsarrat to intercept the incoming strike with the four fighters he then had available. By this time of the day, TG 38.3 had been warding off Japanese land-based aircraft for several hours, and *Princeton* was at that very moment fighting for her life. These factors added to the tension normally experienced in these situations.

Monsarrat watched the inbound "bogies" for a few sweeps of the radar. Months of experience had taught him how to estimate their altitude by noting the way they faded in and out. He then ordered his four interceptors to climb to 22,000 feet as they dashed out on a 035 bearing. It took no vast amount of experience to see that his four fighters were somewhat outnumbered by the sixty-odd blips of light painting across the upper-right-hand portion of his radar scope. Monsarrat asked *Essex* for some help, and soon eight more fighters were following *Langley*'s group out to intercept. At a closing relative speed of close to 600 knots, it was not long before the lead fighter called "Tally-ho," indicating that he had the enemy in sight. Monsarrat felt less than enthusiastic when he ordered the four American fighters to "sail into" the sixty-odd Japanese aircraft, but he quickly added, "Help is on the way, coming up close behind you," referring to the eight *Essex* fighters some ten miles astern.

In the melee that followed, the heavily outnumbered Americans acquitted themselves well. Ozawa's undertrained pilots were quickly dispersed: half were shot down, only a few got to within gunfire range of the ships, and the remainder retreated to airfields on Luzon. In short, the battle wasn't much of one. But something significant did occur in the midst of this minor engagement. It had already been noticed that these planes had come in from a seaward direction, unlike all the previous Japanese attackers, who had arrived from the west or northwest where there was land. Now, while the Americans were engaging this latest group, some of the

American pilots reported back that these aircraft had tail hooks!* This meant that they had probably come from carriers. And those carriers were probably somewhere to the northeast.

In days of old, admirals were forced to rely upon visual means for communications. This meant that no sea commander could control or inform units other than the one upon which he was embarked and those close enough to read his signal flags. If the admiral wished to communicate with a unit beyond his visual range, he would have to rely upon a messenger ship, which would be dispatched to carry his words over the intervening distance. Indeed, even in the close quarters of battle, the commander would sometimes have to rely on ships standing some distance off from the melee to relay his messages to his nearby embattled ships that were obscured in the clouds of cannon smoke enshrouding the battle line.

These cumbersome communications were miraculously supplanted by the invention of radio. By the time World War II was in full bloom, ships could communicate over great distances using relatively small radio sets and a detachment of specially trained "radiomen," rather than having to commit whole ships and great periods of time to the effort. Long messages could be transmitted over long distances using radio personnel and their telegraphic skills. Shorter messages could be transmitted over shorter distances using voice radio, which allowed any man with minimal training in standardized procedures to communicate directly with a counterpart on another ship or in an aircraft. For added security, messages sent by telegraphic means could be encoded by some rather sophisticated encryption methods. But this considerably reduced the timeliness of the communications, since it required the message to be encoded at the sender's end, then transmitted and received by the radiomen, and then decoded at the receiving end.

For all of these great advancements in technology, there were still manifold problems. Radio communications were subject to the whims of nature. Atmospheric conditions, neither constant nor entirely predictable,

---

* Carrier-based aircraft, unlike their land-based counterparts, are fitted with a special hook that comes down from the rear of the aircraft to snag the arresting wire on a carrier's flight deck, permitting them to land in a fraction of the distance required for a normal runway landing.

determined whether messages would get through. All electronic equipment, by its very nature, is complicated and vulnerable to malfunction, and this was particularly true in the pre-transistor days of World War II, when the vacuum tube was an essential, though not always reliable, component of such equipment. The South Seas environment, with its attendant heat and humidity, is not the most conducive to the happiness and well-being of electronic equipment. In short, for myriad reasons these miraculous radio communications could fail. And they often did. Sometimes at the worst of times.

The Japanese, whose complicated plan of attack relied on rather precise timing and coordination, were particularly vulnerable to the failings of communications. In a postwar interview, Kurita said that it sometimes took as long as three hours to receive a reply to a message sent to Admiral Toyoda in Tokyo. Kurita's messages to Ozawa got through for the most part, so that the latter was aware of Kurita's plight in the Sibuyan Sea and did all that he could to divert Halsey's attention. But communications among the other commanders were less than ideal. As the battle progressed, too many messages did not get through.

When Ozawa launched his air strike against TG 38.3, he sent a message to Admirals Kurita and Toyoda to alert them to his actions. However, a faulty transmitter on his flagship, *Zuikaku*, prevented the message from going out.

In another communications failure, Ozawa never received any word back from his aircraft regarding the success or failure of their attack. Since the surviving attackers all landed at shore bases rather than returning to Ozawa's carriers, the admiral was left completely in the dark on this aspect of his operations.

Kurita repeatedly sent messages begging for air support but never received an answer, much less the requested aircraft. Cut off from any meaningful communications other than Toyoda's order to attack "with confidence in heavenly guidance," Kurita began to feel as though he were fighting the entire battle alone.

Nishimura and Kurita, who together made up the all-important pincer that was to close on the landing ships at Leyte Gulf, had only sporadic information as to what the other was doing, and the situation would not improve as the battle progressed.

But the Japanese were not the only ones suffering from poor communications. In the Americans' case it was more a problem of human error than equipment failures or the whims of atmospheric conditions.

In the planning stages of the Leyte invasion, measures were taken to ensure that adequate communications would be provided. Nimitz's orders to Halsey included the words, "necessary measures for detailed coordination of operations between the [Third Fleet and the Seventh Fleet] will be arranged by their . . . commanders." Admiral King sent a message to Kinkaid saying, "I assume that you will command, under MacArthur, all the Naval Forces involved directly in the [Leyte] operations, and that you will coordinate their activities with Admiral Halsey as Commander of the Third Fleet Covering Force." These best intentions aside, the execution fell short of the expectation.

General MacArthur, for reasons known with certainty only to him, had not authorized a direct communications link between his Seventh Fleet commander, Kinkaid, and Nimitz's Third Fleet commander, Halsey. This forced the two naval commanders to rely upon the "Fox schedule," a general fleet broadcast that sent vast quantities of messages out for all ships to copy, rather than a dedicated channel that would have provided greater speed and flexibility. This impediment to efficient communications was exacerbated by the heavy quantity of message traffic being generated by such a gigantic operation. The radiomen at the Naval Communications Station at Manus, who were running the generic Fox schedule, were receiving so much traffic with high precedence indicators that few messages received any kind of priority and most were handled in the order in which they were received, rather than in the order of their importance or urgency. This inability to communicate efficiently with one another would have been unfortunate under any circumstances, but it was particularly deleterious in a scenario where two fleet commanders were operating in the same theater but had no common operational commander, short of COMINCH in Washington, D.C.

One of the ironies of this battle is that atmospheric conditions were such that Admiral Nimitz in Pearl Harbor was kept well informed as to the progress of the battle, and he in turn was relaying the information to Washington, D.C., so Admiral King was also kept abreast of developments in a timely manner. Yet, the Third and Seventh Fleet commanders did not enjoy good communications with each other.

Of the many elements that contribute to the success or failure of a battle, communications between commanders of the same side is one of the most important. The success or failure of this important element can change the course of a battle. Rarely was this more true than at Leyte Gulf.

During the afternoon of the twenty-fourth, Admiral Halsey, as any good commander would, began thinking about contingencies. By 1500, Kurita was still coming on, still apparently headed for San Bernardino Strait, despite the terrible pounding he had been receiving. Halsey decided that it might be wise to have his battleships ready to meet Kurita's force when, and if, it emerged from the strait. Accordingly, at 1512, he sent out a message labeled "Battle Plan" to the ships of his fleet, in which he directed four battleships, two heavy and three light cruisers, and nineteen destroyers to be formed as a new Task Force 34. He sent information copies to Admirals Nimitz at Pearl Harbor and King in Washington. Curiously, he did not include Admiral Kinkaid as an information addressee.* This does not seem to be in the spirit of coordination that was obviously intended by King and Nimitz in their pre-invasion planning messages, but Halsey's message did not have any direct bearing on what Kinkaid was doing, so his omission of the Seventh Fleet commander as an addressee does not appear to be of any great moment.

However, there is a practice in the Navy that has probably been around since the first message was transmitted by a commander at sea. This common practice might be called "reading other people's mail." Captains of ships and admirals of fleets have long insisted that their radiomen copy every message that is flying about in the atmosphere, whether it is addressed to them or not. Whether this electronic eavesdropping should be considered as prudence or nosiness is open to debate, but it is, was, and probably always will be a frequent practice. Admiral Kinkaid was no exception. So, when Admiral Halsey's message setting up Task Force 34 went out omitting Kinkaid as an addressee, it is not surprising that the Seventh Fleet commander was soon reading his own "pirated" copy.

---

* In military communications, a message is typically sent to one or more "action addressees" who are expected to do something in response to the message. Also frequently included are any number of "information addressees" who are provided the message so that they will know what is happening but are not themselves expected to take any action.

Now, all of this may seem rather innocuous, but it was the beginning of a long chain of unfortunate events that was to have very serious consequences. Men were going to die as a result.

The problems began when Admiral Kinkaid misinterpreted Admiral Halsey's message. The latter intended the Task Force 34 message as a contingency plan, not as an order to be immediately carried out. But his wording was vague, listing the ships to be detached from TF 38 and then stating that they "will be formed as TF 34 under V. Adm. Lee," without specifying *when*. Although the use of the future tense in "will be formed" would certainly seem to indicate that Halsey intended the formation of TF 34 to occur at some later time, rather than at the time of the message, that assumption would be based on normal English. The trouble is that the military has a tendency to talk in rather stilted terms, sometimes misusing tenses for effect. For example, it is not uncommon for a commander to issue orders saying something like "Proper military etiquette will be exercised by all personnel aboard this ship." Despite the use of "will be exercised," this order is not intended for later execution but is expected to be carried out immediately. Since Halsey specified no other time or qualifiers (such as "if the enemy comes through San Bernardino Strait") in his message, Kinkaid made the assumption that TF 34 was being formed at the time of the message.

This erroneous assumption was given additional validity by the next line of Halsey's message, which read: "TF 34 engage decisively at long ranges." This sentence, now using the imperative mood, definitely reads like an order to be carried out, not like a contingency plan that might, or might not, happen.

Kinkaid was not alone in assuming that Halsey was then forming TF 34. Other military minds—specifically Nimitz and King—also interpreted Halsey's message that way.

This misunderstanding might have been avoided when Halsey sent out a second, clarifying, message to his forces at 1710 that said, "If the enemy sorties [through San Bernardino Strait], TF 34 will be formed when directed by me." The problem was that this second message went out by shorter-ranged *voice* radio, rather than radio-telegraphy like the previous one, and Admiral Kinkaid did *not* intercept this one. Nor did Nimitz or King.

So it was that Halsey's wording of the 1512 message led Kinkaid, and others, to believe that Halsey's fleet off Leyte Gulf had been reconstituted

into the three carrier task groups *and* the newly formed Task Force 34.*
The first seed of tragedy had been sown.

At 1405, Admiral Sherman's group at last got off his reconnaissance
flights to search the heretofore neglected north. All he could spare for the
search were some bombers without the usual fighter escorts. This was
risky business, but the appearance of tail-hook-carrying aircraft coming
from the northeast made a search mandatory, and the continuing attacks
by Japanese aircraft dictated that he keep as much fighter protection as
possible to cover his force. Also, many of his fighters were, by this time, in
need of reservicing as a result of the day's hectic battles.

At 1640, the search paid off. Sherman's aircraft spotted Ozawa's force
190 miles to the north. At last, the final piece of the puzzle was in place.
Halsey had found his carriers.

The next order of business was what to do about them. It was too late
in the day to launch an air strike, since the attacking aircraft would have
to return to their carriers in the dark.[†] It was apparent that Ozawa's fleet,
dubbed the "Northern Force" by the Americans, would either have to be
engaged at night by surface forces or by air the next day.

An additional problem to consider was that the Japanese carriers
could open the range overnight, putting them at a distance that would
allow them to strike at the Americans with their longer-range aircraft without being within striking distance of U.S. aircraft.

Halsey weighed his options. As he saw it, there were three alternatives
available to him, and he recorded these options in his after-action report
as follows:

(a) Divide the Third Fleet, leaving Task Force 34 (main gunnery
strength) to block San Bernardino Strait, while the carriers with light
screens attacked the Northern Force

---

* The fourth carrier task group, McCain's TG 38.1, was by then returning to
Leyte Gulf from its aborted sojourn to Ulithi, but was still hundreds of miles away.

† The majority of American pilots by this stage of the war were not capable of
making carrier landings at night. While there were some American aviators capable of
night carrier landings, these were specially trained flyers attached to special
squadrons for just that purpose, and they were most often employed in a night reconnaissance role rather than an attack role. USS *Independence*, in Task Force 38, had
such a squadron.

(b) Keep the whole force covering San Bernardino Strait

(c) Strike the Northern Force with whole concentrated strength and leave San Bernardino Strait unguarded

Halsey rejected the first alternative because he wisely considered it imprudent to leave Task Force 34 behind without air cover. He also felt that this alternative "would spread our strength," which, of course, is counter to the Mahan tradition of force concentration.

He rejected the second alternative because "the Northern Force could not be left to operate unmolested, and because destruction of its carriers would mean much to our future operations." One of the most frustrating aspects of the Pacific war to that point had been the Japanese's ability to escape from every battle with a considerable portion of their fleet intact. Even the great victories at Midway and in the Philippine Sea had been marred by this frustration. Halsey and a good portion of the U.S. Navy were most anxious to prevent this from happening yet again.

Halsey accepted the third alternative as his course of action because it "maintained the integrity" of his fleet (that is, kept it *concentrated*) and because it offered the "best possibility of surprise and destruction of the enemy carrier force." He seemed only mildly concerned that this course of action would leave San Bernardino Strait open for Kurita to pass through. While acknowledging that "the Center Force might sortie and inflict some damage," he believed that its fighting ability was "too seriously impaired to win a decision." This assumption was based upon the damage assessments he had received from pilots returning from their strikes on Kurita's force in the Sibuyan Sea.

Those pilots were exuberant. They had lost only eighteen of their own aircraft during the entire day's strikes, and they had seen *Musashi* mortally wounded, limping in circles, bow awash, with a great smear of black oil marking her wake. They had seen *Myoko* retire from the scene early that morning, and they had inflicted numerous hits on other ships all through the day. The result was that their reports tended to overemphasize their success. Men in battle frequently do this. The adrenalin-induced high they experience tends to magnify what they see. This is particularly true of aviators who must view their battles at high speeds, great distances, and very odd angles.

Admiral Halsey accepted these reports at face value, later explaining that "the pilots' reports proved dangerously optimistic, but we had little reason to discredit them at the time." His decision to go north after Ozawa's force "was not based on pilots' reports solely." Halsey and his staff had, for quite some time, discussed and studied and longed for a showdown battle with the Japanese Navy. "We had played it frequently on a game board constructed on the deck of the flag quarters," Halsey said. They had always envisioned this showdown as a clash between carrier forces. "If the rest of the Navy did not then know it, we, in the Third Fleet, were thoroughly cognizant that the carrier had replaced the battleship, and was potentially the strongest and most dangerous naval weapon our opponents possessed."

Although no one in the U.S. Navy was aware of just how impotent Japanese naval air power had become, there had been some speculation on the matter, especially after the poor Japanese showing at Formosa. But Halsey's reasoning was that "we did not know how many planes the Japs had, but we could not take a chance. We knew that the *Princeton* had been attacked and it was reported they were carrier planes." He was, of course, mistaken on this latter point,[*] but the point is well taken nonetheless.

Halsey was also concerned about "shuttle-bombing," a tactic that can be employed when an adversary has airfields (or carriers) on two different sides of the opponent's forces and is then able to fly from one location (such as Ozawa's carriers), strike the enemy in between (Halsey's forces), and then land at the other location (airfields in the Philippines). This process can be reversed and repeated again and again and has the tactical advantage of quicker turnaround times on refueling and rearming as well as giving the attacker two avenues of approach (or "threat axes" in military terminology). It also gives a potential range advantage to the attacker since he is not required to return over the full distance from which he has come. Halsey remembered that "we had been shuttle-bombed many times by the Nips, and only once off Guadalcanal had succeeded in reversing this process."

All of these considerations notwithstanding, perhaps what was foremost in Halsey's mind may well have been the intense criticism suffered by his good friend, Raymond Spruance, after the Battle of the Philippine Sea.

Halsey had just wrapped up his very successful campaign as commander of the South Pacific theater when he arrived at Pearl Harbor in time to watch the progress of the battle from CINCPAC headquarters. From that

---

[*] *Princeton* had been hit by a lone, land-based bomber.

vantage point, Halsey was privy to the assessments of Spruance's performance that were ongoing during and immediately after the battle. Though Halsey never recorded what he had witnessed there (probably because he and Spruance had been longstanding friends,* he would have to be deaf not to have heard the sharp criticisms of Spruance's decision to keep his fleet close to the landing site in the Marianas rather than go after the Japanese Fleet. One of Spruance's more vehement critics was another friend of Halsey's, Vice Admiral John H. Towers, Commander of the Air Force Pacific Fleet, who had been the U.S. Navy's third qualified aviator and a firm believer in the aggressive use of carriers. It seems very likely that Halsey would have been subjected to Towers's rantings about non-aviator Spruance's supposed lack of aggressiveness. So, although it is only speculation, there is ample reason to believe that Halsey would have been influenced by what he heard at CINCPAC headquarters, as well as by the continuing criticism of Spruance that lived on in wardrooms, ready rooms, and Officers Club bars for many months after the battle.

Influenced by all these considerations and armed with the caveat in his original orders that said, "In case opportunity for destruction of major portion of the enemy fleet is offered or can be created, such destruction becomes the primary task," Halsey walked into *New Jersey*'s flag plot, put his finger on the plotted position of Ozawa's Northern Force, and said to his chief of staff, Rear Admiral Carney, "Here's where we're going, Mick. Start them north."

---

* William Halsey and Raymond Spruance had first become acquainted in 1921 when, as U.S. Naval Academy Professor Emeritus Ned Potter puts it, "Lieutenant Commander Ray Spruance commanded the outstanding destroyer of Commander Bill Halsey's outstanding division of the outstanding squadron of the Pacific Fleet destroyers." Despite their very different personalities and leadership styles, they became lifelong friends.

★ Three admirals who would influence the outcome of the Battle of Leyte Gulf. *Left to right:* Chester Nimitz (CINCPAC), Ernest J. King (COMINCH), and William F. "Bull" Halsey (COMTHIRDFLT). *(Naval Institute)*

★ King and Nimitz meet with Admiral Raymond A. Spruance *(extreme left)* at Saipan in the aftermath of the Battle of the Philippine Sea. It was here that King would tell Spruance "you did exactly the right thing" by not going after the Japanese fleet. *(Naval Institute)*

★General Douglas MacArthur (CINCSOWESPAC), President Franklin D. Roosevelt, and Admiral Nimitz pose for photographs on the deck of the USS *Baltimore* in Pearl Harbor. *(Naval Institute)*

★Some of the massive American forces en route to Leyte Gulf for the invasion of the Philippines. Hundreds of U.S. ships would participate in the huge amphibious operation. *(Naval Institute)*

★ Nimitz takes his turn at briefing Roosevelt on Pacific strategy during the meeting in Hawaii. It would be MacArthur who would convince the President that the liberation of the Philippines should be the next strategic priority. *(Naval Institute)*

★ American forces headed for the beach at Leyte Gulf. Japanese resistance to the landing was relatively light, and most American planners believed that the Japanese fleet would not contest the operation. *(Naval Institute)*

★ The Japanese Fleet sorties from Brunei Bay in Borneo, en route to Leyte Gulf. Battleships *Nagato, Musashi,* and *Yamato* lead the way. *(Naval Historical Center)*

★ General MacArthur and Philippine president Sergio Osmena in a landing craft headed for the Philippine shore. Moments later MacArthur would make good on his promise of nearly three years earlier, when he promised the Philippine people, "I shall return." *(Naval Institute)*

★ The aircraft carrier USS *Princeton* explodes after being hit by a single Japanese bomb. The cruiser *Birmingham*, alongside to render assistance, suffered terrible casualties among her topside personnel. *(Naval Institute)*

★ Some of the devastation to USS *Birmingham* is evident from the numerous shrapnel holes peppering her superstructure. *(Naval Institute)*

★ Vice Admiral Marc A. Mitscher (seen here with Nimitz) commanded the air arm of Halsey's Third Fleet during the Battle of Leyte Gulf. *(Naval Institute)*

★ Japanese battleship under attack in Sulu Sea by aircraft from Mitscher's Task Force 38. *(Naval Institute)*

★ Vice Admiral Thomas C. Kinkaid, commander of the Seventh Fleet. Given primary responsibility for the landing operations, his forces would ultimately face the bulk of the Japanese Fleet alone, while Halsey's Third Fleet pursued the northern decoy force. *(Naval Institute)*

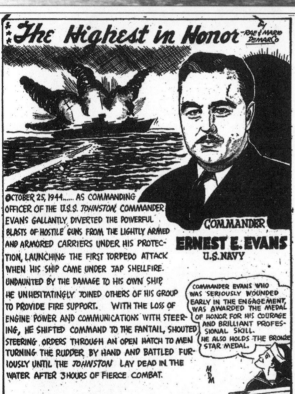

★ Two of the Seventh Fleet escorts lay a smoke screen during the Battle of Samar. *(Naval Institute)*

★ This 1978 vignette appeared in *Navy Times* to commemorate the 1944 heroism of Commander Ernest E. Evans while captain of USS *Johnston* during the Battle of Samar. *(Naval Historical Center)*

★ Lieutenant Commander Robert W. Copeland receives the Navy Cross for heroism while in command of the destroyer escort USS *Samuel B. Roberts*. His ship was one of three escorts lost in the Battle of Samar. *(Naval Historical Center)*

★ U.S. sailors (*foreground*) look on helplessly as the carrier *Gambier Bay* succumbs to Japanese gunfire from a Japanese cruiser (*circled*). (*Naval Institute*)

★ USS *St. Lô*, an American escort carrier, is hit by a *kamikaze*. She would not survive this attack and became the third American aircraft carrier lost in the Battle of Leyte Gulf. (*Naval Institute*)

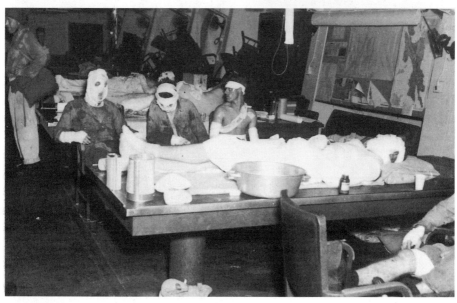

★ American casualties lie on the dining tables in USS *Suwanee*'s wardroom after a successful *kamikaze* attack. Japanese suicide aircraft first appeared in the Pacific War during the Battle of Leyte Gulf. (*Naval Institute*)

★Japanese sailors jettison ammunition from the stricken carrier *Zuikaku* during the Battle of Cape Engano. *(Naval Historical Center)*

★*Zuikaku* crewmembers ignore their ship's heavy list and salute while the battle ensign is lowered. The subsequent sinking of this Japanese aircraft carrier marked the passing of the last of the carriers that had launched the attacks on Pearl Harbor three years earlier. *(Naval Historical Center)*

★Nimitz and Halsey confer aboard a seaplane tender. Despite Halsey's questionable actions during the battle, Nimitz never chastised him for his actions at Leyte Gulf. *(Naval Institute)*

PART V

★ NIGHT OF 24–25 OCTOBER 1944 ★

14

★ Exits and Entrances ★

Roy West was born and raised on two hundred acres of river bottomland in Cherokee County, North Carolina. His father had chosen farming as his life's occupation to make a living, but also because he believed the rigors of farm life to be the best way to keep his nine sons out of trouble. None of the nine ever got into serious trouble, though none became farmers either.

Four of the brothers were of the right age to serve in the armed forces during World War II. One enlisted in the Marine Corps, one joined the Seabees (Naval Construction Battalion), one served in the Army, and Roy, on the day before his eighteenth birthday, enlisted in the Navy and was sent to Bainbridge, Maryland, for basic training. It was August of 1943, nearly two years into the war, when Roy first donned the uniform of his country. Like so many young men of the time, Roy was not old enough to vote when he went off to take part in a world war.

Many of his fellow "boots" at Bainbridge were from North Carolina and, upon graduation, a number of them were assigned to the same ship, USS *McDermut* (DD-677). She was a brand-new destroyer, a 2,050-ton *Fletcher*-class, built in Kearny, New Jersey, and commissioned in November 1943. After a shakedown cruise to Bermuda, *McDermut* sailed for the Pacific. For the next ten months, the ship participated in a wide variety of operations, including shore bombardment, antiaircraft defense, and antisubmarine warfare. She patrolled the waters off Kwajelein and served as part of Spruance's Fifth Fleet during the invasion of the Marianas. By the time the invasion of Leyte was drawing near, *McDermut* and her crew, young men like Roy West for the most part, were functioning as an efficient team, ready for most contingencies.

Shortly before the Philippines invasion, *McDermut* was assigned to participate in the landing operations at Palau. By that time Roy West had become a third class torpedoman's mate and was part of *McDermut*'s torpedo gang, headed by Chief Petty Officer Virgil Rollins. This Navy veteran had survived the attack on Pearl Harbor and the terrible night off Savo Island in the Solomons when so many American ships were sunk that the waters there had been nicknamed "Ironbottom Sound." Such experiences do not breed careless men, and Rollins had long before resolved that maximum preparation was a requirement of getting lucky. When there had been some speculation that the Japanese Navy might show up to challenge the landings at Palau, Rollins directed his men to inspect thoroughly the mechanical and electrical components of the ship's torpedo tubes. To their consternation, the torpedomen discovered that the impulse charges used to eject the torpedoes from their tubes had become corroded and discolored. It was too late at that point to get the materials they needed to refurbish the weapons, so Rollins and his crew sweated out the operations at Palau, hoping they would not be called upon to fire their "fish" until they could link up with a properly equipped repair facility. They had all heard tales of misfires and of torpedoes protruding half-in and half-out of a tube, armed and dangerous and going nowhere. The men's anxiety may have been a bit pessimistic since *McDermut* had not been called upon to fire torpedoes in an actual engagement even once thus far in the war.

But one never knew.

At 2024 in the evening of 24 October, Admiral Kinkaid received a message from Admiral Halsey: "Strike reports indicate enemy [Kurita's force] heavily damaged. Am proceeding north with 3 groups to attack enemy carrier force at dawn."

Years later, Admiral Kinkaid would write an article for the May 1959 Naval Institute *Proceedings* magazine in which he described the essential attributes that a naval officer should possess. One cannot help but wonder if he was remembering the Battle of Leyte Gulf when he wrote: "It is highly *desirable* that a military man speak and write the English language clearly and forcefully. It is *essential* that he be articulate in the formulation of orders and directives."

Had Admiral Halsey* articulated that 2024 message a bit more clearly, the Battle of Leyte Gulf would have turned out very differently. Had he used the word *all* instead of the number 3 to describe what he was taking with him on his trek north, Kinkaid would have realized that San Bernardino Strait was being left unguarded. As it was, Kinkaid interpreted the message to mean that Halsey was leaving Task Force 34 behind to guard the strait and was taking his three carrier task groups north. It must be remembered that all of those who had read Halsey's original Task Force 34 message, and had *not* received the later clarifying voice message, believed that Halsey now had *four* groups under his command in the Leyte Gulf area. So when he radioed that he was taking *three* groups with him, it was natural to assume that one was being left behind.

Why Kinkaid assumed that it was TF 34 being left behind is not entirely clear, since Halsey could have chosen to leave a carrier group. Kinkaid later wrote that he assumed Halsey was leaving behind Task Force 34 because "it was impossible to believe anything else. The proposed composition of TF 34 was exactly correct in the circumstances." This is debatable. If Kinkaid reasoned that leaving TF 34 behind was "exactly correct" because it was nighttime and a surface force was well suited for guarding San Bernardino Strait at night, he was forgetting that daylight would follow, leaving TF 34 vulnerable to the air attacks that had been occurring all day on the twenty-fourth and could reasonably be expected to continue on the twenty-fifth.

Kinkaid was not the only one to assume that Halsey was leaving behind TF 34. Halsey had included CINCPAC as an information addressee on the 2024 message, and Nimitz and his staff also made the same assumption. Nimitz wondered about the lack of air cover for TF 34, but he had long ago—during Halsey's daring raids in the earliest days of the war—learned

---

* There is evidence that this message was not actually written by Halsey, who by that hour had gone to bed after nearly forty-eight hours without sleep, but by one of his staff. This is irrelevant, however. Officers frequently rely on their subordinates to draft reports and messages in their name, just as presidents and other executives do, but they always do so with the understanding that it is they who bear the responsibility for what is written, not the subordinates. Although Halsey, the man, may not have actually chosen the words for this or any other message, it is Halsey, the admiral, who, for all intents and purposes, did.

that it was better to let the on-scene commander call the shots, so he did not question Halsey's decision.

Admiral Spruance, who was following the battle's progress at CINC-PAC headquarters, pointed to the waters just off San Bernardino Strait on the chart and said in his characteristically soft-spoken manner, "I would keep my force right there."

Admiral Kurita could not figure out why the Americans had not come back for more attacks in the remaining hours of daylight. From about 1700 all had been disconcertingly quiet. Kurita had not heard from Ozawa and therefore did not know that Halsey had at last detected Ozawa coming down from the north and had decided to go after him with his entire force.

Despite his concerns, Kurita continued his march across the Sibuyan Sea, at this point seriously behind schedule. There was no way he was going to arrive in Leyte Gulf in the early hours of the morning as originally planned, so at 1830 he sent a message to Nishimura warning him that he had been delayed by the air attacks in the Sibuyan Sea and would not arrive as scheduled for the coordinated pincer attack. It was apparent that *Sho Go** was not happening as planned. Yet there seemed no alternative but to continue on. Retreat was out of the question. Admiral Toyoda's "With confidence in heavenly guidance, all forces will attack!" message saw to that.

At 1951, Kurita ordered the formation to shift from the antiaircraft defensive ring to a column and continue east into the narrowing waters of Ticao and Masbate passes that led into San Bernardino Strait. He was headed for the very spot where Admiral Spruance's finger had touched the chart in CINCPAC's headquarters. The spot where Kinkaid and Nimitz believed there was a powerful American battleship-centered task force waiting. The spot where, in reality, there was only the empty sea.

When Admiral Halsey had ordered his three carrier task groups to concentrate off San Bernardino Strait earlier in the day, Rear Admiral Ralph Davison, commander of Task Group 38.4, had sent a message to Halsey, pointing out that the concentration would draw his force northward

---

* Once the number one (*ichi*) plan had been put into effect it became *the* plan, and the modifier was dropped.

and consequently take him out of range of Nishimura's oncoming Southern Force, which had been discovered and attacked earlier that morning in the Sulu Sea. This did not deter Halsey and, as a result, Nishimura was not molested for the rest of the day. In sharp contrast to Kurita's hellish time in the Sibuyan Sea, Nishimura's passage across the Sulu Sea was peaceful and uninterrupted. He remained on the original schedule and would pass through Surigao Strait under the cover of darkness as planned.

For Vice Admiral Shoji Nishimura this hiatus was a time to reflect upon something more personal. His son, Teiji, who had graduated from the Japanese naval academy at Etajima at the top of his class, had been killed here in the Philippines earlier in the war. For the aging admiral there must have been a touch of irony and a certain appropriateness to come to the site of his son's death on his own mission that many saw as suicidal.

Despite the lack of air attacks, Nishimura had formed his ships into an antiaircraft disposition, with cruiser *Mogami* leading battleships *Yamashiro* and *Fuso* in a column flanked by the four destroyers, two on each side.

As the force drew closer to Surigao Strait in the waning hours of the day, Commander Shigeru Nishino, commanding officer of the destroyer *Shigure*, maintained his station on the port quarter of the formation, wondering what lay ahead. He knew that the battle plan called for this force to enter Leyte Gulf from the south at dawn the next morning to attack the American landing forces. He knew that Kurita was supposed to bring his more powerful force into the gulf from the north at about the same time. But he had seen the messages from Kurita warning that he was under heavy attack and was falling behind schedule. And Nishino knew that Nishimura had not slowed his advance across the Sulu Sea. It was rather apparent that the odds of survival were diminishing.

Sailors are notorious for their beliefs in jinxes, omens, and the like. For *Shigure*, such a belief could serve as a boost to morale, for she was a veteran of the Battle of Vella Gulf in the Solomons. On that dark night of 6–7 August 1943, a group of four Japanese destroyers had lost a night battle with American destroyers for the first time in the war. Three of the four Japanese destroyers had been lost, along with more than a thousand men, but destroyer *Shigure* had been the sole survivor. Nishino had not been in command then, but he could hope that the good fortune that had spared his vessel once before might again bring *Shigure* through her coming trial. In a few hours he would know.

★　★　★

Admiral Kinkaid and his Seventh Fleet staff had received no further word of Nishimura's Southern Force, or of Shima's smaller force coming up behind, since their initial sightings. But it was fairly obvious that they intended to cross the Sulu Sea and enter Leyte Gulf via Surigao Strait, so Kinkaid began making preparations. As he later put it, "We had all day to think about it, to make up our dispositions."

It is rather paradoxical that the battle shaping up for that night promised to be a struggle between surface forces centered around battleships, a duel in which air power would play no significant part. This war in the Pacific had begun with an attack on battleships because the myopic thinking of most naval officers of that time envisioned these great ships as the keystone of naval power. Men like Bull Halsey had changed all that. The aircraft carrier had dominated the war, leaving the battleship commanders to suffer great frustration as the war progressed virtually without them. Now, on this night of 24–25 October 1944, so late in the war, the battleships were at last to get their chance to face one another.

Kinkaid had six of these behemoths in his fleet. USS *Mississippi* was the only one that had not been at Pearl Harbor on 7 December 1941. *Pennsylvania*, *Tennessee*, and *Maryland* had all been heavily damaged in the attack, and *West Virginia* and *California* were actually sunk and subsequently resurrected by salvage teams. They had a big score to settle.

Kinkaid had a lot more than six battleships in his inventory. The Seventh Fleet had been beefed up with a great deal of cruiser and destroyer firepower to provide support to the landing. Also at his disposal were a large number of PT boats.

But Kinkaid had a problem. A premonition of this can be seen in the Seventh Fleet Operation Plan 13-44 of 26 September 1944, which in one part reads: "It is not believed major elements of Jap fleet will be involved in the present operations." In another part of the plan can be found the words, "Participation of Japanese battleships in defense of the eastern Philippines is not considered probable." These expectations affected the logistical planning for the operation.

Among the different types of ammunition used by naval guns are two important varieties: high-capacity (HC) and armor-piercing (AP). HC is well suited for use against shore targets or unarmored ships because of its explosive power, and AP ammunition is more highly specialized, designed with extra penetrating power that makes it effective against the steel sides of modern ships, especially against the armor-plating found on battleships.

Therefore, if one is expecting to conduct shore bombardment, HC is the ammunition of choice, but if one expects to do battle with an enemy fleet, then AP is preferable.

Despite the protests of some of the more prescient officers on the Seventh Fleet staff, the low expectation of a showdown with the Japanese Navy prevailed among the planners, and the combatant ships scheduled to participate in the Leyte operations were loaded with approximately 75 percent HC and only 25 percent AP ammunition. This left them quite prepared to conduct shore bombardment in support of the amphibious operations but precariously underprepared for a major fleet engagement.

Kinkaid ordered Rear Admiral Jesse Oldendorf, commander of the Bombardment and Fire Support Group, to set up a "welcoming committee" for the Japanese ships expected to come through Surigao Strait that night. Kinkaid sent a message to Oldendorf advising him that an estimated force of two battleships, three heavy cruisers, three light cruisers, and ten destroyers could be at the northern end of the strait by as early as midnight.

Oldendorf's command philosophy was that "one duty which was never delegated to my staff was the drafting of battle plans," so he began planning his strategy for that night's engagement. Surigao Strait runs almost due north and south, so Oldendorf decided to set up his main battle line of battleships at the northern end of the strait, in the waters due east of Hingatungan Point. From there the battleships would have plenty of sea room to maneuver, but the narrower waters to the south of his position would keep the approaching Japanese forces from enjoying the same advantage. He then divided the remainder of his forces, the cruisers and destroyers, into two groups that he assigned to take up positions on either flank and somewhat farther south of the main battle line. Because he was concerned that the Japanese might try to slip some of their units past him by making an end run around the eastern side of Hibuson Island, he beefed up his left flank, assigning the heavy cruisers *Louisville*, *Portland*, and *Minneapolis*, the light cruisers *Denver* and *Columbia*, and the nine "tin cans" of Destroyer Squadron 56. To the right flank, Oldendorf assigned the Australian heavy cruiser HMAS *Shropshire*, light cruisers *Phoenix* and *Boise*, and six destroyers, primarily from Destroyer Squadron 24. Six more destroyers were designated as Destroyer Division "XRay" and assigned to screen the main battle line against submarines.

Oldendorf's plan called for the cruisers to be positioned just south of the main battle line in their assigned flank positions, and the destroyers of squadrons 56 and 24 were to take up positions even more to the south on the left and right sides of the strait, respectively.

Oldendorf retained command of the powerful left flank as a second hat, but gave the right flank to Rear Admiral Russell S. Berkey and turned the main battle line over to another subordinate, Rear Admiral G. L. Weyler.

Oldendorf then summoned Berkey and Weyler to join him on his flagship, USS *Louisville*, so that he could explain his plans and solicit their comments. The two subordinate admirals concurred in the soundness of Oldendorf's plan, but there was some concern expressed over the paucity of armor-piercing ammunition. It was agreed that the battleships would place enough AP in their ammunition hoists to permit five uninterrupted salvos, but that HC would also be readily available and used if any targets smaller than battleships presented themselves.

There wasn't time to waste on coding and decoding, but security was obviously important, so Oldendorf communicated his orders visually rather than risk enemy interception of radio signals. Soon, all around Leyte Gulf signal searchlights blinked out the battle plan, and battleships, cruisers, and destroyers began the preparations for battle.

At Manus several weeks earlier, Petty Officer Third Class Roy West and Torpedoman's Mate Second Class Len Wilson had returned from a destroyer tender with fresh black powder to refurbish the torpedo impulse charges. For the next several days the torpedo gang worked on *McDermut*'s torpedo system, installing new detonators, checking and rechecking electrical circuits, and lubricating mechanical components. At last they felt ready for whatever might await them in Leyte Gulf.

On 11 October, the ship got under way from Seeadler Harbor at Manus as one of the many escorts for the troop transports heading for the Philippines. *McDermut* entered Leyte Gulf on the morning of the twentieth, still screening the transports as they approached the Dulag landing area. Several Japanese aircraft made runs on the group but were warded off without serious incident. As the morning wore on, *McDermut* rescued several downed American flyers, and then by mid-afternoon, she had been assigned as part of an anti-torpedo boat screen along with destroyers *Melvin* and *McGowan*. The three ships maintained their stations at the northern end of Surigao Strait for the next several days.

Then, in the early evening of the twenty-fourth, one of the men from the torpedo gang returned to the berthing compartment after standing his watch on the bridge as ship's helmsman. He was out of breath from hurrying down the several ladders from *McDermut*'s bridge. Between excited puffs, the young sailor repeated what he had just overheard while on watch: "The Japs are coming, and they're probably gonna get here tonight!"

The sound of an airplane engine revving up to full power carried across the waters of Leyte Gulf. In another moment, a reconnaissance aircraft was flung into the late afternoon sky from one of the Seventh Fleet battleships. The solitary seaplane skimmed across the water and then climbed slowly as it banked toward land. Similar launchings had been occurring among the cruisers and other battleships for the better part of an hour. It had been decided that flying these fragile planes to the relative safety of land might be prudent since they were prone to damage during gun battles and could serve no useful purpose in an engagement that was shaping up to occur in the darkest hours of night. The cranes normally used to recover these planes were lowered to the decks and lashed down.

The ships of the Seventh Fleet were hard at work getting ready for whatever the night might bring. The words "night battle" had been uttered countless times until they all but echoed off the steel bulkheads of the gray combatants scattered about the gulf. Unnecessary gear was stowed or lashed down so as not to become a missile hazard in the fury of battle. Lifelines were removed, electronic equipment was checked and tuned, and fire hoses were faked down on decks and carefully inspected. Helmets, life jackets, signaling whistles, flashlights, and medical supplies all took on new significance as the sun drew closer to the horizon.

On board USS *Nashville*, Captain Charles Coney had a problem. He naturally wanted his ship to participate in the coming battle, but he had a responsibility that none of his fellow cruiser skippers had. *Nashville* was still flagship for the Commander in Chief of the Southwest Pacific.

Captain Coney went to MacArthur in person and appealed to the general, asking him politely to take his staff and go elsewhere so that Coney could take his ship into battle. MacArthur declined, saying, "No, I do not desire to leave your ship, Captain. I have never been able to witness a naval engagement and this is the opportunity of a lifetime. Proceed to the battle area when you wish."

Coney then turned to Admiral Kinkaid for help. He radioed the Seventh Fleet commander and explained the situation. Kinkaid agreed that *Nashville* should not be permitted to go into direct surface combat with the general embarked, so he diplomatically invited the general to join him on the Seventh Fleet flagship, USS *Wasatch*, a poorly armed command ship that had been built on a merchant hull. MacArthur indignantly replied, "Transfer from a combatant ship to a noncombatant ship? Never!" Despite the reluctance of Coney, Kinkaid, and most of MacArthur's staff to have the supreme commander needlessly endangered, MacArthur stood firm.

Reluctantly, Kinkaid sent a message to *Nashville*, saying "Remain at anchor," and the other combatants steamed southward without her.

Coward was anything but. Perhaps, like the boy named Sue that Johnny Cash would sing about many years hence, Captain J. G. Coward felt compelled to fight in order to counter the stigma of his name. More likely, he was a professional naval officer who could smell a hot battle cooking and was not about to miss it.

"Destroyers can and did do most everything except fly, submerge, or travel overland, but a night torpedo attack is our first love!" Coward once wrote. He spoke with authority on this matter. He had been serving in tin cans throughout the war. As commanding officer of USS *Sterett* he had participated in North Atlantic, Mediterranean, and Pacific operations and had become an authority on night engagements and torpedo attacks. He had fought the Japanese in some of the toughest night surface engagements of the war, doing battle with the "Tokyo Express" in places that veterans would always remember as "The Slot," "Sleepless Hollow," and "Ironbottom Sound."

By the time the Leyte operations were shaping up, Captain Coward had risen to command Destroyer Squadron (DesRon) 54 and was designated as Commander Screen Southern Attack Force and as officer in tactical command of the landing craft movement group of the Southern Attack Force. After escorting about 150 ships to the landing site from Manus, his destroyers provided direct support for the assault craft during the actual landing and then settled into patrol stations at the southern end of the gulf. Several days of relatively routine patrol ensued, though the monotony was periodically broken by Japanese air attacks and the occasional discovery of drifting mines.

By monitoring the TBS radio messages (another example of reading other people's mail) Captain Coward learned, on the twenty-fourth, that an important conference had been called on Oldendorf's flagship. From other information he was able to gather, Coward surmised that a night battle was shaping up in the strait to the south of him. He had not been included in the planning for the battle because his squadron was not assigned to Admiral Oldendorf's Bombardment and Fire Support Group but belonged instead to Vice Admiral Theodore Wilkinson's landing force.

But Coward was not about to sit idly by and miss such a golden opportunity. Especially since his destroyers' patrol stations were such that his ships were already in an ideal position to participate. As Oldendorf's battle line and flanking forces formed up, they were positioning themselves to the north of Coward's position, which left him perfectly positioned to lead the attack down the strait.

"We just had to be in the thick of it," Coward later wrote. He called Admiral Oldendorf on the TBS and declared, "In case of surface contact to southward I plan to make immediate attack with fish, then retire to clear you. If you approve this, I will submit my opplan soon." Oldendorf gave his approval fourteen minutes later. Coward then informed the admiral that "My plan would be to attack from two sides with two groups, one of two and one of three, with one group well to westward and one to eastward. Would that be acceptable?"

Coward's plan was for his flagship, *Remey*, along with *McGowan* and *Melvin*, to attack from the eastern side of the strait, while *Monssen* and *McDermut* would take the western side. His two remaining ships, *Mertz* and *McNair*, would remain on picket patrol at the northeastern exit to the strait, between Desolation Point and Homonhon Island.

Coward ordered his ships to approach the enemy at 30 knots and to use torpedoes only. His experiences at Guadalcanal had taught him that the temptation to use all available weapons was offset by the knowledge that a destroyer's 5-inch guns were virtually useless against the thick hides of battleships and that firing guns at night disclosed one's position. Torpedoes, on the other hand, could do a battleship in and did not give off the telltale flash that guns did.

At 2015, Admiral Oldendorf called Captain Coward on the TBS. "Your last transmission affirmative." Coward was in the fight.

"Give me a fast ship, for I intend to go in harm's way." Those famous words of John Paul Jones, the father of the American Navy, had been adopted as the motto of the diminutive but potent Patrol Torpedo (PT) boats of World War II. These 77-foot, 45-ton, wooden hulled craft had joined the U.S. Navy as an experiment just prior to the outbreak of hostilities. Although half were lashed in cradles on the deck of an oiler when the Japanese attacked, twelve were at Pearl Harbor to return fire with their machine guns. Motor Torpedo Boat Squadron 3 fought a heroic delaying action in the Philippines in those dark early days of the war when little was going the U.S. Navy's way, and it was a PT boat that had carried General MacArthur safely out of the Philippines just prior to their falling to the Japanese. Since then, the PTs had fought an effective campaign in the Solomons and New Guinea and had seen service in the Mediterranean theater as well.

Although most effective against enemy logistical traffic, the PT boats had gone toe-to-toe with Japanese warships on occasion and had held their own, though by war's end sixty-nine had been lost to enemy action, nature's wrath, and friendly fire. They operated most effectively at night, using hit-and-run tactics and earning a reputation as "commandos of the sea." Individual heroism was in no short supply in PT boats, and among the many medals earned by their crews, two were Medals of Honor and one lesser decoration was pinned to the uniform of a future president of the United States.*

In the early afternoon of 24 October 1944, a great many PTs could be seen roaring southward toward Surigao Strait. Admiral Kinkaid had thirty-nine of them at his disposal and had ordered Commander S. S. Bowling to deploy them deep into the strait to serve as early warning pickets for the coming battle.

Lieutenant Commander R. A. Leeson was given tactical command of the boats, and he divided them into thirteen sections of three craft each. Their orders were to "report all contacts, surface or air, visual or radar, and attack independently."

As darkness descended on Surigao Strait, the boats were all on station, laying-to in the glassy waters so as to maximize their radar and radio capabilities and to eliminate their own telltale wakes.

---

* Lieutenant John F. Kennedy was awarded the Navy and Marine Corps medal for his actions in saving members of his crew after their PT-109 had been cut in half by a Japanese destroyer in the Solomons.

At the southern entrance of the strait, one of the three boats guarding the western side of the passage was PT-137, commanded by Lieutenant j.g. Isadore M. Kovar. Murphy's Law* had reared its ugly head on Kovar's boat. Electrical problems had disabled his radio and his radar. He and his crew were going to have to fight using only their eyes and ears as sensors. It could prove to be a harrowing night.

As the evening wore on, the quarter-moon slipped into the sea, and an overcast moved in to squeeze out the light from the stars. Surigao Strait went pitch black.

A light northeast wind fanned the perspiring faces of the PT sailors, and an occasional squall swept down the strait from the north, momentarily interrupting the tense silence with the hiss of falling rain. The hours of waiting had begun.

The small escort carriers of Kinkaid's Seventh Fleet steamed through the darkness east of Leyte Gulf with little to do but watch for submarines. Their aircraft had been rendered impotent by the darkness, but even had it been broad daylight they would have been of minimal use against an enemy force centered around battleships. Like Kinkaid's surface ships, these small carriers had come to the Philippines with the expectation of supporting an amphibious landing rather than engaging an enemy fleet, and they, too, had equipped themselves with ammunition suitable for attacking troops and airfields, instead of the armor-piercing bombs and torpedoes that would be needed against the likes of *Fuso* and *Yamashiro* at that very moment steaming through the Sulu Sea toward Surigao Strait.

Captain Fitzhugh Lee, commanding officer of USS *Manila Bay* (CVE-61), had been monitoring the day's message traffic. He knew that the Japanese were headed for Surigao Strait, and that the Seventh Fleet battleships, cruisers, destroyers, and PT boats were arrayed to meet them. He was also aware that a Japanese force, including carriers, was on its way down from the north, and he was glad to hear that Halsey had headed out that night to intercept this impending threat. He was not aware, however, that while the door was swinging tightly shut on Surigao Strait, the one at San Bernardino Strait was wide open.

---

* "What can go wrong, will."

15

★ Midwatch in Surigao Strait ★

"Never give a sucker an even chance." Such was the philosophy of Admiral Oldendorf, "Oley" among his peers. Partly through an accident of geography and partly as a result of sensible planning, he was certainly not giving his enemy any quarter.

Nishimura's approach through the confined strait on the night of 24–25 October would force him to maintain a narrow formation. Oldendorf's disposition of forces would put the oncoming Japanese force into the jaws of several succeeding pincers as PTs and destroyers gnawed at his flanks along the way. This alone would have been a difficult gauntlet to run, but the array of battleships and cruisers across the northern end of the strait was something out of the oldest textbooks on naval tactics.

Ships, by their necessarily elongated shape, have much more room to place weapons along their sides than on either end. Therefore, it is an axiom of naval warfare that the ideal position for one ship in relation to another, when engaging in battle, is to place one's own ship "broadside" to the enemy's bow or stern. If one pictures an aerial view of such a situation, the two ships form a T, with the advantaged ship as the cap, or top, of the letter. In this way, the capping vessel has all guns along one side clear to fire on the other ship, while the ship making the base of the T can only bring to bear forward or aftermost guns. This advantageous position has for centuries been known among naval tacticians as "capping the T" (or sometimes "*crossing* the T").

This principle can be extended beyond individual ships to include formations. If a naval commander can bring his column of ships across the head of an adversary's column, thus again capping the T, he will have a decided advantage.

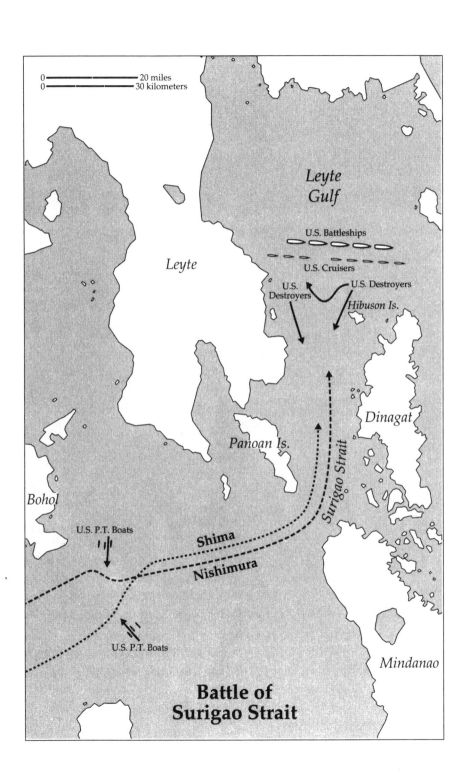

Battle of Surigao Strait

At the Battle of Tsushima in the Russo-Japanese War a half-century earlier, the Imperial Japanese Navy had managed to cross the Russian Fleet's T and achieved a resounding victory. But at Surigao Strait, it was the Japanese who were on the wrong side of the T. Admiral Oldendorf's cruisers and battleships were steaming back and forth across the northern end of the channel in a column, while Admiral Nishimura's ships, by the geography of the area, would be forced to approach in a column, or something close to a column. This amounted to a classic capping the T situation.

At about 2200, aboard the destroyer *Shigure*, Commander Nishino read a message from Kurita advising Nishimura that he did not expect to reach Leyte Gulf until 1100 the next morning. Nishino noted that Nishimura still did not slow down in response to Kurita's message but pressed on in accordance with the original schedule. By this time, they were out of the Sulu Sea and headed northeast across the Mindanao Sea, headed for the approaches to Surigao Strait.

As merely the commanding officer of a destroyer, Nishino was not privy to Nishimura's thinking, but he reasoned that the admiral was continuing with the original schedule because slowing down would have forced him to transit the strait in daylight when they might have to face air attack in addition to whatever else might be waiting for them. Besides, the Japanese had proven themselves generally superior to the Americans in night actions, so that was another reason for them to press on.

At 2215, Nishimura sent cruiser *Mogami* and three destroyers ahead to reconnoiter, leaving *Shigure* back with the two battleships. The latter group altered course to move in closer to the island of Bohol, while the advance force continued on a northeast heading.

Just off Bohol were three of the American PT boats. As the PTs watched and waited, thunder echoed off the island's hills, which were occasionally illuminated in strobes of sheet lightning. At 2236, Ensign Peter Gadd's PT-131 picked up Nishimura's battleship group on radar, and within minutes the three PT boats were charging across the black waters at 24 knots. Lookouts aboard *Shigure* sang out as they picked up the phosphorescent glow of bow waves fast approaching. The Battle of Surigao Strait had begun.

Admiral Nishimura ordered his group to turn toward the oncoming PT boats, and *Shigure* complied. Nishino ordered his searchlight operators to illuminate the attackers, and a shaft of light sliced through the darkness, almost immediately attaching itself to the small boats roaring in from the northeast. Nishino opened fire with his 4.7-inch gun and geysers of water straddled the PTs as they veered violently and began making smoke to counter the searchlight. One of *Shigure*'s shells passed clean through PT-130 without detonating, but PT-152, whose crew had dubbed her the *Lakacookie,* was not so fortunate. She took a hit up forward, killing one man and wounding three others. Flames soon enveloped the forward part of the boat and it seemed that *Lakacookie* was doomed. Then, in a sudden change of fortune, another of *Shigure*'s shells struck the water very near the wounded boat and, miraculously, the great plume of water resulting from the detonation cascaded down over *Lakacookie*'s burning bow and extinguished the flames.

PT-130 moved in to cover the burning *Lakacookie,* and she was also hit. In another stroke of luck, however, the Japanese shell had torn a huge chunk out of one of her torpedo warheads without causing it to detonate.

But *Shigure*'s shooting was too accurate. PT-131, the third boat in the section, was soon riddled with gunfire, and none of the boats were able to set up for a good torpedo shot because of the violent maneuvering required to evade the Japanese gunfire. Soon the PTs were driven off, *Shigure*'s searchlight beam and 4.7-inch shells in hot pursuit.

First round went to the Japanese.

On board the destroyer *McDermut,* Torpedoman's Mate Third Class Roy West sat at his battle station on the ship's torpedo mount amidships, waiting for something to happen. He watched as beads of perspiration traced glistening paths down the face of the man nearest him. The tension had been building ever since the word had come down that the Japanese were coming and *McDermut* received her battle instructions from the squadron commodore, Captain Coward.

Roy West and the other men manning the torpedo mount did not know the details of the battle plan, but they did know that the Japanese were expected to come up through the strait to the south of them and that *McDermut* and the other four ships of DesRon 54 would attack with torpedoes when, and if, they came. The captain had seemed pretty certain that the Japanese would come when he had spoken to the crew earlier over the ship's general announcing system, briefly explaining what was expected to happen and exhorting each man to do his best in the coming battle.

At about 2200, the ship had been ordered to "Condition I Easy," which meant that all battle stations would be manned but that certain designated doors and scuttles could be briefly opened and shut to allow the men limited movement to make head calls or deliver coffee and sandwiches. All around the ship, the men passed the time according to individual needs. Some were quiet, silently praying, while others joked loudly. A few invoked the sailor's ancient rite of complaining and some ventured to predict what the night would bring. Playing cards, letters, and pictures of wives, girlfriends, and dogs emerged from denim pockets, and more cigarettes than usual flared in the ship's interior spaces where there were no munitions.

Amidships, at *McDermut*'s torpedo mount, Roy West listened as a young man nearby talked about the many virtues of his mother, and he watched as another man nervously fingered a small silver cross. One of the men, who consistently wore an air of bravado as though it were part of his Navy uniform, caught Roy's eye and grinned at him as if to say that all was routine and normal. But tiny incongruous strands of spittle between the man's lips said more about what was going on inside than did the forced grin.

The life jackets and helmets that always seemed a burdensome nuisance during drills now brought a mixed sense of foreboding and comfort as the minutes ticked slowly by. Roy West had an almost constant, unsettling feeling of having just stepped in front of a speeding automobile and then having to wait helplessly as the vehicle careened toward him with tires screeching.

And still nothing happened.

The next few rounds of the battle went to the Japanese as well. *Mogami* and the three destroyers that Nishimura had broken off from his battleship group slipped by the next section of PT boats undetected. At 2330, Nishimura sent a message to Kurita, who was by then well into San Bernardino Strait, and to Shima, some thirty miles behind Nishimura, telling them that he was "advancing as scheduled while destroying enemy torpedo boats." This was a bit of an overstatement since he was not exactly "destroying" the attacking PT boats, but it was true that he was advancing unimpeded so far.

As the *Mogami* group continued on, it was attacked by the next section of PTs, two of the three getting off torpedoes, which missed. Again, searchlights and gunfire drove the attackers off, zigzagging and making smoke.

This pattern continued as the two sections of Nishimura's force pressed on. At frequent intervals, sections of three PT boats would make a run at the much larger and more powerful Japanese ships, and each time they would be driven off without achieving any torpedo hits.

But this opening phase of battle was not entirely one-sided. Although the PT boats were not damaging their adversaries, nor even slowing them up appreciably, these diminutive warriors were contributing to the battle in an important way. In the midst of all their wild flailing about in the dark waters, many of the PTs were able to get off reconnaissance reports. Admiral Oldendorf was getting a pretty good picture of the Japanese advance through the information the PTs provided.

In a sea battle as large and multifaceted as the one that occurred in and around Leyte Gulf a half-century ago, where powerful ships such as aircraft carriers, battleships, and cruisers dueled to the death, it is easy to overlook combatants whose length is less than a hundred feet and whose crew numbers only a few men. But those few men should not be forgotten anymore than the thousands of others who ventured into the terrifying world of combat at sea. It was a surreal situation for those PT boat sailors, charging at breakneck speed through pitch black waters toward ominous shadows whose eerie eyes would suddenly blink open, cutting the darkness with frightening beams of harsh light while belching fire like some nightmarish sea dragon. The PTs, casting their torpedoes in a vain attempt to stop their tenacious enemy, would then careen wildly about in a frantic slalom among great geysers of water as shrapnel rained down and dense clouds of smoke billowed in their wakes, absorbing the pursuing tongues of light. This was no moment for the faint of heart.

Nishimura must have been rather pleased at this stage of the action. The Japanese Navy once again was proving its mastery of the night battle. But the old admiral was no fool and probably no optimist. In his next message to Kurita and Shima, he said, "Several torpedo boats sighted but enemy situation otherwise unknown." He might have hoped, but could hardly have expected, that these torpedo boats would be all he would have to face on his way to Leyte Gulf.

Nishimura reunited his two groups at 0040 and placed them in a modified column to better negotiate the narrowing waters ahead. Destroyers *Michishio* and *Asagumo* led the column with battleships *Yamashiro* and

Fuso following and cruiser *Mogami* bringing up the rear. Flared out on each flank, just ahead of *Yamashiro*, were the destroyers *Yamagumo* to starboard and *Shigure* to port.

At about 0200, Lieutenant Commander Leeson, the officer in tactical command of all the PTs, got his chance at the Japanese force. Leeson's boats charged in and his flagship, PT-134, got off the first torpedo shots.

Nishimura had just entered Surigao Strait itself and was altering course to due north. For the narrow waters ahead, he converted the formation to a true column by ordering the flank destroyers, *Yamagumo* and *Shigure*, to move in astern of *Asagumo*. As his ships turned, they spotted the approaching PTs of Leeson's group and immediately showered the attackers with gunfire. Almost simultaneously, Lieutenant John McElfresh's section of three boats closed from the other side of the strait, firing four torpedoes as they came. Once again, none of Leeson's or McElfresh's torpedoes found their mark.

PT-490 was hit by Japanese gunfire, and then 493 took three hits in rapid succession, killing two men and wounding five others. One of the shells tore a hole in the boat's bottom and another blew the crew members completely out of the cockpit area and hurled them back to the fantail. The men returned to their stations and turned the boat toward Panoan Island, hoping to beach her there before she sunk. As 493 headed for the shore, Petty Officer A. W. Brunelle crawled down to the splintered hole, where water was flowing in at a furious rate, and stuffed his life jacket into it to check the flow. This kept the boat afloat long enough for her to reach the shore and run aground. The crew of 493 scrambled ashore and set up a defensive perimeter for the night. They would remain there until sunrise, when high tide would lift their abandoned boat off the rocks, carry it out to deeper water, and then swallow it whole. Dawn would also bring rescue for the surviving crew members of PT-493, when PT-491 came to their aid.

And so it went. More PTs attacked as Nishimura plowed doggedly ahead. More torpedoes splashed into the black waters of Surigao Strait, but remained frustratingly impotent.* More gunfire was sprayed about in the dark, sometimes finding its mark, most times not. And most important, more radio transmissions added electrical activity to the lightning-laced

---

* In the morning, two torpedoes were found on one of the beaches enclosing Surigao Strait, lying helpless like beached whales in silent testimony to the frustration of the PT crews who risked their lives to deliver these fish on target.

air, feeding invaluable information to Oldendorf waiting in ambush at the other end of the strait.

So far the midwatch* aboard *McDermut* had been tense but quiet. Sometime after 0200 the men at the torpedo stations sensed that the ship was no longer pacing monotonously at its patrol station but had changed course and speed. A quick look at the gyro-repeater confirmed they were moving south. Roy West heard someone nearby say, "This is it," and felt the soft rustling of butterfly wings somewhere deep in his stomach.

Torpedoman's Mate Third Class Richard Parker's battle station was on the port bridge wing along with the Torpedo Officer, Lieutenant j.g. Dan Lewis, who was running the port torpedo director. From their vantage point, Parker and Lewis could hear the incoming radio reports, and Parker began passing the "gouge" (navy term for "the word") over the sound-powered phone system to the others at the various torpedo stations. Roy West, whose battle station was gyro setter for torpedo mount number two, looked at his mount captain, Torpedoman's Mate Second Class Harold Ivey as reports came in describing American PT boat attacks against the oncoming Japanese force. Several times the word *battleship* was used and each time, West and Ivey exchanged quick looks.

After a few more minutes, the luxury—or curse—of idleness dissipated as things began to happen. Evidently *McDermut* was closing the enemy because a torpedo firing solution began to take shape. The men on both mounts began quickly matching pointers with the information coming down from the port torpedo director, cranking in gyro angle, alternately engaging and disengaging spindles, and occasionally taking a quick swipe at the beads of perspiration trickling down their faces. Roy West concentrated hard as the glowing dials before him spun in a jerky dance of whirling numbers. As he worked the cranks, just as he had done hundreds of times before in training for this moment, he tried to ignore the thumping cadence of his heart.

McDermut heeled to port as her rudder went over and she came quickly right about 40 degrees. As she steadied up, West knew his ship must be directly paralleling the target's approach course, on the reciprocal, because there was suddenly no gyro error to correct. Assuming that

---

* In the Navy the midwatch is the four-hour watch between midnight and 0400.

the enemy would continue on his present course and speed, this meant *McDermut* had a near perfect firing solution and an optimum chance for success. It also meant that there were Japanese ships closer to Roy West than there had ever been before, and they were probably coming directly at him at a relative speed of nearly 50 knots.

In the subterranean darkness of *Remey*'s Combat Information Center, Captain Coward had been monitoring the reports from the PT boats for nearly two hours. Despite the excited confusion in the reports, one thing was clear: a Japanese force was headed up the strait.

When it appeared that the Japanese had passed the last section of PTs, Coward sent a message to Admiral Oldendorf that he was taking his destroyers down the strait. With *Remey* in the lead and *McGowan* and *Melvin* following, Coward's section of destroyers headed down the eastern side of the strait, while *McDermut* and *Monssen* proceeded southward along the western side. Before long, radar revealed what no human eye could see. Like tiny green ghosts, several faint contacts flared, then faded, on the screen, bearing 184 degrees, range 38,000 yards. Believing that he could better control his destroyers in a night battle from the bridge, Captain Coward left CIC and emerged into the humid night air. It was darker outside than it had been in *Remey*'s CIC.

Soon a report came up from CIC that seven enemy ships could be discerned on the radar. From the relative sizes of the pips, the radarmen evaluated them as two battleships, a cruiser, and four destroyers. As Coward's destroyers raced headlong toward the contacts, excited voices called out the diminishing radar ranges and radio speakers crackled with reports in a chorus as indecipherable to the untrained ear as that heard by the uninitiated at an opera: "Skunks bearing one eight four distance fifteen miles, over." "Standby to execute speed four. Jack Tar and Greyhound One acknowledge." "This is Jack Tar, WILCO." "This is Greyhound One, WILCO." "This is Blue Guardian, I am coming left to zero niner zero to fire fish." And so on.

As the two sections of destroyers converged on the Japanese column, Coward assigned targets to his ships. Five U.S. destroyers, with a total displacement of about 12,500 tons, were about to engage two battleships, a heavy cruiser, and four destroyers, whose tonnage topped a hundred thousand. Undeterred by this unsettling fact, the American destroyers pressed in for the attack.

★   ★   ★

In *McDermut*, Richard Parker passed the word over the sound-powered phone circuit that the three tin cans on the other side of the strait were launching torpedoes at the Japanese.

From his perch atop the torpedo tubes amidships, Roy West peered out over the port side of the ship trying to see if he could make out anything on the eastern side of the strait. His eyes probed the inky darkness as he heard the command to release spindles. Suddenly, there was a burst of light in the sky above *McDermut* as a Japanese star shell ignited. The brightly burning flare hanging from the shrouds of its miniature parachute seemed fixed in the sky above them as it cast an eerie gray-white light on the sea. West glanced about and saw the *Monssen* revealed in the ashen pallor, and he hoped that neither destroyer was as visible to the Japanese. From somewhere ahead, a green searchlight began sweeping the sea and Roy West knew he was in the thick of things.

A moment later, West could feel the expulsion of the five torpedoes beneath him as they were fired electrically from the bridge and leaped from the ship into the boiling sea. Both of *McDermut*'s quintuple mounts fired full salvos. Ten fish swam off into the night in pursuit of Japanese steel. *Monssen* also fired a full salvo of ten more torpedoes, making Surigao Strait a very dangerous place to be.

Roy West and the other torpedomen quickly secured their mounts and gathered around Chief Rollins, who was peering at a stopwatch in the subdued red light of a flashlight. As the group waited anxiously for the expected run-time of the torpedoes to expire, they could feel *McDermut* heeling over sharply as she came about to dash back up the strait. The wind swept across her decks as she came hard to starboard and the whole world seemed to be spinning out of control. Suddenly, West could see the faces of his shipmates in a ghastly green light and knew that the searchlight had found them. He felt the concussion of a nearby detonation and was astonished to see a large column of water rise up out of the sea off *McDermut*'s port side. Several more rounds exploded so close aboard that *McDermut*'s weather decks were drenched in a shower of warm saltwater.

Before the realization of what was happening could steal his reason, West heard Chief Rollins—who was still studying his stopwatch—say in a calm voice, "It's about time for something to happen." And something did.

As if cued by Rollins's words, a huge fireball erupted from the darkness to the southeast. Before the sound of the explosion could reach

McDermut, two more detonations flared from the sea in the same direction. It was a beautiful and a horrid sight, conjuring a strange mix of fear, awe, and elation in Roy West. He could hardly tear his eyes away, but the continued sound of much closer explosions claimed his attention as *McDermut* weaved her way north in a frantic dash for survival.

Roy West did not see the explosions caused by the destroyers on the opposite side of Surigao Strait. All told there were at least six detonations as some of the forty-seven torpedoes of Coward's picket destroyers found their marks. As *Remey*, *McGowan*, and *Melvin* charged up the eastern side of the strait, and *McDermut* and *Monssen* ran up the western side in hasty retreat, the radar plot revealed that the Japanese column had slowed considerably and one of the contacts appeared to be circling.

McDermut and *Monssen*, no longer being chased by Japanese shells, hugged the shoreline of Leyte, trying to hide in the island's radar shadow and leave the strait clear for the succeeding waves of American attackers poised for their turns at the enemy. One group so poised was a section of American PT boats that, in the confusion of battle, did not realize the *Monssen* and *McDermut* were friendly forces. They fired up their powerful engines to full throttle and raced toward the unsuspecting destroyers.

Captain Richard H. Phillips, commander of Destroyer Division 108, had commanded the two western destroyers during the attack. From *McDermut*'s bridge, he had been constantly monitoring the PT boats' tactical circuit as well as his own. When he heard that there were PT boats on an attack run, he quickly surmised from the range and bearing information they were passing on the radio that his ships were the target. In the nick of time, he was able to get ahold of the errant PTs and deflect them from what might have been a terrible tragedy. After that near-miss, *McDermut*, *Monssen*, and the destroyers on the eastern side of the strait continued their exodus unmolested.

Coward's Picket Patrol was only the first of several waves of attackers. Once the DesRon 54 destroyers had completed their attacks and were retreating up the sides of the strait, the right flank destroyers of DesRon 24 moved in for an attack. They approached the Japanese force in two groups of three each. As they neared their quarry, the *Yamagumo*, which had been hit by one of *McDermut*'s torpedoes, exploded, illuminating the other Japanese ships so that they made clear targets for the oncoming second wave of destroyers. At 0323, the Australian destroyer *Arunta* fired four torpedoes at *Shigure*, which was by now leading the Japanese column. All four missed. *Killen* launched five torpedoes at *Yamashiro*. One struck and temporarily slowed the big battleship, but did not stop her. *Beale* fired five more torpedoes, but all of them missed.

The second group of right-flank destroyers moved in by circling to the south of the Japanese and then coming back north for the attack. They, too, launched a barrage of torpedoes and also opened fire with their guns. Two torpedo wakes of unknown origin, but assumed to be Japanese, crossed *Daly*'s bow as the destroyers pressed the attack. Several detonations were observed among the Japanese ships during this attack, but it was impossible to tell if they were hits by the latest wave of American torpedoes or if they were secondary explosions resulting from Coward's attacks. Some observers even believed that what they were seeing was the flash of *Yamashiro*'s heavy-caliber guns as she retaliated.

The Japanese column was falling apart. The radar picture became confused as both Japanese and American ships veered about in every conceivable direction trying to unmask batteries or to escape the deadly fire of an adversary. At one point, *Hutchins* launched five torpedoes at the destroyer *Asagumo*, but when she successfully evaded, the American torpedoes continued on their way and struck the unfortunate *Michishio*. She blew up and immediately sank.

Admiral Oldendorf called off the right-flank destroyers, fearing that they were getting too entwined with the Japanese ships and might foul the range for his cruisers and battleships that were still waiting for their turn at the enemy.

As the final hour of the midwatch began, the natural darkness of Surigao Strait was marred by the flames of burning ships, and the stillness that normally would have reigned in these wee hours of the night was broken by the ominous rumbling of hostile gunfire and exploding ships. And still the battle was not over.

16

★ Curtain Call ★

Roy West and the other torpedomen remained clustered together near *McDermut*'s torpedo tubes as the destroyer charged northward. Japanese shells were no longer falling close aboard and there was little to do besides bask in the exhilaration that often follows when one has survived the dangers of combat.

Suddenly, one of the torpedomen said, "Would you look at that?" His voice was full of wonderment. "Over there. Off the starboard side. In the sky." Roy West peered in the direction indicated and saw several crimson streaks of light flash across the sky from north to south like meteors. Several more followed almost immediately. A throaty rumble like distant thunder, felt more than heard, rolled in from the north. "The heavies are shooting," someone said.

Oldendorf's cruisers and battleships had indeed begun their barrage. The admiral and his staff had been monitoring the PT and destroyer attacks by radio and could actually see the flare of some of the hits far to the south, especially the big one caused by *McDermut*'s first torpedo. Then, on search radar, they had picked up the advancing Japanese and tracked them as the right-flank destroyers had played their part.

Oldendorf would have preferred to wait until all the destroyers had completed their attacks before allowing the gun batteries of the cruisers and battleships to enter the fray, but the Japanese were getting too close. In order to maximize the effectiveness of his early salvos of armor-piercing ammunition, it was necessary to begin firing before the Japanese got inside the 26,000-yard envelope. So when the first Japanese ship had reached that point and the fire-control radars of the big ships were locked on target, Oldendorf ordered, "Commence firing." With a tremendous roar, some of the most powerful artillery pieces in the world breathed fire into the night and hurled gargantuan projectiles—some of them weighing more than a ton each—at a sensed, but as yet unseen, enemy.

In the meantime, there was yet another group of destroyers moving in for the attack. Captain Smoot's DesRon 56, making up the left flank, had gotten the word "Launch attack—get the big boys" at 0335 and had headed southwest in three sections of three destroyers each. Smoot's plan of attack was to fan out the three sections, sending one down each side of the Japanese force and the third down the middle. The effect would be to "funnel" in the Japanese so that evasion would be all but impossible.

As the destroyers raced along, Captain Smoot heard a strange sound overhead and looked up. In the black sky above he saw the tracer shells of the cruisers and battleships arcing their way southward. "It was quite a sight," he later said. "It honestly looked like the Brooklyn Bridge at night—the taillights of automobiles going across Brooklyn Bridge."

Smoot pressed his attack much closer to the crippled Japanese force than the earlier destroyer attacks had. The section of three destroyers that he had chosen to make the run down the middle of the strait consisted of USS *Richard P. Leary*, USS *Albert W. Grant*, and his flagship, USS *Newcomb*. As they charged along, Smoot noted that *Grant* was lagging behind. He called her on the radio and told her to speed up, but saw that instead she was falling farther behind. *Grant* was apparently having some engineering difficulty and this put the destroyer in a very precarious position. Alone in the strait, yet so close to the Japanese force, she was picked up on radar by one of the American cruisers and mistaken for an enemy ship. The cruiser opened fire on *Grant*, and, to make matters worse, so did the Japanese.

While the rest of Smoot's destroyers were firing their torpedoes in a close-in attack, *Grant* was caught in a murderous crossfire. Eleven 6-inch shells from the American cruiser and nine 4.7-inch Japanese shells rained down on the unlucky destroyer. The first round struck her on the fantail at 0407 and exploded among a stack of expended shell casings. Several more rounds hit amidships, doing heavy damage to her forward engineering spaces, causing a great cloud of pressurized steam to roar out of her forward stack. The ship's log recorded her continuing agony in concise and lurid detail:

0408½ Additional shell hits began to riddle ship. Hit forward at water line flooded forward storeroom and forward crew's berthing compartment. Hit in 40mm gun #1 exploded 40mm ammunition and started fire. Hit through starboard boat davit exploded killing ship's doctor, Lieutenant Charles Akin Mathier, five radiomen, and almost entire amidships repair party. Other hits in forward stack, one hit on port motor whaleboat, one hit and low order explosion in galley. One hit in scullery room, one hit in after crew's berthing compartment, and one hit in forward engine room. All lights, telephone communications, radars, and radios out of commission. Steering control shifted aft.

It is difficult to imagine what was *not* hit on that ship.

With *Grant* dead in the water, her captain, Commander T. A. Nisewaner, felt no great need to remain on her bridge, so he went below to see what could be done to save his ship. Discovering that the forward engine room had been one of the hardest hit areas, he climbed down the ladder in the access trunk to assess the damage there. In so doing, he entered a nightmarish world of flickering flames, choking smoke, and the warning hiss of escaping steam. He groped through the darkness and rising seawater toward the groans of wounded sailors. When he came upon the first man, who was badly hurt, Commander Nisewaner hefted the injured sailor onto his back and carried him out of the hell-like space. He went back in several times and repeated the process until he had rescued all the men he could find.

Meanwhile, in the crew's after head, the ship's sole surviving pharmacist's mate, W. H. Swaim, struggled valiantly by the dim light of battle lanterns to administer first aid to more than eighty dying and wounded men. He was assisted by a young sailor, J. C. O'Neill, Jr., whose only medical "training" had been watching his father, a practicing physician, at work. It is safe to say that young O'Neill's observances had never quite equaled what he dealt with that night. He improvised tourniquets from available materials, bound up bloody stumps, injected morphine, and rigged an emergency oxygen tent for a man suffering terribly from severe burns.

In the wardroom, Chief Commissary Steward L. M. Holmes turned his skills from cooking to medical pursuits as he, too, filled the void left by the deaths of the ship's doctor and leading pharmacist's mate. One of his many patients, Radioman First Class W. M. Selleck, whose legs had been torn off, looked up at Chief Holmes with his life ebbing away, and said,

"There's nothing you can do for me. Go ahead and do something for those others."

And out on deck, Watertender Third Class W. G. Hertel, himself seriously wounded, asked to be propped up against the base of a boat davit so that he could administer syrettes of morphine to those suffering men within his reach.

Such stories go on and on. Nearly every man in the crew, living and dying, was cited in the ship's battle report for varying degrees of heroism under these most terrible circumstances.

Among the legion of heroes were the men who tended to the wounds of their ship. Fighting fires, stuffing mattresses into gaping shell holes, shoring up damaged bulkheads with tables, pumping and bailing by hand, and working in darkness and fear to repair damaged machinery, *Grant*'s repair parties were able to keep her afloat. Before morning's light she would be taken under tow by *Newcomb* and would live to fight again in later battles of the Pacific war.

The other destroyers of Captain Smoot's DesRon 56 had moved in very close to the Japanese force and scored at least two hits on battleship *Yamashiro*. By now the Japanese were staggering badly from the many punches delivered by the incessant waves of American destroyers. And they had yet to endure the U.S. cruisers and battleships with their 6-, 8-, 14-, and 16-inch guns.

Log entries for battleship *West Virginia*; night of 24 October 1944:

0332: Received orders from Commander Battle Line to open fire at 28,000 yards.

0333: 4,000 yards to go; Gunnery Officer reports range 39,000 and has solution with large target.

0351: Cruisers on right flank have opened fire. Gunnery Officer says he has had same big target for a long time and that it is an enemy. Commanding Officer ordered commence firing.

0352: First eight-gun salvo at 22,800 yards, AP projectiles.

0353: Could hear Gunnery Officer chuckle and announce that first salvo hit. Watched the second salvo through glasses and saw explosions when it landed.

0354: Our salvos very regular at about 40 seconds interval. Other BBS*
opened after our second or third salvo.

0358: Gunnery Officer reports target is stopped and [radar] pip is getting
small.

0402: BBS of Battle Line turned 150 degrees on signal to course 270.
Ordered cease firing. Have to think about small amount of ammunition on
board. CIC reports targets turned left and reversed course.

0411: Pip reported to "bloom" and then fade.

0412: Target disappeared. Can see ships burning. One is a big fire.

This rather laconic account of the gunfire phase of the Battle of Surigao Strait captures the essence of what occurred. What it does not
describe is the awesome power of those many ships delivering terrible
devastation in the form of heavy-caliber seagoing artillery. What it only
hints at—by the mention of the gunnery officer's chuckle—is the high
level of emotion felt by the men delivering those blows. What it refers to as
a pip blooming, then fading, is actually the catastrophic loss of a giant
ship and the hundreds of men crewing her. Yet, perhaps most significant of
all, what the log entries fail to mention is that this moment was an epoch of
history.

In those brief and terrible minutes, surface ships fought surface ships
without the intrusion of those interlopers from the sky that had stolen the
show from the gunships in this war. Battleships were at last unleashed to
wreak the havoc for which they were designed. Yet it was not the grand
show long dreamed about. Despite their frightful destructive power, in this
showdown in Surigao Strait these leviathans were outdone by their little
brothers, the destroyers. It was the torpedo—for all its development problems at the beginning of the war and in spite of its inability to measure up
to the pyrotechnic glamor of gunfire—that had done the most damage in
the last surface action. The great guns spoke in anger that night, not
merely at an enemy with whom they had a score to settle but also at their
own impotence, and this one final gasp of pent-up fury would serve as a
ceremonial salute to their own passing.

★   ★   ★

---

* BBS is the abbreviation for "battleships."

By the time Nishimura's force had reached the northern extent of the strait, it was a mere shadow of the striking power it had represented when it entered the narrow waters to the south. Only three ships remained: battleship *Fuso*, cruiser *Mogami*, and destroyer *Shigure*. The rest had been sunk or scattered about Surigao Strait as limping or totally disabled hulks. Battleship *Yamashiro*, Nishimura's flagship, had been blown in half, and each half was burning furiously like a Viking funeral pyre. The American destroyers had done their work well.

At 0351, Admiral Oldendorf had ordered the cruisers to commence firing and two minutes later, the battleships. The three Japanese ships continued their approach, suffering a terrific pounding as they drew closer to the American lines. *West Virginia*, *Tennessee*, and *California* were equipped with modern fire-control radars and their shooting was particularly accurate. "WeeVee," as *West Virginia*'s crew fondly called her, shot 93 rounds of 16-inch armor-piercing ammunition, while the other two together expended 132 rounds of 14-inch AP. The other three battleships, without the newer fire-control radars, had difficultly finding targets. After the shooting started, *Maryland* was able to pick up the splashes from Wee-Vee's rounds on radar and fired 48 rounds of 16-inch in the same vicinity. *Mississippi* got off only one salvo, and *Pennsylvania* fired no shots at all.

From the bridge of *Shigure*, Commander Nishino tried to keep his wits about him as explosion after explosion resounded in his ears and great walls of water rose and fell all around him. Every clock, compass, and gauge on the ship had been rendered useless by the concussions of the exploding shells. The radios were out as well. Through the curtains of cascading water he caught glimpses of a burning ship (or part of a ship—he wasn't sure) looking much like a glowing hot iron just out of a steelworker's furnace.

Amid the chaos and cacophony of war, Nishino wondered why Nishimura had come up the strait in a simple column, making such an easy target for the Americans. Why had the admiral not staggered the formation and approached using zigzag maneuvers instead of presenting to their enemy a fire-control officer's dream? On his own initiative, Nishino was by now maneuvering violently in a struggle for survival. Despite the incredible number of shells raining down, *Shigure*'s luck was holding. All but one of the rounds were near-misses. The one shell that had found its mark punched a small hole in the ship's fantail and plunged into an oil storage tank where it failed to explode.

By this time, Nishino had lost visual contact with the other Japanese ships and, without radios, could not call them. Nishino came about and headed south at high speed.

After several minutes of charging along at 30 knots, the enemy shell-fire diminished and Nishino soon saw *Mogami*, barely crawling along and burning furiously amidships. Then he saw *Fuso*, lying broadside to the enemy shellfire, apparently helpless as round after round chewed her to bits. Nishino continued south, leaving the firing and the awful images behind. Suddenly, his helmsman cried out that he no longer had control of the rudder. There was nothing to do but come to a stop and effect repairs.

Shigure lay to in the dark waters of Surigao Strait. Anxious moments passed while her crew worked at repairing the steering cables that had been damaged by one of the near-misses. She was the proverbial sitting duck as she lay motionless in those hazardous waters. The men worked feverishly at their repairs, while Nishino and everyone else topside peered out into the foreboding darkness hoping to see nothing. Then, the tense silence was broken by a lookout's report. Nishino peered into the gloom in the direction indicated by the lookout. Dark shadows were barely visible, stealing up from the south. Unquestionably they were ships. From one of them came the focused beam of a shaded signal lamp, beating out the message: "I am the *Nachi*."

It was Shima.

One light and two heavy cruisers, escorted by three destroyers, passed by *Shigure*, headed north. One of the destroyers of Vice Admiral Shima's force had been hit by a torpedo from one of the PT boats operating farther south and was no longer part of the formation, having been slowed to a mere 10 knots and noticeably down by the bow. The remainder of Shima's force was now navigating the same waters traveled by Ferdinand Magellan nearly four hundred years earlier, when the famed explorer was halfway through his historic circumnavigation of the earth. More significant, however, Shima's force was following the same track taken by Nishimura *barely an hour before*, the same track that had led to disaster.

Nishino responded to Shima's flagship message "I am the *Nachi*" by signaling, "I am the *Shigure*. I have rudder difficulties." This laconic message is rather astounding. Nishino said nothing of what had just transpired farther up the strait where Shima was headed. No warning of the ambush that lay ahead. No mention of the apparent loss of two battleships, a cruiser, and three destroyers just a few miles up the strait. No warning of the waves of destroyers flanking the channel and the heavy gunships capping it.

In a postwar interview, Commander Nishino explained this lack of communication as follows: "The reason I did not communicate directly with Admiral Shima and inform him of the situation was that I had no connection with him and was not under his command." Nishino added, "I assumed that Shima knew conditions of the battle . . . by sighting the burning ships *Fuso* and *Mogami*, and by seeing me on a retiring course."

Perhaps equally astounding is that Shima made no attempt to query *Shigure* about what lay ahead. He just proceeded on up the strait, past the burning remnants of his predecessor's fleet, toward the area where the darkness was diluted by arcing tracers, bursting star shells, and the incandescent glow of burning ships.

Commander Kokichi Mori had been in the Imperial Japanese Navy for fifteen years. He had commanded two destroyers since war began and was a graduate of the naval staff college. In February 1944 he had been assigned as torpedo officer on Vice Admiral Shima's staff. Now, in the dark morning hours of 25 October, he was peering out through the bridge windows of the cruiser *Nachi*, trying to make some sense of the strange and ominous scene ahead.

Two large fires flared against the velvet-black backdrop, and in their glow Mori could make out two smoke screens on either side of the burning ships, like curtains flanking a stage. Although *Nachi*'s unreliable radar showed nothing ahead, Mori guessed that behind those curtains lurked American ships. There were flashes of gunfire visible through the smoke, and red tracers plunged into the pall with great frequency.

Mori had been concerned from the start of the operation that there might be difficulties. He knew that the American Fleet waiting at Leyte Gulf was no pushover. Earlier, sketchy reconnaissance reports had told of a formidable force, including seven or eight battleships and a large number of torpedo boats. Shima's force had already encountered the torpedo boats and had left the destroyer *Abukuma* behind as a result. Mori had watched as the only clue to the PT boat's existence had been twinkling machine guns—until *Abukuma* had been hit by a torpedo and signaled that thirty of her crew were dead and that she could only make about 10 knots.

Mori knew that *Sho Go* called for Kurita and Nishimura to arrive at opposite ends of Leyte Gulf at about the same time, and he was aware that Kurita had been slowed by American air attacks. It was difficult, however, to know what Nishimura was doing since the communications plans that had been set up prior to the commencement of the operation did not provide a common channel for Nishimura and Shima to talk to one another. Each was steaming into battle along the same approach, more or less ignorant of each other's intentions or actions. It was not the best of arrangements, but it was not Mori's place to question such things. His concern was the execution of an effective torpedo attack by Shima's force when the time came for it.

That time had come as Shima formed his ships into a column with *Nachi* leading the other two cruisers and the three destroyers following behind. Once again, there was the column, when a more diverse formation would have complicated the Americans' fire-control solution. The problem was that the Japanese had enjoyed great success with columnar attacks when using torpedoes at night earlier in the war, so it was natural that they would resort to this disposition now. But American fire-control radar had improved a great deal and the old tactics were in need of a new look.

As Shima's force drew nearer the curtain of smoke, they passed close enough to the burning *Mogami* to identify her. By now, Shima had a solid radar contact farther up the strait and was intent upon attacking. He ordered "Combat to port" and brought his column right to position his torpedo batteries on the target, plunging through the clouds of smoke as he went. Everyone was intent upon the attack. No one noticed that *Mogami* was not dead in the water but was making way at about 8 knots. The muffled thunder of big guns farther north was audible as Shima's ships raced along toward the northeast, calculating the attack.

The cruisers launched their torpedoes, and then Mori returned his attention to the burning *Mogami*. To his horror, the cruiser was much closer than he had expected, and the thin ribbon of white water near her bow told all. She was making way! The bearing was constant and the range diminishing rapidly—the mariner's worst nightmare. Mori heard "Hard starboard!" shouted out, but it was too late. With the sickening sound of grinding metal, *Nachi* and *Mogami* collided.

As the two ships drifted along in the unwanted embrace, a voice called from a megaphone on *Mogami*'s bridge. "This is *Mogami*!" said the excited voice, as if it somehow mattered. "Captain and executive officer killed. Gunnery officer in charge. Steering destroyed. Steering by engine." And then, in one of those great understatements that lend comic irony to an otherwise tragic situation, the voice said, "Sorry."

Nachi carefully extracted herself from *Mogami*'s grasp, the sound of tearing metal almost unbearable to hear. *Nachi* left a good portion of her port bow aboard *Mogami* and was consequently forced to limit her speed to about 20 knots. Shima still wanted to press the attack. His destroyers had not yet fired their torpedoes and he still had his guns. Mori objected, saying, "Admiral, up ahead the enemy must be waiting for us with open arms. Nishimura's force is almost totally destroyed. It is obvious that we, too, will fall into a trap." Shima pondered for a moment, then agreed. He ordered his force to come about and head south.

The Battle of Surigao Strait was, for all intents and purposes, over.

As the sun rose next morning, several columns of thick black smoke towered into the brightening sky like remnants of the black shroud that had engulfed Surigao Strait the night before. The morning light revealed clusters of men clinging to the debris that littered the waters of the strait, and large smears of oil stretched for miles. As U.S. destroyers moved in to pick up the Japanese survivors, most swam away or disappeared beneath the oily water, shunning rescue in a final act of defiance.

Those drifting sailors were not the only ones with resistance still in them. Destroyer *Asagumo*, whose bow had been blown off by one of Captain Coward's torpedoes several hours earlier, was still exchanging gunfire with several American destroyers when daylight arrived. She fought on when two U.S. cruisers moved in to join the fray, and her after gun mount continued to fire as her bow slipped beneath the surface of the sea. Finally, her American adversaries watched in awe as the stern slipped into the sea with the after gun mount still firing!

And then there was *Mogami*. Despite the fearful pounding she had endured, the fire that all but engulfed her midships section, the loss of her commanding and executive officers, and the ignominy and further damage caused by her collision with *Nachi*, the resilient cruiser was still afloat, still under way, and still able to fight. Incredibly, she had endured still more hits from the American cruisers *Louisville*, *Portland*, and *Denver* just after dawn when Admiral Oldendorf had taken his left flank cruisers down the strait in pursuit of the retiring Japanese units.

As if this were not enough, *Mogami* was spotted by PT-491 as she steamed south at 6 knots. The PT boat began trailing her while trying to get off a contact report by radio. Not yet down for the count, the limping Japanese cruiser commenced firing with her 8-inch guns and came very close to hitting the pursuing boat. After firing two torpedoes that missed, the PT boat retired with *Mogami*'s guns still dropping rounds dangerously close.

Farther down the strait, another PT engaged *Mogami*, and this one, too, was driven off by gunfire. By this time, the seemingly invincible Japanese cruiser had effected repairs to her engineering plant and was making good speed once again.

But the feisty cruiser had used up all nine of her lives. With the daylight came American attack aircraft. Left out of the night's furious action, they now chased after the remnants of the Japanese forces. The planes came upon struggling *Mogami* and, within minutes, had delivered the mortal blow she had somehow evaded all night. A bomb crashed into her engine room and soon there was nothing left to do but abandon her to the sea. Her gunnery officer, now captain by default, ordered the men off and the valiant ship soon slipped beneath the waves.

Ironically, the loss of *Mogami* left *Shigure* as the only ship of Nishimura's force to survive the action. History had repeated itself by sparing *Shigure*, since she had been the sole survivor of the Japanese force at Vella Gulf little more than a year earlier.

As Shima's ships retired from Surigao Strait, they, too, were pursued by American ships and aircraft. *Nachi* was accosted by the meddlesome PTs, but she was able to strike one last blow for the Emperor by scoring a direct hit on one of the attackers, seriously wounding the section commander and two other men. Destroyer *Abukuma* was hit by a torpedo fired by one of the PTs, which did not prove fatal, but she was later finished off by U.S. Army Air Force bombers. Air attacks on the rest of Shima's force yielded little damage.

In Leyte Gulf itself, American sailors had spent the night watching in fascination and some dread as the flashes of gunfire reflected off the clouds to the south of them. They need not have worried. The scorecard for this battle was an impressive one, and notably one-sided.

With the exception of *Shigure*, Nishimura's fleet had been annihilated, and Nishimura had joined his son in death, going down with *Yamashiro*. Shima's force had fared better, but before another ten days could pass, *Nachi* would be sunk by American carrier-based aircraft, leaving only cruiser *Ashigara* and four destroyers as survivors of the original force that had entered Surigao Strait. All told, the Japanese had lost two battleships, three cruisers, and four destroyers as a result of this last of the great gun and torpedo battles. By comparison, one American destroyer and several PT boats had been damaged. One of the PTs was sunk, but no other U.S. vessels had been lost.

Exact personnel casualty figures for the Japanese are unknown, but they were in the thousands. The Americans had lost but 39 men, with another 114 wounded, most of them in USS *Albert W. Grant*.

An interesting footnote to this great engagement is found in the names of two of the young officers serving in Captain Smoot's left-flank destroyers. Elmo R. Zumwalt served as evaluator in USS *Robinson* and James L. Holloway III was USS *Bennion*'s gunnery officer. Both men would one day rise to the U.S. Navy's highest command position, Chief of Naval Operations.

As 25 October 1944 got under way, the U.S. Navy had dealt another devastating blow to its Imperial Japanese counterpart. But the Battle of Leyte Gulf was not over. What naval historian Samuel Eliot Morison would later dub "the main action" had not yet occurred. And the Japanese were about to unveil a new weapon which would eventually kill more American sailors than any other so far used in the war. There were only a few more hours left to this greatest of all sea battles, but before they were over, many more ships and men, both Japanese and American, would perish.

17

★ Friction and Fog ★

While the battle raged in Surigao Strait, the Third Fleet spent a relatively quiet night. The gargantuan force steamed north toward Ozawa's Northern Force, and many of the men not actually on watch had little to do but rest up for the next day's anticipated activities. Foremost on that agenda was an attack on the Japanese carrier force.

At a little before midnight, Halsey had ordered his fleet to slow down to 16 knots. "The purpose of this was to avoid overrunning the Northern Force's daylight circle," he later wrote. This "daylight circle" was determined by drawing an arc from Ozawa's last known position, using his maximum speed and the hours left until dawn to define the radius. By not crossing that arc, Halsey ensured that Ozawa could not effect an end run to get by him during the night. "If [Ozawa] slipped past my right flank," Halsey explained, "he would be able to shuttle-bomb me—fly from his carriers, attack me, continue on to his fields on Luzon for more bombs and fuel, and attack me again on the way back." This concern makes sense, since Halsey did not realize how weakened Ozawa's air power was. "If the enemy slipped past by my left flank, between me and Luzon," Halsey added, "he would have a free crack at the transports." This concern for the Seventh Fleet's transports in Leyte Gulf is less understandable, and ironic at best, since Halsey had left San Bernardino Strait open for Kurita, who was much closer to the gulf.

Halsey continued north, sending *Independence*'s night reconnaissance aircraft out ahead to search for the Japanese carrier force. At 0208 he got his first contact report. Then, six minutes later, a second group was detected by the "night snoopers." Ozawa had split his force into two groups, enhancing his role as decoy by making detection that much more likely.

Upon discovering the location of Ozawa's force, Halsey at last ordered Task Force 34 formed and sent it out ahead of the carriers to a point ten miles in the van. CINCPACFLT's report of the battle for Leyte Gulf to Admiral King explains Halsey's reasoning for this move:

> The Commander Third Fleet's plan for pushing strong surface forces ahead of his carrier groups and toward the enemy was a logical piece of tactics to attempt. Our expectation, based on past achievements, is that in an exchange of carrier attacks between fleets, it will be our enemy's fleet that takes the worst of it, and starts retiring while still at a distance many times greater than gun-range. The only possibility then of closing and capitalizing on our gun power is to overtake cripples or ships of naturally low speed.

Nimitz agreed with Halsey that by sending the gunships out ahead of the carriers, the odds of their catching up to the Japanese were greatly increased.

There were, however, risks associated with such a move. Keeping in mind that Halsey's main justification for going after the Japanese carrier force was that he still considered it a significant danger with a potent air strike capability, sending the gunships out, away from the carrier force, would deprive his carriers of a major antiaircraft capability. This loss of defensive fire support was offset somewhat by the proven effectiveness of Task Force 38's fighter protection, but the loss of *Princeton* the day before removes some of the validity of this argument, since she supposedly enjoyed this protection when she was mortally wounded by a Japanese aircraft.

Furthermore, if the approaching Japanese force had been a truly operational entity instead of a mere decoy, Task Force 34, if it had been detected by Japanese air reconnaissance as it lunged out ahead of the rest of the fleet, might have scared them off. And Halsey would again miss his chance at a big carrier battle.

In his flag plot aboard USS *Franklin*, Rear Admiral Ralph Davison, commander of Task Group 38.4, disagreed with this latest move by Halsey, but for a different reason. He and his chief of staff, Captain James Russell, stood over the round screen of the ship's surface search radar, watching as the tiny points of light representing Halsey's powerful battleships and their escorts slowly separated themselves from the Third Fleet mass and surged ahead. Both men believed that those ships should be headed south instead of north, and Davison looked up at his chief of staff, his face illuminated by the ghostly green light of the radar scope. "Jim," said the admiral, "we're playing a helluva dirty trick on the transports in Leyte Gulf." Russell nodded his agreement, then asked, "Do you wish to say anything to Admiral Mitscher?" Davison shook his head resignedly and answered, "He must have more information than we do."

After Halsey detached TF 34, he then ordered the carriers to prepare to launch a strike at the first glimpse of dawn's light and to make ready a second strike to follow as soon as possible. Halsey did not intend to pull any punches. These Japanese carriers were not going to get away. No "Spruance nuance" for Bull Halsey!

In Halsey's flag plot aboard USS *New Jersey*, members of his staff were watching over things as the admiral slept in his cabin one ladder below. Men clad in chambray, denim, and khaki were hunched over tables that were covered with nautical charts, polar-coordinate maneuvering boards, stacks of messages, coffee-stained operation orders, and dog-eared tactical publications. Vertical status boards lined the bulkheads, displaying a wealth of relevant information, including the disposition of the entire Third Fleet, the best-guess disposition of Ozawa's fleet, equipment status of the various ships and aircraft, last known positions of downed aviators, voice radio call signs, fuel and water percentages, and ammunition loads. The hiss of high-frequency radios along with the hum of ventilators and the steady thrum of *New Jersey*'s powerful turbines melded into a symphony as familiar to these twentieth-century sailors as the sounds of groaning wood, creaking rigging, and flapping canvas would have been to mariners of an earlier time.

In this crowded compartment, with its constant pall of cigarette smoke, and where the aroma of coffee always hung thickly in the air, many of the important decisions of the war had been made by the "Dirty Tricks Department." Halsey's staff had dubbed themselves with that unusual sobriquet early in the war when someone at one of the staff meetings had casually said, "I wonder what dirty tricks we can play on the little sons of bitches today."

But on the night of 24–25 October, it was the "little sons of bitches" who were pulling the dirty tricks. Ozawa's decoy force was doing its job by luring Halsey away from Leyte Gulf, and Kurita was, at that very moment, navigating the channel through San Bernardino Strait toward the void left by the northbound Third Fleet.

The potential for disaster loomed rather large at that moment, and the inevitability factor grew as the night wore on and the powerful Third Fleet got farther and farther away from Leyte Gulf. With Halsey's massive striking power lured northward and Kinkaid's Seventh Fleet punch drawn southward to cover Surigao Strait, the landing forces in the gulf were left virtually unprotected. The troops ashore were depending upon many of those ships in the gulf for continued logistical support, and those soldiers were, at that moment, particularly vulnerable since a great percentage of their supplies were still stacked on the beaches where they would be easy targets for a marauding force of gunships, like the one on its way through San Bernardino Strait.

The only element left between Kurita and the easy pickings in the gulf were the Seventh Fleet escort carriers and their accompanying destroyers. Any tactician worth his salt could see that these were no obstacle of any great moment. The CVEs were, after all, merely cheap imitations of the larger and more potent CVs and CVLs. These tiny carriers had played a tremendously important role in the war by serving as ferries for replacement aircraft and by providing air support for the amphibious landings, but they were hardly a match for the likes of Kurita with his still formidable array of battleships and cruisers. With no armor-piercing bombs or torpedoes to speak of, the CVEs would be wasting their time and, quite possibly, their lives by attacking Kurita's ironclads with bombs and rockets designed to handle the very different targets found ashore during an amphibious landing.

By a combination of clever tactical deception and dogged determination on the part of the Japanese, and poor communications and some misjudgment on the part of the Americans, the greatly outclassed Japanese Fleet had managed to set themselves up for what, just days before, seemed impossible. Despite the costly setbacks in Palawan Passage, the Sibuyan Sea, and Surigao Strait, the Japanese had achieved the main objective of their elaborate plan. The door was open to Leyte Gulf.

But for the Americans all hope was not lost. In the early hours of the all-night trek, the Third Fleet, or a part of it, could still be recalled to get back in time to "plug the hole" *if* the "Dirty Tricks Department" would just realize the grave potential danger. An opportunity for that realization came before midnight.

USS *Independence*, a CVL in Admiral Bogan's Task Group 38.2, had one of the U.S. Navy's few night-flying squadrons of World War II. In those still-fledgling days of naval aviation, the techniques of night carrier operations were not yet commonplace, and only a relatively few pilots had the requisite training and skills necessary. These men were organized into special squadrons, and two of these, one fighter and one torpedo, resided in *Independence* as Night Air Group 41.

As TG 38.2 moved north with the other Third Fleet task groups, the *Independence* night-flyers were launched for an "over-the-shoulder" look. As these nocturnal snoopers flew near San Bernardino Strait, they discovered that the navigation lights marking the channel had been turned on. This was a bad omen, to say the least. Navigation lights had been extinguished over most of the world when war had come, elevating tactical considerations to a higher precedence than normal navigational safety. That these lights had been turned on in San Bernardino Strait, in defiance of the wartime blackout, could mean only one thing. The risk that these lights represented must be outweighed by a larger tactical consideration. Such as the passage of a powerful fleet on a critical mission.

In the days of Napoleon, a Prussian general by the name of Carl von Clausewitz decided to write a book about war. He titled the lengthy treatise, rather appropriately, *On War*, and it has become one of the classic works on the subject, earning Clausewitz the reputation of "philosopher of war" and making his work required reading among actual and would-be strategists. In a chapter entitled "Friction in War," Clausewitz coined the term *friction* to describe conditions with which all warriors are familiar, whether they have read *On War* or not. Simply put, friction is a collective term that means all that can go wrong in a battle. In another chapter, entitled "Intelligence in War," Clausewitz described the confusion and difficulty of obtaining accurate information in the midst of an engagement, something other writers have termed the "fog of war."

These elements are present in virtually all battles, but at Leyte Gulf, friction was abundant and the fog of war was particularly thick. A little before midnight, Admiral Bogan, embarked in his flagship, *Intrepid*, received a TBS call from Captain Edward C. Ewen, commanding officer of

Independence. Ewen told the admiral about the navigation lights in San Bernardino Strait and that the *Independence* night-flyers had also actually sighted Kurita's force coming east through the channel. Bogan drafted a message to Halsey, warning him of what the night reconnaissance had discovered and recommending that Halsey detach Task Force 34 and Bogan's TG 38.2 from the rest of the Third Fleet so that these forces could return to the San Bernardino Strait area and wait for Kurita to emerge. Bogan tried to call Halsey by tactical voice radio to deliver his message, but because the admiral was resting, Bogan got one of Halsey's staff standing watch in flag plot instead. Bogan began to read the message he had drafted, beginning with the night reconnaissance information regarding San Bernardino Strait. When he got to the part about the navigation lights, the anonymous voice representing the Third Fleet retorted with an impatient "Yes, yes, we have that information." Bogan took that retort as "a brush off" and decided not to say anything more.

One opportunity to correct the error had come and gone. The entire Third Fleet continued unhesitatingly north.

On board USS *Washington*, one of the powerful Third Fleet battleships steaming northward with Halsey, some members of the staff of Vice Admiral Willis A. Lee, Commander Battleships Pacific Fleet, had been discussing this trek northward and were having some grave doubts. They were worried that this Japanese Northern Force might be a decoy to lure the Third Fleet away from Leyte Gulf. They went to Lee and advised him that they believed the admiral should call Halsey and warn him of the imprudence of leaving San Bernardino Strait open. In the discussion that followed, the politics of inter-admiral relations were evaluated. The consensus appeared to be that Admiral Halsey was not the easiest man to approach with an idea counter to his own. It was feared that if Lee told Halsey what he thought should be done, Halsey might very well do the opposite. Sometimes it was better to keep quiet and let Halsey and his staff come to their own conclusions. But to these men the situation seemed potentially disastrous, so they urged Lee to take a chance and make the call to Halsey.

Lee agreed with his staff and believed that Kurita's force could be handled by a detachment of battleships deployed across the entrance of San Bernardino Strait to cap the T just as Oldendorf was doing at that very moment in Surigao Strait. He was only mildly concerned about the vulnerability to air attack such a force might suffer when daylight arrived, and concluded that the detachment of only one or two of Halsey's light aircraft carriers would be sufficient to counter that threat.

By both signal light and voice radio, Lee attempted to call Halsey and express his concerns. To both messages he answered with a perfunctory "Roger" and nothing more.

One of Lee's staff expressed the concern that they might not be dealing with Halsey himself, but instead with a watch officer acting as a buffer while the admiral slept. When the night reconnaissance report from *Independence*'s night-flyers came in, Lee tried again. An abrupt "Roger" was again the only response.

Lee, too, gave up.

Admiral Mitscher had also gone to bed. Like Halsey and many others in the fleet, this commander of Task Force 38 was tired from many months of arduous operations. There is even reason to believe that his health was poor, adding to his fatigue. And then there was the matter of his having been squeezed out of his command responsibility by Admiral Halsey. There simply was not much for Mitscher to do with Halsey at the reins of the fleet.

But Mitscher's chief of staff, Commodore Arleigh Burke, was not asleep. And the more he thought about what was transpiring, the less he liked it. He couldn't understand what the Japanese were trying to accomplish by bringing in their carriers separately from the other forces. He reasoned that the Marianas Turkey Shoot must surely have convinced the Japanese they could not hope to prevail in a toe-to-toe carrier battle with the Americans. And there were the reports that most of the Japanese planes that had come in from the north had not gone back that way but had flown on to land bases in the Philippines. It had to be a ruse, he concluded. The northern carrier force must be a decoy. And they were taking the bait.

When the second message arrived, confirming the presence of Kurita's force in San Bernardino Strait, Burke and the staff operations officer, Commander James Flatley, decided to wake Mitscher. The two officers went to the admiral's cabin and entered. Mitscher, who was once described by a fellow officer as not looking a day over eighty, woke from his sleep looking very weary. Burke and Flatley explained their concerns, emphasizing that they believed Halsey should either turn around or at least detach a force to go back and guard San Bernardino Strait. When Flatley produced the messages from *Independence*'s night-flyers, the admiral's crease-lined eyes widened perceptively. "Does Admiral Halsey have that report?" he asked.

"Yes, he does," replied Flatley.

Mitscher, resting on one elbow in his bed, thought for a moment, his leathery features even more furrowed than usual, and said, "Admiral Halsey has all the information we have. He may have more. He is a very busy man in the midst of planning and executing a complex operation. Any suggestions we send to him gratuitously will add to his problems and won't help him." In a tired voice, Mitscher added, "If he wants my advice, he'll ask for it." Then he rolled over to go back to sleep.

The third opportunity to correct the error was lost.

These three failed attempts by Halsey's subordinates are indeed tragic in light of what transpired the following morning. In two of the cases, it was the lack of receptivity from Halsey's staff watch that had short-circuited attempts to warn Halsey of his mistake. Bogan felt rebuffed by the curt and apparently impatient response, "Yes, yes. We have that information," and Lee could get no response other than the simple radio codeword "Roger," meaning only "I have received your radio transmission." One might argue that Admiral Bogan should not have been so quick to give up, but Admiral Mitscher's point that Halsey was a busy man and "any suggestions we send to him gratuitously will add to his problems and won't help him" has validity and would give any subordinate pause when contemplating giving unsolicited advice. It is not an easy undertaking for a subordinate to tell his boss that the latter may be making a mistake, and there is a natural reluctance to press the point once offered and apparently not received with enthusiasm.

In Mitscher's case, it is difficult to decide with certainty what was truly behind his reluctance to call Halsey with unsolicited advice. Was it indeed predicated upon his realization (from experience, no doubt) that such advice can be a worrisome irritation to a commander who is indeed on top of the situation with a better picture of what is happening than is available to his subordinates? Or was it simply that Mitscher was piqued by Halsey's rather insensitive assumption of command, leaving Mitscher out of the chain of command for most of the battle? The response "If [Halsey] wants my advice, he'll ask for it" can be taken either way.

Another question that arises is whether Halsey himself was aware of and, therefore, rejecting the significance of the *Independence* night-flyers' reconnaissance reports, or was it his staff watch, serving as buffer for the sleeping admiral, that insulated him from this crucial information and therefore deprived him of the opportunity to reconsider his decision to go north with his entire fleet. His after-action report, submitted to King, via Nimitz, immediately after the battle, admits that he "recognized the possibility that the Center Force [Kurita] might come through San Bernardino Strait and on to attack Leyte forces," but goes on to explain that he "was convinced that the Center Force was so heavily damaged that it could not win a decision, while the possible maximum strength of the Northern Force . . . constituted a fresh and powerful threat." This report by no means clears up the question of whether Halsey knew, the night of 24–25 October, about the reconnaissance reports of Kurita's transit of San Bernardino Strait, but his use of the phrase "*might* come through San Bernardino Strait" indicates that he did not know of the reports confirming the Japanese force in the strait. But Halsey's discounting of Kurita's force as being "so heavily damaged that it could not win a decision" makes the question irrelevant.

In his postwar autobiography, Halsey explained his decision to take his whole fleet north based on the perceived threat and his desire to preserve "my fleet's integrity," making no mention of the *Independence* reports. From the moment he decided to go after Ozawa, his attention was focused on the north, and there was no further mention of Kurita's force until the following morning, when it was too late.

Later, in his appended comments to an article about the Battle of Leyte Gulf by Hanson W. Baldwin, Halsey admitted that "night snoopers not only scouted the Northern Force but also the Sibuyan Sea and made reports of Kurita turning once again to the eastward." But then Halsey added, "A report of this was directed sent [*sic*] to Kinkaid around 2100 or 2130 that night." This second statement makes it clear that Halsey felt no personal responsibility for Kurita's Central Force; that he believed Kinkaid could and should handle Kurita; that, at this point, he saw his responsibility as only that defined in the caveat to his orders from Nimitz, which said, "In case opportunity for destruction of major portion of the enemy fleet offers or can be created, such destruction becomes the primary task." One might argue that invoking that caveat was appropriate since Halsey did not know Ozawa's force was a decoy and believed that he had indeed discovered "a major portion of the enemy fleet." But the question immediately arises—was not Kurita's force also "a major portion of the enemy fleet"? And did not Halsey's orders also direct him to "cover and support [Kinkaid's] forces"?

Merely to forward to Kinkaid the information that Kurita was on his way through San Bernardino Strait is not the action of a prudent commander. Halsey should have at least queried Kinkaid about his ability to handle both the Southern and Central Japanese forces while he, Halsey, took all of his much more powerful force to cover only the one Japanese force coming down from the north. There is too much assumption in this action. Halsey assumed that Kurita was so badly damaged as to no longer pose a serious threat to the Seventh Fleet. Yet, if that were true, why, then, was Kurita still coming? Halsey also assumed that since he heard no protest from Kinkaid regarding his move north, then Kinkaid must have approved. It apparently did not occur to Halsey that there might be some misunderstanding causing Kinkaid's lack of protest, or that perhaps Kinkaid had not even received all the information Halsey had sent him. It is unlikely that Halsey would have tolerated such assumptions from his subordinates. His rise to power in the U.S. Navy was not based on such careless behavior.

It is difficult to see this situation as Halsey must have been viewing it at the time. Perhaps, in his commendable early recognition of the carrier's dominance in modern naval warfare, Halsey had forgotten that the battleship could still be a potent weapon under the right circumstances. Perhaps it was Halsey's unsated thirst for the big victory at sea that blinded him to the reality of the situation and caused him to charge off so recklessly after Ozawa's carrier force. Or maybe Bull Halsey was just plain tired.

Whatever the explanation, Halsey and his entire fleet were headed north, while Kinkaid's fleet had gone south and Kurita's fleet was once again steaming east.

Of course, Halsey and the "Dirty Tricks Department" were not the only ones making assumptions that night. On board the Seventh Fleet flagship *Wasatch*, Kinkaid and his staff were assuming that Halsey was covering San Bernardino Strait. They, too, had not made any attempt to confirm what they assumed.

But, in the case of the Seventh Fleet, this lack of thoroughness did not persist throughout the night. As the action in Surigao Strait was drawing to a close, Admiral Kinkaid called a meeting of his staff to review the night's events. Kinkaid wanted "to see if there was anything we had forgotten to do or anything that we were doing that was wrong." As the meeting drew to a close, somewhere around 0400, Kinkaid's operations officer, Captain Richard H. Cruzen, spoke up. "Admiral," he said in a voice laced with weariness, "I can think of only one thing. We've never asked Halsey directly if Task Force 34 is guarding the San Bernardino Strait." Kinkaid considered that for a few seconds and then agreed. Within a few minutes, a message was on its way to Halsey asking him to confirm the presence of TF 34 at San Bernardino Strait. It seemed that, at last, the "fog of war" was about to lift. But Clausewitz's ever-present friction intervened. Because of the roundabout communications channels that had been set up between Halsey and Kinkaid, this message did not get to Halsey for another two and a half hours. Too late to stave off disaster.

After the meeting broke up, Dick Cruzen and the staff intelligence officer, Art McCollum, lingered to discuss the situation. Neither was convinced that Halsey was guarding San Bernardino Strait and one of them said, "Well, my lord, we ought to find out about this thing." Together, they drew up a reconnaissance plan that called for the so-called "Black Cats"* to scout the area around the strait and then convinced Kinkaid to approve the plan. But, again, friction reared its ugly head and somewhere between plan and execution, the search coordinates were transposed, and the reconnaissance was carried out over a useless sector to the west instead of the critical one devised by Cruzen and McCollum.

And the fog of war remained, thick and dangerous as ever.

---

* A land-based night reconnaissance squadron that flew specially configured versions of the PBY Catalina seaplane.

PART VI

★ 25 October 1944 ★

18

★ "Charge of the Light Brigade" ★

Wednesday, 25 October 1944. Sunrise 0627. Partial squalls in the morning. Second day of the decisive battle. Taking advantage of the dim moonlight of her seventh lunar night through a cloudy sky, we passed San Bernardino Strait without incident at 0035 and formed Alert Formation No. 19 on an easterly course.

So began Vice Admiral Ugaki's diary entry for the early hours of the twenty-fifth, describing the unimpeded passage of Kurita's force through San Bernardino Strait. His entry of the night before reflected Ugaki's frequent optimism despite the traumatic loss of *Musashi* and the heavy air attacks he himself had witnessed from the bridge of *Yamato*. He wrote of "enough confidence to deal with an enemy once we could approach and reach it." But he also expressed his concern for what lay ahead by adding, "What I fear is that the enemy which detected our movements continuously tonight will concentrate their attacks upon us . . . after dawn comes." Ugaki believed that unless they could count on support from their land-based air forces, "All of our fighting strength will be reduced to nothing at the end."

Ugaki's commander, Takeo Kurita, agreed with that estimation and, during the night, sent a message appealing once again for air support the following day. He also sent a message declaring, "Braving any loss and damage we may suffer, the First Striking Force will break into Leyte Gulf and fight to the last man."

Commander Tonosuke Otani, Kurita's staff operations officer, had spent the night expecting that the force would have to fight its way out of the strait when they emerged on the eastern side. He was surprised but not

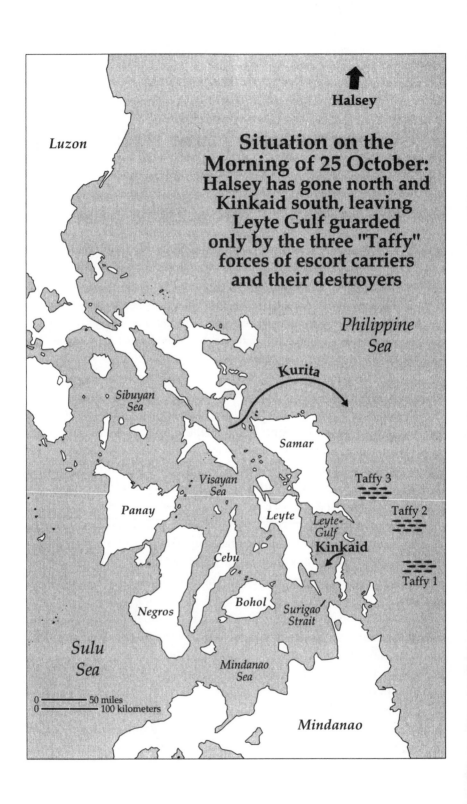

Luzon

**Situation on the
Morning of 25 October:**
Halsey has gone north and
Kinkaid south, leaving
Leyte Gulf guarded
only by the three "Taffy"
forces of escort carriers
and their destroyers

Halsey

Philippine
Sea

Kurita

Sibuyan
Sea

Samar

Visayan
Sea

Taffy 3

Panay

Leyte

Taffy 2

Leyte
Gulf

Kinkaid

Cebu

Taffy 1

Negros

Bohol

Surigao
Strait

Sulu
Sea

Mindanao
Sea

0 ——— 50 miles
0 ——— 100 kilometers

Mindanao

much relieved when they steamed out of the narrow waters and found the sea ahead to be empty. He remained convinced that it was only a matter of time before the hammer fell. His first concern was that the apparently vacant waters meant that the Americans had opted for a submarine ambush. When anxious minutes passed with no underwater contacts and no reports of torpedo wakes, Otani surmised that they would run into the Americans before they reached the southern tip of Samar.

Kurita, too, had expected his ships to have to fight their way out of San Bernardino Strait and had ordered all units to man battle stations as they emerged from the confining waters. When the force steamed out unopposed, Kurita was too tired to have any noticeable reaction. He stared dully at the empty sea and simply ordered the mission to continue, forming the ships into a night search disposition. He placed the battleships in the center with the cruisers and then the destroyers grouped in columns on the flanks, somewhat ahead of the battleships. The entire formation had a front extending over thirteen miles.

For the next six and a half hours, Kurita's Central Force steamed on toward Leyte Gulf, the monotony broken only by several messages from the Japanese forces in Surigao Strait. The first two messages had revealed little of what was occurring, but the last one, arriving about 0530, reported that the battleships had been destroyed and that cruiser *Mogami* had been seriously damaged and was on fire.

For Kurita's ships, the lack of enemy opposition was both welcome and unsettling. The inactivity made staying alert difficult, yet the continued expectation of an American attack by submarine or surface force haunted the Japanese throughout the night, keeping the tension level at a draining high. All through the early morning hours, worried eyes strained to pierce the darkness, scanning the surface of the sea for ominous shadows, while weary ears listened to the strange chorus echoing in the ocean's depths, trying to discern manmade sounds from the natural ones residing there. As the sky brightened in the east, the tension level increased. Soon the skies, too, would be potentially hostile as American warbirds left their nocturnal roosts to begin their diurnal search for prey.

At 0623, *Yamato*'s radar picked up several aircraft and Kurita sent a signal reforming his fleet into an antiaircraft disposition. The large force had begun to reorient itself into the new, circular position when lookouts spotted several masts piercing the horizon to the southeast. They were the telltale thin masts of American ships, and as Kurita turned his formation toward them, more masts appeared. It soon became clear that there was a sizable American force ahead.

That force was actually Taffy 3, but reports began pouring in describing the American force as consisting of full-size carriers, cruisers, and even battleships. Why the Japanese mistook the tiny CVEs and destroyers and destroyer escorts for much larger units is not entirely clear. Perhaps it was because the long-range nature of carrier warfare had prevented Japanese and American naval forces from getting close enough to actually see one another except on rare occasions during the war, so that the Japanese were unfamiliar with the appearance of their enemy's ships. Another explanation might be that the Japanese fully expected Halsey's Third Fleet to be waiting for them at Leyte Gulf, since they had not heard anything to the contrary from Ozawa, and after all they had been through, it was only natural to assume the worst when they at last sighted their adversary.

Whatever the reason, the Japanese had forfeited a great psychological advantage by their mistaken identification. Instead of entering the battle with the confidence that should have accompanied such a tremendous tactical advantage, they moved in with a fatalistic feeling of sacrifice and little hope of ultimate victory.

Even so, there was some cause for celebration. Attacking a full-blown American carrier force was a far more desirable option for Kurita than risking his fleet over the inglorious target of amphibious shipping in Leyte Gulf. Although his primary mission was to attack the American transports in the gulf, his orders, like Halsey's, included a caveat that permitted him to attack any American task forces that he might encounter along the way. His chief of staff, Tomiji Koyanagi, upon receiving the lookouts' reports that there were American carriers on the horizon, thought, "God has come to our assistance." Tears of joy trickled down the jubilant faces of many of the younger officers as they realized they had been given the opportunity to fight a worthy opponent after all.

Kurita did not hesitate. He ordered his fleet to engage the enemy. Within minutes, *Yamato*'s mighty 18.1-inch guns were preparing to fire for the first time at enemy ships. The huge barrels trained outward and aimed at the nearly defenseless American ships.

As darkness had given way to morning light on 25 October, the wind barely whispered across the calm surface of the Philippine Sea. Intermit-

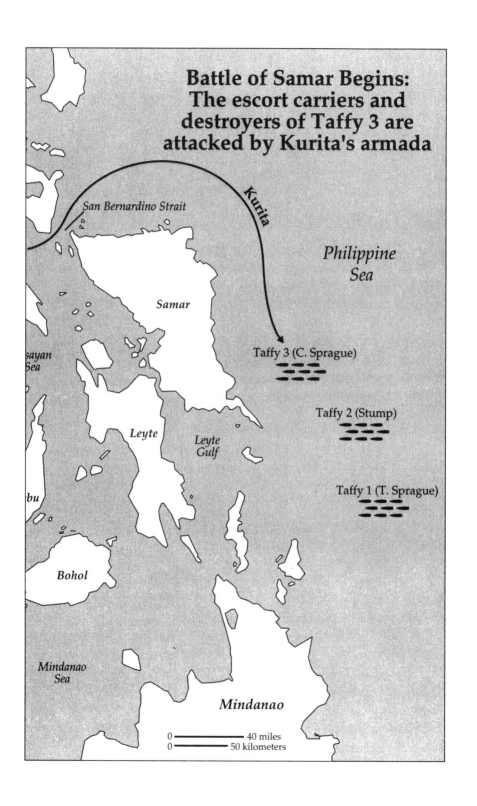

tent rain squalls occasionally disturbed the otherwise tranquil scene, but provided the six CVEs, three destroyers, and four destroyer escorts of Taffy 3 with "freshwater wash-downs" that rinsed some of the glistening salt from their weather decks.

This northernmost of the three Seventh Fleet escort carrier task groups had been steaming all night east of the island of Samar, waiting for daybreak so that flight operations could be resumed. To the southeast, the other two task groups had passed a relatively quiet night as well, Taffy 2 staying in an area almost due east of Leyte Gulf and Taffy 1 steaming off northern Mindanao. Another day of routine operations in support of the troops ashore at Leyte lay ahead for the flyers and crews of these mini-aircraft carriers.

Aboard USS *Samuel B. Roberts*, one of the small destroyer escorts assigned to Taffy 3, the crew was just securing from dawn general quarters and headed for breakfast. The captain, Lieutenant Commander Robert W. Copeland, should have taken advantage of the uneventful night by getting some sleep—one never knew when such an opportunity might come again—but he and the executive officer, Lieutenant Bob Roberts, had spent most of the night with the watch team in CIC, their ears glued to the TBS radio, listening to the talk of the ships slugging it out in Surigao Strait. It had been difficult to tell exactly what was happening. The radio chatter only gave hints of the action, and the distance and the intervening islands involved sometimes blocked or garbled the transmissions. Despite these handicaps, the picture that emerged from these electronic clues left no doubt that there had been a major engagement and that the Japanese had been routed. By daylight it was clear that the remnants of the Japanese Fleet were in full retreat.

This was exciting fare for the men of the "Sammy B," since the invasion of Leyte was the ship's first real wartime operation. *Roberts* had been built at Brown Shipbuilding in Houston, commissioned the previous April, and had joined the Pacific Fleet after a shakedown cruise in the Caribbean and a final fitting-out in Boston. To date, her most exciting moments had occurred in the midst of a typhoon that had preceded the Leyte landings.

The captain left CIC and headed for the wardroom in search of a cup of fresh coffee to help get the morning off to a proper start. He was just about to descend the ladder leading to officers' country when he was summoned to the bridge. The watch had just received a sighting report from one of the task force's Avengers flying early-morning reconnaissance. The pilot reported seeing a number of Japanese battleships, cruisers, and destroyers northwest of *Roberts*'s position. Almost simultaneously, the ship's lookouts reported seeing antiaircraft bursts in the sky to the northwest.

The captain and the executive officer casually watched the smudges of smoke popping out in random patterns among the cumulus clouds. Then a lookout reported, "Object on the horizon. Bearing two five zero relative. Looks like the mast of a ship." Lieutenant Bill Burton, the gunnery officer, had been trained in ship recognition techniques at a stateside school before reporting to *Roberts*. He peered through binoculars in the direction indicated by the lookout. What he saw looked something like a Japanese pagoda. He knew instantly that it was the fighting-top of a Japanese cruiser.

The captain and executive officer were remarkably calm under the circumstances. They had just spotted an enemy warship for the first time in either one's experience and had, just moments before, received an air reconnaissance report of a Japanese force not far away. Yet neither man seemed the least perturbed and neither made a move to prepare the ship for action. It seemed that the executive officer was about to react as one would expect when he stepped over to the ship's general announcing system microphone and activated the system. He leaned in to the mike and spoke. "Now hear this!" he said, using the Navy's standard phraseology to call for the crew's attention. "All hands desiring to see the fleeing remnants of the Japanese fleet, lay up topside."

After spending the night listening to the action in Surigao Strait, both the captain and the executive officer assumed that what they were seeing must be the whipped remainder of the Japanese Southern Force. It did not occur to them that what they were seeing was an entirely different fleet, Kurita's Central Force, nor did it occur to them that they might be in great danger at that moment. And probably among the last thoughts that might have occurred to either man was that, before the day was over, they would be swimming for their lives in the shark-infested waters of the Philippine Sea.

Sailors emerged from the various hatches and doors about the ship, some only half-clothed and wearing beards of shaving cream on their faces, others with cheeks puffed with breakfast. Everyone stared curiously to the northwest, looking for a glimpse of the "fleeing" Japanese so that they might someday see the awe in the eyes of others as they related how they had once been within sight of the enemy. But the Japanese were not fleeing. They were, in fact, coming on at 30 knots, and it didn't take an expert lookout to discern that the curiosities to the northwest were getting larger.

As the captain and XO watched and absorbed new data, such as the speed-up of the carriers to flank speed and the shifting of course to the east, the real situation began to dawn. Copeland ordered "General Quarters" and soon the men of *Roberts* were racing back to battle stations.

Three minutes later, bursts of green and purple water seemed to leap out of the sea between *Roberts* and the nearest carrier, *Fanshaw Bay*. Japanese shells, with their individually dye-marked bursts, were raining in.

Boatswain's Mate First Class Red Harrington watched as the colored bursts climbed into the morning sky off the ship's starboard bow. "Fleeing my ass!" he said.

With the morning light had come the resumption of flight operations for the CVEs. Rear Admiral Clifton A. F. "Ziggy" Sprague was the commander of Taffy 3 and had his flag in USS *Fanshaw Bay*, one of the so-called "Jeep carriers." These diminutive floating airfields had many other unofficial names. To the men in the fleet they were frequently referred to as "baby flattops," "Kaiser coffins,"* "tomato cans," and "wind wagons." They were what the sailors called "thin-skinned," meaning they had no double hulls, no armor, no torpedo blisters for defense. They were also very slow. Captain Walter Karig aptly described their speed capabilities when he wrote: "In a calm sea and with a following breeze these little ships might make 18 knots provided the engineering officer had been leading a good life."

Sprague watched from the bridge of *Fanshaw Bay*, as planes took off from the short flight deck, some loaded with depth charges in case any Japanese submarines appeared in the area, and others carrying antipersonnel bombs and strafing ammunition for use against targets ashore on Leyte Island.

At 0637, one of the men in *Fanshaw Bay*'s CIC, who had been monitoring the interfighter director net, began hearing voices speaking in what sounded like Japanese. He turned to the man next to him and said, "What do you make of that?" The second man listened for a moment, then said,

---

* Because many were built by Henry Kaiser's shipyards.

"Somebody's playing a joke." The first man shrugged and said, "Yeah, maybe. Or it could be long-range jamming." Taffy 3 continued the morning's routine.

Sprague looked out the bridge windows at the sea, now quite bright in the morning light. Ahead of *Fanshaw Bay* were the other CVEs under his command: *Kalinin Bay*, *White Plains*, *St. Lô*, *Kitkun Bay*, and *Gambier Bay*, all launching aircraft as the group headed northeast into the light morning wind. Screening the carriers were the destroyers *Johnston*, *Hoel*, and *Heerman*, and the destroyer escorts *Samuel B. Roberts*, *Dennis*, *Raymond*, and *John C. Butler*.

At about 0745, an excited voice called from CIC, reporting that one of the pilots had spotted an enemy surface force of four battleships, seven cruisers, and eleven destroyers just twenty miles northwest of the task group and closing at 30 knots. Sprague leaned over the "squawk box" and pressed the lever. "Air plot, tell that pilot to check his identification." Sprague's voice reflected the irritation he felt. The last thing he needed was for some overzealous aviator to get everybody excited by a misidentification of one of Halsey's task groups.

A moment later, air plot called the bridge. "The pilot insists that these ships are Japanese. He says they have pagoda masts!"

Sprague looked northwest and could see puffs of antiaircraft fire above the horizon. "Come to course zero-niner-zero," Sprague barked. "Flank speed. Launch all aircraft." Taffy 3 turned due east in response and puffs of black smoke from the CVE stacks signaled their increase in speed.

Away to the northwest, the pilot who had spotted the Japanese fleet dove in on the nearest enemy cruiser and released his weapons. They were depth charges meant for submarine targets. But they were all he had.

A few minutes later, the Japanese ships had closed to within eighteen miles of Taffy 3 and several colored geysers appeared within two thousand yards of the fleeing carriers. The next salvo fell even closer. It was only a matter of time before these deadly projectiles would find their mark. Closer still, the rounds walked in, and Admiral Sprague wondered what he could possibly do to save his task group.

Aboard the destroyer *Johnston*, Lieutenant Ed Digardi, the ship's communications officer and navigator, was not as surprised as some of the others in the task group by the Japanese shells cascading in from the northwest. He and the other officers in *Johnston*, monitoring the nighttime reconnaissance reports, had correctly deduced that Kurita was coming through San Bernardino Strait. Still, he could not help staring in awe as the great plumes of water climbed skyward about them. *Johnston* was the closest American ship to the oncoming Japanese force, and many of the Japanese shells were falling in her vicinity.

Digardi was the officer of the deck in *Johnston* whenever she went to battle stations; no small honor when bestowed by the likes of *Johnston*'s captain, Commander Ernest E. Evans, a full-blooded Cherokee Indian with a reputation as a formidable fighter. Evans's nickname—bestowed at the Naval Academy years earlier—not surprisingly was "Chief." This caused no small amount of confusion since, in the Navy, a chief is a senior enlisted man.

Evans was a short, barrel-chested man with a booming voice whom nearly everyone described as a born leader. He had earned his fighting reputation while aggressively hunting submarines in the Pacific and at Kwajalein, where he had taken his ship in close to shore to destroy some Japanese shore batteries that had been posing a serious threat to the landing forces there.

One of Ed Digardi's earliest impressions of Evans was formed when the captain spoke at the commissioning ceremony for USS *Johnston* on 27 October 1943. He told the crew and assembled guests that when war had broken out in the Pacific, he had been serving in an old, World War I–vintage destroyer, USS *Alden*, in the Java Sea near the Dutch East Indies. He explained that after the heavy cruisers *Houston* and *Marblehead* had been eliminated by the Japanese Navy, and the situation had become hopeless for the remnants of the U.S. Asiatic Fleet, *Alden* had been forced to beat a hasty retreat out of the Java Sea. "Now that I have a modern fighting ship,"—Evans indicated the bunting-draped *Johnston*—"I intend to go in harm's way," he promised, quoting John Paul Jones. Speaking with a conviction that Digardi sensed was sincere and irrevocable, Evans then said, "I will never again retreat from an enemy force."

Almost a year to the day from that moment, Evans was about to get the chance to prove just how sincere he had been. With Japanese ships closing on Taffy 3 and USS *Johnston* directly in their path, Evans's moment had come. He began issuing the orders that would take his ship "in harm's way."

Just below the bridge on the port side, Bill Mercer, who routinely worked in the ship's laundry, sat at his battle station as trainer for one of the twin 40-mm gun mounts. From that position he could hear the captain giving orders up on the bridge. Having seen the masts of Japanese ships poking above the horizon off *Johnston*'s port quarter when he first arrived at his station, Mercer was most gratified to hear the captain order, "All engines ahead flank." Heading away from the enemy as fast as possible seemed like an excellent idea to the eighteen-year-old Mercer. His happiness was short-lived, however. Before long he heard the captain's booming voice order, "Left full rudder," and watched as *Johnston*'s bow swung rapidly around *toward* the Japanese ships. Mercer began strapping on his life jacket.

As officer of the deck, Ed Digardi was preparing the ship for battle and carrying out the captain's specific instructions. Evans ordered a smoke screen and Digardi called the engineers and instructed them to begin making black funnel smoke while the ship's smoke generator detail began producing cottony white clouds that seemed to cling to the sea like a heavy fog.

Captain Evans instructed Digardi to bring the destroyer about and start zigzagging between the Japanese ships and the fleeing carriers. The object was to lay a curtain of smoke that would obscure the CVEs from view. While accomplishing this, Evans assured the crew, over the ship's general announcing system, that Admiral Halsey's Third Fleet would soon arrive to take over. He then ordered his 5-inch guns to commence firing on the nearest Japanese cruiser. Soon Digardi could see hits registering on the enemy cruiser's superstructure, which prompted the Japanese to retaliate. Giant splashes began falling closer to *Johnston*. Evans "chased the splashes" by steering the ship toward the last shot to fall, a tactic based on the theory that the shooting ship will correct a missed shot, making the site of the last shot a relatively safe place to be.

Quartermaster-striker Robert M. Billie watched the colored geysers leaping out of the sea from his lookout station on the port side of the flying bridge.* Because he hadn't seen any enemy ships since assuming his general quarters station as one of *Johnston*'s lookouts, Billie had been wondering if the reports of a Japanese Fleet in hot pursuit had been false. He no longer doubted as he watched the ship veering rapidly about in pursuit of

---

* The flying bridge on a ship is located above the regular bridge and is completely open to the air. Because of its additional height and less-obstructed view, this bridge is sometimes used by the conning officer for maneuvers requiring added visibility. It is also an excellent location for the stationing of lookouts.

the last enemy shell burst. It was the only time he could remember wanting to dig a foxhole.

As most of the carriers disappeared from view behind the smoke curtain, more of the Japanese ships turned their guns on *Johnston* in frustration. Lieutenant Digardi listened in awe as battleship rounds passed overhead, sounding like a fast-moving freight train as they roared by. It was becoming more and more evident that their chances of survival were poor at best and rapidly diminishing.

Pastel splashes began closing in on the destroyer from all sides, and Evans also must have been thinking in terms of the ship's demise, for he turned to Digardi and said, "We can't go down with our fish aboard." True to his reputation and his commissioning-day promise, Evans ordered, "Stand by for a torpedo attack." He then told Digardi to head directly for the formation of cruisers still bearing down from the northwest. As the ship came about, guns still firing at a furious rate, Digardi could clearly see the massive cruisers ahead, their dull gray forms highlighted by the flashes of gunfire. Beyond them he could make out the ominous forms of an echelon of battleships. This was sheer madness! One tiny destroyer charging an armada of some of the world's most formidable firepower.

As *Johnston* closed the enemy at an alarming rate, Lieutenant Jack Bechdel, the torpedo officer, took the conn and steered the ship according to the firing solution provided by the torpedo director's analog computer, using the lead cruiser, *Kumano*, as his point of aim. Soon a strange language, laced with mathematical and nautical terminology, was echoing about *Johnston*'s bridge:

"Range thirteen thousand yards. Target speed two-five knots. Train mount one to one-one-zero relative; mount two at one-two-five relative. Range twelve thousand yards. Target angle zero-four-zero. Set running depth at six feet. Range eleven thousand yards. One degree spread. Mount one, three-five degrees right gyro angle. Mount two, two-five degrees right gyro angle. Tube offset two-point-five degrees. Three second interval. Range ten thousand yards."

All the while, Japanese shells fell all about *Johnston*, miraculously none finding their target, but the odds of such continued good fortune diminishing with each near-miss.

While the ship charged headlong at the enemy, Lieutenant Digardi stood on the port wing of the bridge near the torpedo officer, the captain, a third-class signalman, and the squadron recognition officer who had boarded at Manus just before *Johnston* departed for the Philippines. Bechdel fired all ten of the ship's torpedoes and returned control to Digardi, who stepped into the pilothouse to give orders to the helm. He steered *Johnston* into her own smoke screen to gain some respite from the cascading Japanese gunfire. Moments later, the sound of distant underwater explosions indicated that some of the torpedoes had found their mark.

Johnston emerged from the smoke screen and those crew members who could look were treated to the welcome sight of flames burning brightly on *Kumano*'s fantail. But any elation felt at that moment was quickly extinguished as *Johnston*'s phenomenal luck ran out. Three 14-inch shells slammed into the destroyer's after engine and fire rooms, followed by a 6-inch salvo that struck *Johnston*'s port bridge wing and penetrated her 40-mm magazine. The ship immediately lost steering control and all power to her after gun mounts.

On the flying bridge, a piece of shrapnel struck the mouthpiece of Robert Billie's sound-powered phone, shattering the instrument and filling the young sailor's mouth with blood and broken teeth. Billie looked down and could see several dead and wounded men scattered about the deck below. A subsequent explosion lifted Billie into the air and slammed him down on the steel deck, knocking him unconscious. Upon reviving, he saw his shoes, still neatly tied, lying next to his head.

A few minutes after the rounds hit *Johnston*, Bill Mercer heard someone above him call, "Stand by below." Mercer watched as a pair of khaki-clad legs dangled into view. Someone on the bridge was lowering one of the officers to the main deck. As the khaki shirt appeared, Mercer could see that it was covered with blood. The lowering paused for a moment, and then Mercer saw to his dismay and horror that the officer's body had no head.

The decapitated squadron recognition officer was not the only victim on the bridge. Lieutenant Digardi had rushed out of the pilot house to the port bridge wing right after the shells had crashed into *Johnston*. He found terrible carnage. Besides the headless officer, Digardi discovered that the torpedo officer had lost a leg and the signalman had been blown to bits. The captain was still alive but bleeding from shrapnel wounds to his neck, chest, and hand.

On the flying bridge one deck up, Robert Billie discovered that he was bleeding from every limb and that the only one he could move was his left arm. In a state of shock, he again lost consciousness.

As Bill Mercer looked about the mangled ship, trying to forget the image of the headless body that had dangled in front of him, he saw that mount 52, one of the forward 5-inch gun mounts, was still firing at a furious rate but that the deck around the mount was filling up with expended brass shell casings that threatened to inhibit the mount's rotation. Mercer and another 40-mm gunner, J. B. Strickland, ran forward and began jettisoning the brass casings as fast as they could. When they had cleared most of the brass from the deck, Mercer and Strickland returned to their guns. Almost immediately after their departure from the mount 52 area, the gun took a direct hit.

On the bridge, which one observer later described as looking "like a kid's BB target," the ship's doctor tried to minister to the captain's wounds. But Evans, whose shirt and helmet had been blown off his body, refused treatment, saying, "Don't bother me now. Help some of those guys who are hurt." Ignoring the wounds to his neck and chest, Evans then wrapped his bleeding hand in a handkerchief and returned to the business of fighting his ship.

Admiral Sprague had few options in this one-sided battle. His ships were vastly outgunned and his carriers could not even run away since their top speed was only about half that of their pursuers'. In desperation, he sent out a plain-language radio message at 0701 giving his position and that of the enemy force and asking for help from anyone who could provide it.

Trying to offer some reassurance, Admiral Felix Stump, commander of Taffy 2 farther south, called his friend Sprague on the TBS. "Don't be alarmed, Ziggy," he said. "Remember, we're back of you. Don't get excited. Don't do anything rash!" Those who heard the call from Stump remembered that, despite the reassuring words, the admiral's voice was anything but reassuring, rising in pitch and volume as he spoke.

Sprague quickly ordered all ships to begin making smoke, hoping that a thick blanket of it might hinder the Japanese fire-control solution. Some of the ships were equipped with special smoke generators made specifically for this purpose, and they began pumping out billows of thick, white smoke. The other ships improvised by reducing the air-to-fuel ratio of their power plants, which had the normally undesirable effect of belching great clouds of heavy, black smoke into the atmosphere. The heavy, humid air blanketing the Philippine Sea kept the smoke screens close to the surface, so that the area was soon belted with layers of black and white smoke.

But the smoke did not thwart the Japanese gunfire. Flagship *Fanshaw Bay* and USS *White Plains* were the closest CVEs to the approaching Japanese force and both were in serious trouble. *Yamato*'s shells began falling menacingly about *White Plains*, raising tall plumes of pink-dyed water into the air. Then *Kongo*'s rounds began hitting nearby as well, and fountains of yellow-tinted water leaped upward. Soon these were joined by geysers of red, green, blue, and purple water as other Japanese ships tried to hit *White Plains*. A young sailor watching the colorful spectacle from the CVE's flight deck suddenly shouted, "They're shooting at us in Technicolor!"

The kaleidoscopic shooting was becoming more accurate with each salvo. Soon *White Plains* was straddled by four shells, two forward and two aft, and all very, very close. Some of the colorful water cascaded down onto the CVE's fight deck, and one round hit so close astern that her captain believed she had taken a hit and immediately reported as much to Admiral Sprague. The detonation jarred one of the ship's planes out of its chocks, and as it surged forward, its spinning propeller sheared off a sizable piece of the wing of the fighter just ahead of it. The near-miss also caused *White Plains* to lose steering control, and the ship began careening haphazardly. With clouds of smoke pouring forth and the ship staggering about with her rudder temporarily useless, she must have appeared down for the count, because moments later the Japanese shifted their fire away from *White Plains* and onto other inviting targets in the vicinity.

While the American ships were struggling to survive, the aircraft that had been hurriedly launched by the CVEs were doing their best to fight back against the oncoming Japanese marauders. In their haste to get airborne, many had taken off armed with fragmentation bombs and some were armed with depth charges. Some had only machine-gun bullets to throw at their thick-skinned Japanese adversaries. And some had no ammunition at all. Even with these handicaps, the pilots bore in on their enemies as though they were armed to the teeth. The bombs and bullets they did have, while doing no serious damage, could not be ignored entirely. The Japanese were forced to devote a measure of their attention to antiaircraft fire, and men at exposed gun stations and on the bridges of the Japanese ships were frequently forced to keep their heads down because of the constant buzzing by persistent American aircraft. It was a situation not unlike that experienced by people harassed by small flying insects; while there is no serious threat, there is enough irritation to be terribly distracting.

Even those flyers who had taken off with no ammunition, and others who quickly expended what they had on board, flew into the face of heavy Japanese gunfire[*] in order to keep up the pressure. There was no shortage of courage among these men as they braved the intense fire in a desperate attempt to keep the Japanese at bay. It is difficult to imagine the kind of fortitude required for such an act. In tribute to his enemy, Commander Otani, Kurita's operations officer, later described what he witnessed from *Yamato*'s bridge: "The attack was almost incessant but the number of planes at any one instant was few. The bombers and torpedo planes were very aggressive and skillful, and the coordination was impressive; even in comparison with the great experience of American attack that we had already had [the day before in the Sibuyan Sea], this was the most skillful work of your planes."

But it was going to take more than the courage of some persistent aviators to prevent Kurita from doing a great deal of damage to the vulnerable Taffy 3. With the giant *Yamato*, three other battleships, and a potent force of cruisers and destroyers still under his command—all of which had a considerable speed advantage over the fleeing CVEs—Kurita was in a position to do more harm to the U.S. Navy than had been done since the attack on Pearl Harbor.

Far to the north, Commander David McCampbell, who had shot down the record-setting nine enemy aircraft the day before, was again airborne. This time he was flying as target coordinator for a large group of Third Fleet aircraft, headed for Ozawa's sacrificial force.

Halsey had ordered the air armada to take off at the first glimpse of dawn's light. By the time they were airborne, Halsey, in his flagship *New Jersey*—now a part of Task Force 34—was miles ahead of the carriers.

The Japanese Northern Force was by then located off the northern tip of Luzon, opposite a jut of land known as Cape Engaño. The battle about to take place there would forever be remembered by the name of that cape. In one of those incredible ironies that have no logical explanation, the

---

[*] It should be remembered that because Kurita knew, before embarking on this mission, that he could count on little air support, he had equipped his ships with more antiaircraft guns than were usually allocated and had spent a great deal of time training his gun crews in antiaircraft procedures.

Spanish word *engaño* translates to "trick," "deceit," or "fraud" in English. How appropriate to the decoy mission of Admiral Ozawa!

Ozawa's chief of staff, Captain Toshikazu Ohmae, was certain that an American attack was forthcoming. He even knew the approximate range of his enemy. In his experience of fighting the Americans, he had learned that they had certain predictable patterns. He knew that his foe nearly always sent out reconnaissance patrols at about a half-hour before sunrise. When he received a report that morning of aircraft snooping around the force, he calculated that the American Fleet must be about a hundred miles away.

Besides McCampbell, there were twenty-six other aces in the strike group that first reached Ozawa's force. Little wonder that the eighteen Japanese fighters they encountered flying combat air patrol over Ozawa's carriers were quickly eliminated.

With no fighters to oppose them, the American aircraft had only the ship's antiaircraft fire to contend with. Within minutes, Ozawa's ships were enveloped by flocks of attack aircraft, and soon their wakes were marked with streaming oil and long tails of black smoke.

As target coordinator for the strike, McCampbell flew above the action, using his radio call sign "Rebel 99" while directing the swarms of planes to the wildly maneuvering Japanese ships below. One of the destroyers was hit and sank immediately. The light carrier *Chitose* was the first of the flattops to succumb. At 0937 she disappeared into the Philippine Sea, a great froth of white water momentarily marking the fluid grave site.

Ozawa was embarked in *Zuikaku* during these attacks. This veteran carrier was one of the last surviving ships that had participated in the raid on Pearl Harbor, and she had fought in nearly every major battle of the Pacific since. But this would be her last. The early attacks completely disabled her communications capability and damaged her rudder, so Admiral Ozawa shifted his flag to the light cruiser *Oyoda* as soon as there was a lull in the fighting.

The second strike arrived from the Third Fleet carriers and McCampbell directed them as well. With the arrival of the third strike, it was time for McCampbell to go back to his ship, so he was relieved on station by Hugh Winters, commander of *Lexington*'s air group. Winters had brought with him the largest strike of the day, numbering more than two hundred aircraft, and soon these fresh attackers had *Zuikaku* on the ropes.

From his new flagship, Ozawa watched the old carrier endure still more damage as the American aircraft hammered at her relentlessly. Whether he thought of it at that precise moment is not known, but later Ozawa would lament the Imperial Japanese Navy's earlier decision to commit the bulk of his air complement to the defense of Formosa. Had he been able to retain those planes and pilots, undertrained as they may have been, the Battle of Cape Engaño might have been less one-sided. As it was, all the Japanese ships could do was maneuver violently about and fight back with their antiaircraft guns. These were tactics proven ineffective time and again during the war. Given enough attacking aircraft, ships had very little hope of surviving for long without supporting aircraft of their own. *Zuikaku* was no exception. By the afternoon she was gone.

Fortunately for the Americans, Kurita was not in his best fighting trim and was not taking full advantage of his overwhelming superiority off Leyte Gulf. Upon first sighting the U.S. carrier force, he had not formed his ships into a battle line, which would have made him most potent by allowing his larger ships to coordinate their fire while the destroyers led the attack with torpedoes. Instead, he ordered a "general attack" which, in essence, meant a "free-for-all," causing his attack to be chaotic and wasteful.

This by no means meant that Taffy 3 was going to survive, however. Uncoordinated as the Japanese might be, they pressed the attack, coming ever closer to the fleeing Americans, their 8-, 14-, 16-, and 18.1-inch guns hurling literally *tons* of metal and high-explosive at the thin-skinned carriers and their diminutive escorts. It seemed that nothing could save the ships of Taffy 3, that it was only a matter of time—and not much of that—before the American ships would be pulverized by the heavy-caliber shooting of Kurita's Central Force.

Then Mother Nature took pity on the outclassed Americans by providing a brief respite. A sizable squall swept down from the north providing what one military historian has aptly described as a "seagoing foxhole." Sprague and his carriers jumped into it, taking advantage of the cover provided by steering headlong into the storm. Once enveloped by the squall, the small carriers became temporarily invisible to the eyes and radar of their foe, and for a little while they were safe from the Japanese gunfire. But Kurita's ships continued to close the distance, and the squall was moving south faster than the CVEs could keep up. It was only a matter of time before the squall would move on, exposing the American ships once again to almost certain destruction.

Regardless of the one-sided battle going on just over the northern horizon off Cape Engaño, there was no jubilation in Halsey's flag plot aboard USS *New Jersey*. Something was amiss.

The first hint of trouble had come a little before 0700, when Halsey had received a message from Kinkaid, which from the date-time group had obviously been sent much earlier. It informed Halsey that Kinkaid's forces were engaging an enemy surface force in Surigao Strait. Well enough. But at the end of the message there was a question from Kinkaid that bewildered Halsey: "Is TF 34 guarding San Bernardino Strait?"

This was the first indication that Halsey had that Kinkaid was even aware of Task Force 34, since the commander of the Seventh Fleet had not been included as an addressee on any of the messages Halsey had sent regarding the creation of this force. He was further dismayed that Kinkaid apparently believed that TF 34 was guarding San Bernardino Strait. After all, Halsey *had* included Kinkaid on his message informing everyone that he was "proceeding north with 3 groups."

The puzzled Halsey immediately sent a reply to Kinkaid informing him of what Halsey thought should be obvious. He said that Task Force 34 "is with our carriers now engaging enemy carriers."

More than an hour passed in which the only other communication from Kinkaid was a report that all was going well in Surigao Strait. But then a third message arrived, stating that "Enemy BB and cruiser reported firing on TU 77.4.3 from 15 miles astern." Halsey wondered how Kinkaid had allowed Ziggy Sprague to get caught like this. But Halsey was still not alarmed—he figured that the eighteen CVEs in Task Group 77.4 could protect themselves until Oldendorf's gunships could come to their rescue.

But eight minutes later, Halsey's expectations were dashed when yet another message arrived from Kinkaid. "Urgently need fast BBs Leyte Gulf at once," the message read. Halsey was surprised by this plea. He later wrote that "it was not my job to protect the Seventh Fleet. My job was offensive, to strike with the Third Fleet, and we were even then rushing to intercept a force which gravely threatened not only Kinkaid and myself, but the whole Pacific strategy."

Despite Halsey's belief that he was not responsible for protecting

Kinkaid's amphibious fleet, he immediately sent a message off to Vice Admiral McCain, whose Task Group 38.1 was en route from the Ulithi area to rejoin with the other elements of TF 38. Halsey ordered McCain to divert his force "at best possible speed" to the Leyte Gulf area to aid Kinkaid.

At 0900, another plea from Kinkaid read, "Our CVEs being attacked by 4 BBs, 8 cruisers, plus others. Request Lee [commanding TF 34] cover Leyte at top speed. Request fast carriers make immediate strike." Halsey's response was to "become angrier" since there "was nothing else I could do."

Several more messages flew back and forth between Kinkaid and Halsey, in which Halsey gave his position so that Kinkaid could see the impossibility of his requests, and Kinkaid repeated his pleas, growing more strident with each succeeding one. Finally, Kinkaid, in apparent desperation, sent a message in plain language without the usual time-consuming coding. This one practically shrieked, "Where is Lee? Send Lee."

Halsey, quite exasperated by now, was about to send yet another negative response, when he suddenly received another message. This one was not from Kinkaid, and it was a message he would remember for the rest of his life. It was from Nimitz.

On the twenty-fifth of October in the year 1854, a battle occurred at a place called Balaclava in the Crimean Peninsula of the Ukraine. This engagement was part of a war the world has all but forgotten, and the Battle of Balaclava would itself have certainly been forgotten—since it was of no great tactical or strategic significance, had occurred as the consequence of miscommunications among commanders, and was decidedly one-sided—except that a man known as Alfred Lord Tennyson chose to immortalize the engagement in a poem. That literary masterpiece describes the courageous attack of a small and lightly armed British cavalry unit, numbering only six hundred men in an age when armies took the field by the thousands. This diminutive unit of horsemen had no hope of victory, yet thundered its way along the floor of a valley overlooked by Russian heavy artillery. Tennyson's poem extolled the selfless courage and sacrifice of the moment. He called that poem "The Charge of the Light Brigade."

Ninety years later—*to the day*—the escorting ships of Taffy 3 faced similar circumstances, and they, too, responded with selfless courage and made the noble sacrifice for which there is no equal.

The squall, which had provided temporary shelter for the fleeing Americans, moved on to the south, leaving Taffy 3 vulnerable once again to the Japanese onslaught. Admiral Sprague ordered the destroyers and destroyer escorts of his force to conduct a torpedo attack against Kurita's oncoming armada.

"Forward the Light Brigade!
Charge for the guns!" he said:

It was a desperate call, but Sprague had little alternative under the circumstances. Despite the reassurances Captain Evans had given the men of *Johnston*, Halsey was *not* coming to their aid, and the fate of this unimpressive little force would be decided entirely by its own actions.

"Forward the Light Brigade!"
Was there a man dismayed?
Not though the soldier knew
Someone had blundered:

Aboard heavily damaged USS *Johnston*, steering had to be accomplished by emergency cables and the destroyer was under way on only one engine, reducing her to half-speed and half-power. She had no gyrocompass, her search radar antenna was dangling uselessly from the mast, and, although power had been restored to two of the three after gun mounts, mount 54 was reduced to firing manually in local control.

From his vantage point in the gun director, Lieutenant Robert C. Hagen, the ship's gunnery officer, could see *Hoel, Heerman,* and *Samuel B. Roberts* racing by at full speed in response to Admiral Sprague's order to "Form one eight for torpedo attack." It was obvious to Hagen that Sprague's order did not apply to *Johnston*, since she had already expended all her torpedoes and, with her speed reduced to only 17 knots, had no hope of keeping up with the other escorts. But the "Chief" had other ideas. In his booming voice, Captain Evans ordered his ship to fall in astern of the other escorts to provide gunfire support. As he prepared to direct *Johnston*'s gunfire, Lieutenant Hagen said to himself, "Oh, dear Lord, I'm in for a swim."

Theirs not to make reply,
Theirs not to reason why,
Theirs but to do and die:
Into the valley of Death
Rode the six hundred.

Lieutenant Digardi, too, had assumed that the order for a torpedo attack did not apply to *Johnston* and had headed her south once her steering had been restored. When Evans had ordered Digardi to come about and head back toward the enemy, he had been momentarily surprised until he remembered the captain's words at the commissioning ceremony: "I will never again retreat from an enemy force."

As the four American escorts charged boldly at their formidable Japanese adversaries, both sides were firing at one another at a furious rate. Tiny 5-inch shells bounced off the thick hides of Kurita's ships, while heavy-caliber rounds roared through the air and peppered the water all around the Taffy 3 escorts, some of them slamming into the already wounded *Johnston*. Still generating smoke, the three escorts with torpedoes remaining charged in to deliver these more potent weapons, while the limping *Johnston* valiantly struggled to keep up, firing her remaining guns with amazing persistence.

> Flashed all their sabres bare,
> Flashed as they turned in air
> Sabring the gunners there,
> Charging an army . . . :

Bill Mercer had been driven from his battle station by a raging fire that had engulfed his gun mount. He and seven or eight other men were huddled under a gun tub as the relentless pounding of Japanese shells continued. Suddenly, for no discernible reason, Mercer headed forward, leaving the other men still huddled beneath the gun tub. When he had gotten a few yards away, he heard and felt a tremendous explosion behind him. When the smoke cleared sufficiently, he saw that a Japanese round had landed directly beneath the gun tub, killing all of the men who had just seconds before been his companions. Turning away from the awful sight, he again started forward. But another round detonated close aboard *Johnston*, this one forward of Mercer's location. He immediately felt a searing heat to his face as he saw cascades of water, dyed the color of blood, pouring over *Johnston*'s gray superstructure.

> Stormed at with shot and shell,
> Boldly they rode and well,
> Into the jaws of Death,
> Into the mouth of Hell

The tenacious courage displayed by the American escorts was not wasted. The cruiser *Kumano* was out of the battle, licking the wounds inflicted by *Johnston*'s earlier torpedo attack. The cruiser *Suzuya* also withdrew from the battle in order to transfer the commander of Heavy Cruiser Division Seven and his staff from crippled *Kumano*. This latest torpedo run by the other escorts had scored several hits and forced *Yamato* to turn away and temporarily head north, taking with her the longest-range guns in the force and losing about seven miles in her pursuit of the carriers, as well as removing the Japanese Fleet commander from the battle for a time.

Plunged in the battery-smoke
Right through the line they broke;
Cossack and Russian
Reeled from the sabre-stroke

Confusion reigned on both sides during this wild melee. As *Johnston* emerged from the pall of smoke that by now had been woven in a tangled pattern all about the area, the starboard lookout suddenly yelled to Digardi, his voice filled with apprehension. The young lieutenant turned in the direction indicated by the lookout and saw that *Heerman* was off his starboard bow, close aboard and heading right for *Johnston* at full tilt. Both ships immediately rang up "All engines back full," though for *Johnston* this meant only one engine could respond. The two destroyers surged at each other as though drawn by some evil magnetic force, both vessels shuddering under the strain of propellers beating frantically in reverse. Then, by a margin of less than ten feet, the two ships managed to miss one another. With no time for even an exhalation of relief, the men of *Johnston* and *Heerman* immediately refocused their attention on the enemy.

Digardi turned away from *Heerman* only to see the battleship *Kongo* looming out of the smoke at a range of seven thousand yards. By now the only way *Johnston* could be steered was by sending the orders by sound-powered phone from the bridge to the after steering compartment, where exhausted sailors were laboring to operate the rudder's hydraulic system by hand. With such poor steering capability, *Johnston* was not able to effect her turn until she was within five thousand yards of *Kongo*. The destroyer's 5-inch guns continued to hammer away at the huge battleship as the two ships closed on one another. Incredibly, *Johnston* got in so close to *Kongo* that the great vessel's guns were unable to depress their elevation enough to aim at the small gray irritant so close aboard. For a brief moment, *Johnston* was able to strike at will at an enemy that was unable to retaliate.

Meanwhile, *Hoel* had been scampering about for quite some time, engaging Japanese ships without sustaining any major damage to herself. But her luck ran out and she found herself surrounded by a battleship and several heavy cruisers who began to chew at her mercilessly. Firing over five hundred rounds in defiance, *Hoel* eventually succumbed to the more than forty hits she received over the next twenty minutes. Listing heavily to port with one magazine on fire and her engines completely knocked out, she was ordered abandoned by her captain at approximately 0830.

Cannon to right of them,
Cannon to left of them,
Cannon behind them
Volleyed and thundered;
Stormed at with shot and shell,
While horse and hero fell,
They that had fought so well

As *Hoel* endured her death throes, the destroyer escort *Samuel B. Roberts* steamed by, her captain resisting the urge to come to *Hoel*'s aid despite the emotional devastation of the act. Captain Copeland knew that to succumb to that humanitarian temptation would probably do little good for the men of the stricken destroyer and would only spell doom for his own ship and crew, who were, at that exact moment, engaged in a running gun battle with a Japanese cruiser.

Early in the battle, *Roberts* had hit one of the Japanese ships with several of her torpedoes and had been dealing with this vengeful cruiser ever since. Just as *Johnston* had done, *Roberts* had managed several times to get so close to the Japanese ship that the latter had been unable to lower her guns enough to get a proper bead on her tiny adversary. *Roberts*'s gun crews had been firing for so long and so continually that they had given up worrying about what type of ammunition to use. The men in the ammunition handling rooms beneath her two 5-inch gun mounts had been grabbing whatever was closest at hand and feeding it to the blazing guns above. As a result, the Japanese cruiser was being hit with all sorts of strange rounds, including some designed as illumination projectiles and even some dummy practice rounds loaded only with sand.

Six minutes after passing by the mortally wounded *Hoel*, Copeland heard one of his lookouts yell, "Captain, there's fourteen-inch splashes coming up astern!" From the pattern he saw astern, Copeland knew that the next rounds would hit him if he didn't do something fast. He immediately ordered "All engines back full," and *Roberts* began to tremble violently as the astern bell was answered by the alert engineers down below. The ship shuddered to a halt so quickly that her fantail was nearly engulfed by her own wake wave. A second later, a 14-inch round roared overhead and struck the sea just ahead of the ship, confirming the wisdom of Copeland's quick reaction.

But *Roberts* had pushed the odds as far as they would go. In avoiding the approaching battleship rounds she had made herself vulnerable to the cruiser who had been her particular nemesis for the better part of two hours. Three 8-inch armor-piercing shells struck her on the port side forward. Because *Roberts*'s hull contained no armor, the Japanese shells did not detonate, but instead passed completely through the ship, entering the port side and exiting the starboard, leaving neat, round holes at each location. While preferable to the terrible destruction that would have occurred upon internal detonation, these rounds were not without serious consequences. Two of the shells exited below the waterline causing flooding in the forward ammunition handling room and in the compartment containing the ship's master gyro. The latter damage was more serious since it shorted out all electrical power to the radios, radars, and gun mounts. It also took the lives of two electricians who were trapped in the small compartment and drowned. But the most serious damage was done by the third round, which cut right through the ship's main steam line in the forward fire room. High-pressure steam roared into the fire room instead of into the turbines where it was meant to be, instantly killing three of the five men on station there. The other two men were scalded, one of them doomed to a lingering and extremely painful death, the other, an eighteen-year-old by the name of Jackson McKaskill, destined to survive as a hero. Although already burned by the ferocious steam, McKaskill made his way through the intense heat and confusing darkness to shut off the air and fuel supplies to the offending boiler. He then removed the sound-powered phones from one of his dead shipmates and reported the damage and casualties. By the time he had completed these level-headed actions, all the flesh had been seared from the bottoms of both feet.

With half her engine power gone, *Roberts* lost much of the agility that had kept her alive for so long. Almost simultaneously, four more rounds smashed into the wounded destroyer escort. Captain Copeland heard the detonation and turned in time to see several bodies hurled outward from the spot where once there had been a 40-mm gun mount and now there was only unidentifiable wreckage and a massive cloud of smoke. Another round sapped still more of *Roberts*'s power and her speed was further reduced. Then round after round crashed into the hapless ship, piercing her flimsy hull, ripping into her inner compartments, smashing her vital equipment, and tearing apart her human components.

Captain Copeland was trying to assess his damage—his guns had fallen silent for the first time since the battle had begun—when out of the swirling bands of smoke came the spectral image of USS *Johnston*. By now her bridge was a total shambles, smoke and flames adorned her almost everywhere, her mast was bent double, and her large radar antenna dangled loosely, banging against her superstructure with every roll of the ship. One of her gun mounts had been completely obliterated and there was only a hole where one of the torpedo mounts had once resided. But to Copeland's utter amazement, *Johnston* was still under way, still firing at the enemy.

As the mangled destroyer passed close by *Roberts*, Copeland could see her Cherokee skipper on the fantail, shouting conning orders down through the hatch leading to the after steering compartment. Evans was stripped to the waist and covered with blood. As *Johnston* steamed by, Evans looked up at Copeland and casually waved. Copeland returned the gesture, not realizing at the time that he was waving farewell to this incredibly brave man.

As *Johnston* disappeared into the veils of smoke as hauntingly as she had appeared, Copeland began getting his damage assessments. Both 5-inch gun mounts were finished. The after mount had gone out in a particularly tragic and awe-inspiring manner. During most of the long engagement the after mount had fired manually when power had been lost. This required not only that pointing and training had to be laboriously done by hand, but that the 28-pound powder cases and 54-pound projectiles had to be manually lifted up from below decks in order to be loaded. Despite this handicap, the gun crew had kept the gun firing at an incredible rate, and with the relentless firing, the gun had become quite hot. When the crew was down to their last seven rounds, they abruptly lost the compressed air supply to the gun. This air was essential to the safe firing of the weapon because it was used to clear the barrel of dangerously hot gases between rounds. To fire such a hot gun without the ejecting air would be a very hazardous undertaking. Shunning the danger, the men had continued to fire the weapon. As they were loading the final powder charge, it "cooked off" before they could close the breech, blowing the mount apart and killing or fatally wounding all but one of the ten-man crew. When a member of the repair party entered what was left of the shattered gun mount, he found the gun captain, Gunner's Mate Third Class Paul Henry Carr, torn open from neck to crotch with most of his internal organs exposed to view. Carr, still alive, was holding the last projectile, begging for someone to load it in the gun and fire it. He died a short while later, lying next to the gun he had served so well.

With so much damage, no weapons left with which to fight, enemy shells still raining in, and his ship sinking beneath him, there seemed no alternative for Copeland but to order, "Abandon ship." This was not an easy decision for the captain of this tiny destroyer escort, and he later recounted his thoughts at that moment:

> You have a love for a ship and it's difficult for you to abandon your ship because she seems to be a living thing. Besides, it's hard to order men to go out and jump into the water. We were out in the Philippine [Sea], about seven miles deep. It was a pretty rugged place. It was like jumping out of the frying pan into the fire, but we knew the frying pan; we were going to burn in there and we didn't know whether the fire would go out or not.

Copeland gave the onerous order and men began helping their wounded shipmates over the side while others went about the business of destroying classified material. As the last of the crew was leaving the ship, Captain Copeland took one final turn about his ship's main deck, making certain that everyone who was still alive had left or been removed. As he passed beneath the ship's wrecked motor whale boat, he paused for a moment and looked up. What he saw, for some reason, stuck in his memory:

> I could look from the deck up through the bottom of the boat. It was a sight I will never forget. That one picture summed up the whole desolate destruction of a living ship with living men coming into the emptiness of nothing. I realized I was the only person alive on that side of the ship. A feeling of utter loneliness came over me. It made me shudder. . . . Down

on the deck there lay three men, two of whom I could identify and one I couldn't. They were dead.

Copeland moved on, so wrought with emotion that he could not pay attention to where he was walking. Suddenly his feet slipped out from under him and he went down hard on the deck in a sitting position. His hands had instinctively broken the fall and as he lifted them from the wet deck, he saw that they were covered with blood. He realized he was sitting in a rather large pool of fresh blood. As he started to get up, trying not to slip in the crimson puddle, the seat of his trousers soaking wet and his shoes painted red, he felt something like rain spattering down on him. He looked up and saw the headless corpse of a man draped over the wreckage of one of the 20-mm guns, the last vestiges of blood dripping from the lifeless body.

Shakily, Copeland got to his feet and moved on. In his haste to escape the dreadful sight, he nearly fell into the gaping maw of a shell hole that had laid open his ship's engine room. Through the big hole Copeland could see water pouring into the space while flames crackled and spat in protest.

All the while, Japanese shells fell on and around the dying ship. A single destroyer was by now their only tormentor.

Copeland headed for the bow of the ship and leaped off it into the sea. *Roberts* was left alone to die. Or nearly so. As a dozen sailors clung to one of the life rafts, they suddenly realized they were being drawn back toward the ship. Seawater rushing into a gaping wound on the ship's side had formed a current as strong as a rushing river, and the raft was being swept along toward the jagged hole. Flames flickered within the dying ship as the men paddled frantically against the current, trying to escape being sucked back into the sinking ship. But they were unable to stem the tide, and soon the raft was at the gaping hole. Some of the men desperately clutched the torn metal that framed the opening while others paddled for their lives. They were still in that precarious position when the current subsided enough to allow the twelve Jonahs to escape Leviathan's grasp, and they quickly paddled away as the ship slowly disappeared from sight.

As *Roberts* gave up the ghost, *Johnston*, too, was mortally wounded. Like hungry wolves, a pack of Japanese cruisers and destroyers had closed in on the gallant destroyer and were pounding her into submission. She had fought long and hard, several times interposing herself between the attackers and the helpless CVEs still fleeing for their lives. She had endured the intense barrage much longer than anyone could ever have imagined. But her time had run out and Captain Evans at last gave the order for her crew to leave her.

As communications officer, Lieutenant Digardi was responsible for carrying out the destruction and disposal of classified materials. With three men to assist him, Digardi went to the radio shack, where he found a total shambles and all the men dead. He quickly destroyed a coding machine that had somehow survived the devastation and then headed for his stateroom where he kept a number of classified documents and publications. Placing these in weighted canvas bags designed for the purpose, he and the other men tossed them into the sea. As explosions continued to rock the ship, Digardi and the three sailors then filled a mattress cover with the remaining materials, weighted the large sack with several 5-inch shell casings, and jettisoned this as well.

The party of four men then started to return to the bridge when Digardi was summoned to the wardroom by the ship's doctor. Digardi told the other three to go back to the bridge. As he started for the wardroom, he saw a shell slam into *Johnston*'s side, killing the three sailors he had just sent to the bridge.

In the wardroom, the doctor told Digardi that he needed some life jackets to put on the wounded he had been treating. Digardi went out to the main deck in search of the jackets and immediately saw the torpedo officer, Jack Bechdel, trying to get himself over the ship's rail. The stump where his leg had been was dressed, but the lieutenant was too weak to get himself over the side of the ship. Digardi grabbed him by the back of the neck and seat of the trousers and helped him over the rail. As he watched his friend splash into the sea, there was a direct hit just behind Digardi, and he, too, left the ship, hurled into the air and flying some thirty feet from *Johnston* before slapping into the water.

Meanwhile, amid all the destruction and carnage, Robert Billie had regained consciousness. He could barely move and was unable to talk, and he lay helpless as several men passed by him, apparently assuming him dead. With only his left arm functioning, he pulled himself slowly across the deck. Each pull was agonizing, and his many shrapnel wounds oozed blood with each exertion, leaving a red smear to mark his path. At last he reached the rail, but like Bechdel, he was too weak to pull himself over. And like Digardi, Billie was assisted by the Japanese. A close salvo hit lifted him over the side and threw him into the sea.

Bill Mercer had left *Johnston* in a more conventional manner, jumping off the port side amidships and swimming quickly away where he joined up with a friend who, supported by his kapok life jacket, was neatly combing his hair. When the sailor had finished the task, he tossed the comb into the water saying, "I don't guess I'll ever need that again."

As the survivors of *Johnston* floundered about in their new environment, watching their ship slowly disappearing into the sea, they saw a Japanese destroyer bearing down on them. Fearing they were about to be strafed, many slipped out of their life jackets and dove beneath the water for protection. Others feared being depth-charged and tried to float on their backs, believing they would sustain less injury this way. Still others watched in fatalistic terror as the Japanese vessel rapidly approached.

But the Japanese ship did not strafe and did not depth-charge these men. Instead, some of the crew tossed cans of food to their enemies now floating helplessly in the water. And many of *Johnston*'s survivors then witnessed something they would never forget. There on the bridge-wing of the Japanese destroyer, an officer stood watching as *Johnston*, his mortal enemy of just moments before, slipped beneath the waves. As the noble ship went down, this Japanese officer lifted a hand to the visor of his cap and stood motionless for a moment . . . saluting.

> When can their glory fade?
> O the wild charge they made!
> All the world wondered.
> Honour the charge they made!
> Honour the Light Brigade,
> Noble six hundred!

19

★ "The World Wonders" ★

While the battles were raging off Samar and off Cape Engaño in the Philippines, Admiral Nimitz, three thousand miles away at Pearl Harbor, was pitching horseshoes. Early in his tenure as CINCPAC, Nimitz decided that one way to quell some of the hysteria that followed on the heels of the Pearl Harbor attack was "to create an atmosphere of quiet determination and orderly planning at CINCPAC Headquarters." He set up a pistol range just outside his office, and near his living quarters a half-mile away, he had a horseshoe court built. "I spent a lot of time at both places," Nimitz later said, "and I often invited war correspondents to join me. I hoped they would report the confident, relaxed atmosphere. And they did!"

Nimitz continued this practice as the war progressed and October 1944 was no exception: "During the Battle of Leyte Gulf, one of the most crucial sea battles in history, all of us at CINCPAC Headquarters eagerly awaited news of the outcome. I was on pins and needles but couldn't show it. So I went to my quarters to pitch horseshoes, telling my staff, 'If word comes, you can reach me there.'"

But, by the time Kinkaid had sent his plain-language "Where is Lee? Send Lee" message, Nimitz could stand the tension no longer and went back to his gray concrete headquarters building at Makalapa Crater. Nimitz's anxiety grew as he read the messages from Kinkaid describing the perilous situation of Sprague's Taffy 3 CVEs, and his confusion grew as he read Halsey's responses. Like so much of the U.S. Navy, Admiral Nimitz had assumed that Halsey had left Task Force 34 behind to guard San Bernardino Strait.

Nimitz concluded that it was time to give Halsey a gentle nudge. He decided to send a message that would remind Halsey that others were monitoring the situation with some concern. This might also alert the Third Fleet Commander that there was indeed some confusion about what Halsey had been doing.

Nimitz instructed his chief of staff, Admiral Forrest Sherman, to draft a message asking Halsey to clarify the position of Task Force 34. Sherman dictated the brief message to a yeoman who scribbled it out in typical Navy form, using all upper-case letters to avoid confusion and, noting the emphatic tone in Sherman's voice, inserted a repeat function for added emphasis, so that the message read, WHERE IS RPT WHERE IS TASK FORCE THIRTY FOUR. The message was then sent down to the communications facilities in the basement of CINCPAC headquarters for immediate coding and transmission. It was down in these communications spaces that an ensign assigned to Nimitz's staff—who has managed to remain anonymous—would have an inadvertent but terribly significant effect upon the Battle of Leyte Gulf.

During the war, Pacific Fleet communications doctrine required that any brief message prepared for encryption was to have additional phrases added as "padding" at the beginning and end of the message to complicate the decryption efforts of the enemy. Such added phrases were to be deliberately and obviously meaningless so as to be clearly distinct from the actual message, and, as an additional precaution against confusion, the meaningless phrases were to be set apart from the real message by a pair of repeated letters. For example, if a commander wished to send an encrypted message to a subordinate saying "attack the enemy at dawn," the actual message might go out as RAIN MAKES MUD PUDDLES QQ ATTACK THE ENEMY AT DAWN LL PUPPY DOG TAILS. Anyone familiar with these procedures who read such a message would know which parts of the message were padding and which part was the actual intended communication. It was common practice for decoding officers on the receiving end of such a message to remove the extraneous phrases before forwarding the decrypted message to their commanders.

The anonymous ensign, whose fortune it was to be the officer on watch that day while the battles off Samar and Cape Engaño were going on, took Nimitz's message for Halsey and began preparing it for encoding and transmission. As called for by doctrine, he dutifully added the phrase TURKEY TROTS TO WATER to the beginning of the message, followed by a pair of G's. So far so good. But at the end of the message he added a phrase that by unhappy coincidence was to alter the course of the two battles raging in the Philippines. Not realizing the danger of misinterpretation, he chose the seemingly innocuous phrase THE WORLD WONDERS. There is some debate as to whether it was incredibly ironic coincidence or whether this ensign had actually realized that this day was the anniversary of the Battle of Balaclava and had recalled this phrase from Tennyson's "The Charge of the Light Brigade," where it does appear. Either way, the damage was done.

When the fateful message, TURKEY TROTS TO WATER GG WHERE IS RPT WHERE IS TASK FORCE THIRTY FOUR RR THE WORLD WONDERS, arrived aboard Halsey's flagship, the decoding officer removed the phrase preceding the GG separator. But, because the phrase THE WORLD WONDERS seemed to fit the text of the actual message, the decoder—who has also managed to remain anonymous—failed to remove the phrase and included it on the copy sent to Halsey. Two compounding errors—the use of a phrase at the transmitting facility that was not clearly nonsensical, and the failure of the receiving facility to remove it, despite the two-letter separator RR— were compounded a *third* time by Halsey's failure to notice the two-letter separator when the message was handed to him aboard USS *New Jersey*. So instead of reading Nimitz's intended gentle nudge, Halsey read what he interpreted as a sarcastic slap, WHERE IS RPT WHERE IS TASK FORCE THIRTY FOUR THE WORLD WONDERS.

Enraged and hurt by what he interpreted as stinging criticism from his friend and advocate, Chester Nimitz—criticism that would be witnessed by both Kinkaid and Admiral King, who were both information addressees on the message—Halsey lost his self-control. Tears poured from his weary eyes as he yanked his cap from his head and threw it to the deck. It was all too much.

His chief of staff, Mick Carney, grabbed the admiral by the shoulders. "Stop it!" Carney said. "What the hell's the matter with you? Pull yourself together!"

Halsey did. But it was through a blind rage that he made his next decision. Still smarting from what he believed to be Nimitz's stinging criticism, and finally recognizing that his responsibilities lay in two different areas, Halsey at last divided his forces. He detached the battleship group, Task Force 34, and Bogan's Task Group 38.2 to head south for Leyte Gulf. He left behind Sherman's TG 38.3 and Davison's TG 38.4 to deal with Ozawa's Northern Force.

With Ozawa's battleships a mere forty-two miles from the guns of his own dreadnoughts (which had a range of half that distance), Halsey, embarked in battleship *New Jersey*, turned south. With that change of course, Bull Halsey forever denied himself the opportunity to engage the enemy in a surface fight, something he had dreamed of since his earliest days at the Naval Academy.

And because he was so far north, time and distance dictated that he would not reach Leyte Gulf until the next morning. What he would find upon his arrival there he could not be sure, but one thing was clear—he was not going to arrive in time to have any effect on the battle then being fought off Samar. He compounded his error by taking along the screening destroyers, which were low on fuel. This required his whole force to slow down while the destroyers replenished their fuel from the larger ships.

By his rash decision, made in a state of anger and disappointment, Halsey had condemned himself to a kind of limbo, steaming on a tranquil sea between the battles of Samar and Engaño. The situation was described well by novelist Herman Wouk in his monumental work, *War and Remembrance*, when his protagonist, "Pug" Henry, watches the agonizingly slow process of refueling from the bridge of his mighty battleship and laments his plight. "It was a bitter sight; bitter to be becalmed in this great Battle Line in the midst of vast engagements, not yet having fired a shot."

Regardless of the noble efforts of the screening destroyers and destroyer escorts, the escort carriers of Taffy 3 were still in serious trouble. Flagship *Fanshaw Bay* had been hit several times, USS *St. Lô* had been hit six times, and *Kalinin Bay* had received at least double that number of hits. *Kitkun Bay* was straddled several times but remained unhit, while *White Plains* had been surrounded by so many near-misses that she had been obscured from view by towering splashes much of the time—not a single Japanese shell had actually struck her. But it was USS *Gambier Bay* who was in the most serious trouble.

When Taffy 3 had involuntarily emerged from the protective squall, *Kalinin Bay* and *Gambier Bay* were at the rear of the formation and, therefore, closest to the oncoming Japanese force. For about a half-hour, Captain W. V. R. Viewig, commanding officer of USS *Gambier Bay*, was able to prevent his ship from being hit by using the "chasing salvos" tactic. At 0741, the CVE's only weapon, a single 5-inch gun, opened fire on the pursuing enemy. At 0810, *Gambier Bay* received her first hit. Before long, she was hit again. And again.

Just as with the thin-skinned escorts, the CVEs had nothing substantial enough to cause detonation of the Japanese armor-piercing rounds raining down on them, so that these shells passed completely through without exploding. While this was undeniably fortunate, the large number of rounds striking *Gambier Bay* was having its effect. Captain Copeland of *Roberts* had caught a glimpse of *Gambier Bay* during the battle and described this unfortunate CVE as looking like a colander.

Some of the more serious damage resulted from a near-miss that hit near the waterline and ruptured *Gambier Bay*'s hull plating near the forward engine room. Water poured into the engine room at an estimated rate of 19,000 gallons per minute, far too much for the de-watering pumps, which had a maximum capacity of 1,200 gallons per minute. The ship began to list noticeably as the incoming water took its effect. Soon *Gambier Bay* was reduced to a speed of a mere 11 knots, and her pursuers drew closer at a much faster rate.

From the catwalk surrounding *Gambier Bay*'s flight deck, Photographer's Mate Second Class Allen C. Johnson watched helplessly as Japanese shells of various sizes flew through his ship. He also saw some of the projectiles skip across the flight deck without penetrating or detonating and could feel still others hitting inside the ship beneath him. One internal hit detonated, and Johnson was amazed to see the flight deck undulate like a wave at the seashore. It was about that time that the young petty officer decided it was time to go get his dress blue uniform. Months before he had listened with deep interest as an older sailor had told him of his woes after surviving the sinking of his ship. The veteran had spun a sad tale of not being able to go on liberty for months after he had been rescued because he had lost all his dress uniforms when the ship had gone down. Johnson was not about to let that happen to him, and since it was becoming increasingly clear that *Gambier Bay* was not going to survive this beating, Johnson headed for the ship's photo lab where he had stowed a set of dress blues, neatly rolled into a tight package for just such a purpose as this.

He opened one of the light lock doors leading to the interior of the ship from the catwalk. A great deal of black smoke poured forth from the open door, so Johnson paused for a moment to let the smoke clear. When he could see, Johnson saw that the deck was missing a few feet inside the passageway. He was glad he had not rushed in.

His way to the photo lab blocked, Johnson abandoned his quest for the dress uniform and turned back to the catwalk to return to his station.

Along the way, he encountered a young seaman from the fire rescue team sitting on the catwalk deck, his arms crossed in front of him and tears pouring down his cheeks. As Johnson got closer he heard the seaman saying, "I'm ruined, I'm ruined," over and over. Johnson saw that the young man's abdomen had been torn open and he was trying to hold in his intestines.

Johnson moved on and encountered another man staring glassily into space, apparently uninjured but with trickles of saliva seeping from his mouth. The man did not acknowledge Johnson as he passed by but kept staring with uncomprehending eyes.

In sharp contrast to this understandable but nonetheless unsettling sight, Johnson next came upon a lookout sitting casually in a chair looking for all the world as if the day's activities were as routine as any other. With the roar of Japanese shells in the air, the ship shuddering under the impact of hit after hit, the pungent smell of smoke permeating the atmosphere, and dead and wounded men within sight, this young lookout was peering through his binoculars, periodically reporting what he saw over sound-powered phones, and humming a tune to himself between reports. As Johnson approached him, the lookout turned and casually asked, "How ya doin'?"

Astonished, Johnson answered, "Fine," then added, "how're *you* doing?"

"Okay," the lookout said calmly. "Pardon me," he added, then spoke into his sound-powered phone set. "*Tone*-class cruiser bearing zero six zero now three thousand yards," the man said as though reporting the weather rather than an enemy ship. With a friendly smile, the lookout turned back to Johnson. "What were you saying, pal?"

About that time, a salvo of shells tore into *Gambier Bay* with great impact, one of them ripping into the after engine room, causing extensive damage. The men in the engine room had no choice but to secure what they could and get out as quickly as possible to avoid drowning in the great rush of water that poured into the space like a raging river. With that hit, *Gambier Bay* had lost all propulsive power. She wallowed to a stop and, symbolically, her ragged ensign drooped forlornly from the gaff, the loss of relative wind taking all the starch out of the national colors. There could be no doubt. She was a doomed ship.

Captain Viewig surveyed the situation and came to the inescapable conclusion that his only option was to abandon his ship. Listing, burning, powerless, and pathetic, *Gambier Bay* had no hope of survival. Viewig was the last man off the ship and, as he left her, a Japanese cruiser was less than a mile away, still firing. At 0911, *Gambier Bay* capsized to port and went down, settling into one of the deepest valleys in the Pacific Ocean.

It was the first time an American aircraft carrier had been sunk by gunfire. The Japanese had claimed another U.S. ship, the fifth so far. And they were not through yet.

Southeast of the action off Samar, Rear Admiral Felix B. Stump had begun preparing his Taffy 2 aircraft to join the fray the moment the earliest reconnaissance reports had come in warning of the approaching Japanese ships. Although Stump had not anticipated the attack by Kurita's force, he had foreseen the potential need for attacks on the remnants of the Japanese force in Surigao Strait and had warned his crews to be prepared to load their aircraft with ordnance suitable for antiship action on short notice. As a result, many of the Avengers on his CVEs were loaded with torpedoes, rockets, and general-purpose bombs in relatively short order.

Under the circumstances, the choice of any prudent commander would have been to steer his vulnerable force away from the Japanese force. But because the wind was from the northeast, Stump had no choice but to order his formation to steer in that direction to get enough wind across the decks to launch the heavily loaded aircraft. He was thus forced to bring his ships much closer to the attacking Japanese force, giving up some of the safety margin he had enjoyed by being positioned farther away when the battle had begun. On the bridge of his flagship *Natoma Bay*, Stump discussed this predicament with one of his staff officers, Ben Grosscup, while the launches were taking place. "When I was at the Academy as a midshipman," Stump said, his eyes fixed on the ominous horizon to the northeast, "we used to talk about the deathless statements of our old naval heroes, and I've often wondered just what sort of deathless statement I would make at the appropriate time. The one that sticks in my mind is that of John Paul Jones, who said, 'No naval commander makes a tactical error in laying his ship alongside that of the enemy.'"* At that moment, the sig-

---

* Admiral Stump's knowledge of naval history was admirably patriotic but nonetheless flawed. He attributes the saying to the wrong naval hero. It was not the American John Paul Jones who uttered this famous saying, but the British admiral Horatio Nelson who actually said, "No captain can do very wrong if he places his ship alongside that of the enemy."

nal flag representing flight operations dropped from the yardarms of the carriers, indicating that the launch was complete. Grosscup said, "Fox is down on all ships, Admiral." Stump, still staring in the direction of the oncoming Japanese Fleet, said, "John Paul Jones to the contrary notwithstanding, the time has come to get the hell out of here." Stump then ordered flank speed in the opposite direction.

The aircraft launched from the Taffy 2 ships joined the fray, adding their limited but very welcome capabilities to the fight. Stump had instructed the pilots to fan out and hit as many Japanese ships as possible, rather than bunch up on just a few. They complied, and Taffy 2 aircraft were soon swooping all over Kurita's formation, mingling with the planes of Taffy 3 and enduring the heavy Japanese antiaircraft fire. Before the battle was over, they would lose fewer aircraft than the beleaguered Taffy 3, but twelve Avengers and eleven Wildcats would not return.

From the bridge of *Yamato*, Admiral Ugaki followed the progress of the battle. He listened to reports from battleship *Kongo* that she had sunk an *"Enterprise*-class carrier," not knowing that this was not a full-size carrier as reported, but the CVE *Gambier Bay* instead. He heard reports from *Yamato*'s officers that they had sent a "cruiser" to the bottom, again not knowing that this was the destroyer *Hoel*. He absorbed the report from the commander of the Tenth Destroyer Squadron that his ships had torpedoed and sunk one *"Enterprise*-class carrier" as well as severely damaging another. Ugaki had no way of knowing at the time that those Japanese destroyers had actually made *no* hits on *any* American ships in that torpedo attack, much less *"Enterprise*-class carriers."

Even in the face of all these inflated reports, Ugaki did not feel that Kurita was making the best use of his assets. As evidenced by his diary, he did not understand some of Kurita's actions: "Though its reasoning was unknown, the fleet order called for battleship divisions and heavy cruiser divisions to attack and the destroyer squadron to follow. The fleet's attacking directions were also conflicting and I feared the spirit of all-out attack at short range was lacking."

Ugaki shared his feelings with Kurita's chief of staff, Koyanagi, who passed them on to Kurita. Ignoring Ugaki's protests and effectively silencing them, Kurita directed Ugaki to concentrate on his own Battleship Division One.

When the American torpedoes caused *Yamato*, under Kurita's direction, to turn away and head north, losing ground on the enemy forces they were pursuing, Ugaki could not hide his impatience. "It was about ten minutes," he wrote in his diary, "but it seemed like a month to me."

Koyanagi, too, followed the battle from *Yamato*. He was impressed by the effectiveness of the Americans' use of smoke. Japanese radar was not very efficient and this utilization of smoke had made gunfire accuracy a difficult thing to achieve. Still, he had seen with his own eyes an American aircraft carrier hit many times and could see that it was sinking. And there were reports of others as well.

One thing that worried Koyanagi was the fuel state of the force. Hot pursuit at high speed was consuming the precious asset at an alarming rate. What was worse, for all of this high speed and consequent burning of huge quantities of fuel, it did not appear to the chief of staff that they were gaining on the Americans.

Kurita shared Koyanagi's concerns about the fuel consumption, and he, too, felt they were making little if any progress in their chase. This is puzzling because a review of the American accounts of the battle, as recorded in logs and veterans' testimonies, reveals the opposite view—that the Japanese were, in fact, quite obviously gaining. The speed differential between Kurita's warships, the slowest of which was 24 knots, and the Taffy 3 carriers, whose maximum speed was 17 knots (under the best of circumstances), establishes the American view as correct. But what is often paramount in war is not what actually *is* the truth, but what is *perceived* as the truth.

The inflated reports from his subordinates notwithstanding, Kurita was feeling less than enthusiastic about the battle raging about him. He had lost cruisers *Kumano*, *Suzuya*, *Chikuma*, and *Chokai* to torpedo and bomb attacks delivered by American aircraft and ships he believed to be part of a powerful American task force. He was certain that more task forces must surely be lurking not too far away, and it would be only a matter of time before those additional forces could be brought to bear. Indeed, his lookouts had reported seeing still more masts on the horizon, presumably those of Taffy 2.

In an attempt to gather more information, Kurita ordered *Yamato*'s two search aircraft to be launched and sent one northward and one to the Surigao Strait area. Neither aircraft returned and only the aircraft searching northward reported back by radio, saying that there was nothing to be seen.

All these factors weighed heavily on a very tired Admiral Takeo Kurita. Trying to see through the fog of fatigue caused by an event-filled and harrowing three days, this weathered-looking Japanese admiral could not see that his adversary was pinned against the ropes, bleeding above the eyes, and staggering under the force of every punch. Kurita was winning the fight of his life but didn't know it.

As the battle off Samar continued on, the outclassed American forces were doing what they could.

Although *Hoel*, *Johnston*, and *Samuel B. Roberts* were lost that day, the other destroyer escorts and *Heerman*, the only surviving destroyer, did what they could for the nearly helpless carriers. At one point, the Japanese cruisers *Chikuma* and *Tone* had gotten dangerously close to the Taffy 3 flagship, *Fanshaw Bay*. As they approached the carrier's port quarter, *Raymond*, already on that side of the ship, was joined by *Dennis* and *John C. Butler*, who had been on the carrier's starboard side. All three fired their guns at the much larger cruisers who retaliated in kind. *Tone* put a shell into *Dennis* that passed through without detonating. Two more hits quickly followed, knocking out *Dennis*'s 40-mm gun director and one of her two 5-inch guns. *Butler*, in the meantime, had survived several very near-misses, but was beginning to run out of ammunition, so Admiral Sprague sent her ahead of the formation to lay more smoke.

Heerman, for quite some time, had been trying to draw fire away from the suffering *Gambier Bay* but had been unsuccessful. When the shattered CVE began to burn furiously and developed a serious list, the cruiser *Chikuma* and three Japanese destroyers turned their attention away from *Gambier Bay* and concentrated on *Heerman*. Before long, a Japanese shell struck *Heerman*'s pilothouse, killing three men and fatally wounding a fourth. As it happened, one of those killed was a pilot from *Gambier Bay* who had been rescued the day before after crash-landing in the sea. The destroyer began taking a severe beating from the Japanese ships, but good damage control procedures and a measure of luck prevented her from sharing the fate of her sisters, *Johnston* and *Hoel*. Though battered and suffering serious casualties, *Heerman* would survive the battle.

After the CVEs had launched their aircraft, there was little they could do but scamper about trying to make difficult targets for the Japanese gunners. The only defensive weapon each of these ships had, besides a number of antiaircraft guns, was one 5-inch gun that had neither the range nor the punch to have much effect on the attackers. But they fired them anyway. As related by the commanding officer of *Kitkun Bay*: "Being able to fire that one 5-inch contributed greatly to the morale of the crew because they felt that at least we were able to throw something at the enemy. It was pretty tough for the men because all the 40-mm and 20-mm gun crews, all the flight deck personnel, and other topside personnel had nothing to do except watch the progress of the battle."

The 5-inch guns were not just good for morale. *Kalinin Bay*'s 5-inch gun crew, firing at an oncoming Japanese torpedo, was able to divert it away from the ship. This rather impressive feat was similarly accomplished by a pilot who stopped two torpedoes coming up astern of *Kalinin Bay* by detonating them with his machine guns.

On board *White Plains*, an officer who was in charge of one of those underemployed 40-mm gun crews referred to by the captain of *Kitkun Bay*, watched helplessly as the Japanese ships grew ever larger with each passing minute. He pointed out to his men that their idleness would not last forever: "Just wait a little longer, boys," the officer said sardonically, "we're sucking them into 40-mm range."

But such was not to be. Just when the situation seemed bleakest to most Americans fighting this hopeless battle, when countless numbers of men had resigned themselves to either an early death or the dreaded trial of trying to survive in the hostile sea, the Japanese ships ceased fire and turned away.

Many a jaw hung down in testimonial disbelief to what they were witnessing. Many a prayer of thanksgiving rose from that battered fleet. Many a cheer could be heard in the stillness that followed the silencing of the guns. But most memorable of all the reactions to this apparent miracle were the words of a young signalman aboard Admiral Sprague's flagship, who saw his formidable Japanese adversaries turning away and said, "Goddammit, they're getting away!"

While the Seventh Fleet—intended from the outset to be an amphibious landing support force—fought the primary fleet-to-fleet engagements near Leyte Gulf, the Third Fleet—the most powerful fleet to roam the seas in all of World War II—tried desperately to get into the fight.

One element of the Third Fleet, Task Group 38.1, under Vice Admiral John S. McCain, had been racing toward the action at Leyte Gulf at 30 knots. Over the last several days, this task group was first ordered to proceed to Ulithi for replenishment, then directed to rejoin with the rest of the Third Fleet, then redirected to head for Leyte Gulf to rescue the endangered CVEs of the Seventh Fleet. Listening to Kinkaid's pleas for help stimulated McCain to order one of the longest carrier strikes of the war. Several times he attempted to find out whether his planes would be able to land at Tacloban airfield after delivering their strike, but could not get confirmation that the airstrip was yet secure. Consequently, McCain was forced to equip the aircraft with wing tanks loaded with fuel in order to ensure that they would be able to make the long trip back. This meant that they could not be armed with heavy torpedoes but would instead have to carry bombs, which were considerably lighter but would be less potent against Kurita's force. A weak strike was perhaps better than no strike, so McCain's aircraft were launched when they were still about 335 miles from the Japanese force.

The first strike hit Kurita after he had broken off his pursuit of Taffy 3. Only the cruiser *Tone* was hit by the attackers, and that one hit turned out to be a dud. In subsequent strikes, the Americans claimed many hits, but the Japanese did not confirm these after the war, so there is no way to know with certainty which version is correct. Fourteen of McCain's aircraft were lost in the strikes, costing twelve American lives. Overall, this attack was inconsequential except that it may have reinforced Kurita's belief that he had made the right decision to break off his attack. It also had an ironic significance in that it was the only role played by Third Fleet forces in the battle off Samar.

In the meantime, Halsey, with Task Force 34 and Task Group 38.2, continued to head south toward a battle that would be over long before he could arrive, while the remainder of his fleet, Task Groups 38.3 and 38.4, now under Mitscher's command, continued to attack Ozawa off Cape Engaño.

In that northernmost battle, Mitscher's force launched six different strikes at Ozawa's decoys. The first three were the most telling, causing the majority of the damage that ultimately claimed all four of Ozawa's carriers, one of his cruisers, and two destroyers. But the rest of Ozawa's Northern Force escaped, including the two "hermaphrodite" carrier-battleships, *Ise* and *Hyuga*. At the end of the battle, Captain Ohmae, Ozawa's chief of staff, evaluated what he had witnessed: "I saw all this bombing and thought the American pilot is not so good." While veterans of Midway, the

Marianas, and Formosa might take justified exception to this remark, there was some undeniable truth in that assessment here at Engaño. Mitscher had plenty of force available, especially considering that his adversary had no air power remaining and could only employ evasive maneuvering and shipboard antiaircraft guns to thwart the oncoming waves of hundreds of American aircraft. But just as Kurita was surely exhausted, so must have been the American pilots. It seems probable that the reason for this less than spectacular performance was the toll taken by the many months of combat operations this powerful but not omnipotent force had endured. Mitscher himself had fairly well predicted such a performance when, just before the commencement of the Leyte operations, he noted, "No other force in the world has been subjected to such a period of constant operation without rest or rehabilitation."

The battle off Cape Engaño served as a kind of anticlimax to what had become the biggest naval battle in history. Indeed, some appreciation of the magnitude of the Battle of Leyte Gulf is realized when one considers that an engagement in which four aircraft carriers, a cruiser, and two destroyers were sunk can be reasonably described as an anticlimax. But with no insult intended toward those who fought there, the battle between Mitscher and Ozawa was almost mundane when compared to the other actions associated with Leyte Gulf. It was unquestionably one-sided, yet it was indecisive in its outcome. It was fought by unquestionably brave men, yet there were no *unusual* feats of bravery recorded. It was the result of a successful diversion on the part of Ozawa, yet Kurita's failure to press his advantage in Leyte Gulf robbed the diversion of its real import. And because of Halsey's reaction to the misunderstood "THE WORLD WONDERS" message from Nimitz, taking Task Force 34 south on a fruitless chase, his final chance for a battleship engagement was lost. Although Halsey would never admit his mistake in going north after Ozawa's decoy force, he would later lament his decision to head south, saying, "I am in agreement that I made a mistake in bowing to pressure and turning south. I consider this the gravest error I committed during the Battle of Leyte Gulf."

Halsey was not the only admiral to make questionable decisions during the Battle of Leyte Gulf. Why Kurita chose to turn away from Taffy 3 when victory seemed so certain is difficult to assess accurately. To do so requires going into the mind of a taciturn Japanese admiral whose few contributions on the matter are, at best, confusing. From the existing evidence, it appears that Kurita's reasoning was as follows:

As already noted, Admiral Kurita did not realize that he had his enemy almost completely at his mercy, that he could have annihilated the entire Taffy 3 force and perhaps even gone on to do similar damage to Taffy 2 as well, had he only understood the true nature of his situation and kept up the pursuit.

But Kurita did *not* have a clear picture at all. For some inexplicable reason, he and other members of his staff continued to believe that they were not gaining on the Americans sufficiently. After the war, he told an interviewer that he honestly believed the American carriers were making 30 knots during the chase. Added to that were his concerns over several messages that Japanese communicators had intercepted. These messages were in fact the desperate, plain-language appeals for help from Kinkaid, but the pessimistic side of Kurita deduced from these dispatches that help was indeed on the way and it was only a matter of time before it arrived.

Accepting Kurita's version of what was occurring, what, then, were his options? Lingering in the same area in a hostile environment is rarely advisable for a force having mobility as one of its important assets, particularly when reports seem to indicate that more enemy forces are on the way. Even less appealing is the prospect of a mobile force entering a confined area where its maneuverability may be severely hindered, and where any newly arriving enemy forces might be able to trap the confined force. Kurita saw his original task of going into Leyte Gulf as foolhardy by this stage of the game. He believed that the delay of several days between the landing of American troops on Leyte and his arrival had allowed the Americans time to firmly establish themselves ashore, and he considered it likely that the transports which had brought the invasion force may even have left the area by this time. Another problem he perceived was based upon his observation of U.S. aircraft flying toward Leyte. In actuality, these planes were merely elements of Taffy 2 and 3 that were running out of fuel and were forced to land at Tacloban airfield since their parent carriers were unable to recover them while under attack. But to Kurita these were aircraft gathering at Leyte for a major strike against him once he entered the gulf.

At the height of the battle, Kurita received a report of another American carrier task group to the north of him; this report erroneously informed him that this group was within his reach. Because Kurita believed he had inflicted serious damage on a full-size carrier force, he was tempted to move off and do the same to another one. Surely that would do more for the war effort than attacking a landing force that by now had landed its troops and may even have departed the area. Kurita later admitted that "The destruction of enemy aircraft carriers was a kind of obsession with me, and I fell victim to it." While chasing after another carrier force would undoubtedly invite still more American air attacks, Kurita preferred facing them in open water to the alternative of enduring the same in the confines of Leyte Gulf.

As can best be discerned from postwar testimony, it was these factors that persuaded Kurita to abandon his attack of Taffy 3 and head away from Leyte Gulf. The trouble is that Kurita's own accounts are varied and unclear. At one point during a postwar interrogation by American military personnel, Kurita first said that he decided "to go north and join Admiral Ozawa for coordinated action against your northern task force." But in the same interview, he later contradictorily asserted that "I considered my mission to go north and seek out your carrier task force and bring it under engagement with the assumption that Admiral Ozawa would thereby be assisted by it. But it was not to join forces with Admiral Ozawa." Kurita also told his interrogators that "If I didn't find anything up [north], I would withdraw through San Bernardino Strait." Yet he later clouds this issue by saying, "Secondarily or overall, I wanted to be at San Bernardino Strait at sunset to get through and as far to the west as possible during the night." Whether the phrase "secondarily or overall" suffers from translation or obfuscation, deliberate or unintentional, by Kurita, is indeterminable now. But the two words are incompatible and, taken separately, give very different meaning to what follows. Was an exit through San Bernardino Strait a "secondary" or an "overall" consideration? Kurita's severest critics choose the latter, saying that he had no intention of further engagements, that his only real goal was to get away. This assertion is strengthened by Kurita's subsequent withdrawal back through San Bernardino Strait, without any noticeable attempt to seek out additional enemy forces to the north. But to call this man a coward on the basis of this evidence alone is presumptuous. This is too serious a charge to be made recklessly.

There are other inconsistencies in Kurita's explanation of his actions. It is possible that these are the flaws that often accompany a concocted story or that Kurita was deliberately vague because the truth was too painful to face. More likely, the explanation lies in Kurita's state of exhaustion at the time he was facing these important decisions. Rather than revealing deliberate obfuscation, it is equally possible that his testimony reflects the state of confusion he was in at the time caused by his lack of rest, the great responsibility he bore, and the strain of very heavy combat endured for the better part of three days. Kurita himself later admitted, "I did not feel tired at the time, but under great strain and without sleep for three days and nights, I was exhausted both physically and mentally." It is plausible that this sleepless, battered old admiral was not at all certain *why* he took the actions he did.

Whatever the explanation, Kurita's decision was not received with enthusiasm by some of his fellow Japanese officers. Admiral Ugaki, sharing his ship, *Yamato*, with Kurita and his staff, noted in his diary: "I felt irritated on the same bridge seeing that they [Kurita and his staff] lacked fighting spirit and promptitude." And when Captain Ohmae, Ozawa's chief of staff, learned of Kurita's decision to head northward, away from Leyte Gulf, he said, "[Kurita] should have been braver and gone on to Leyte."

The Americans, however, saw Kurita's disengagement in a somewhat different light. To all but the most optimistic, Taffy 3 was doomed until Kurita made his fateful decision. Admiral Sprague appropriately summed up the American reaction to Kurita's decision in his after-action report:

> The failure of the enemy . . . to wipe out all vessels of this task unit can be attributed to our successful smoke-screen, our torpedo counterattack, continuous harassment of the enemy by bomb, torpedo, and strafing air attacks, timely maneuvers, and the definite partiality of Almighty God.

20

★ "Divine Wind" ★

Two hours had passed since the expected rising of the sun, but the skies remained dark and foreboding. Heavy clouds rolled angrily across the leaden sky and the howl of the wind masked all other sound. The ships of the huge armada with their cargoes of battle-ready soldiers struggled frantically in the angry sea, and some began to founder as the screaming gale pushed mountainous waves across their decks. Spots of blood marked the frightened faces of the men who dared face the sandblast effect of the wind, and flying debris maimed those unlucky enough to be in its path. It soon became apparent that the invasion would have to be aborted, and for the second time in seven years, Japan had been spared by the intervention of a great typhoon.

The first storm had struck in the year 1274 and destroyed more than two hundred of the Mongol emperor Kublai Khan's ships, causing his invasion force to retreat to the Asian mainland. This second attempt at the conquest of Japan was occurring in August of 1281, when a Sino-Mongol army of 140,000 men embarked in thousands of ships bound for Japan. But the great Khan's powerful fleet was again bludgeoned and scattered by the fury of a Pacific typhoon, and this time fewer than one in five of the would-be invaders escaped to their homeland.

Years of dissension and internal wars had weakened the Japanese and they were in no shape to repel the Mongol invaders. Having resigned themselves to either death or slavery, the fortuitous appearances of the typhoons were hailed as an intervention by *Ise*, the wind god. A legend was born that would carry over the centuries, strengthening the Japanese belief that they were a divinely protected people, convincing them that their destiny had been ordained by the gods and that they had been saved by what they called the "divine wind"—*kamikaze* in Japanese.

In the early evening of 19 October 1944, a black limousine rolled along a dust-covered road on the island of Luzon in the Philippines. The automobile had traveled the fifty miles from the capital city of Manila to Mabalacat airfield, part of the large Clark air complex once belonging to the Americans and now in the hands of the Japanese. A yellow pennant fluttering at the front of the car signified that inside was an officer of flag rank.

As the twilight faded into darkness, the black limousine stopped in front of a cream-colored house with green trim that had originally been the home of a prosperous Filipino family but now served as the headquarters of the Japanese 201st Air Group. Several Japanese naval officers emerged from the car and went into the building. Inside, the fine furnishings that once adorned the spacious rooms had been replaced by a maze of folding canvas cots draped in the mesh of mosquito netting, and flight gear and personal belongings were scattered about. The entourage of officers threaded their way among the cots and proceeded upstairs to a small room on the second floor where they gathered around a table and sat down.

At the head of the table sat Vice Admiral Takijiro Onishi, a round-faced man with close-cropped hair and a down-turned mouth, who had just days before been named commander of First Air Fleet, giving him responsibility for all Japanese naval air forces in the Philippines. What was left of them.

A single light bulb hung above the large table from a twisted wire, its dim light exaggerating the deep creases in the admiral's face. All eyes were on Onishi as he began to speak: "As you know, the war situation is grave," he began in a subdued tone. "The appearance of strong American forces in Leyte Gulf has been confirmed. The fate of the Empire depends upon the outcome of the *Sho* operation, which Imperial General Headquarters has activated to hurl back the enemy assault on the Philippines. Our surface forces are already in motion." So far, Onishi had told these men nothing they did not already know. "Vice Admiral Kurita's Second Fleet, containing our main battle strength, will advance to the Leyte area and annihilate the enemy invasion force. The mission of the First Air Fleet—" several of the officers leaned closer to the admiral at the mention of their air fleet—"is to provide land-based air cover for Admiral Kurita's advance and make sure that enemy air attacks do not prevent him from reaching Leyte Gulf."

No one in the room could have had any illusions about this mission. While it was perfectly logical that they should support Kurita in his quest for Leyte Gulf, it was also quite impossible. Heavy losses of aircraft in the Formosa air battle, combined with the American air strikes on the Philippines that had preceded the landing and destroyed so many aircraft, had left Japanese air strength seriously depleted. Here at Mabalacat, where the bulk of the remaining fighter strength had been concentrated, only about thirty aircraft were able to take to the sky. Arrayed against an American striking force that seemed to have an infinite supply of aircraft flown by well-trained pilots, the mission, as stated by Onishi, would be virtual suicide for those required to carry it out.

Admiral Onishi's eyes blazed with intensity as he continued. "In my opinion, there is only one way of assuring that our meager strength will be effective to a maximum degree." There was utter silence in the room as the group of officers waited expectantly for the admiral's solution to their dilemma. "We must organize suicide attack units composed of Zero fighters armed with bombs, with each plane to crash-dive into an enemy carrier." He paused for a moment, then asked, "What do you think?"

This was not the first time that such an idea had been considered. Suicide tactics had been suggested at various times by aviators frustrated with their inability to overcome their powerful American enemy. And suicide attacks had been actually employed by aviators of both sides, most frequently by flyers who, convinced of their inability to survive a particular mission because of damage to their aircraft, would try to crash their plane into an enemy ship rather than merely die fruitlessly by crashing into the sea. There were even some flyers *not* faced with certain death who, in a moment of patriotic fervor or for other reasons known only to them, chose to fly their aircraft into the enemy as a means of ensuring maximum possible damage.

But this *was* the first time that suicide tactics had been officially sanctioned by the commander of an air unit. If agreed upon, it would be the first time that pilots would be trained, briefed, and sent into the air with the expressed expectation that they would deliberately kill themselves in the service of their country. Military men have always risked death, and some missions have been virtually suicidal by their nature—the odds of returning very poor indeed. But this was most unusual. Onishi's plan called for the organization of whole units whose men would not only *risk* death but would *seek* it.

Contrary to legend, these Japanese officers did not lust for the opportunity to kill themselves. But their special kind of honor and the desperate nature of their situation made their answer to Onishi all but a foregone conclusion.

The next morning an announcement was posted for all the flyers to see. It was signed by Admiral Onishi and called for the organization of a special attack corps whose mission would be to "destroy or disable, by 25 October if possible, the enemy carrier forces in the waters east of the Philippines." The unit would be "divided into four sections, designated as follows: *Shikishima* [a poetic name for Japan], *Yamato* [the ancient name for Japan], *Asahi* [morning sun], and *Yamazakura* [mountain cherry blossoms]." Overall, this special attack corps would be known as *Kamikaze*, meaning "divine wind."

On the morning of 25 October, while Taffy 3 was fighting for its life, and Taffy 2 was sending aircraft to help in the fray, Taffy 1, about 130 miles to the south, was about to have problems of its own.

At sunrise, the six aircraft making up the *Asahi* unit of the *Kamikaze* Corps took off from an airfield at Davao and headed east. They had no confirmed reports of specific locations of American units in the area, but what intelligence they had received indicated that there were so many U.S. ships operating in Philippine waters that they would probably have no difficulty locating targets. So on they flew, determined to be the first members of the newly formed Special Attack Corps to die for their Emperor.

Gunner's Mate Third Class John B. Mitchell, gun captain of mount number five aboard USS *Santee*, was at his station when the word was passed over the sound-powered phone system that there were "bogies" in the area. He immediately began scanning the sky looking for the hostile aircraft.

Beneath the sea, Lieutenant Commander Masahiko Morinaga peered through the eyepiece of his periscope at his target, an American aircraft carrier. Morinaga was commanding officer of the submarine designated I-56 and had been stalking the American task force for quite some time. Now, he was about to shoot.

The "divine wind" emerged from the clouds above the American task group and plummeted downward toward their adversaries. One of the pilots selected *Santee* as his target and bore in. He began firing his machine guns as his aircraft roared downward.

Hearing *Santee*'s gunnery officer yell that a bogey was diving in from astern, John Mitchell spotted the plane almost immediately and ordered his pointer and trainer to bring the 40-mm gun around to bear on the target. The aircraft was adorned with the twinkling light of machine guns firing as it grew larger. Mitchell stared at the oncoming plane in disbelief. It was obvious that the plane was not pulling out of its dive. He knew it was not because the pilot had been killed or wounded since none of *Santee*'s guns were firing at him. Mitchell screamed, "Pull out, you bastard, pull out!" But to no avail. The plane flew right into the flight deck just a few feet forward of the after elevator. A great flurry of debris swirled upward and outward as plane and ship violently merged. The aircraft virtually disappeared into the ship, driving its way through the flight deck and continuing on into the hangar bay where its bomb exploded. Shrapnel sprayed among the aircraft and men in the hangar bay, some of it tearing open depth bombs that were waiting to be loaded on planes. High-explosive material poured out of these gutted weapons but fortunately burned without exploding.

On deck, Mitchell had been tossed into the air by the crash of the *kamikaze*. He came down in his gun tub, which had filled with water when *Santee* had heeled over from the impact. He thought he had been tossed into the sea and began trying to swim before he realized he was still on board.

At about the same time that *Santee* was hit, other Japanese planes were diving on other carriers in Taffy 1. One headed straight for *Suwanee*, but the CVE's antiaircraft fire was so intense that the pilot broke off the attack and looked for another, more accommodating, target. He picked out *Sangamon* as his alternate victim. Before he could reach this new target, however, a 5-inch round found its mark and blasted him to pieces. Fragments of the destroyed aircraft rained across *Sangamon*'s flight deck, killing one man and wounding two others.

Another would-be *kamikaze* headed for *Petrof Bay*, but this one, too, was decimated by antiaircraft fire and crashed into the sea, so close that it threw water up on the carrier's flight deck.

The *kamikaze* that had succeeded in striking *Santee* had torn a thirty-foot gash into the flight deck, killed sixteen men, wounded twenty-seven others, and started several fires on the ship. But *Santee* had not been mortally wounded. Damage-control parties began fighting the fires and soon had them under control.

Off *Santee*'s starboard side, at a depth of about thirty feet, Lieutenant Morinaga had his firing solution. He gave the order and a spread of torpedoes emerged from the tubes of his submarine and sped off toward *Santee*. At 0756, one torpedo slammed into the ship's starboard side, abreast the after elevator.

The destroyer *Trathen* charged in to attack the subsurface intruder. She began sowing the sea with depth charges in a barrage that would last for nearly a half-hour but would prove to be a wasted effort. The I-56 escaped and made her way safely back to Japan.

The torpedo hit on *Santee* proved to be a glancing blow that damaged the carrier enough to give her a 6-degree starboard list, but was not serious enough to sink her. This "Combustible-Vulnerable-Expendable" ship had absorbed a torpedo and a direct hit by a *kamikaze*, but would not succumb.

Taffy 1's worries were not over, however. Another Japanese aircraft, piloted by a man determined to die, was taken under fire by American guns. A trail of smoke from the plane indicated that it had been hit, but that was not going to be enough to thwart the pilot from his mission. Careening down at a 45-degree angle, this plane proved unstoppable, and, at 0804, crashed into *Suwanee*'s flight deck. Like the one that had struck *Santee*, it was swallowed by *Suwanee*'s flight deck and found its way to the hangar bay, where its bomb detonated. Damage to the ship was remarkably light considering what had just occurred. She lost the use of her after elevator and temporarily lost her ability to steer, but within a relatively short period of time damage-control parties were able to patch the hole in her flight deck, and the ship was once again conducting flight operations.

These first *kamikaze* attacks had been harrowing to be sure, but the results were not spectacular, prompting one of the American captains to file an action report that reflected his contempt for this new tactic. The commanding officer of *Petrof Bay* wrote that a suicide dive "is a stupid way to attack *because it has less chance of getting home* than other types of bombing." He argued that the plane made a bigger target and that it had less penetrating power than a bomb. This contempt would not be shared, however, by the captain of USS *St. Lô*, operating far to the north with Taffy 3.

For four consecutive days the pilots of the newly formed *Shikashima* unit had prepared for their final flights by the ritual of ceremonial farewells, prayers before a sacred shrine, and the donning of *hachimaki*.*
On every one of the four days the pilots had returned to their base frustrated by bad weather and their inability to locate the enemy. On 21 October, one lieutenant, less patient than his comrades, had taken off by himself, determined to fly to Leyte Gulf in search of a target upon which to expend himself. He was never heard from again, and since no American ships reported being attacked by a suicide pilot that day, it can only be surmised that he crashed into the sea. Finally, on 25 October, at 0725, the *Shikashima* pilots took off on what would prove to be a more fruitful mission.

By luck, these *kamikaze* pilots discovered the ships of Taffy 3 just after Kurita had broken off his attack. The crews of the Taffy 3 ships were just beginning to unwind from the close brush with death they had all experienced. Their guard was down.

On board the destroyer escort *Raymond*, Vernon Kimmel, the leading fire controlman, was still at his battle station when the "divine wind" began to blow. *Raymond* had survived the battle with Kurita's fleet with little serious damage. Despite the destroyers' gun battles with the fearsome Japanese ships, *Raymond* had come out of the engagement with a lot of shrapnel holes but no personnel casualties. Kimmel looked over at the nearest CVE, USS *St. Lô*. She, too, had come out of the battle well off compared to some of her sisters. From Kimmel's vantage point he had a good view of the nearby carrier and could see no apparent damage. When one considered what had happened to *Gambier Bay*, who was now at the bottom of the sea, *St. Lô* was indeed fortunate.

The time was 1053 when the *kamikazes* seemed to appear out of

---

* *Hachimaki* were bandanna-like cloths worn tied around the forehead of the suicide pilot. In the days of the ancient Samurai, warriors tied white cloths around their heads signifying their expectation of fighting to the death. The *Kamikaze* Corps adopted this tradition, adding poetic calligraphy and a red sun symbol to the white cloth.

nowhere. Lookouts on *Raymond* were the first to spot them and the ship opened fire at the marauders. The Japanese planes fanned out, heading for different targets. One tried to hit the bridge of *Kitkun Bay* but missed and landed in the ship's port catwalk instead. Its bomb exploded, peppering the carrier's flight deck with shrapnel, but only seventeen men were injured, one fatally. Another of the *kamikazes* nearly hit *White Plains* but exploded just off her port side causing only minor damage and injuring only eleven men.

A second *kamikaze* headed for *White Plains* was hit by antiaircraft fire. Trailing smoke, the plane veered away from *White Plains* and headed instead for *St. Lô*. As the plane headed for its new target, the guns on *Raymond* tried desperately to knock it down. Soon it was too close to the carrier and *Raymond*'s guns were forced to cease firing rather than chance hitting *St. Lô*. The *kamikaze* pressed the attack and crashed into *St. Lô*'s flight deck a split-second after releasing its bomb. The aircraft shattered on impact, its many pieces careening along the flight deck then sliding off the ship's bow into the water. The bomb, however, had penetrated the flight deck and exploded in the hangar bay below. Within three minutes, gasoline fires were burning furiously inside the ship.

Vern Kimmel had been watching from his station in *Raymond*'s gun director as ugly black smoke began pouring from several places on *St. Lô*. He was wondering how serious her damage was, when there was a tremendous explosion. Kimmel watched in horrified fascination as *St. Lô*'s huge aircraft elevator sailed across the water. He later said that it looked "like a giant Frisbee." Debris and smoke climbed hundreds of feet into the air, escorted by a huge ball of flame. Great chunks of the ship rained down into the sea for hundreds of yards all around.

A major portion of *St. Lô*'s flight deck had been blown off by the explosion. Another twenty-five feet of it had been peeled back and folded over on itself. A series of explosions then followed, and it soon became apparent that *St. Lô* was not going to survive. The captain gave the order to abandon ship, and those who had survived the terrible explosions and had not already been blown overboard began leaving the ship by whatever means they could find. By this time the ship was a raging inferno and many men were forced to leap from the flight deck, rather than use the preferred method of climbing down ropes.

St. Lô had been listing to port for most of her ordeal, but the final explosion was so violent it threw the carrier over on her starboard side.

The life had been irrevocably knocked out of her, and soon she was lying completely on her side, her flight deck perpendicular to the water, a great gaping hole in her bottom. She began sliding backward into the sea and, before long, she was gone. One hundred and fourteen men went with her.

Another ship had been sunk in the Battle of Leyte Gulf.

PART VII
★ AFTERMATH ★

21

★ Long Nights ★

As night descended upon the waters surrounding the Philippine islands, there was an air of peace on those tropical seas. Gone were the tense expectations of battle, for all the battles were over. Gone were the sounds of salvos fired in anger, the screams of diving aircraft, the cacophony and confusion of combat, the whispered prayers of men seeking deliverance from hell itself. Palawan Passage, where Kurita had suffered the first blows of battle in this epic confrontation just three nights earlier, had returned to its deceptively placid state, except that new victims now reposed in the waters so aptly called "Dangerous Ground." The Sibuyan Sea, where Halsey's air armada had swarmed over the persistent Japanese Central Force, now served as the path of retreat for the remnants of that battered fleet. And Surigao Strait, where powerful battleships had thundered in anger, was as quiet as the night Ferdinand Magellan had first brought European influence to this part of the world. The sounds of war had faded from these waters, never to be heard on such a scale again.

But for some the struggle was not yet over. In the dark waters off Samar, the survivors of the "Light Brigade" clung to life rafts, floating debris, and each other in a new battle for survival. The men who, just hours before, had crewed the nobly charging United States ships *Johnston*, *Hoel*, and *Samuel B. Roberts*, along with the hundreds of others who were the survivors of the lost carriers *Gambier Bay* and *St. Lô*, had not been rescued while daylight remained on 25 October. And with the night came new dangers.

Robert Billie was too weak to keep his head above water, even with a life jacket on. His many shrapnel wounds had taken their toll. Someone tied him to one of the stronger men to keep him from drowning. He drifted in and out of consciousness as the hours went by.

Bill Mercer was in better shape, but he knew something Billie did not. He had spotted a large shark late that afternoon.

Ed Digardi was worried. The expected quick rescue had not come. They had seen U.S. aircraft several times in the afternoon, but no American ships had come to pluck them from the water. Some of the men were badly wounded and could not last much longer under such arduous conditions. Several life rafts had been located, but the fresh water that was supposed to be stored in them was putrid. As darkness descended, Digardi saw the dreaded fins of sharks circling nearby in the fading light.

As the hours went by, some of the badly wounded gave up the fight. Once it was certain a man was dead, he was slipped out of his life jacket and allowed to descend into the deep. Two men Bill Mercer knew as "Cooper" and "Walker" had been badly burned aboard *Johnston* and both died shortly after dark. Mercer helped remove their life jackets and watched his shipmates sink, their pallid faces barely visible in the eerie moonlight. He suddenly felt like "an eighteen-year-old boy going on forty."

The sharks hit after the moon had gone.

On the afternoon of the twenty-fifth, Captain Charles Adair, who had played such a key role in the planning of the amphibious assault on Leyte, was already working on plans for the expected invasion of Luzon. He was hard at work aboard Admiral Barbey's flagship in Leyte Gulf, surrounded by stacks of paper and piles of reconnaissance photographs. As was his habit, he had switched on the screen that displayed messages as they came in and was periodically glancing at it to see if anything of importance was going on.

At about 1500, Adair happened to look up when the words "many men in the water" caught his eye. It was a report from an aircraft that had been flying about 110 miles northeast of Leyte Gulf. Adair knew that there had been several American ships lost that afternoon, although he wasn't sure how many. What disturbed him was that he could find no indication that anyone had done anything to rescue the survivors. Armed with a copy of the message, Adair went to see his boss, Admiral Daniel E. Barbey, commander of the Northern Attack Force, Task Force 78.

Adair showed the message to Barbey, then recommended forming a rescue force using the landing craft and patrol vessels at their disposal.

The LCIs seemed particularly suited to the task because their ramps could be lowered to assist bringing aboard survivors. Barbey approved the plan and Adair went to work.

At Captain Adair's direction, Task Group 78.12 was formed in less than an hour, consisting of two PCs (Patrol Craft) and five LCIs under the command of Lieutenant Commander J. A. Baxter. Adair arranged for a doctor and a pharmacist's mate to accompany the tiny task group on its mission, and soon they were under way, headed for the waters off Samar. They would not get there until the next morning.

Bill Mercer felt the shark brush up against him as it swam swiftly by. He kicked at it and used language his mother would not have appreciated. A faint trail of phosphorescence marked the predator's passage just below the surface.

Out of the darkness came the curses and splashes of other men fighting off the intruders, and there were occasional screams of agony and terror as some of the sharks succeeded in their attacks. Ed Digardi could hear the dreadful thrashing sounds of sharks as they tore apart the dead who had been cast adrift.

Spared some of the nightmare night by his periodic lapses into unconsciousness, Robert Billie was still tied to a man whose name he didn't know. Sometime during the night, Billie was aware enough of his surroundings to feel a sudden jolt. Before he could even realize what was happening, he and his companion were dragged beneath the surface and thrashed wildly about. Saltwater poured into his mouth and nostrils as he was whipped about like a rag doll. When he realized what was happening, he wanted to scream but could not. He was certain he was going to die, but suddenly he felt his head break the surface and he gasped for breath. Just as quickly as the attack had begun, it ended. Billie lay helpless, choking on the ingested water, trying to catch his breath. And then he realized with great horror that he was alone.

When morning came, Task Group 78.12 had arrived at their destination and found nothing except floating debris and an occasional oil slick. For most of the day, they continued to find only the detritus of war. In the late afternoon, they at last spotted a survivor clinging to a wooden box but were disappointed to find he was Japanese. They recovered him, searched him for weapons, then gave him food, water, and medical attention.

The would-be rescuers watched the sun descend into the sea with heavy hearts. The survivors, if there still were any, would most likely have to spend another night in the water.

Baxter continued the search on into the night, combing the area as best he could, knowing that the odds were long at best that they would be able to find anything in the darkness.

Then, at 2220, the lookouts on PC-623 sighted several red, white, and green flares off to the west. They headed toward the pyrotechnics and within fifteen minutes began recovering survivors from *Gambier Bay*.

For the next several hours the rescue force picked up survivors in varying numbers. By 0348, they had accumulated more than two hundred men, some of them in serious need of medical attention. Baxter detached PC-1119 to take the survivors back to Leyte Gulf and then, with his remaining force, continued his search.

All the men so far recovered had been from *Gambier Bay*. Four other American ships had gone down in the battle and, so far, not one man of their crews had been recovered.

The second night in the water was worse than the first for the *Johnston* sailors. More of the wounded died and sharks continued to attack sporadically, but now the sailors had a new enemy: thirst. Some of the men began succumbing to the temptation to drink the seawater and were paying the price. Hallucinations and ravings became more common as the ingested saltwater took its toll. Adding to their problems, many of the kapok life jackets were becoming waterlogged and it became a struggle for many of the men to stay afloat. Sleep became a constant enemy because men who gave in and fell asleep frequently drifted away from the others and had to be brought back, at no small exertion. Some drifted away and were not missed in time to be recovered. Sometimes a man disappeared and no one was certain just what had happened to him.

Ed Digardi struggled all night trying to keep the men together and their morale up. His friend, Lieutenant Jack Bechdel—the one-legged torpedo officer whom Digardi had helped over *Johnston*'s rail just before he himself had been blown off the ship—died sometime during the night. At one point, a sailor who had apparently ingested saltwater went berserk and Digardi had to knock him out and tie him to a floater net to prevent him from harming himself and others in the group.

At about noon of the day before, Bill Mercer and several other men had decided to leave the rest of the group and try to swim to Samar. Along the way they discovered a life raft with two other *Johnston* men in it. They clambered aboard and shared some of the rations that were in the raft. They decided to remain with the raft rather than continuing their swim to Samar.

Mercer and J. B. Strickland made a pact that called for one to sleep while the other stayed awake. Since both men feared going to sleep without the security of someone watching over them, this seemed like a workable arrangement. Strickland went to sleep first, his head on Mercer's shoulder. After awhile—what seemed like hours to Mercer but, by his own admission, was probably more like five minutes—Mercer woke Strickland and said it was his turn to sleep. Strickland agreed, and Mercer laid his head on his companion's shoulder. But Strickland had immediately gone back to sleep and both men rolled off the raft into the water. They decided not to try that again.

Johnston's survivors, dwindling in number with each passing hour, spent a long night in the dark Philippine waters. In those terrible hours they fought the numbing cold of the water, battled with their own exhaustion, feared the carnivores lurking among them, witnessed the passing of many of their shipmates, and clung desperately to life when death seemed an easier alternative. For those who would live to remember, this would be the longest night of their lives, not only for the obvious reasons, but because they would relive it again and again in their dreams for the rest of their lives.

Ed Digardi rejoiced when dawn arrived on the twenty-seventh. The warmth of the sun was most welcome, and he knew that their chances of being rescued increased dramatically with the arrival of daylight. Most of the men seemed unaware of the changes morning had brought. As a result of their exhaustion, injuries, lack of food and water, and mental depression, many were nearly catatonic. It was apparent that many would not survive another hellish night like the previous two.

As the sun climbed over the horizon, Digardi peered down into the sea, watching the sun's rays dance about in the deep blue water beneath them. It was a beautiful sight despite his terrible situation. The water looked so cool and bright, it was difficult to remember that it was unfit to drink.

While Digardi was staring into the mesmerizing water, he suddenly realized there was something else down there. Drifting very slowly along in the shadow cast by the cluster of floating men, was a large group of sharks.

It was nearly 0900 when PC-623 picked up the first *Johnston* survivor. The last man would not be recovered until the early afternoon. Ed Digardi's group was among the last.

When Robert Billie was helped aboard one of the LCIs, he told his rescuers he could walk on his own. One step, and he fell to the deck. Later, he nearly lost one of his shrapnel-filled legs to a surgeon's saw.

When Bill Mercer first sighted the approaching LCIs, he was afraid they were Japanese ships, but when one turned broadside and he saw the red, white, and blue flag flying from her gaff, he knew his ordeal was over.

Digardi removed his life jacket before climbing the cargo net that had been slung over the side of the LCI. He watched as the life jacket sank out of sight and wondered exactly when it was that he had started keeping *it* afloat.

Once aboard the PCs and LCIs of Task Group 78.12, many of the men fell instantly asleep. Some did not stir even when a Japanese aircraft roared out of the sky and began strafing the tiny task group.

It was not until the next day that all the survivors of *Johnston*, *Hoel*, *Samuel B. Roberts*, *Gambier Bay*, and *St. Lô* were safely aboard hospital ships being treated for their wounds, exposure, and exhaustion. There were over a thousand of them—hundreds more than might have been saved had not Captain Charles Adair taken the action he did. And perhaps hundreds fewer than might have been saved had someone thought of these men before they came to the attention of Adair.

22

★ Epitaph ★

Finally, the Commander Third Fleet can confidently report that this action and the brilliant operations of the Seventh Fleet resulted in (a) utter failure of the Japanese plan to prevent the re-occupation of the Philippines, (b) the crushing defeat of the Japanese Fleet, and (c) the elimination of serious naval threat to our operations for many months, if not forever.

—W. F. HALSEY

This conclusion to Admiral Halsey's after-action report to COMINCH via CINCPAC is a fairly accurate summation of the Battle of Leyte Gulf. The Japanese did indeed fail in their attempt to prevent the reoccupation of the Philippines by American forces, their fleet was certainly defeated, and the Japanese navy had unquestionably been eliminated as a serious threat, with Halsey's projection of "forever" more accurate than his lesser alternative of "for many months."

But if there is to be a truly accurate assessment of this great battle, more must be said than what appears in Halsey's report. His description of the Seventh Fleet's contribution as "brilliant" is only partially true, and very different adjectives come to mind when attempting to describe the performance of the Third Fleet. His use of the word "crushing" when describing the defeat of the Japanese Fleet is overstated and invites a more telling assessment. And there are many other aspects of the battle, both positive and negative, that are not addressed and must be if this great event is to take its proper place in history.

To begin with, a more penetrating assessment of the strategic significance of the battle is in order. Leyte Gulf was not a decisive battle in the same sense that the Battle of Midway had been. The course of the war had not been altered by what occurred there in Philippine waters. But, perhaps just as significant, the course of the war was permitted to *continue* as a result of the Leyte Gulf battle. This does not have the same dramatic appeal as a reversal but, from the American point of view, is no less important. Had the Japanese prevailed in their fairly modest goal of disrupting the landings, the impact on American conduct of the war could have had some far-reaching consequences. Admiral Morison, in his monumental and widely revered fifteen-volume *History of United States Naval Operations in World War II*, probably goes too far when, in assessing what might have happened had the Japanese succeeded with *Sho Go*, he writes that "General MacArthur's Army would have been cut off, like that of Athens at Syracuse in 413 B.C.," and adds that "Third Fleet alone could not have maintained its communications." But Sparta was in a far stronger position in 413 B.C. than was Japan in A.D. 1944. It is difficult to imagine the Japanese Navy—with no air power left at this point in the war—able to prevent the Third Fleet from doing anything it was tasked to do. In a purely military sense, it is doubtful that a Japanese success at Leyte Gulf would have accomplished anything other than a delay, albeit a significant one, in the American march across the Pacific.

It was in the political arena that a potential for an American disaster was greatest. A defeat in the Philippines, even a temporary one, could have had significant reverberations on the homefront. The late October occurrence of this battle placed it just before a presidential election. By late 1944, the American public had grown accustomed to victories; any sudden dramatic change in that trend could have had serious consequences for Roosevelt's unprecedented bid for a fourth term. At worst, he might have been defeated. A lesser consequence might have been his loss of a clear mandate for his policies. Either of these setbacks might have forced a change in American prosecution of the war, allowing the political opposition to force an abandonment of Roosevelt's "unconditional surrender" policy and a resort to negotiated settlement with the Japanese.

A more far-reaching consequence of an American setback in the Philippines might have been the postwar status of the United States in the Far East. MacArthur warned Roosevelt of the ramifications of bypassing the Philippines; a similar loss of credibility could well have resulted from an American defeat there.

The American victory at Leyte Gulf was also strategically significant because it ensured the recapture of the Philippines. For the Japanese this was tantamount to ultimate defeat. Admiral Mitsumasa Yonai, Japanese navy minister, said after the war, "When you took the Philippines, that was the end of our resources." Because of the American submarine threat, the Japanese were having enough difficulty getting oil from the south to the home islands *before* the American landings at Leyte. Once they lost the Philippines, that tenuous supply line was severed and defeat became an inevitability.

At the conclusion of the Battle of Leyte Gulf, the U.S. Navy was supreme in the Pacific. Never again would the Imperial Japanese Navy be able to mount any meaningful resistance to the American march to the Japanese homeland. This is not to say, however, that the war was over for the U.S. Navy. More American sailors would die in the Battle of Okinawa in April 1945 than in any other battle of the war in the Pacific. But those casualties would result primarily from the "divine wind" tactic introduced at Leyte Gulf, not from any actions taken by ships of the Imperial Japanese Navy. That once-proud service, for all intents and purposes, ceased to exist after the great sea battle off the Philippines.

In its last attempt at the great decisive battle, Japan lost four aircraft carriers, three battleships (including one of her super dreadnoughts), nine cruisers, and a dozen destroyers. Hundreds of aircraft were lost and thousands of airmen and sailors died. It was a tremendous defeat by any standard.

On the American side the battle was less costly, but not without serious consequence. Three aircraft carriers, two destroyers, one destroyer escort, and a submarine did not survive the battle. Hundreds of Americans died in the action and many more were wounded.

Considering that the two American fleets vastly outnumbered their opponents, and that the Japanese had no meaningful air power with which to oppose the Americans, the Japanese did surprisingly well. From a purely statistical standpoint, the U.S. Navy should have decimated the Japanese at Leyte Gulf, but because Ozawa's decoy worked, American capability was effectively reduced. With the entire Third Fleet removed from the equation by Halsey's dash northward, the Japanese should have fared well against the remaining forces at Leyte Gulf. With that in mind, it is the Japanese who must be chastised for their disappointing performance. The sinking of so few American ships off Samar in the face of such great potential was a humiliating circumstance for a navy that had once dominated in the world's largest ocean.

In point of fact, Admiral Ozawa was the only Japanese admiral who accomplished his mission at Leyte. By luring Halsey away from the focus of the battle, he gave the Japanese Navy its one and only chance for success under the circumstances. Unfortunately for the Japanese, Nishimura, Shima, and Kurita were unable to capitalize on this golden opportunity.

Nishimura made a series of errors that not only failed to take advantage of the opportunity offerred by Ozawa's successful ruse but also cost him his fleet and his life. By not merging his force with that of Shima, he condemned both forces to hopeless impotence. By not slowing down when he received word that Kurita had been delayed in the Sibuyan Sea, Nishimura forfeited the advantage a coordinated arrival at Leyte Gulf would have afforded and allowed Kinkaid to concentrate his forces at the head of Surigao Strait, where one of the greatest ambushes in history was effected.

Shima barely factors into the battle at all. His force, unmerged with Nishimura, was relatively insignificant, and his late arrival at the scene lent little but confusion (and an embarrassing collision) to an already disastrous situation. Shima's unwillingness to communicate, either with Nishimura before the battle, or with the commanding officer of retreating *Shigure* during it, is difficult to understand. Perhaps the only credit Shima is due is for his decision to retire from Surigao Strait before he shared the fate of Nishimura. Under the circumstances, this retreat makes more sense than anything else Shima did.

Kurita is the true enigma of the battle. On the one hand, his tenacity in the face of the setbacks in Palawan Passage and the Sibuyan Sea is admirable. On the other, his sudden withdrawal from the battle off Samar—*when victory was within his grasp*—is difficult to reconcile. Had he then charged off to the north, eventually running into Halsey's southbound force, much of the controversy would have been removed, even if he had been annihilated by Halsey. His actions would have been attributed to an error in judgment and nothing more. But his subsequent departure through San Bernardino Strait makes his motive suspect. The temptation to call him a coward arises, and his confusing postwar explanations do not help the matter.

Takeo Kurita's war record is not one of notable intellectual brilliance, but there is not the slightest hint of cowardice to mar his performance in the several years of combat he endured before Leyte Gulf. To attribute his actions at Samar to cowardice is simply not warranted in light of available evidence. Exhaustion is a far more plausible explanation for Kurita's actions. There can be no argument that this man had been pushed to the limits of human endurance by his experiences over the three days of battle. Submarine and air attacks, the sinking and abandonment of his flagship, the pressures of command, the lack of air support, poor communications, and the steady attrition of his forces all add up to an incredibly draining ordeal.

Kurita, for the most part, refused to comment on the Battle of Leyte Gulf after the war, but Masanori Ito, a Japanese journalist, convinced Kurita to grant him an interview nearly a decade after the battle. Disappointingly, Kurita's responses in that interview shed little additional light on his motives. He contended, as before, that his reason for breaking off the attack at Samar was to head northward in search of another carrier force, and that when he failed to find that force he decided to retire through San Bernardino Strait. Ito asked Kurita if he had considered going back to Leyte Gulf once he realized he was not going to encounter another carrier force.* Kurita answered, "By that time I believe that Leyte was no longer in my thoughts. As I recall, my mind was filled with such problems as enemy air attacks in the Sibuyan Sea next day, and the state of our fuel supply." Kurita then conceded that he had erred by going after the carrier force, explaining that "Leyte Gulf was stationary, the enemy task force was not, and so the chances of finding it were an unknown quantity."

Ito recorded that he "then asked his [Kurita's] opinion on such subjects as the basic operation orders. . . . To these questions Admiral Kurita remained silent and merely smiled a wry smile." Behind that wry smile may be another explanation for Kurita's actions. It is quite possible that he did not really believe in his mission to begin with, that he was carrying out his orders halfheartedly. This would explain his reluctance to go into Leyte Gulf and would account for his decision to reenter San Bernardino Strait rather than continue north in search of the other carrier task group. Kurita was perhaps hinting at this earlier in the Ito interview when he said, "I had been given orders and, as a military man, I should have carried them out."

While Admiral Kurita was able to admit his error in judgment, Admiral Halsey was not. Soon after the battle ended, Halsey sent a message to Nimitz and King explaining his actions: "As it seemed childish to me to guard statically San Bernardino Strait, I concentrated Task Force 38 dur-

---

* Kurita's navigational track reveals that he turned south again for a while in the afternoon of the twenty-fifth—as though headed back to Leyte Gulf—before reversing course again and entering San Bernardino Strait.

ing the night and steamed north to attack the Northern Force at dawn. I believed that the Center Force had been so heavily damaged in the Sibuyan Sea that it could no longer be considered a serious menace to the Seventh Fleet."

Nimitz expressed his concern over the matter in a letter to King two days after the battle, in which he said he regretted "that the fast battleships were not left in the vicinity of Samar when Task Force 38 started after the striking force reported to be in the north. . . ." Nimitz added that "It never occurred to me that Halsey, knowing the composition of the ships in the Sibuyan Sea, would leave the San Bernardino Strait unguarded, even though the Jap detachments in the Sibuyan Sea had been reported seriously damaged." But Nimitz never formally chastised Halsey directly and was willing to let the matter rest.

Several months later, Halsey and King met face to face. When the subject of Leyte Gulf came up, King cut Halsey off by saying, "You don't have to tell me any more. You've got a green light on everything you did."

With his two immediate superiors willing to close the matter there, Halsey might well have enjoyed a happy ending to his story. But, though he was losing his hearing as age crept up on him, Halsey was not deaf to the criticisms of his tactics that could be heard in naval circles. So in 1947 when Halsey was invited to publish his autobiography in the *Saturday Evening Post*, he made several tactical errors that in some ways were more serious than those he committed at Leyte Gulf.

The first six installments of the autobiography were well received by an adoring public, except that some of his remarks regarding the consumption of alcohol brought protestations from a national temperance society and he ruffled some feathers in military circles when he criticized an Army Air Corps commander who was still living. But, all in all, the project seemed to be going well.

In the seventh installment, Halsey had to face the prickly problem of Leyte Gulf, and it was here that he steamed full speed into a mine field. Halsey decided that a national magazine would make an excellent forum in which to vindicate himself. By doing this he brought to national attention a controversy that until then had been kept within fairly tight circles. Had he just left the matter alone by glossing over the business of his northward trek, or had he just admitted that he had been suckered by the Japanese and should not have gone north with his entire fleet, the matter might well have been ignored or forgiven and forgotten. But proud men often make the fatal error of refusing to admit mistakes, and Bull Halsey was certainly no exception to that unfortunate characteristic. As a result of his adamant refusal to admit he was wrong and, worse, his inability to just let the matter lie undisturbed, Halsey stirred up one of the great controversies of naval history—one that would haunt him throughout the remainder of his life and become an indelible blemish on an otherwise sterling career.

His first tactical error was to blame the problems at Leyte Gulf on the divided command situation. Although technically correct in his assessment that the lack of a common commander had led to the difficulties experienced by the Americans at Leyte, he was firing shots at his superiors, and this is rarely a clever thing to do, especially when those superiors have been defending you. Nimitz had no responsibility for the divided command situation and was probably too much the gentleman to be lured into a controversial situation anyway, so he remained silent in the wake of Halsey's shots. King was another story. Halsey's criticism of the command structure was throwing shrapnel King's way and he, unlike Nimitz, was never too much the gentleman to keep his feelings to himself.

Halsey's more serious error in the seventh installment was to make Kinkaid the scapegoat. Halsey's version of the battle made his old friend Kinkaid out to be the one who had erred in allowing his Taffy 3 ships to be attacked by Kurita. Such comments as "I wondered how Kinkaid had let Ziggy Sprague get caught like this" left little room for misunderstanding of Halsey's intent; he was clearly determined to shift the blame for the debacle at Samar away from himself no matter whose head would roll.

Perhaps out of respect for his friendship with Kinkaid, or because he sensed that he might have gone too far in his criticisms, Halsey added the following contradiction to his account:

> I have attempted to describe the Battle of Leyte Gulf in terms of my thoughts at the time, but on rereading my account, I find that this results in an implication grossly unfair to Tom Kinkaid. True, during the action, his dispatches puzzled me. Later, with the gaps in my information filled, I not only appreciate his problems, but frankly admit that had I been in his shoes, I might have acted precisely as did he.

This is amazing. Halsey first fired a broadside at Kinkaid, then appeared to realize that he was being "grossly unfair to Tom Kinkaid" after "rereading my account." But instead of tearing up what he had previously written, he let it stand alongside this confusing rejoinder and gave it to the world to wonder about. Halsey seemed naively unaware that he could not have it both ways.

When the installment appeared in the *Saturday Evening Post*, it was not long before King responded with a stinging letter to Halsey in which he said, "Personally, I must say that I did not like the tenor of the installment, neither as to Kinkaid . . . nor as to the command set-up. . . ." King added, "You would do well to review—and rewrite—the matter contained in the 7th installment. . . ."

Halsey had burned one bridge by his attack on Kinkaid—the friendship was destroyed and was replaced by a bitter animus that both men would take to the grave—and now he burned yet another by responding to King's letter with "I have given your letter and my article much thought and study, and have asked for and received counsel. I regret that your point of view and mine do not coincide."

In the matter of his turning south when almost within gun range of Ozawa's ships, Halsey made a weak gesture of accepting the blame, writing, "Although Ernie King later assured me that [my orders to head south] were the right ones, I am convinced that they were not." Halsey admitted that he had given the orders "in rage," but further watered down his admission of error by explaining that the CINCPAC encoder who had added the "world wonder" phrase was "either drowsy or smart-alecky" and that "Chester [Nimitz] blew up when I told him about it; he tracked down the little squirt and chewed him to bits, but it was too late then; the damage had been done."

So even this error, which Halsey said he was accepting responsibility for, is really the fault of a "little squirt" on Nimitz's staff. While there is truth in this claim, it fails as a noble gesture when put this way.

At about the same time that Halsey's seventh installment appeared, Bernard Brodie published in the *Virginia Quarterly Review* an article entitled, "The Battle for Leyte Gulf." Although Brodie gave Halsey his due by recognizing the admiral's boldness and acknowledging that "[Halsey's] accomplishments prior to the Battle for Leyte Gulf were spectacular," he was downright insulting in his assessment of Halsey's performance at Leyte. "[Halsey's] judgments were not equal to his boldness" and "The U.S. Navy will have learned the greatest lesson of the Battle for Leyte Gulf if it concludes that in the supreme commander it is brains that matters [*sic*] most," Brodie wrote.

Then in November, *Life* magazine, one of the most widely read magazines in America at the time, published an article by Gilbert Cant, the very title of which cut Halsey to the quick. "Bull's Run: Was Halsey Right at Leyte Gulf?" placed the whole matter into the glaring spotlight of national attention. Cant's article, though not insulting as Brodie's had been, nonetheless caused Halsey's ego no small pain when it asked in extra large, bold print "Did a Japanese blunder save an American Army and Fleet from a Halsey mistake?" Photographs of Halsey and Kinkaid appeared above the title, juxtaposed to suggest that the two were staring at one another in adamant defiance.

The controversy continued for years with periodic flare-ups that rankled Halsey and sometimes spurred him to action and other times did not. On 31 October 1953, a New York *Herald-Tribune* article, "Leahy Hits Halsey on Leyte Battle," quoted Admiral Leahy, Roosevelt's chief of staff, as having said about Halsey's northward trek, "We didn't lose the war for that but I don't know why we didn't." Leahy concluded his comments with "Halsey went off on a little war of his own." Halsey did not respond to this, though it must have been difficult for him to restrain himself.

Admiral Kinkaid, through all this, remained quiet. For a decade, he made no public comment in response to Halsey's allegations. In 1949, King, writing from his room at Bethesda Naval Hospital while recovering from a stroke, began querying Kinkaid about his actions at Leyte Gulf in a series of letters that spanned several months of back-and-forth correspondence. King seemed obsessed with finding out why Kinkaid had not sent out his own aircraft to search the San Bernardino Strait area instead of assuming that Halsey was there on guard. The letters have the underlying tone of a witch hunt, though the actual wording is cordial. Admiral King seemed intent upon fixing at least some of the blame for the Samar debacle on Kinkaid.

In Kinkaid's final letter to King, he wrote: "I believe that Halsey made a serious mistake and I regret that he did not acknowledge it in his book instead of his shabby references to me. I have refused to be drawn into a controversy on the subject because no good could come of it."

But in 1955, Kinkaid relented and decided, at last, to fight back. Hanson Baldwin published an account of the battle in his book, *Seafights and Shipwrecks*, and for added interest invited both Halsey and Kinkaid to append their comments to his account. Both agreed, and the two locked horns indirectly over Baldwin's piece.

Halsey's tone was strident and defensive but he refrained from any further attacks on Kinkaid. Kinkaid, on the other hand, vented some of his long pent-up fury with comments like "[Halsey] apparently overlooks the fact that the absence of TF 34 from San Bernardino Strait precluded the total destruction of Kurita's force on the spot, to say nothing of the loss of American lives and ships of the CVE force."

Kinkaid spoke out again in a 1960 interview. This time he was less confrontational, perhaps because Halsey had died the year before. "Halsey spent ten years or more trying to justify his action. . . . Some of his efforts to justify it were at my expense. I don't mind that so much, but I don't think his logic was very good."

The argument did not just take place between Halsey and Kinkaid. Many others had their own views and expressed them. John Thach, McCain's air operations officer during the battle and a highly respected aviator, supported Halsey's decision to go north, believing that Halsey had had the vision to look beyond the landings at Leyte. Thach said, "If I were Halsey and had the whole thing to do over again, even knowing what's been written in all the books, I'd still go after those carriers." In an interview conducted as part of the U.S. Naval Institute's oral history program, Admiral Bogan, who commanded Halsey's Task Group 38.2 at Leyte Gulf, summed up his thoughts on the matter by saying, "It's a long story and it will never be resolved, except that I'm clear in my own mind that it was a great mistake on Halsey's part."

With a half-century gone by in which to make a judgment, and realizing that no judgment will ever be final in this matter, what should history record in terms of this Halsey-Kinkaid controversy? Who is to be praised and who is to bear the burden of error? And just what errors were committed?

The answer is that both men are to be praised for much of what they did, but both must also bear a measure of the blame for what went wrong.

Kinkaid erred by making assumptions. The reasons for these erroneous assumptions are understandable. But, as Carl von Clausewitz noted, much friction lies waiting for the incautious commander, and the fog of war is thick under even the most routine circumstances. In war, assumptions must never be made if there are any means of verification available.

Kinkaid assumed that Halsey was covering San Bernardino Strait. In light of the vague messages sent by Halsey (and Kinkaid could not have known they were vague), this assumption makes sense. But in the final analysis it was a *mistaken* assumption and Kinkaid's fault lies in not attempting verification until it was too late to have the desired effect.

Halsey's error was the more egregious. Without Halsey's mistake, Kinkaid's error is erased and the Battle of Leyte Gulf has a significantly modified outcome. One is tempted to point to a number of Halsey's actions and classify them as errors: his misunderstanding of his mission; his going north after a decoy force; his vague communications; his misreading of Nimitz's "Where is TF 34?" message; his emotional response to Nimitz's message; his attempts to fix the blame on Kinkaid. But in truth all of these points lose their significance in light of a single error Halsey made. Had Halsey divided his forces before going north, had he left part of his tremendous combat capability behind at San Bernardino Strait, instead of taking the entire Third Fleet with him, *all of the other errors would be canceled out.* It would not have mattered that Halsey saw his mission as offensive rather than defensive. No one would have cared that Ozawa's force was an impotent decoy. His vague messages would not have mattered and would have remained folded away in the yellowed pages of communication logs rather than being subjected to the scrutiny of the world. Nimitz would never have been compelled to write his misunderstood message. And Bill Halsey and Tom Kinkaid would have remained friends until death. In short, the world would never have wondered what went on at Leyte Gulf.

If Halsey's reluctance to divide his fleet was at the heart of the matter, what was it that caused him to make that tragic decision? His Mahanian War College training was most likely an ingredient in his thinking. Seven years after the war, Halsey explained his reasoning in the U.S. Naval Institute's *Proceedings* magazine:

> I could guard San Bernardino with Task Force 34 while I struck the Northern Force with my carriers. Rejected. The heavy air attacks on Task Group 38.3 which had resulted in the loss of the *Princeton* indicated that the enemy still had powerful air forces and forbade exposing our battleships without adequate air protection. *It is a cardinal principle of naval warfare not to divide one's force to such an extent as will permit it to be beaten in detail.* If enemy shore-based planes joined with his carrier planes, together they might inflict far more damage on my half-fleets separately than they could inflict upon my fleet intact. [Emphasis added]

At the time of the battle, Halsey did not know how severely hampered was Japanese air power, so he cannot be blamed for overestimating the capability of his enemy. The loss of *Princeton* must have been a sobering event, and it is no wonder that Halsey factored that into his thinking. And what he says about dividing the fleet "to such an extent as will permit it to be beaten in detail" is certainly true. But to assert that the Third Fleet could not be divided without risking its being "beaten in detail" is unreasonable. This was a tremendously potent force that could well afford to be divided. Fleets are, after all, meant to be divided. Otherwise, why have that complicated system of task forces, groups, units, and so on? Why have other admirals in the fleet?

Halsey's point about leaving the battleships at San Bernardino Strait without air cover is well taken and is something apparently overlooked by Kinkaid in his continual assertions that leaving TF 34 behind was "exactly correct in the circumstances." But why not leave behind an air group to defend the battleships when daylight returned? Admiral Lee's suggestion that one or two CVLs would be all that was needed has a great deal of merit.

There may be another factor in this equation. Halsey was embarked in a battleship. Since the night approach of Kurita called for the gunships of the Third Fleet as the logical counter, breaking off the battleships to remain behind at San Bernardino would have required Halsey to remain as well. Halsey's belief that Ozawa's Northern Force represented the "big battle," coupled with his frustration at having missed all of the other large fleet engagements of the war, may well have motivated him to send the battleships, including his flagship, *New Jersey*, and therefore *himself*, north.

This is, of course, speculation, and there is no way to know for certain what caused Bull Halsey to make that fateful decision. The world will continue to wonder.

In 1936, the Naval War College published *Sound Military Decision*, a book that included the observation that in naval warfare "mistakes are normal, errors are usual; information is seldom complete, often inaccurate, and frequently misleading." This was certainly true at Leyte Gulf, and the War College, in the spirit of gleaning lessons learned, embarked upon a special postwar project, headed by Commodore Richard W. Bates, the purpose of which was to prepare a detailed "strategical and tactical analysis" of the Battle of Leyte Gulf. The foreword to the study explains the need for the analysis "because of the nature of the Allied victory at Leyte Gulf and the numerous controversies which have arisen concerning it. . . ." The resulting study was indeed detailed—consisting of more than two thousand pages—and promised to be a valuable document that would achieve the stated purpose of provoking "earnest thought among prospective commanders and thus to improve professional judgment in command." Unfortunately, the study ended at the Battle of Surigao Strait; the controversy over the action at Samar was never analyzed. The foreword to the fifth and final volume explained the sudden termination of the project as follows: "For reasons beyond the control of the Naval War College, the Chief of Naval Operations decided to conclude the battle analyses with the Battle of Surigao Strait and to discontinue all other planned volumes."

This was a most unfortunate decision. Any organization does well to encourage introspection and self-criticism of a constructive nature. The Navy probably cheated itself of a valuable document by terminating Commodore Bates's project before it got to the stages of the battle most needing such a look.

Halsey and Kinkaid were not alone in their errors at Leyte Gulf. Nimitz shares a small measure of the blame for allowing the caveat to be appended to Halsey's orders and for not recognizing the danger signs so apparent in Halsey's letter to CINCPAC before the battle. MacArthur should not have permitted the awkward communications setup between Halsey and Kinkaid that allowed so much delay and confusion. Bogan, Lee, and Mitscher should have pressed Halsey with their concerns when they felt he was making a mistake. And Sprague should have seen to the rescue of the men who were forced to abandon his ships during the action off Samar.

While it is important for the sake of learning to remember and evaluate the errors made, it is also important for the sake of the nation's heritage to remember what was achieved. Admiral Halsey, for example, deserves a great deal of credit for keeping the Japanese off balance by his bold actions. It was Halsey who caused the acceleration in schedule that brought the Americans to the Philippines before the Japanese had completed their preparations, and it was his aggressiveness that caused his enemy to commit their precious air assets at Formosa. On 6 January 1945, President Roosevelt delivered what would prove to be his last State of the Union Address. Among the many things he reported to the Congress on that wintery day was the following:

> Last September . . . it was our plan to approach the Philippines by further stages, taking islands which we may call A, C, and E. However,

Admiral Halsey reported that a direct attack on Leyte appeared feasible. . . . Within the space of 24 hours, a major change of plans was accomplished which involved Army and Navy forces from two different theaters of operations—a change which hastened the liberation of the Philippines and the final day of victory—a change which saved lives which would have been expended in the capture of islands which are now neutralized far behind our lines.

No small accolade from no small man.

Admiral Kinkaid, like Halsey, deserves a great deal of credit for his performance of duty before Leyte Gulf, and *at* Leyte his leadership, overall, was excellent. The amphibious landings, which were the primary mission of U.S. forces there, were superbly handled. His postwar reticence to participate in the dispute between Halsey and himself is admirable, and his eventual change of heart on that is fortunate for historians because it sheds some additional light on the controversy.

Without General MacArthur there might not have been a battle at Leyte Gulf. His persistence was instrumental in bringing about the liberation of the Philippines at an earlier time than would otherwise have occurred, and his ability to sway Roosevelt was pivotal to the whole matter.

Admiral Spruance conducted a brilliant campaign in the Marianas, though his decision to stay close to the islands to defend the amphibious forces was then, and is even today, a controversial one. The irony is that Spruance was criticized for doing exactly the opposite of what Halsey was criticized for doing at Leyte Gulf. The comment has been made many times, once by Halsey himself, that the war in the Pacific would have been better served had Halsey commanded at the Marianas and Spruance at Leyte Gulf.

Admiral Oldendorf's conduct of the battle in Surigao Strait was outstanding. His planning was flawless and his execution nearly so. Only the understandable errors that led to the unfortunate damage to *Albert W. Grant* mar an otherwise perfect performance.

Admiral Clifton Sprague deserves recognition for his conduct at Samar. Responding to a desperate situation with no time to plan and with few assets at his disposal, he managed to keep a cool head and made the best of a very bad situation.

One is reluctant to begin singling out individual ships and their commanders because all played important roles and because there are many examples of outstanding performance that deserve recognition. But in the case of the Taffy 3 escorts, an exception would be in order. What the men in those ships did on that October morning off Samar deserves to be a focal point of the nation's naval heritage, ranking with John Paul Jones's epic "I have not yet begun to fight" battle. Commander Ernest E. Evans received the Medal of Honor, posthumously, for his incredible courage while taking the *Johnston* "in harm's way." One of the buildings at the Navy's Surface Warfare Officers School in Newport, Rhode Island, rightfully bears his name. But there should be more tributes. A statue commemorating the deeds of those ships and the men who crewed them in the Battle of Leyte Gulf should be erected in the nation's capital so that all Americans will be reminded of the kind of courage and sacrifice this nation can produce when circumstances require.

War is probably mankind's greatest folly. It is wasteful, tragic, and frequently unnecessary. But when it does occur, in an ironic twist, it brings out what is in some ways *best* about mankind. Many brave men, American and Japanese, fought at Leyte Gulf. Too many died there, while others live even today as flesh-and-blood monuments to those virtues that shine forth from the wreckage and tragedy of war. Admirals Halsey, Kinkaid, and Sprague, General MacArthur, Captain Adair, Commanders Evans and McCampbell, Lieutenant Digardi, Petty Officer Roy West, Seaman Billie, and the thousands of others like them are to be honored just for being there at Leyte Gulf—for doing their jobs under arduous circumstances, for serving and sacrificing for their country. The causes for which these men fought and sacrificed have faded with time; the machines they used to carry out their deadly business are now rusted relics of another era; the sands have swallowed their footprints and the waters show no trace of their wakes. But the glory of their deeds will never be tarnished by time.

Source Notes

Many of the books I have read or consulted about the Second World War have helped shape my understanding of the subject but do not appear here or in the bibliography because I made no direct use of them in the writing of this book. Among the many works that cover the whole war or a large part of it, several are noteworthy for their treatment of the Battle of Leyte Gulf. Probably the most readable account is John Toland's *The Rising Sun*, which provides a reasonable amount of detail and presents the battle primarily from the Japanese point of view. Ronald H. Spector's *Eagle Against the Sun* is also an excellent, relatively recent rendition of the battle. Samuel Eliot Morison's *The Two-Ocean War* does the battle justice and is very readable, but his more focused and detailed book, *Leyte*, from his fifteen-volume study, *History of United States Naval Operations in World War II*, is the most complete account of the American side of the battle, suffering only from its age; Morison could not access some of the then-classified materials that have since come to light. My former colleagues in the Naval Academy's history department and professional historians everywhere will cringe at what I am about to say, but a truly wonderful (accurate and insightful) account of the battle is included in Herman Wouk's novel *War and Remembrance*.

There have, through the years, been a number of works devoted specifically to the Battle of Leyte Gulf. The most recent was a book by Adrian Stewart entitled simply *The Battle of Leyte Gulf*, which is a limited, popular rendition of the battle. C. Vann Woodward's *The Battle for Leyte Gulf* is a well-written, accurate account that suffers only from its age (like Morison, Woodward did not have full access to all pertinent information). Probably the best writer in the group, Stanley L. Falk, an associate professor of National Security Affairs at the Industrial College of the Armed Forces, titled his work *Decision at Leyte*. This work focuses on the land campaign as well as the sea battle, which makes for a more diversified treatment but results in a slight dilution of the naval aspects. James A. Field's *The Japanese at Leyte Gulf* presents the battle from the Japanese point of view, relying heavily on postwar testimony provided by Japanese naval officers during the Strategic Bombing Survey conducted by the Naval Analysis Division shortly after the war ended. Edwin P. Hoyt's *The Battle of Leyte Gulf* is one of the few works on the battle that is still in print, still available in a somewhat watered-down paperback version. Of the other mentioned works, only Morison's are still in print.

Many other works cited in the bibliography provided background and helped me to keep things within a World War II context; calling the ship-to-ship voice radio net by its World War II "TBS" rather than the more modern "PRITAC," for example.

Specific references follow and are arranged by chapter for convenience.

Chapter 1: CINCSOWESPAC

The opening scene is based primarily upon Douglas MacArthur's *Reminiscences*, D. Clayton James's *The Years of MacArthur*, William Manchester's *American Caesar*, and Gavin Long's *MacArthur as Military Commander*. MacArthur's feelings and words come from his *Reminiscences*, the political-strategic background referred to is covered by all the works here mentioned and especially Eric Larrabee's *Commander in Chief*. The PT boat escape is covered in Robert J. Bulkley's *At Close Quarters*.

Roosevelt's dinner party appears in James's *The Years of MacArthur* (page 128 of volume 2) and the many honors heaped upon MacArthur are listed on page 135 of that same work and on page 329 of Larrabee's *Commander in Chief*. Details provided in the footnotes regarding the JCS and the CCS are from Samuel Eliot Morison's monograph *Strategy and Compromise*. The argument that an admiral rather than a general should direct the Pacific war is addressed best in James (page 117) and the quote from Roosevelt's doctor is on pages 128–129 of that same volume. The Leahy quote is taken from his autobiographical *I Was There* (page 65) and the Roosevelt quote calling MacArthur "our worst politician" can be found in Manchester's *American Caesar*. Eric Larrabee discusses in some detail the potential political rivalry between Roosevelt and MacArthur on page 12 of his *Commander in Chief*. The compromise solution of what to do with MacArthur is discussed on pages 117–125 of James and pages 1 and 2 of M. Hamlin Cannon's *Leyte: Return to the Philippines*.

The discussion of Pacific strategy that makes up the last section of the chapter is gleaned from Morison's *History of United States Naval Operations in World War II* and his *The Two-Ocean War*; James's *The Years of MacArthur*; E. B. Potter and Chester Nimitz's collaborative *The Great Sea War*; C. Vann Woodward's *The Battle for Leyte Gulf*; Ronald H. Spector's *Eagle Against the Sun*; Dan Van Der Vat's *The Pacific Campaign*; and Edwin P. Hoyt's *MacArthur's Navy*.

Chapter 2: COMINCH

The account of the suicide leaps off Marpi Point is recounted in John Toland's *The Rising Sun* (pages 588–590), Spector's *Eagle Against the Sun* (pages 317–318), Morison's *The Two Ocean War* (page 290), Van Der Vat's *The Pacific Campaign* (page 328), and most graphically in Major Frank Hough's account, "End in Saipan" included in Don Congdon's *Combat World War II (Pacific Theater of Operations* volume, pages 455–456). These sources do not agree as to the number of people committing suicide: Toland says 22,000; Morison says "hundreds"; Van Der Vat says 8,000; and Spector says "almost two thirds of the 12,000 total noncombatants." Toland is probably the most correct because he was closer to Japanese sources than were the others. Morison's account, as noted earlier, suffers from its age.

Admiral Spruance is re-created from information found in Larrabee's *Commander in Chief*, Thomas B. Buell's *The Quiet Warrior*, and E. P. Forrestel's *Admiral Raymond Spruance, USN*.

The Battle of the Philippine Sea is covered in a large number of sources, but the focus of this account is based primarily upon Morison's *The Two Ocean War*, Eric Grove's *Fleet to Fleet Encounters*, William T. Y'Blood's *Red Sun Setting: The Battle of the Philippine Sea*, Charles A. Lockwood's *Battles of the Philippine Sea*, and Spector's *Eagle Against the Sun*. The references to "unsinkable aircraft carriers" and the malarial problems of Japanese forces are addressed in Yoichi Hirama's "Japanese Naval Preparations for World War II."

The quote, "if you get shot now, you were hit in your own rear areas," is taken from Toland's *The Rising Sun* (page 588) and the exchange between King and Roosevelt over the COMINCH title is related in Potter's *Nimitz* (page 311). Other details about King were taken from Larrabee, Robert Love's *The Chiefs of Naval Operations*, and Robert Spiller's *Dictionary of American Military Biography*. The Love quote concerning King's weaknesses and the quote of King's daughter are drawn from Larrabee (page 155). King's reassuring words to Spruance regarding the latter's actions during the Battle of the Philippine Sea resides on page 320 of Buell's *The Quiet Warrior*. The Nimitz lamentations on things that might have been comes from his Summary of Action for June 1944, submitted to King and included among King's papers on microfilm at Nimitz Library at the U.S. Naval Academy (also quoted on page 303 of Potter's *Nimitz*).

The evaluation of King as a strategist is reflected in many World War II analyses but is summed in Spiller's *Dictionary of American Military Biography* (page 564). King's trip around Saipan is recounted in Potter's *Nimitz* (pages 312–314) and the unappetizing story about the Saipan flies appears on pages 320–321 of Buell's *The Quiet Warrior*.

The comments on differing Pacific strategies were derived from Cannon's *Leyte: Return to the Philippines* and Morison's *History of United States Naval Oper-*

ations in World War II. The MacArthur radio message can be found on page 4 of Cannon.

Chapter 3: CINCPAC

The rubber contraceptive story was originally related by Lamar (pages 8–9) and is included in Potter's *Nimitz* (page 186).

Much of the material in this chapter is taken from Potter's *Nimitz*. The original letter to Nimitz's wife regarding Drew Pearson is in the Special Collections of Nimitz Library at the Naval Academy. The framed photograph quote is drawn from page 222 of Potter's *Nimitz*.

The description of Roosevelt at sea is derived from James MacGregor Burns's *Roosevelt: Soldier of Freedom* and Larrabee's *Commander in Chief*. The Burns quote describing Roosevelt's vulnerability to the voters is on page 496 and Fala's tribulations are described on page 488.

The material on "Dusty" Rhoades comes from his published diary, *Flying MacArthur to Victory*. The loyal disciple quote is on page 133.

Roosevelt's triumphant entry into Pearl Harbor is described in many works, including Burns, Leahy, and Potter's *Nimitz*. Leahy's quote about the lack of remaining evidence of the attack appears on page 249 of his *I Was There*.

The activities during the President's visit to Pearl Harbor and the Roosevelt-Leahy-MacArthur-Nimitz dinner are described in varying detail in Manchester, Leahy, Larrabee, Burns, MacArthur, and Potter's *Nimitz*. Leahy's quoted observations appear on pages 250–251 and MacArthur's comment on Roosevelt's neutrality during the after-dinner discussions come from page 251 of his *Reminiscences*. MacArthur's warning to Roosevelt about the potential of voter vengeance is taken from Burns (page 489). The letter from Roosevelt to MacArthur appears on page 217 of the latter's *Reminiscences*.

The details of the luncheon at Nimitz's quarters are taken from Lamar and Potter's *Nimitz*. The reference to "MacArthur's victory luncheon" appears in Potter's *Bull Halsey* (page 275). The MacArthur quote about seeing "eye to eye" is on page 319 of Potter's *Nimitz*.

Chapter 4: COMTHIRDFLT

The opening section of the chapter is derived from information in the Halsey/Bryan biography, Potter's *Bull Halsey*, and *Born to Fight* by Ralph B. Jordan.

The Halsey quote about the nickname "Bull" comes from the Halsey/Bryan book and Halsey's utterance about the Japanese language is in many sources including Potter's biography (page 13). The various names that Halsey had assigned his enemies are covered on pages IX–X of Jordan. The Arleigh Burke quote can be found on page 24 of the booklet, *The Best of Burke*. The observations by Merrill concerning Halsey's intellectual capabilities are included in *The Dictionary of American Military Biography* (pages 427–428). Halsey's words concerning his "report" and his avoidance of philosophy and politics appear on page 1 of his autobiography. Nimitz's defense of Halsey is covered in Larrabee (pages 391–392) and Potter's *Bull Halsey* (page 35). The Halsey "stagecoach" quote appears on page 197 of his autobiography. Descriptions of the Third Fleet abound, but the material for this one comes from *Battles of the Philippine Sea* (pages 63–64) and C. Vann Woodward's book on Leyte Gulf (page 27). The description of the At Sea Logistics Group is derived from *The Great Sea War* by Potter and Nimitz (page 365), Larrabee (page 391), and Spector (page 423).

Halsey's box score of the Philippine raids in September is recorded on page 199 of his autobiography. The reconnaissance information is taken from page 375 of a Naval Institute oral history of the memories of John Thach and from page 571 of Admiral King's *A Naval Record*. Halsey's dilemma and subsequent decision are described in his autobiography (pages 199–200) and in Potter's *Bull Halsey* (page 277).

The process of JCS acceptance of Halsey's proposal to accelerate the landing schedule is described well in Morison's *History of United States Naval Operations in World War II* (volume 12). Halsey's point of view is in his autobiography on pages 200–201. The Marshall quote appears in the Halsey autobiography on page 201, and comes from the "Biennial Report of the Chief of Staff of the United Army to the Secretary of War, July 1, 1943 to June 30, 1945," submitted by General of the Army George C. Marshall.

Chapter 5: "We Will Fight You All!"

Much of this chapter is drawn from Admiral Ugaki's diary, published as *Fading Victory*. His musings in the aftermath of the battle of the Philippine Sea are found on pages 415–416, his reflections on the suicides at Marpi Point are on page 437, and his declaration of "We will fight you all!" is on page 441.

The Fuchida quote is taken from page 131 of *Interrogations of Japanese Officials* conducted after the war by the Naval Analysis Division as part of the Strategic Bombing Survey. Morison discusses the contrasting figures regarding American flyers in his *The Two-Ocean War* (pages 280–281). The deterioration of Japanese aircraft production and maintenance is discussed by the Japanese themselves in the *Interrogations*. C. Vann Woodward covers the logistics problems of the Japanese on pages 14–15 of his book. The Japanese intention to reunite their fleet is covered in the *Interrogations* (pages 219–220). The significance of Halsey's acceleration of the schedule is acknowledged by Morison in his *History of United States Naval Operations in World War II* (volume 12, pages 66–67), by Woodward (pages 22–23), and by the Japanese themselves on pages 38 and 153 of the *Interrogations*.

Chapter 6: King Two

The reminiscences of Charles Adair are in his Naval Institute oral history. The observation that more American sailors would be at Leyte than had been in the entire U.S. Navy in 1938 is Morison's, in his *The Two-Ocean War* (footnote on page 370).

The information on Admiral Kinkaid comes from his papers, which reside in the Naval Historical Center in Washington, D.C. The 1908 *Lucky Bag* can be found in Nimitz Library at the U.S. Naval Academy, where there is a complete collection of these college yearbooks.

Edwin Hoyt's *MacArthur's Navy* provides some information on that topic and his *The Men of the Gambier Bay* gives a good description of CVEs. Other carrier types are covered in detail in Norman Friedman's *U.S. Aircraft Carriers: An Illustrated Design History*. Morison, Woodward, Congdon, and the CINCPAC papers all provide insight into the planning for King Two. Professor Potter's incisive analysis of the caveat to Halsey's orders is found on pages 279 and 402 of his *Bull Halsey*. Halsey's interpretations and his correspondence with Nimitz appear in his autobiography and in Potter's biography.

Chapter 7: "We Sailed Quietly East in the Dark of Night"

Much of the first section of this chapter is drawn from "Design and Construction of *Yamato* and *Musashi*" by K. Matsumoto and M. Chihaya. The reference to the picture of *Mogami* appears in Woodward (page 35); *Haruna*'s history is mentioned on page 617 of Toland; and *Shigure*'s is found in Paul Dull's *A Battle History of the Imperial Japanese Navy*. The Japanese decision to build superior ships to the American Navy's is discussed in Toshiyuki Yokoi's "Thoughts on Japan's Naval Defeat" (page 73). Building the super-battleships so that any U.S. copies would be unable to use the Panama Canal is revealed in the Matsumoto article (page 1104). Details of the building of the super-battleships are found on pages 1109–1110 of Matsumoto. Admiral Kurita's claim that he was not permitted to know the top speed or caliber of the big ships' guns appears on page 52 of the Naval Analysis Division *Interrogations*. Details of the blast effect and ammunition types of the guns are on pages 1107–1109 of the Matsumoto article. The Ugaki quote at the end of the section comes from page 479 of his diary (*Fading Victory*).

Details of the meeting in Tokyo are found in Harries' *Soldiers of the Sun* (page 403) and Toland. The quoted conversations appear on page 610 of the latter.

The comparison of chess and go is my own observation but was inspired by a comment in Stanley Karnow's *In Our Image*, in which he calls the Japanese Philippine strategy "as complex as a *Go* game" (page 313). The observation regarding Japan's lost ability to trade space for time is taken directly from page 6 of Field's book. The Miyazaki quote is included in MacArthur's *Reminiscences* (pages 244–245). The *Sho* plans are discussed in many sources, but particularly useful are Field's book (page 9), Congdon (page 610), and the Naval Analysis Division's *Interrogations* (page 294).

The reasoning behind Halsey's pre-Leyte attacks on Okinawa, Formosa, and the Philippines is discussed on pages 1440–1442 of W. D. Puleston's article "Modern War and Ancient Maxims," page 119 of Hoyt's *The Carrier War*, and in Morison's *The Two-Ocean War* (page 362). Kusaka's activation of *Sho Ni Go* is discussed in Hoyt's *The Carrier War* (pages 119–121) and in Morison's *History of United States Naval Operations in World War II* (volume 12, page 69). The latter is also the source of the Fukudome reaction to the Formosa attacks (page 93). Toland reveals the Toho Motion Picture Company's efforts on page 607 of *The Rising Sun*. The Carney quote appears in Hoyt's *The Carrier War* (page 123). The effects of Halsey's raids are discussed in Spector (page 424), Woodward (page 22), and Morison's *History* (page 104). The Japanese point of view of the effects can be found on pages 131 and 220 of the Naval Analysis Division's *Interrogations*. Field speculates on the differences of Ozawa and Kurita on pages 29–34 of his book.

The final section of the chapter is based upon Ugaki's diary (pages 480–485).

Chapter 8: "Strike!"

The focus on Rhoades in this section is based upon his memoirs, *Flying MacArthur to Victory*. His approach to Leyte comes from pages 296–297 and the discussion between him and MacArthur is recounted on page 260.

Joseph St. John's observance of the landing is recounted on pages 186–187 of his memoir, *Leyte Calling*.

MacArthur on the bridge of Nashville is based on a description appearing on page 348 of Frazier Hunt's *The Untold Story of Douglas MacArthur* and page 251 of MacArthur's *Reminiscences*.

The section relating to St. John's experiences as a fugitive and guerrilla in the Philippines comes from pages 40, 62, 113–114, 128–310, and 186–188 of his memoir.

The final section of the chapter is based upon Rhoades (pages 297–298) and MacArthur (pages 252–253).

Chapter 9: Of Sorties, Submarines, and Coffee

Details of U.S. submarine activities are included in the three-volume study of the battle by Richard Bates, entitled *The Battle of Leyte Gulf, October 1944* (pages 50–57 and 135). Some details are also found in Morison's *History* (volume 12, page 168). Information on the *Ise* and *Hyuga* "hermaphrodites" can be found in the Naval Analysis Division *Interrogations* (page 277), Congdon (page 614), Spector (pages 431–432), and most especially in *The Hybrid Warship* by Layman and McLaughlin. Their condition upon heading south is detailed in the *Interrogations* on pages 154 and 221.

Details of Andy Kerr's experiences are found in his wonderful book *A Journey Amongst the Good and the Great* and his oral history done by the Naval Institute in 1983–1984. The number of Japanese aircraft in the Philippines at the time of the American return is discussed in Field's book (pages 255–256), Woodward's (page 40), and Morison's *History* (volume 12, page 165). These figures are, as Morison puts it, "still a matter of guess," because there was so much shuffling of assets between the Philippines, Japan, and Formosa as a result of the activation of *Sho*. On page 8 of his book, Woodward makes the observation about the scattering of aircraft among the many islands of the Philippine archipelago. The experiences of Leon Garsian are recorded in a footnote on page 146 of volume 12 of Morison's *History*, and the mistaken identity of *Honolulu* is covered on pages 145–148 of that same work.

Details of the Japanese meeting aboard the cruiser *Atago* and the discussions of strategy are taken from Toland (page 618), Karnow (page 313), Ugaki (pages 484–485), and Kenneth Macksey's *Military Errors of World War II* (page 220). The naval historian and analyst quoted ("one leg ashore, one leg afloat") is W. D. Puleston and that wonderful phrase is found in his article "Modern War and Ancient Maxims" appearing in the December 1945 issue of *Proceedings* magazine (page 1441).

Chapter 10: Dangerous Ground

The American point of view of the engagement in Palawan Passage is well covered in R. C. Benitez's two articles "Battle Stations Submerged" and "Prelude to the Battle of Leyte Gulf" as well as Theodore Roscoe's *Submarine Operations of World War II*. The Japanese point of view can be found in Ugaki's diary, Field's book, the Naval Analysis Division's *Interrogations*, and Janusz Skulski's *The Battleship Yamato*. An area of some confusion is whether a rendezvous between Nishimura and Shima was ever intended. Field admits that this issue is "somewhat obscure" (page 257), but Ugaki's diary seems to confirm that no rendezvous was ever intended (page 486).

Chapter 11: TG 38.3

The Halsey quote regarding "changing the drivers" is taken from his autobiography. Locations of the various forces described in the opening section of the chapter are established in many sources; of particular use for this book were Larrabee (page 391), Woodward (page 43), and John Monsarrat's *Angel on the Yardarm* (page 43). On page 426 of his *Eagle Against the Sun*, Spector discusses Halsey's reasoning in sending two of his task groups to Ulithi in the midst of the invasion.

In his *Proceedings* article appearing in May 1952, Halsey explains his tactics during the search phase of the battle and Woodward sheds some additional light on pages 47–48 of his book. Admiral Sherman discusses his concerns on page 292 of his book, *Combat Command.*

The Japanese point of view is gleaned from the Naval Analysis Division's *Interrogations.* Specifically, the Yamaguchi quote appears on page 180 and the Kurita rebuttal is on page 38.

The account of reconnoitering the Sibuyan Sea is a product of the material in Halsey's autobiography; Woodward; Sherman; and Theodore Taylor's biography, *The Magnificent Mitscher.* Details are abundant in Air Group Eighteen's official history.

The Halsey "burned into my brain" quote is on page 128 of his autobiography. The exchange of messages between Halsey and Nimitz regarding Halsey's desire to head into the inland seas of the Philippines is covered in Potter's *Nimitz* (page 331) and his *Bull Halsey* (page 287). The Halsey "Strike" message comes from pages 213–214 of his autobiography.

Admiral Sherman's inability to carry out the Halsey strike order is explained in Sherman's memoirs (*Combat Command,* pages 213–214).

The McCampbell story is covered well in Edward H. Sims's *Greatest Fighter Missions* (pages 195–219) and Barrett Tillman's *Hellcat* (pages 139–141). McCampbell also has an oral history in the Naval Institute's collection.

The *Princeton* sinking is covered in a number of sources, including Morison's *History* (volume 12), but there are some significant details available in Nimitz's summary of operations for the month of October (copy available in Nimitz Library Special Collections). The executive officer's letter is quoted there. The information on Paul Drury was provided to me by Mr. Drury in an interview conducted on 13 March 1993 (with several follow-up conversations for additional detail). Other information is available in the Time-Life Books' *Return to the Philippines* volume in their World War II series, Hanson Baldwin's "The Sho Plan: The Battle of Leyte Gulf" (reprinted in Congdon), Halsey's autobiography, and Sherman's memoirs.

Chapter 12: Sibuyan and Sulu Seas

The ideas concerning Halsey and his adherence to Mahan doctrine are my own but are based upon my readings of Halsey and of Mahan. The discussion of the Naval War College is based upon information found in *Sailors and Scholars: The Centennial History of the U.S. Naval War College* by John Hattendorf et al., *The U.S. Naval War College, 1919–1941: An Institutional Response to Naval Preparedness* by Gerald J. Kennedy, *The Blue Sword: The Naval War College and the American Mission, 1919–1941* by Michael Vlahos, and "The Naval War College and the Origins of War Planning Against Japan" (*Naval War College Review,* July–August 1980) also by Vlahos. The Pratt quote is included in *Sailors and Scholars* (page 144). The Mahan quotation concerning concentration can be found on page XIX of Hattendorf's *Mahan on Naval Strategy*. The Kalbfus quote comes from his *Sound Military Decision* (reprinted as part of the Naval Institute's *Classics of Sea Power* series, page 68). The Halsey quote from his Naval War College thesis can be found in that document in the Naval War College Library (titled "The Relationship in War of Naval Strategy, Tactics, and Command" and dated 16 May 1933). The Halsey "cardinal principle of warfare" quote is from his May 1952 *Proceedings* article, "The Battle of Leyte Gulf."

Much of the section dealing with the *Enterprise* comes from Edward P. Stafford's *The Big E* (also reprinted as part of the Naval Institute's *Classics of Naval Literature* series in 1988). The Fred Bakutis story is recounted in Eric Hammel's *Aces Against Japan* and Barrett Tillman's *Hellcat*.

The section dealing with American reconnaissance and the concern over the absence of Japanese carriers is drawn from Potter's *Bull Halsey* (page 294) and Halsey's autobiography (page 216).

Details of the air battles in the Sibuyan Sea are found in Toland, Field, Ugaki, the Naval Analysis Division's *Interrogations*, Wilbur H. Morrison's *Above and Beyond*, and Tomiji Koyanagi's article "With Kurita in the Battle of Leyte Gulf."

Chapter 13: "Start Them North"

The opening section of the chapter is based primarily on Field's book (pages 62–63).

The next section comes from Monsarrat (pages 33–35 and 103–104), Hoyt's *The Carrier War* (page 129), the Naval Analysis Division's *Interrogations* (pages 130, 156–157, and 221–222), the oral history account of George Van Deurs (page 490), and Sherman's *Combat Command* (pages 294–295).

The section dealing with communications is based on Field (page 70), Potter's *Bull Halsey* (page 290–293), and Halsey's autobiography (page 214). Nimitz's message concerning coordination of operations can be found on page 615 of Congdon and the message from King to Kinkaid is on page 130 of William M. Leary's *We Shall Return!: MacArthur's Commanders and the Defeat of Japan*. Kinkaid's assumption that Halsey had formed Task Force 34 is discussed in many sources but can be found in its most original form in his after-action report, a copy of which is kept in the Special Collections section of Nimitz Library. Also at Nimitz Library (on microfilm among the King papers) is a copy of Halsey's COMTHIRD-FLT 240612Z OCT 44 message telling TF 34 to "engage decisively at long ranges."

Sherman's problems are discussed on page 295 of his *Combat Command*. Halsey's three options are discussed in his autobiography but in a more original form in his after-action report to Nimitz (copy among his papers at the National Archives and on microfilm among the King papers at Nimitz Library). Halsey discusses his reasoning behind accepting the aviators' estimates of damage in the Sibuyan Sea in his *Proceedings* article (page 490). His professed ignorance of the number of planes Ozawa had and his concerns about shuttle-bombing are quoted from Congdon (page 651). Halsey's friendship with Spruance and his presence at CINCPAC headquarters during the Marianas campaign are discussed on pages 176–178 of Potter's *Arleigh Burke*. The "Start them north" quote appears on page 217 of Halsey's autobiography.

Chapter 14: Exits and Entrances

The opening section and later references to Roy West are based on information he provided to me during several personal interviews. It should be noted that Mr. West's only hesitancy in helping me was that he felt his name would appear a disproportionate number of times in the book. "I'm no hero, and it's not fair to the other men who fought at Leyte to put so much emphasis on me," he said with complete sincerity.

The Kinkaid quote regarding the importance of clear communications appears in his article entitled, "A Naval Career" (page 47). There seems to be some uncertainty as to who actually drafted the confusing messages. Robert Love, in his recent *History of the U.S. Navy*, states that it was Halsey's chief of staff Carney who did the writing and that may well be true. But the responsibility, in any case, is Halsey's. Kinkaid's belief that Halsey had left TF 34 behind is stated on page 643 of Congdon. Nimitz's and Spruance's reactions (including the Spruance quote that "I would keep my force right there") are on page 336 of Potter's *Nimitz*.

The death of Nishimura's son is revealed in Toland (page 632). The battle history of destroyer *Shigure* is recounted in Paul Dull's *A Battle History of the Imperial Japanese Navy, 1941–1945*.

Details of the Seventh Fleet Operation Plan, and the attitudes contained therein, are discussed in Charles Adair's oral history account (pages 399–405 of transcript). The problems with the ammunition load-out are discussed by Adair (page 403) and by Kinkaid himself in an interview included in John T. Mason's *The Pacific War Remembered: An Oral History Collection* (page 269). Oldendorf's claim that he never delegated the drafting of battle plans comes from his "Comments on the Battle of Surigao Strait" (page 105).

The section dealing with Captain Coward comes from his article "Destroyer Dust," Morison's *History*, and an article, also by Morison, entitled "The Battle of Surigao Strait." The voice messages quoted in the section are taken directly from *McDermut*'s TBS log, a copy of which was provided to me by Roy West.

Background on the use of PT boats in World War II can be found in Norman Polmar's *World War II: America at War* and Robert J. Bulkley Jr.'s *At Close Quarters: PT Boats in the United States Navy*. Details of the PT boat preparations for battle are in Morison's "The Battle of Surigao Strait" (page 35).

The concluding section, dealing with Fitzhugh Lee comes from his oral history.

Chapter 15: Midwatch in Surigao Strait

The battle in Surigao Strait is reconstructed by careful comparison of the accounts of Morison, Toland, Spector, Woodward, Coward, Bulkley, Kinkaid (oral history), Oldendorf ("Comments" in *Proceedings*), and Walter Karig et al., *Battle Report*. Careful examination of the TBS radio logs of the various ships and their dead-reckoning trace charts helps to corroborate and resolve differences. Roy West's memories were very helpful as well, especially for the sections dealing with him and the others in *McDermut*.

Chapter 16: Curtain Call

This is a continuation of chapter 15, continuing and concluding the battle of Surigao Strait. Sources include those accounts mentioned for the previous chapter plus the monthly CINCPAC/CINCPOA report for October 1944, the oral histories of Joshua Cooper and Roland Smoot, Field's book, the accounts of Mori and Nishino as provided during the Naval Analysis Division *Interrogations*, a press conference with Admiral Kinkaid (transcript among Kinkaid's papers in Naval Historical Center in Washington, D.C.), Kinkaid's article ("A Naval Career"), and the comments of Vice Admiral T. D. Ruddock appearing in *Proceedings* (November 1959).

Chapter 17: Friction and Fog

The first quotation is taken from Nimitz's formal report to King on the battle (copy among King's papers on microfilm at Nimitz Library). The discussions between Davison and Russell are recorded in the latter's oral history.

The accounts of Bogan's and Lee's reservations about Halsey's actions are taken from the transcript of Bogan's oral history (page 109) and Ivan Musicant's *Battleship at War* (pages 290–294), respectively. Burke's and Flatley's doubts and their visit to Mitscher's cabin are related in *The Best of Burke* (page 17), Potter's *Burke* (page 206), and Taylor's *The Magnificent Mitscher* (page 262). Professor Potter was also kind enough to share his vast knowledge and insights with me.

Also useful in writing this chapter were Halsey's autobiography and Arthur McCollum's oral history (pages 645–646). The latter's account provides the details of the meeting of Kinkaid's staff and the resulting actions of that conference.

Chapter 18: "Charge of the Light Brigade"

Background for this chapter comes from a number of sources with good accounts of the battle off Samar, most notably Toland, Karig, and Field. The poetry comes from the *Oxford Book of War Poetry*.

The opening quote is from Ugaki's diary (page 492). Kurita's message beginning "Braving any loss . . . " is included in Koyanagi's account in *The Japanese Navy in World War II*, edited by David C. Evans. Otani's memories are drawn from the Naval Analysis Division's *Interrogations* (pages 171–172). Kurita's formation is diagrammed on page 39 of the latter work and Kurita's caveat is discussed there as well (page 224).

The early-morning discovery of the Japanese by the men of USS *Roberts* is recounted in Edward P. Stafford's *Little Ship, Big War* (pages 136–137).

The accounts of Ed Digardi, Bill Mercer, and Robert Billie are based upon conversations with these men and with their published accounts in *The Fighting and Sinking of the USS Johnston, DD-557*, edited by Bill Mercer. Some of the information about *Johnston* and Evans was taken from an article by Robert C. Hagen, "We Asked for the Jap Fleet—And Got It," which appeared originally in the *Saturday Evening Post* and is reproduced in aforementioned Mercer book.

The Otani quote appears in the Naval Analysis Division's *Interrogations*.

Ohmae's observation about the American predictable pattern of sending out reconnaissance planes a half-hour before sunrise is also in the *Interrogations* (page 158).

The "seagoing foxhole" is Karig's (page 388).

The messages from Kinkaid to Halsey, and the latter's replies, are included as an addendum to Halsey's after-action report submitted to Nimitz (copy among King's papers on microfilm in Nimitz Library).

Details on *Roberts*'s demise are found in Karig and Stafford.

The Japanese naval officer saluting as *Johnston* went down is recounted in Toland and confirmed by many of the *Johnston* survivors in their book (Mercer).

Chapter 19: "The World Wonders"

Much of this chapter comes from the *Interrogations*, Ugaki's diary, Toland, William T. Y'Blood's *The Little Giants*, Morison's *History of United States Naval Operations in World War II* (volume 12), and Clark Reynold's *The Fast Carriers*, and an oral history by Joseph J. Rochefort.

The Nimitz quote at the beginning of the chapter comes from page 7 of his booklet, *Some Thoughts to Live By*, published by the Nimitz Foundation. The "world wonders" fiasco is carefully derived from a number of sources: Halsey's article (page 492), Kinkaid's letters to Potter, Bernard Brodie's article "The Battle of Leyte Gulf" (pages 459–460), and the actual message logs (among King's papers at Nimitz Library). The Wouk quote at the end of the section is from page 1041 of *War and Remembrance*.

The focus on *Gambier Bay* comes from Edwin Hoyt's *The Men of the Gambier Bay*.

The Stump quote regarding John Paul Jones is on pages 194–195 of *The Little Giants*.

The Ugaki quote, questioning Kurita's reasoning, is from his diary (page 497).

The words of the commanding officer of *Kitkun Bay* are from page 395 of Karig and the gun hits on torpedoes are also recorded in Karig (page 398). The two wonderful quotes from sardonic American sailors ("We're sucking them into 40-mm range" and "Goddammit, they're getting away!") appear in a number of accounts including Toland and Y'Blood.

Captain Ohmae's evaluation of the American pilots at Engaño is on page 158 of the Naval Analysis Division's *Interrogations*. Halsey's admission of error in turning south is on page 658 of Congdon (Halsey's appended comments to Hanson Baldwin's article about the battle).

Adrian Stewart talks about the Japanese faulty perception of relative speed on page 179 of his book, and it is confirmed in various places in the *Interrogations*. The wonderful "pygmies/giants" quote is from Field's book (page 126). Kurita granted a rare interview (outside of that of the Naval Analysis Division's) some years after the war, which appears on pages 165–167 of *The End of the Imperial Japanese Navy* by Masanori Ito and Roger Pineau. His admission that the destruction of carriers was "a kind of obsession with me" comes from that interview. Kurita's claim that he was going north to join Ozawa appears in the *Interrogations* (page 44). His contradictions appear in that same interview. His comment about being tired is from page 166 of the Ito and Pineau interview. Ugaki's criticism is from page 497 of his diary and Ohmae's is on page 159 of the *Interrogations*.

Chapter 20: "Divine Wind"

Toland writes of the origin of the Japanese reverence for the "divine wind," but his dates do not match other sources consulted, such as the *Encyclopedia Britannica* and several college texts on Japanese history. This must be a misprint in Toland's book because his mastery of Japanese facts is otherwise flawless and most impressive.

The origins of the *kamikaze* as a weapon are well covered in *The Divine Wind* by Rikihei Inoguchi et al.; *Suicide Weapons* by Arthur J. Barker; *Divine Thunder* by Bernard Millot; Toland's *The Rising Sun*; and Spector's *Eagle Against the Sun*.

The first *kamikaze* attacks at Leyte Gulf are described in the aforementioned sources and in Y'Blood's *The Little Giants* and Hoyt's *The Kamikazes*.

The firsthand experiences of Vern Kimmel are based upon conversations with him and on materials he very kindly sent to me.

Chapter 21: Long Nights

The experiences of the men in the water are from the recollections of those men as told to me during interviews and as recorded in Mercer's compilation, *The Fighting and Sinking of the USS Johnston, DD-557*. Charles Adair's role in their rescue is reconstructed from his and R. D. Tarbuck's oral histories.

Chapter 22: Epitaph

As is fitting for a final chapter of a work such as this, much of what appears here are my own conclusions. However, certain specifics need to be addressed.

The Halsey quote at the beginning of the chapter comes from his after-action report to Nimitz and King (copy available in King papers in Nimitz Library at the U.S. Naval Academy). As stated in the text, the quote comparing Leyte to Syracuse comes from Admiral Morison's *History* (volume 12, page 337), and the words of Yonai are from page 338 of that same work. The already mentioned Ito interview (on page 167 of his and Pineau's work) is relied upon again and the note about Kurita's navigational track is based upon information found in Dull's book. The Halsey quote explaining his reasoning for leaving San Bernardino Strait unguarded is from Potter's *Bull Halsey* (page 307). The Nimitz letter to King was dated 28 October 1944 and is available among King's papers at Nimitz Library. The "green light" quote is from Halsey's autobiography (page 226). Professor Potter gives the best account of Halsey's postwar activities in his biography. The quotes used are identified in the text. The letters between King and Kinkaid are among the Kinkaid papers at the Naval Historical Center in Washington and make fascinating reading. The Baldwin article with its appended comments by Kinkaid and Halsey is reprinted in its entirety in Congdon. The 1960 Kinkaid interview appears in Mason's *The Pacific War Remembered* (quote from page 274). The Thach quote is from his oral history conducted by the Naval Institute in 1971 (pages 387–388 of the transcript). Bogan's words come from his oral history transcript (page 86). The Halsey quote from the *Proceedings* article is on page 490. The Leyte Gulf study done by Commodore Bates for the Naval War College is available from the Defense Technical Information Center and a copy resides on the shelves of Nimitz Library in Annapolis. The Roosevelt State of the Union quote is included in Halsey's autobiography (page 201).

Bibliography

Books

Adams, Henry H. *Witness to Power: The Life of Fleet Admiral William D. Leahy*. Annapolis, Md.: U.S. Naval Institute Press, 1985.

Baldwin, Hanson. *Sea Fights and Shipwrecks*. Garden City, N.Y.: Hanover House, 1955.

Ballentine, Duncan S. *U.S. Naval Logistics in the Second World War*. Princeton, N.J.: Princeton University Press, 1949.

Barbey, Daniel E. *MacArthur's Amphibious Navy: Seventh Amphibious Force Operations 1943–1945*. Annapolis, Md.: U.S. Naval Institute Press, 1969.

Barker, A. J. *Suicide Weapon*. New York: Ballantine Books, 1971.

Bates, Richard W. *The Battle of Leyte Gulf, October 1944*. Springfield, Va.: National Technical Information Service, 1953–1957.

Battle Stations! Your Navy in Action. New York: William H. Wise, 1946.

Baudot, Marcel, et al., eds. *The Historical Encyclopedia of World War II*. New York: Facts on File, 1980.

Belote, James B., and Belote, William M. *Titans of the Seas: The Development and Operations of Japanese and American Carrier Task Forces During World War II*. New York: Harper & Row, 1975.

Blair, Clay, Jr. *Silent Victory: The U.S. Submarine War Against Japan*. Philadelphia: J. B. Lippincott, 1975.

Breuer, William B. *Retaking the Philippines: Americans Return to Bataan and Corregidor, October 1944–March 1945*. New York: St. Martin's Press, 1986.

Brodie, Bernard. *A Layman's Guide to Naval Strategy*. Princeton, N.J.: Princeton University Press, 1942.

———. *War & Politics*. New York: Macmillan, 1973.

Buell, Thomas B. *Master of Sea Power: A Biography of Fleet Admiral Ernest J. King.* Boston: Little, Brown, 1980.

————. *The Quiet Warrior: A Biography of Raymond A. Spruance.* Annapolis, Md.: Naval Institute Press, 1988.

Bulkley, Robert J., Jr. *At Close Quarters: PT Boats in the United States Navy.* Washington, D.C.: Naval History Division, 1962.

Burke, Arleigh. *The Best of Burke: Some Wit, Wisdom and Advice from Admiral Arleigh "31-Knot" Burke, USN (Ret.).* Fredericksburg, Tex.: Admiral Nimitz Foundation, 1986.

Burns, James MacGregor. *Roosevelt: The Soldier of Freedom.* New York: Harcourt Brace Jovanovich, 1970.

Cannon, M. Hamlin. *The War in the Pacific, Leyte: The Return to the Philippines.* Washington, D.C.: Office of the Chief of Military History, 1954.

Carter, Worrall Reed. *Beans, Bullets, and Black Oil: The Story of Fleet Logistics Afloat in the Pacific During World War II.* Washington, D.C.: Government Printing Office, 1952.

Churchill, Winston. *The Second World War: Triumph and Tragedy.* Vol. 6. Boston: Houghton Mifflin, 1953.

Congdon, Don, ed. *Combat WWII: Pacific Theater of Operations.* New York: Arbor House, 1983.

Conway's All The World's Fighting Ships 1922–1946. Annapolis, Md.: Naval Institute Press, 1979.

Costello, John. *The Pacific War 1941–1945,* New York: Quill, 1982.

Craig, William. *The Fall of Japan.* New York: Dial Press, 1967.

D'Albas, Andrieu. *Death of a Navy.* New York: Devin Adair, 1957.

Dictionary of American Naval Fighting Ships, 6 vols. Washington, D.C.: Naval Historical Division, 1959.

Dorwart, Jeffrey M. *Conflict of Duty: The U.S. Navy's Intelligence Dilemma.* Annapolis, Md.: Naval Institute Press, 1983.

Dulin, Robert O., Jr., and Garske, William H., Jr. *Battleships: United States Battleships in World War II.* Annapolis, Md.: Naval Institute Press, 1976.

Dull, Paul. *A Battle History of the Imperial Japanese Navy, 1941–1945.* Annapolis, Md.: Naval Institute Press, 1977.

Evans, David C., ed. *The Japanese Navy in World War II.* 2d ed. Annapolis, Md.: Naval Institute Press, 1986.

Falk, Stanley L. *Decision at Leyte.* New York: W. W. Norton, 1966.

————. *Liberation of the Philippines.* New York: Ballantine, 1971.

Farley, Edward I. *PT Patrol: Wartime Adventures in the Pacific and the Story of PTs in World War II.* New York: Exposition Press, 1957.

Fetridge, William Harrison. *The Navy Reader.* New York: Bobbs-Merrill, 1943.

Field, James A., Jr. *The Japanese at Leyte Gulf: The Sho Operation.* Princeton, N.J.: Princeton University Press, 1947.

Forrestal, James. *The Forrestal Diaries.* Edited by Walter Millis. New York: Viking, 1951.

Forrestel, E. P. *Admiral Raymond A. Spruance: A Study in Command.* Washington, D.C.: Government Printing Office, 1966.

Francillon, Rene J. *Japanese Aircraft of the Pacific War.* Annapolis, Md.: Naval Institute Press, 1970.

Frank, Benis. *Halsey.* New York: Ballantine, 1974.

Friedman, Norman. *U.S. Aircraft Carriers: An Illustrated Design History.* Annapolis, Md.: Naval Institute Press, 1983.

————. *U.S. Cruisers: An Illustrated Design History.* Annapolis, Md.: Naval Institute Press, 1984.

————. *U.S. Destroyers: An Illustrated Design History.* Annapolis, Md.: Naval Institute Press, 1982.

————. *U.S. Small Combatants: An Illustrated Design History.* Annapolis, Md.: Naval Institute Press, 1987.

Gray, Colin S., and Barnett, Roger W., eds. *Seapower and Strategy.* Annapolis, Md.: Naval Institute Press, 1989.

Greenfield, Kent R. *American Strategy in World War II: A Reconsideration.* Baltimore: Johns Hopkins Press, 1963.

Greenfield, Kent Roberts, ed. *Command Decisions.* Washington, D.C.: Office of the Chief of Military History, 1960.

Grove, Eric. *Fleet to Fleet Encounters: Tsushima, Jutland, Philippine Sea.* London: Arms and Armour Press, 1991.

Halsey, William F., and Bryan, J., III. *Admiral Halsey's Story.* New York: McGraw Hill, 1947.

Hammel, Eric. *Aces Against Japan: The American Aces Speak.* Vol. 1. Novato, Calif.: Presidio Press, 1992.

Harries, Meirion, and Harries, Susie. *Soldiers of the Sun: The Rise and Fall of the Imperial Japanese Army.* New York: Random House, 1991.

Hattendorf, John B., ed. *The Influence of History on Mahan.* Newport, R.I.: Naval War College Press, 1991.

————, ed. *Mahan on Naval Strategy: Selections from the Writings of Rear Admiral Alfred Thayer Mahan.* Annapolis, Md.: Naval Institute Press, 1991.

Hattendorf, John B., Simpson, B. Mitchell, III, and Wadleigh, John R. *Sailors and Scholars: The Centennial History of the U.S. Naval War College.* Newport, R.I.: Naval War College Press, 1984.

Hattori, Takushiro. *The Complete History of the Greater East Asia War*. Tokyo: Hara Shobo, 1966.

Hayes, Grace P. *The History of the Joint Chiefs of Staff in World War II: The War Against Japan*. Annapolis, Md.: Naval Institute Press, 1982.

Hindle, Brooke. *Lucky Lady and the Navy Mystique: The Chenango in World War II*. New York: Vantage Press, 1991.

Holmes, Wilfred J. *Double-Edged Secrets: U.S. Naval Intelligence Operations in the Pacific During World War II*. Annapolis, Md.: Naval Institute Press, 1979.

Hough, Richard. *The Longest Battle: The War at Sea, 1939–1945*. New York: William Morrow, 1986.

Howarth, Stephen. *The Fighting Ships of the Rising Sun: The Drama of the Imperial Japanese Navy, 1895–1945*. New York: Atheneum, 1983.

—————. *To Shining Sea: A History of the United States Navy 1775–1991*. New York: Random House, 1991.

Hoyt, Edwin P. *The Battle of Leyte Gulf: The Death Knell of the Japanese Fleet*. New York: Weybright and Talley, 1972.

—————. *The Carrier War*. New York: Avon, 1972.

—————. *How They Won the War in the Pacific: Nimitz and His Admirals*. New York: Weybright and Talley, 1970.

—————. *Japan's War: The Great Pacific Conflict, 1853 to 1952*. New York: McGraw-Hill, 1986.

—————. *The Kamikazes*. New York: Arbor House, 1983.

—————. *MacArthur's Navy*. New York: Orion, 1989.

—————. *The Men of the Gambier Bay*. Middlebury, Vt.: P. S. Eriksson, 1979.

Hughes, Wayne P., Jr. *Fleet Tactics: Theory and Practice*. Annapolis, Md.: Naval Institute Press, 1986.

Hunt, Frazier. *The Untold Story of Douglas MacArthur*. New York: Manor Books, 1977.

Inoguchi, Rikihei, Nakajima, Tadashi, and Pineau, Roger. *The Divine Wind: Japan's Kamikaze Force in World War II*. Annapolis, Md.: Naval Institute Press, 1958.

Ito, Masanori, with Pineau, Roger. *The End of the Imperial Japanese Navy*. Translated by Andrew Y. Kuroda and Roger Pineau. New York: W. W. Norton, 1956.

James, D. Clayton. *The Years of MacArthur*. Boston: Houghton Mifflin, 1975.

Japanese Naval Vessels of World War Two as Seen by U.S. Naval Intelligence. Annapolis, Md.: Naval Institute Press, 1987.

Jentschura, Hansgeorg, Jung, Dieter, and Mickel, Peter. *Warships of the Imperial Japanese Navy 1869–1945*. Annapolis, Md.: Naval Institute Press, 1977.

Jordan, Ralph B. *Born to Fight: The Life of Admiral Halsey*. Philadelphia: David McKay, 1946.

Kahn, David. *The Code Breakers*. New York: Macmillan, 1967.

Kalbfus, E. C. *Sound Military Decision*. Annapolis, Md.: Naval Institute Press, 1992.

Karig, Walter, Harris, Russel L., and Manson, Frank A. *Battle Report: The End of an Empire*. New York: Rinehart & Company, 1948.

Karnow, Stanley. *In Our Image: America's Empire in Philippines*. New York: Random House, 1989.

Kennedy, Gerald John. *United States Naval War College, 1919–1941: An Institutional Response to Naval Preparedness*. Newport, R.I.: Naval War College Center for Advanced Research, 1975.

Kerr, Andy. *A Journey Amongst the Good and the Great*. Annapolis, Md.: Naval Institute Press, 1987.

King, Ernest J. *The War Reports of General of the Army George C. Marshall, General of the Army H. H. Arnold and Fleet Admiral Ernest J. King*. New York: J. B. Lippincott, 1947.

King, Ernest J., and Whitehill, Walter Muir. *Fleet Admiral King: A Naval Record*. New York: Da Capo Press, 1987.

Lamar, H. Arthur. *I Saw Stars: Some Memories of Commander Hal Lamar, Fleet Admiral Nimitz' Flag Lieutenant, 1941–1945*. Fredericksburg, Tex.: Admiral Nimitz Foundation, 1985.

Larrabee, Eric. *Commander in Chief: Franklin Delano Roosevelt, His Lieutenants, and Their War*. New York: Harper & Row, 1987.

Launer, Jay. *The Enemies' Fighting Ships*. New York: Sheridan House, 1944.

Layman, R. D., and McLaughlin, Stephen. *The Hybrid Warships: The Amalgamation of Big Guns and Aircraft*. Annapolis, Md.: Naval Institute Press, 1991.

Leahy, William D. *I Was There: The Personal Story of the Chief of Staff to Presidents Roosevelt and Truman Based on Notes and Diaries Made at the Time*. New York: McGraw-Hill, 1950.

Leary, William M., ed. *We Shall Return! MacArthur's Commanders and the Defeat of Japan 1942–1945*. Lexington, Ky.: University of Kentucky Press, 1988.

Lebourgeois, Julien J. *The United States Naval War College*. New York: Newcomen Society in North America, 1975.

Livezey, William E. *Mahan on Sea Power*. Norman: University of Oklahoma Press, 1981.

Lockwood, Charles A., and Adamson, Hans Christian. *Battles of the Philippine Sea.* New York: Thomas Y. Crowell, 1967.

Long, Gavin. *MacArthur as Military Commander.* Princeton, N.J.: D. Van Nostrand, 1969.

Love, Robert William, Jr. *The Chiefs of Naval Operations.* Annapolis, Md.: Naval Institute Press, 1980.

————. *History of the U.S. Navy.* Harrisburg, Pa.: Stackpole Books, 1992.

MacArthur, Douglas. *Reminiscences.* New York: McGraw-Hill, 1964.

Macintyre, Donald G. *The Battle for the Pacific.* New York: W. W. Norton, 1966.

————. *Leyte Gulf: An Armada in the Pacific.* New York: Ballantine, 1973.

Macksey, Kenneth. *Military Errors of World War Two.* London: Arms and Armour Press, 1988.

Mahan, Alfred Thayer. *The Influence of Sea Power Upon History, 1660–1783.* Mineola, N.Y.: Dover Publications, 1987.

Manchester, William. *American Caesar: Douglas MacArthur 1880–1964.* Boston: Little, Brown, 1978.

Mason, John T. *The Pacific War Remembered: An Oral History Collection.* Annapolis, Md.: Naval Institute Press, 1986.

Mercer, William E. *The Fighting and Sinking of the USS Johnston, DD-557.* Euless, Tex.: Johnston/Hoel Association, 1991.

Merrill, James M. *A Sailor's Admiral: A Biography of William F. Halsey.* New York: Crowell, 1976.

Miller, David. *Submarines of the World.* London: Salamander, 1991.

Miller, Edward S. *War Plan Orange: The U.S. Strategy to Defeat Japan, 1897–1945.* Annapolis, Md.: Naval Institute Press, 1991.

Millot, Bernard. *Divine Thunder: The Life and Death of the Kamikazes.* Translated by Lowell Bair. New York: Pinnacle Books, 1970.

Mitsuru, Yoshida. *Requiem for Battleship Yamato.* Seattle, Wash.: University of Washington Press, 1985.

Monsarrat, John. *Angel on the Yardarm: The Beginnings of Fleet Radar Defense and the Kamikaze Threat.* Annapolis, Md.: Naval Institute Press, 1985.

Morison, Samuel E. *History of United States Naval Operations in World War II.* Boston: Little, Brown, 1947–1962.

————. *Strategy and Compromise.* Boston: Little, Brown, 1958.

————. *The Two-Ocean War.* Boston: Little, Brown, 1963.

Morison, Wilbur H. *Above and Beyond.* New York: Bantam, 1986.

Morris, Ivan. *The Nobility of Failure: Tragic Heroes in the History of Japan*. New York: Holt, Rinehart, and Winston, 1975.

Motley, John J., and Kelly, Philip R. *Now Hear This*. Washington, D.C.: Infantry Journal Press, 1947.

Musicant, Ivan. *Battleship at War: The Epic Story of the USS Washington*. New York: Harcourt Brace Jovanovich, 1986.

Naito, Hatsuho. *Thunder Gods: The Kamikaze Pilots Tell Their Story*. New York: Kodansha International, 1989.

Naval Analysis Division, United States Strategic Bombing Survey (Pacific). *The Campaigns of the Pacific War*. Washington, D.C.: Government Printing Office, 1946.

―――. *Interrogations of Japanese Officials*. Washington, D.C.: Government Printing Office, 1946.

Nimitz, Chester W. *Some Thoughts to Live By*. Fredericksburg, Tex.: Admiral Nimitz Foundation, 1985.

Parrish, Thomas, ed. *The Simon & Schuster Encyclopedia of World War II*. New York: Simon & Schuster, 1978.

Pemsel, Helmut. *A History of War at Sea*. Annapolis, Md.: Naval Institute Press, 1979.

Polmar, Norman, and Allen, Thomas B. *World War II: America at War 1941–1945*. New York: Random House, 1991.

Poolman, Kenneth. *Allied Escort Carriers of World War Two in Action*. Annapolis, Md.: Naval Institute Press, 1988.

Potter, E. B. *Admiral Arleigh Burke: A Biography*. New York: Random House, 1990.

―――. *Bull Halsey*. Annapolis, Md.: Naval Institute Press, 1985.

―――. *Nimitz*. Annapolis, Md.: Naval Institute Press, 1976.

Potter, E. B., and Nimitz, Chester W., eds. *The Great Sea War: The Story of Naval Action in World War II*. Englewood Cliffs, N.J.: Prentice-Hall, 1960.

Pratt, Fletcher. *Fleet Against Japan*. New York: Harper Brothers, 1946.

Puleston, W. D. *The Influence of Sea Power in World War II*. New Haven: Yale University Press, 1947.

Reynolds, Clark G. *The Fast Carriers: The Forging of an Air Navy*. New York: Robert E. Krieger Publishing, 1978.

―――. *History and the Sea: Essays on Maritime Strategies*. Columbia, S.C.: University of South Carolina Press, 1989.

Rhoades, Weldon E. *Flying MacArthur to Victory*. College Station, Tex.: Texas A & M University Press, 1987.

Robison, S. S. *The History of Naval Tactics.* Annapolis, Md.: Naval Institute Press, 1942.

Roscoe, Theodore. *Destroyer Operations in World War II.* Annapolis, Md.: Naval Institute Press, 1953.

————. *Submarine Operations in World War II.* Annapolis, Md.: Naval Institute Press, 1949.

Sato, Kenryo. *The Greater East Asia War Memoirs.* Tokyo: Tokuma Shoten, 1966.

Sherman, Frederick C. *Combat Command: The American Aircraft Carriers in the Pacific War.* New York: E. P. Dutton, 1950.

Sims, Edward H. *Greatest Fighter Missions of the Top Navy and Marine Aces of World War II.* New York: Harper & Brothers, 1962.

Skulski, Janusz. *The Battleship Yamato.* Annapolis, Md.: Naval Institute Press, 1988.

Smith, Robert R. *Triumph in the Philadelphia.* Washington, D.C.: Office of Chief of Military History, 1963.

Smith, S. E., ed. *The United States Navy in World War II.* New York: William Morrow, 1966.

Spector, Ronald H. *Eagle Against the Sun: The American War with Japan.* New York: Free Press, 1985.

Spiller, Robert J., ed. *Dictionary of American Military Bigoraphy.* 3 vols. Westport, Conn: Greenwood Press, 1984.

Stafford, Edward P. *The Big E.* New York: Random House, 1962.

————. *Little Ship, Big War: The Saga of DE-343.* New York: William Morrow, 1984.

Steinberg, Rafael, and the editors of Time-Life Books. *Return to the Philippines.* Alexandria, Va.: Time-Life Books, 1980.

Stewart, Adrian. *The Battle of Leyte Gulf.* New York: Scribner, 1980.

Stillwell, Paul. *Battleship New Jersey: An Illustrated History.* Annapolis, Md.: Naval Institute Press, 1986.

St. John, Joseph F., as told to Handleman, Howard. *Leyte Calling. . . .* New York: Vanguard Press, 1945.

Takagi, Sokichi. *History of Naval Battles in the Pacific.* Tokyo: Iwanami Shoten, 1949.

Taylor, Theodore. *The Magnificent Mitscher.* New York: W. W. Norton, 1954.

Terasaki, Ryuji. *Navy Spirit: Life of Commander Jisaburo Ozawa.* Tokyo: Tokuma Shoten, 1967.

Tillman, Barrett. *Hellcat: The F6F in World War II.* Annapolis, Md.: Naval Institute Press, 1979.

Toland, John. *The Rising Sun: The Decline and Fall of the Japanese Empire.* New York: Bantam, 1971.

Treadwell, Mattie E. *The Women's Army Corps.* Washington, D.C.: Office of the Chief of Military History, 1954.

Ugaki, Matome. *Fading Victory: The Diary of Admiral Matome Ugaki 1941–1945.* Translated by Masataka Chihaya. Edited by Donald M. Goldstein and Katherine V. Dillon. Pittsburgh, Pa.: University of Pittsburgh Press, 1991.

Utley, Jonathan G. *An American Battleship at Peace and War: The USS Tennessee.* Lawrence, Kans.: University of Kansas Press, 1990.

Van Der Rhoer, Edward. *Deadly Magic: A Personal Account of Communications Intelligence in World War II in the Pacific.* New York: Charles Scribner's Sons, 1978.

Van Der Vat, Dan. *The Pacific Campaign.* New York: Simon & Schuster, 1992.

Vlahos, Michael. *The Blue Sword: The Naval War College and the American Mission, 1919–1941.* Newport, R.I.: Naval War College Press, 1980.

Watts, Anthony J., and Gordon, Brian G. *The Imperial Japanese Navy.* Garden City, N.Y.: Doubleday, 1971.

Wolfert, Ira. *American Guerilla in the Philippines.* New York: Simon & Schuster, 1945.

Woodward, C. Vann. *The Battle for Leyte Gulf.* New York: Macmillan, 1947.

Wouk, Herman. *War and Remembrance.* Boston: Little, Brown, 1978.

Y'Blood, William T. *The Little Giants: U.S. Escort Carriers Against Japan.* Annapolis, Md.: Naval Institute Press, 1987.

———. *Red Sun Setting: The Battle of the Philippine Sea.* Annapolis, Md.: Naval Institute Press, 1981.

Articles

Ahlstrom, John D. "Leyte Gulf Remembered." *U.S. Naval Institute Proceedings,* August 1984, pp. 45–53.

Andidora, Ronald. "Admiral Togo: An Adaptable Strategist." *Naval War College Review,* Spring 1991, pp. 52–62.

"Battle of the Pacific." *Time,* 30 October 1944 (Pacific Pony Edition), pp. 9–14.

Benitez, R. C. "Battle Stations Submerged." *U.S. Naval Institute Proceedings,* January 1948, pp. 25–32.

————. "Prelude to the Battle of Leyte Gulf." *Submarine Review*, April 1985, pp. 21–27.

Brodie, Bernard. "The Battle for Leyte Gulf." *Virginia Quarterly Review*, Summer 1948, pp. 455–60.

Burke, Arleigh. "Admiral Marc Mitscher, A Naval Aviator." *U.S. Naval Institute Proceedings*, April 1975, pp. 54–63.

Cant, Gilbert. "Bull's Run: Was Halsey Right at Leyte Gulf?" *Life*, 14 November 1947, pp. 73–90.

Coward, J. G. "Destroyer Dust." *U.S. Naval Institute Proceedings*, November 1948, pp. 1373–83.

Deac, Wilfred P. "The Battle Off Samar." *American Heritage*, December 1966, pp. 20ff.

Feldt, E. A. "Coastwatching in World War II." *U.S. Naval Institute Proceedings*, September 1961, p. 72.

Field, James, Jr. "Leyte Gulf: The First Uncensored Japanese Account." *U.S. Naval Institute Proceedings*, March 1951, pp. 255–65.

Halsey, William F. "The Battle for Leyte Gulf." *U.S. Naval Institute Proceedings*, May 1952, pp. 487–95.

Hamilton, Andrew. "Where is Task Force Thirty-Four?" *U.S. Naval Institute Proceedings*, October 1960, pp. 76–80.

Hirama, Yoichi. "Japanese Naval Preparations for World War II." *Naval War College Review*, Spring 1991, pp. 63–81.

Howard, Warren S. "The Kongos in World War II." *U.S. Naval Institute Proceedings*, November 1948, pp. 1401–7.

Hughes, Wayne P. "Naval Tactics and Their Influence on Strategy." *Naval War College Review*, January–February 1986, pp. 2–17.

Karig, Walter, Harris, Russell, and Manson, Frank A. "Jeeps Versus Giants." *U.S. Naval Institute Proceedings*, December 1947, pp. 1444–53.

Kinkaid, T. C. "A Naval Career." *U.S. Naval Institute Proceedings*, May 1959, pp. 43–47.

Koyanagi, Tomiji. "With Kurita in the Battle of Leyte Gulf." *U.S. Naval Institute Proceedings*, February 1953, pp. 118–33.

MacDonald, Scot. "Small Boys Off Samar: Survival Could Not Be Expected." *Surface Warfare*, February 1980, pp. 12–23.

Matsumoto, L., and Chihaya, M. "Design and Construction of *Yamato* and *Musashi*." *U.S. Naval Institute Proceedings*, October 1953, pp. 1103–7.

Miller, V. J. "Fleet Units Lost During World War II." *U.S. Naval Institute Proceedings*, January 1960, p. 90.

Moore, Lynn Lucius. "Shinano: The Jinx Carrier." *U.S. Naval Institute Proceedings*, February 1953, pp. 142–49.

Morison, Samuel E. "The Battle of Surigao Strait." *U.S. Naval Institute Proceedings*, December 1958, pp. 31–53.

Moskow, Shirley. "The Battle for Leyte Gulf." *Sea Classics*, August–September 1985, pp. 64–72.

Newmann, William L. "Franklin D. Roosevelt: A Disciple of Admiral Mahan." *U.S. Naval Institute Proceedings*, July 1952, pp. 713–19.

Nimitz, Chester W. "Naval Tactics." *Naval War College Review*, November–December 1982, pp. 8–13.

Oldendorf, Jesse B. "Comments on the Battle of Surigao Strait." *U.S. Naval Institute Proceedings*, April 1959, pp. 104–7.

Oldendorf, Jesse B., as told to Daniel, Hawthorne. "The Battle of Surigao Strait." *Blue Book Magazine*, March 1949, pp. 17–24.

Parker, R. C. "Some Special Uses of Smoke Screens." *U.S. Naval Institute Proceedings*, July 1940, pp. 953–61.

Potter, E. B. "Command Personality." *U.S. Naval Institute Proceedings*, January 1969, pp. 18–22.

Puleston, W. D. "Modern War and Ancient Maxims." *U.S. Naval Institute Proceedings*, December 1945, p. 1435.

Reynolds, Clark G. "The Maritime Strategy of World War II: Some Implications?" *Naval War College Review*, May–June 1986, pp. 43–50.

Ruddock, T. D. *Comment & Discussion* on Samuel Eliot Morison's "The Battle of Surigao Strait." *U.S. Naval Institute Proceedings*, November 1959, p. 102.

Sprague, C. A. F., and Gustafson, Lt. Philip H. "The Japs Had Us on the Ropes." *American Magazine*, April 1945, pp. 26–35.

Stacy, C. P. "The 18-Inch Gun." *U.S. Naval Institute Proceedings*, March 1954, pp. 334–35.

Toyama, Saburo. "Japanese Use and Misuse of History in the Pacific War." *Naval Aspects of Naval History: Selected Papers from the 5th Naval History Symposium*, Nautical and Aviation Publishing, 1985, pp. 183–88.

Vlahos, Michael. "The Naval War College and the Origins of War-Planning Against Japan." *Naval War College Review*, July–August 1980, pp. 23–41.

Vuillez, Albert. "The End of the Japanese Fleet." *History Today*, June 1977, pp. 375–79.

West, Fred. "At the Battle of Surigao Strait—'Straits of Hell.'" *Sea Classics*, March 1979, pp. 58–63.

Williams, John Hoyt. "Leyte Gulf, 1944: A Periscopic View." *The Retired Officer Magazine*, October 1984, pp. 33–37.

Winters, Hugh T. "Recollections of the Second Battle of Leyte Gulf." *Naval Aviation Museum Foundation*, Fall 1985, pp. 19–28.

Wylie, J. C. "Reflections on War in the Pacific." *U.S. Naval Institute Proceedings*, April 1952, p. 351.

Yokoi, Toshiyuki. "Thoughts on Japan's Naval Defeat." *U.S. Naval Institute Proceedings*, October 1960, pp. 68–75.

Unpublished Documents

Commander in Chief Pacific, *Operations in the Pacific Ocean Areas During the Month of October 1944*, 31 May 1945, Nimitz Library Special Collections, U.S. Naval Academy, Annapolis, Md.

Commander in Chief United States Fleet, *Amphibious Operations: Invasion of the Philippines, October 1944 to January 1945*, 30 April 1945, Nimitz Library Special Collections, U.S. Naval Academy, Annapolis, Md.

Commander in Chief United States Fleet, *Battle Experience Bulletins*, 1944, Naval War College, Newport, R.I.

Papers of Admiral Thomas C. Kinkaid, Naval Historical Center, Department of the Navy, Washington, D.C.

Papers of Fleet Admiral Ernest J. King, USN (microfilm copy), Nimitz Library Special Collections, U.S. Naval Academy, Annapolis, Md.

Papers of Fleet Admiral William Leahy, USN (microfilm copy), Nimitz Library Special Collections, U.S. Naval Academy, Annapolis, Md..

Papers of Fleet Admiral Chester W. Nimitz, USN, Nimitz Library Special Collections, U.S. Naval Academy, Annapolis, Md.

Potter, E. B., letter to author, 10 May 1993.

Oral Histories and Interviews by Author

Adair, Charles. Tape recording and transcript, 1975. U.S. Naval Institute Oral History Program, Annapolis, Md.

Billie, Robert. Interviews with author, 1993.

Bogan, Gerald F. Tape recording and transcript, 1969. U.S. Naval Institute Oral History Program, Annapolis, Md.

Cooper, Joshua. Tape recording and transcript, 1973–1974. U.S. Naval Institute Oral History Program, Annapolis, Md.

Digardi, Edward M. Interviews with author, 1993.

Drury, Paul. Interviews with author, 1993.

Kerr, A. A. Tape recording and transcript, 1983–1984. U.S. Naval Institute Oral History Program, Annapolis, Md.

Kimmel, Vern. Interviews and correspondence with author, 1992–1993.

Kinkaid, Thomas C. Tape recording and transcript, 1956. Naval Historical Center Oral History Program.

Lee, Fitzhugh. Tape recording and transcript, 1970. U.S. Naval Institute Oral History Program, Annapolis, Md.

McCollum, Arthur H. Tape recording and transcript, 1971. U.S. Naval Institute Oral History Program, Annapolis, Md.

Rochefort, Joseph J. Tape recording and transcript, 1969. U.S. Naval Institute Oral History Program, Annapolis, Md.

Russell, James S. Tape recording and transcript, 1974. U.S. Naval Institute Oral History Program, Annapolis, Md.

Smoot, Roland N. Tape recording and transcript, 1970–1971. U.S. Naval Institute Oral History Program, Annapolis, Md.

Tarbuck, R. D. Tape recording and transcript, 1970–1971. U.S. Naval Institute Oral History Program, Annapolis, Md.

Thach, John S. Tape recording and transcript, 1971. U.S. Naval Institute Oral History Program, Annapolis, Md.

Van Deurs, George. Tape recording and transcript, 1969. U.S. Naval Institute Oral History Program, Annapolis, Md.

West, Roy. Interviews with author, 1993.

Acknowledgments

To the point of being trite, it has often been said that the life of a writer is a solitary one. This is undeniable to be sure, for many hours are indeed spent alone, mining great quantities of documents that to the rest of the world are only so much paper, peering into the cold light of a cathode-ray tube in search of just the right word or phrase, staring out windows at worlds that only the writer can see. But no one ever accomplishes anything completely alone—especially not the writer of history. I am indebted to many people for the creation of this book.

I must first acknowledge the contributions of Jim Charlton, Buz Wyeth, and Florence Goldstein, without whom this book would never have come to pass. These experts in the complex world of publishing made this endeavor not only easier and more professional, but more enjoyable.

I am particularly grateful to the many veterans of the Battle of Leyte Gulf who responded to my advertisements for help. I stand in awe of their courage and their actions in October 1944, and I am deeply in their debt for their willingness to help me in 1992–1993. Without them both battle and book would have been far different. The contributions of the men whose stories appear in the book should be apparent and I will not name them individually here. But I would like to acknowledge especially the *many* veterans who offered to help but were not included in this narrative because of space and time limitations. To these unsung individuals I extend a special thanks and a hope that each will be as generous when the next author comes asking for help.

Many of the research personnel at the Naval Academy's Nimitz Library, the Naval Historical Center in Washington, D.C., and the Admiral Nimitz Foundation in Fredericksburg, Texas, were particularly helpful. I am especially grateful to Barbara Manvel at the Nimitz Library, who is both a friend and a valuable ally.

As always, I am indebted to my colleagues in the Naval Academy History Department who serve as my inspiration and whose support, criticism, and friendship have been invaluable. Jack Sweetman was particularly encouraging and Craig Symonds's contributions were consistent with the generosity and friendship I have come to count on but never take for granted. And I am especially indebted to Professor Emeritus E. B. Potter, who very generously shared his vast knowledge with me.

Many of the wonderful people who make the Naval Institute the outstanding organization that it is went way beyond the call of duty in supporting me in this endeavor, especially Paul Stillwell, Linda O'Doughda, Mary Beth Straight, John Miller, Fred Schultz, Scott Belliveau, Dorothy Sappington, Susan Artigiani, LeAnn Bauer, Tanje Quarto, Mark Gatlin, and Fred Rainbow.

I offer a special thanks to Stacy, Tom, Chris, and Ryan Gernentz who opened their home to me, providing an ideal atmosphere for the contemplation necessary in the early stages of this book. They also listened patiently to my ideas and encouraged me as only loving friends can.

My first book was dedicated to my wife, Debby, whom I therein described as "typist, editor, critic, and loving wife." She deserves each of these titles yet again. This book could never have come to be were it not for her patience, support, valued opinions, superb word-processing skills, love, and encouragement.

So, even though this work is affixed with the name of but one author, it is truly the product of the selfless efforts of many. Each of them has my sincere gratitude.

Index

Page numbers in *italics* refer to maps.

334 ★ Index ★

Gabilan